The Letters of Demosthenes

The Letters of
DEMOSTHENES

Jonathan A. Goldstein

1 9 6 8

Columbia University Press

NEW YORK AND LONDON

JONATHAN A. GOLDSTEIN is
Associate Professor of History and Classics
at the University of Iowa

886.01
D387xg

Copyright © 1959, 1968 Columbia University Press
Library of Congress Catalog Card Number: 67–19652
Printed in the United States of America

Preface

IN THIS STUDY I WISH to establish the authenticity of Demosthenes'
Epistles 1 to 4 and to extract all possible historical information
from them. Chapter 8 and Part V of my book are running commentaries; the rest of the book is organized to follow the logic of the arguments on authenticity. The reader who wishes commentary should
consult first Chapter 8 for matters of rhetoric. Part V, with full cross-
references to everything not in Chapter 8, treats all other matters. In
Chapter 5 the chronological order of the letters is established as Ep. 3,
Ep. 2, Ep. 4(?), Ep. 1, and this order is followed in the translation
and the running commentaries. Chapter 8 is both a running commentary and an attempt to prove authenticity. I hope those interested
in the proof will not find the length of Chapter 8 forbidding and that
those seeking a rhetorical commentary will find it convenient to use.

In the translation and throughout I have used Rennie's *Oxford
Classical Text* of Demosthenes. My few departures from it are treated
in Part V.

The bibliography is a selected list of the works referred to in the
notes. Section F omits some works cited only once and all encyclo-
pedia articles bearing titles that are names of persons and places. The
absence of several of the more recent studies of Demosthenes means
only that in my eyes they are not necessary for treating the problems
of Demosthenes' letters. On the other hand, in Sections A, B, and E
of the bibliography every effort has been made to include everything
of any importance.

Manfred Fuhrmann's new edition of Anaximenes' *Ars rhetorica*
(Lipsiae: B. G. Teubner, 1966) came to my attention after my book
had been set in type. Fuhrmann's *conspectus* (pp. 99–102) collating
the pages of his edition with those of Hammer's will make reference
easy. I have taken note of his views on how the types of oratory were

v

originally classified in Anaximenes' work (below, Chap. 7, n. 20). His textual alterations do not change the meaning of the texts I have cited. The manuscript authority for the reading adopted below at p. 147, n. 87, becomes A^2.

This book is based on my doctoral dissertation written under Professor Elias Bickerman (Columbia University, 1959). My debt to Professor Bickerman goes far beyond what I can note here. It was he who suggested the topic to me. His earlier study of the problem suggested many of the directions of my research. His guidance and encouragement are responsible for much of whatever is valuable in this book. His generous criticism has helped me remove mistakes and infelicities.

I am deeply indebted to Professor Saul Lieberman of the Jewish Theological Seminary and to the American Academy for Jewish Research. Professor Lieberman's example and encouragement turned me to the study of the ancient world, and he saw to it that the Academy, then under his presidency, granted me the fellowship under which the original version of this book was written.

I am grateful to the late Professor John Day, who introduced me to epigraphy and papyrology, disciplines important for this work. I shall always remember him for his kindness.

I am grateful also to my parents, Rabbi and Mrs. David A. Goldstein, for their unfailing support and encouragement, and especially to my wife, Dr. Helen Goldstein, whose courage, wisdom, scholarship, and devotion saw me through the birth-pangs of this book.

No part of this work has caused me, a relative late-comer to classical studies, more difficulty than the translation. If it lacks a Demosthenic ring, that is because I lack an oratorical talent. It is as accurate as I could make it. I am grateful to Professors Morton Smith, Rosalie Colie, and Frederic Will and to Mr. R. J. Macfarlane for reading the translation at various stages and making valuable suggestions.

During my work I have received valuable help from many persons, some of whom I do not know by name. To all of these I here give thanks.

The publication of this book has been made possible by generous grants from the Graduate College of the University of Iowa and from the Stanwood Cockey Lodge Foundation of the Classics Department of Columbia University; to both of them I here record my thanks. I am grateful to Professor Gilbert Highet and to the late Professor Moses Hadas for consideration shown me.

My relationship to the Columbia University Press through Mr. Henry Wiggins and Miss Sarah Redwine has been a most amicable one. I thank them for lending their resources and skill to the difficult task of getting this book into print.

January 1968   JONATHAN A. GOLDSTEIN

Abbreviations

THE READER UNFAMILIAR with the abbreviations of the authors and titles of ancient texts will have no trouble deciphering them with the help of the Bibliography, Section C.

AJP	*American Journal of Philology*
ABSA	*Annual of the British School at Athens*
Arch. Ephem.	Ἀρχαιολογικὴ Ἐφημερίς
BCH	*Bulletin de correspondance hellénique*
BGU	*Berliner griechische Urkunden*
BPhW	*Berliner philologische Wochenschrift*
BVSAW	*Berichte über die Verhandlungen der Sächsischen Akademie der Wissenschaften zu Leipzig: philologisch-historische Klasse*
Busolt-Swoboda	G. Busolt, *Griechische Staatskunde* (Vol. II, ed. H. Swoboda)
CP	*Classical Philology*
CQ	*Classsical Quarterly*
CR	*Classical Review*
FD	*Fouilles de Delphes*
F. Gr. Hist.	*Die Fragmente der griechischen Historiker*, ed. Felix Jacoby
GHI	*A Selection of Greek Historical Inscriptions* (Vol. I, 2d ed.), ed. M. N. Tod
IG	*Inscriptiones Graecae*
IG ²	*Inscriptiones Graecae*, editio altera
JHS	*Journal of Hellenic Studies*
Lipsius	J. H. Lipsius, *Das attische Recht und Rechtsverfahren*
NJb	*Neue Jahrbücher für philologie und Pädagogik*
P. Berol.	*Berlin Papyri*
PhW	*Philologische Wochenschrift*
POxy.	*Oxyrhynchus Papyri*

Pros. Att.	J. Kirchner, *Prosopographia Attica*
RE	*Realencyclopädie der classischen Altertumswissenschaft,* ed. Pauly-Wissowa-Kroll-Mittelhaus
REA	*Revue des études anciennes*
REG	*Revue des études grecques*
REL	*Revue des études latines*
Rh. Mus.	*Rheinisches Museum für Philologie*
Riv. fil.	*Rivista di filologia e d'istruzione classica*
RPh	*Revue de philologie, d'histoire et de littérature anciennes*
*SIG*³	*Sylloge inscriptionum graecarum,* 3d ed.
TAPA	*Transactions and Proceedings of the American Philological Association*
Vit. X orat.	[Plutarch] *Vitae decem oratorum* in Plutarch *Moralia* 832b–852e

Contents

PART I

Introductory Studies

CHAPTER 1

The Problem of Authenticity

S IX LETTERS OF Demosthenes have come down to us in Byzantine manuscripts.[1] The first four in our printed editions, addressed to the Council and the People of Athens, purport to have been written by Demosthenes from exile after his condemnation in the Harpalus affair in 323. He asks exoneration for himself and for his condemned political allies. Ep. 5 is a private letter, addressed to an otherwise unknown Heracleodorus; ostensibly, it was written by Demosthenes in his youth.[2] Ep.6 purports to have been sent by Demosthenes to the Council and People of Athens in 322 during the Lamian war.

The success of Richard Bentley in 1697 in proving the epistles of Phalaris and of other ancient worthies to be forgeries[3] cast doubt on the authenticity of all collections of letters attributed to Greek celebrities. Thus, in 1759 John Taylor could state, as the general and sure judgment of scholars, that Demosthenes' letters were fictions.[4] In 1875, however, Friedrich Blass protested that the problem of the authenticity of Demosthenes' letters had not been studied.[5] The

---

[1] See below, p. 8.

[2] Ep. 5. 5.

[3] *A Dissertation upon the Epistles of Phalaris, Themistocles, Socrates, Euripides, etc., and Aesop's Fables* (London, 1697).

[4] In the preface to his edition of the letters of Aeschines (reprinted in *Oratores Attici*, ed. W. S. Dobson, XII, 294): "Nemo hodie in Re Literaria reliquus est qui Demosthenis Epistolas confictas atque isti nomini temere assutas esse non crediderit: Adeo nunquam de ea re vel minima exstiterit dubitatio."

[5] "Über die Echtheit der Demosthenes' Namen tragenden Briefe," *Jahresbericht über das Königliche Wilhelms-Gymnasium zu Königsberg i. Pr.* (1875), pp. 1–11.

3

controversy has continued ever since.[6] Until the present time there has been no work giving a detailed interpretation of these texts and from it drawing conclusions as to their authenticity. Both in content and in the history of the transmission of the text Epp. 1–4 constitute a unity.[7] If authentic, they are the latest extensive documents from the orator's hand to survive.[8] On the other hand, Epp. 5 and 6 stand apart in the history of their transmission and differ stylistically from the others.[9] Both are very brief. Their content, even if true, is of interest more for biographical curiosities than for history, and the case for their authenticity is vastly weaker than that for Epp. 1–4.[10] In this work, therefore, I shall give a detailed interpretation of Epp. 1–4 and discuss afresh their authenticity, touching only incidentally on Epp. 5 and 6.

The several approaches of this study will converge to support strongly the authenticity of Epp. 1–4. Hence, it is well to present at the outset an outline of the arguments against authenticity, so that they can receive a fair hearing in their full cumulative force. The arguments known to me are the following:

1. The chronology presupposed by Ep. 3. 1, 39 is contradicted by Plutarch *Dem.* 26–27 and by the provisions of Athenian law.[11]

2. There is a *vaticinium ex eventu* at Ep. 2. 20.[12]

3. Ep. 3. 31 implies that Philocles was convicted of bribe-taking in the Harpalus affair of 324/3 B.C., contrary to epigraphic evidence.[13]

4. Ep. 3. 31 implies that Charidemus, who was killed in 333, was alive in 324/3.[14]

5. At the time of Demosthenes' exile, no one could have described Pytheas in the terms used at Ep. 3. 29–30.[15]

[6] For the literature on the problem, see bibliography, sec. E.

[7] See below, Chaps. 2 and 5.

[8] Even if D. 25 were proved to be authentic, it would give us little information about Demosthenes. Cf. C. H. Kramer, *De priore Demosthenis adversus Aristogitonem oratione*, and Piero Treves, "Apocrifi demostenici," *Athenaeum*, n.s., XIV (1936), 252–58.

[9] See below, Chaps. 2 and 3.

[10] See Appendix I.

[11] See below, pp. 65–68.

[12] See below, pp. 68–73.

[13] See below, Chap. 5, n. 60, and p. 65.

[14] See commentary to Ep. 3. 31–32.

[15] See commentary *ad loc.*

6. Ep. 3. 16–18 falsely implies that Moerocles was an archon in 324/3.[16]

7. Epp. 1–4 lack factual content reflecting the events of 324/3 and parrot the earlier works of Demosthenes.[17]

8. The letters contain errors on earlier events of the fourth century which Demosthenes would not have made.[18]

9. The letters could not possibly have served Demosthenes' purposes in 324/3: there was no way in which they could have received a hearing; and, if heard, they could have aroused only hostility.[19]

10. The letters show traces of being written against a background later than Demosthenes' death.[20]

11. The arguments and rhetorical technique of the letters are undemosthenic and in places thoroughly inept.[21]

12. The form and language of the letters depart from the rules of fourth-century epistolography.[22]

13. The language and style of the letters are undemosthenic and in places thoroughly inept.[23]

---

[16] See below, Chap. 5, n. 101.

[17] See below, pp. 29–30, and Parts II, III, and V.

[18] See commentary to Ep. 3. 19 and to Ep. 2. 7-12.

[19] See below, pp. 129–30, 52–63; Chaps. 6 and 8.

[20] See below, pp. 76–94; commentary to Ep. 4. 5–7. (One might think that the interest in the Cappadocians and the Syrians was prompted by the wars of the diadochi.)

[21] See below, Part III.

[22] See below, pp. 98–100, 176–78.

[23] See below, Chap. 3.

CHAPTER 2

The Transmission of the Text

D EMOSTHENES' LETTERS as a group were known to Cicero and Quintilian, and Cicero refers clearly to Ep. 5.[1] The text of Ep. 3 1–38 is preserved on a papyrus of Cicero's time.[2] Ep. 2 is alluded to by Plutarch[3] and preserved in part on a papyrus of the second

[1] Quint. x. 1. 107 (comparing Cicero's works with those of Demosthenes): "In epistulis quidem quamquam sunt utriusque, . . . nulla contentio est." Cf. Photius *Epp.* ii. 44, Vol. CII, col. 186 Migne. Cicero *Brutus* 31. 121: "Lectitavisse Platonem studiose, audivisse etiam Demosthenes dicitur; idque apparet ex genere et granditate verborum. Dicit etiam in quadam epistula hoc ipse de sese." *Orator* 4. 15: "Cuius ex epistulis intellegi licet quam frequens fuerit Platonis auditor."

Actually, at Ep. 5. 3 the author expresses only admiration for the school of Plato. Hence, if Cicero was alluding to our Ep. 5, his inference was somewhat inaccurate. Doubtless he was quoting from memory; even had he wished, he probably could not have checked the reference. On the vicissitudes of Cicero's library, see C. Wendel, "Das griechisch-römische Altertum," chap. ii of Fritz Milkau and Georg Leyh (eds.), *Handbuch der Bibliothekswissenschaft*, III, 113–15, 141. Cicero was probably influenced also by a prevalent legend about Demosthenes as a student of Plato. See Schaefer, I, 311–14, 321–24; K. Kalbfleisch, "Plato und Demosthenes," *Rh. Mus.*, XCII (1944), 190–91. Olympiodorus, *Scholia ad Platonis Gorg.* to p. 515c, made the same erroneous inference from Ep. 5. 3.

[2] F. Kenyon, *Classical Texts from Papyri in the British Museum*, pp. 56–62 and Plate III. It is probably the oldest papyrus fragment of the Demosthenic corpus and may even be older than the time of Cicero; see R. A. Pack, *The Greek and Latin Literary Texts from Greco-Roman Egypt* (2d ed.), pp. 34–36, and P. J. Sijpesteijn, "Les parchemins et les papyrus de Démosthène trouvés en Egypte," *Chronique d'Egypte*, XXXVIII (1963), 299, n. 3, and 305, n. 1. Since Ep. 3 existed in Cicero's time, it is unnecessary to consider the possibility that Cicero refers to letters different from those in our possession.

[3] *Dem.* 26. 2: "αἰσχύνη τῆς αἰτίας φησὶ καὶ δι' ἀσθένειαν τοῦ σώματος οὐ δυναμένου φέρειν τὸν εἰργμὸν ἀποδρᾶναι." Cf. D. Ep. 2. 17: "μετέστην . . . πρῶτον μὲν τοὐνειδος τῆς εἱρκτῆς χαλεπῶς τῷ λογισμῷ φέρων, εἶτα διὰ τὴν ἡλικίαν οὐκ ἂν οἷός τ' ὢν τῷ σώματι τὴν κακοπαθίαν ὑπενεγκεῖν." Plutarch, who speaks of the insufficiency of his library (*Dem.*

6

century A.D. Ep. 1 is preserved in part on a papyrus of the second century A.D.[4] The author of the letters attributed to Aeschines, who wrote in the second century A.D., makes unmistakable references to Epp. 1–4.[5] Ancient rhetoricians[6] and lexicographers[7] often quote Epp. 1–4. Only the very short Ep. 6 is not attested in ancient sources. On the other hand, ancient critics often denied the authenticity of speeches ascribed to Demosthenes.[8] To our knowledge, no one in

2. 1), may have been relying on his memory, or he may have derived his information indirectly from Ep. 2, for only the excellent Codex Matritensis N 55 (Graux's M^a) presents the reading φησί. The other mss. have φασί. Plutarch most likely derived from D. Ep. 2. 20 the picture of Demosthenes at *Dem.* 26. 4: "'Ήνεγκ δὲ τὴν φυγὴν μαλακῶς, ἐν Αἰγίνῃ καὶ Τροιζῆνι καθεζόμενος τὰ πολλὰ καὶ πρὸς τὴν Ἀττικὴν ἀποβλέπων δεδακρυμένος." Plutarch's vague τὰ πολλά leaves it possible that Ep. 2. 20 was one of several sources lying before him as he wrote, but the failure to mention Calauria suggests again that he was relying on his memory or derived his information indirectly.

[4] Ep. 2: *Papyri Osloenses* Inv. No. 1471, published by S. Eitrem and L. Amundsen, *Eranos*, LIV (1956), 101–8. Ep. 1: POxy. xxxi. 2549.

[5] See Appendix II. On the letters of Aeschines and their date, see F. Blass, *Die attische Beredsamkeit*, III 2, 185–86; the introduction to *Aeschinis quae feruntur epistolae*, ed. E. Drerup, and the review by L. Radermacher, *Literarisches Zentralblatt*, LV (1904), 1432–33; Karl Schwegler, *De Aeschinis quae feruntur epistolis*, and the review by Drerup, *Deutsche Literaturzeitung*, XXXVI (1915), 1280–84. F. Houthuys, *Over de Zoogenaamde Brieven van Aeschines* (Thèse de lic.; Louvain: 1947), is inaccessible to me. Radermacher insisted that the author of Ps.-Aesch. Epp. 11–12 was different from the author of Epp. 1–9, and his view was upheld by Schwegler (pp. 8–16), but Drerup's review of Schwegler presents a good refutation. Even if Radermacher's view were correct, the letters except for Ep. 10 constitute a unit, for according to Radermacher the supposed second author composed Epp. 11 and 12 in order to complete the collection; cf. Schwegler, pp. 16, 76. Ep. 10 seems to have nothing to do with Aeschines and probably slipped into the collection from outside. See Drerup's review of Schwegler, p. 1281.

[6] In the second century A.D., Aelius Aristides quoted Ep. 3. 45, wrongly citing it under the title "On Concord" of Ep. 1 (Aristides 23 [42]. 71, p. 792 Dindorf: "Δημοσθένης δὲ ἐπιστέλλων Ἀθηναίοις περὶ τῆς ὁμονοίας τὴν μὲν ἐν τοῖς τοιούτοις ἥτταν καλὴν καὶ προσήκουσαν ἔφη νίκην παρὰ τοῖς εὖ φρονοῦσι κρίνεσθαι, λέγων ἣν γονέων υἱεῖς ἡττῶνται, εἰ καὶ πολῖται συγχωροῦσιν ἀλλήλοις"). With Ps.-Aesch. Ep. 11, this is the earliest attestation of Ep. 1. Allusions to Epp. 2–3 in ancient rhetorical handbooks: Ps.-Aristides *Rh.* i. 45, 47 Schmid; Hermog. *Id.* i. 7, ii. 8; Apsines, p. 309 Hammer; see also the Byzantine scholiasts, *Rhetores Graeci*, ed. Christian Walz, V, 495; VI, 253–57, 438; VII, 993; and the anonymous *De figuris, ibid.*, VIII, 631.

[7] Pollux ii. 129 ascribes the word αἰσχρορρημοσύνη to Demosthenes; it occurs only at Ep. 4. 11. Apart from Ps.-Aesch. Ep. 7, this is the sole ancient reference to Ep. 4. For other citations of the letters in ancient lexicographers, see commentary to Ep. 3. 12, τῆς ἀξίας; to Ep. 3. 30, φθόης; and to Ep. 2. 11, 14.

[8] See Blass, III 1, 54–63.

7

antiquity ever questioned the authenticity of Demosthenes' letters.[9] Particularly significant is the testimony of Cicero, for in going beyond the mention of "a certain letter" of Demosthenes to speak of a body of "his letters," he implies that among the groups into which the corpus of Demosthenes' works was divided[10] stood a collection of letters. If Cicero had no suspicions concerning Ep. 5, this entire collection must have been an accepted part of the corpus long before his times.

Demosthenes' letters are found in the two families of medieval manuscripts of the corpus which have the most authority. Epp. 1–5 appear in *Codex Parisinus* **S**, and all six in *Codex Marcianus* **F** and its contemporary of the same family, *Codex Marcianus* **Q**. All three manuscripts are well-written pieces dating from the tenth century. The absence of the letters from the families headed by *Codex Augustanus* **A** and *Codex Parisinus* **Y** may be discounted since the corpus as presented in these two families is clearly incomplete.[11] The textual analyses of G. Pasquali indicate that all four manuscript families go back to archetypes compiled probably in the second

[9] Other ancient attestations of the letters: below, Chap. 5, n. 106, and commentary to Ep. 3. 6, τῷ φῆσαι Λυκ.; Ep. 3. 42, οὐ μὴν οὐδὲ κτλ.; Ep. 3. 44; and Ep 2. 10, μόνου. The statement at Ps.-Plut. *Vit. X orat.* 847e, that there were 65 authentic *logoi* of Demosthenes, may indicate that he or his authority included Epp. 1–4 in the Demosthenic corpus. Eliminating Philip's letter (D. 12) and counting the *Prooemia* as a single oration, on the basis of the extant corpus, we could conclude that Pseudo-Plutarch's 65 included 61 orations and four letters. *Logos* as used by Pseudo-Plutarch can mean "work," not merely "oration"; see *Vit. X orat.* 836a–b, where the *logoi* of Lysias include letters and rhetorical textbooks, and see also G. Pasquali, *Storia della tradizione e critica del testo*, p. 301, on the figures of the *logoi* of Isocrates at *Vit. X orat.* 838d. However, even in antiquity some of the extant orations of Demosthenes were regarded as spurious, and at least one lost oration was considered authentic by Callimachus (see below, n. 63). Hence one cannot be sure what works were included in Pseudo-Plutarch's figure. See also Blass, III 1, 50.

[10] Such subdivided corpora are a natural growth from the conditions of ancient book-making. See Appendix III. Here we may note the earliest direct attestations of groups of the Demosthenic corpus. Only the *Philippics* (D. 1–11 and probably 13—see below, p. 15) are attested earlier as a group than the letters, being mentioned in the second century B.C. by Panaetius (Plut. *Dem.* 13. 4). The speeches to the Assembly on Hellenic affairs (D. 14–16) are first mentioned as a group by Dion. Hal. *Amm. I.* 10, Vol. I, p. 268 U.-R.; see also Didymus, *Kommentar zu Demosthenes*, ed. H. Diels and W. Schubart, pp. 63–65. The public forensic speeches (D. 18–24) are first so attested by Dion. Hal., *loc. cit.*; and the "epitropic" orations (D. 27–31) by *Vit. X orat.* 839f.

[11] See the *Codicum catalogus* in *Demosthenis Orationes*, ed. S. H. Butcher, I, xvii–xx, and Pasquali, pp. 292–93.

century A.D.[12] Nevertheless, peculiarities of our manuscripts afford a glimpse into the earlier history of the text.

One feature in the manuscript tradition of Demosthenes far ante-dates the second Christian century: the stichometric notations. Indeed, this usage can be traced back to the early stages of Greek book-making. The first Greek books of which scribes produced copies for a sizable public were the epics of Homer. When a scribe copied epic poetry it was natural for him to measure the quantity of his work in terms of hexameter lines, or *stichoi*. The inclusion of a note recording the number of hexameter lines also afforded the pur-chaser of a roll a way of determining whether the work was complete. Hence the scribes adopted the practice of appending such sticho-metric notes to their work. The hexameter line thus became estab-lished as the unit of measure, and when prose works found a public, the scribes continued to measure by hexameter lines.[13] Athenian prose authors of the fourth century B.C. measured the length of their works in this manner.[14]

The stichometries in the manuscripts of the Demosthenic corpus are of a well-defined type.[15] In the margins of many of the works of the corpus "partial" stichometries occur, by which every hundredth *stichos* is indicated by a letter of the Ionian Greek alphabet, begin-ning with alpha and ending with omega. If more than twenty-four letters are needed, the alphabet is repeated. At the end of most of the works of the corpus, stichometric notes occur giving the total number of *stichoi* in Attic "acrophonic" numerals.[16] The marginal letters are simply the means by which the scribe who computed the total stichometry recorded the intermediate stages of his counting.[17]

---

[12] Pasquali, p. 288. See his entire discussion, pp. 269–94.

[13] See E. G. Turner, *Athenian Books in the Fifth and Fourth Centuries, B.C.*, and the most comprehensive treatment of ancient stichometries, Kurt Ohly, *Sticho-metrische Untersuchungen*, to be supplemented by Carl Wendel, *Die griechisch-römische Buchbeschreibung*, pp. 34–44.

[14] Isoc. 12. 136; Theopompus, *F. Gr. Hist.* No. 115, F 25.

[15] For the most complete collection of the stichometries of the Demosthenic corpus, see F. Burger, *Stichometrische Untersuchungen zu Demosthenes und Herodot*.

[16] On Greek acrophonic numerals, see M. N. Tod's articles, *ABSA*, XVIII (1911–12), 98–132; XXVIII (1926–27), 141–57; XXXVII (1936–37), 236–57; XLV (1950), 126–39.

[17] Ohly, pp. 84–85; Wendel, *Buchbeschreibung*, pp. 42–43. On the anomalous marginal stichometries of D. 19 and 59, see below, n. 44.

The marginal letters and the totals in acrophonic numerals are both indices of antiquity. Even in the archaizing usage of the Athenian inscriptions, the familiar numeral system based on the 27-letter alphabet[18] practically superseded acrophonic numerals by the middle of the first century B.C.[19] Outside Athens, with few exceptions, the acrophonic numerals were already out of use in the third century B.C.[20] and in Egypt under Ptolemy I.[21] The marginal letters, too, belong to an earlier numeral system which was superseded by the 27-letter alphabet.[22] Unlike the 27-letter system, the acrophonic numerals were used only as cardinals, never as ordinals. Before the introduction of the 27-letter alphabetic system, for a Greek the only means, other than fully written words, to indicate an ordinal was to use the letters of the alphabet, alpha representing first and omega twenty-fourth, if the local alphabet was the Ionian. This system, to which Tod has given the name of "letter labels," is known first from inscriptions of the fifth century B.C., but it did not reach high development at Athens until the second half of the fourth century, during the period of Demosthenes' and Lycurgus' activity.[23]

[18] In the 27-letter alphabet, alpha stands for 1, digamma (or stigma) for 6, etc. On the history of this system, see Tod, "The Alphabetical Numeral System in Attica," *ABSA*, XLV (1950), 126–39.

[19] *Ibid.*, p. 138, where Tod also enumerates the few sporadic later occurrences of acrophonic numerals. Herodian Περὶ τῶν ἀριθμῶν (printed in H. Stephanus, *Thesaurus Linguae Graecae* [3d ed; Paris: Firmin Didot, 1831–65], Vol. VIII, appendix, col. 346) knows of acrophonic numerals in Athens only in total stichometries and in the laws of Solon and old inscriptions.

[20] See Tod's articles cited in n. 16. The latest epigraphic example outside Attica is from Rhodes (first century B.C.). On the archaizing use of acrophonic numerals in "Euthalian" manuscripts of Acts and the Catholic and Pauline Epistles see B. Hemmerdinger, "Euthaliana," *Journal of Theological Studies*, n.s., XI (1960), 349–54, and "Les chiffres attiques du *Parisinus Gr.* 223 des Épîtres pauliniennes," *REG*, LXXVI (1963), 204–5.

[21] Wendel, *Buchbeschreibung*, pp. 34–35.

[22] So already W. Christ, *Abhandlungen der philosophisch-philologischen Classe der Königl. bayerischen Akademie der Wissenschaften*, XVI, 169–70.

[23] See Wilhelm Larfeld, *Griechische Epigraphik*, pp. 297–98; V. Gardthausen, *Griechische Palaeographie*, II, 358–59; M. Tod, "Letter Labels in Greek Inscriptions," *ABSA*, XLIX (1954), 1–8. In measuring a stichometry, no confusion would result from simply repeating the alphabet if more than twenty-four ordinals were needed. Where confusion might arise, there were several methods to indicate unequivocally second and later sequences of twenty-four, such as "AA, BB, . . .," for the second sequence, "AAA, BBB, . . .," for the third, etc.; or "AA, AB . . .," for the second, "BA, BB, . . .," for the third, etc. Both methods are known from fourth-century Athens; see Tod, *ABSA*, XLIX, 1–8.

Strictly speaking, the intermediate stages of a scribe's count in reckoning a stichometry are not cardinal totals, but ordinal labels ("the four-hundredth *stichos*"). In any case, acrophonic cardinals, requiring five figures to represent "900," were too cumbersome to use in a narrow margin. The 27-letter system was used both for cardinals and for ordinals[24] and could express any number up to 1,000 in three figures or fewer, but it was not in use in Athens of the fourth and early third centuries.[25] Hence the only convenient means available then in Athens for a scribe to record the intermediate stages of his count was to number every hundredth *stichos*, using the system of letter labels. The use of marginal stichometries in letter labels and total stichometries in acrophonic numerals thus became the established procedure of Athenian scribes; and the Hellenistic world, including the Alexandrian libraries and book trade, merely took it over from Athens.[26]

Like acrophonic cardinals, letter labels as a method for expressing ordinals were abandoned with the introduction of the 27-letter system, except in certain stereotyped usages which had become well established before the 27-letter system was in general use.[27] Stichometries were one such area of survival. The editions of Thucydides used by Dionysius of Halicarnassus evidently had a marginal stichometry expressed in letter labels,[28] and the stichometries to his rolls of Demosthenes' orations also were probably of the original Athenian type.[29] Even works written in the first century B.C. were provided

[24] One can hardly avoid the assumption that the previously existing ordinal system of alphabetic "labels" paved the way for the ordinal use of the alphabetic 27-letter system.

[25] See Tod, *ABSA*, XLV, 137–38.

[26] See Wendel, *Buchbeschreibung*, p. 34.

[27] See Appendix IV.

[28] Dion. Hal. at *Thuc.* 10, Vol. I, p. 339 U.-R. gives accurately the length of Th. i. 1–87 as 2,000 *stichoi* and gives other correct stichometric data at *Thuc.* 13, Vol. I, p. 344; 19, Vol. I, p. 353; and 33, Vol. I, p. 379. See Ohly, pp. 10–11. It is hard to believe that Dionysius counted the lines himself or arrived at his figures by guessing. Moreover, at *Thuc.* 10, Vol. I, p. 340, Dionysius says that Th. i. 88–117 has less than 500 *stichoi;* actually it has about 700. The error becomes more understandable if Dionysius was following a marginal stichometry and became confused because a repetition of the alphabet began between the twentieth and twenty-seventh marginal letters.

[29] At *Dem.* 57, Vol. I, p. 250 U.-R., Dion. Hal. estimates the total length of Demosthenes' works as 50,000 to 60,000 *stichoi;* to be more accurate he might have had laboriously to add up the figures of the total stichometries at the end of each part of the corpus; hence he was content with a rough estimate. See Ohly, p. 20.

with marginal stichometries in letter labels and total stichometries in acrophonic numerals.[30]

The 27-letter system soon encroached upon the areas where the other two survived.[31] A later Athenian writer on numeral systems did not even mention latter labels.[32] The encroachment appears even in the stereotyped stichometries. A papyrus fragment of a comedy from about 200 B.C. already exhibits the marginal numeral rho, "one-hundredth," in the 27-letter system, rather than the letter label alpha.[33] Even where the old method of numbering each hundredth line by an ordinal is preserved, the numerals used tend to become those of the 27-letter system, with digamma or stigma rather than zeta for "sixth," as in the Bankes *Iliad* of the second century A.D.[34]

Very few papyri with total stichometries have been found. A document of about 160 B.C., our earliest containing a total stichometry, has it in the 27-letter system.[35] Since it is a private exercise rather than a book, this document proves little about the book trade and about fine editions. But a papyrus fragment of the *Iliad* of about 200 A.D. has a total stichometry in the 27-letter system.[36] Study of the stichometries found in papyri and in medieval manuscripts of ancient works demonstrates that a sharp line can be drawn near the beginning of the Christian era. Works composed later do not have marginal stichometries expressed in letter labels; and, except for three isolated and late instances of scribal archaism, they have total stichometries only in the 27-letter system, not in acrophonic numerals.[37]

[30] See Ohly, "Die Stichometrie der herkulanischen Rollen, *Archiv für Papyrusforschung*, VII (1924), 191.

[31] See Appendix IV. The lists of Peripatetic works in Diogenes Laertius express the book numbers in the 27-letter system, and the scribes of the manuscript tradition of Aristotle are often confused by the letter labels.

[32] Herodian (see above, n. 19).

[33] *Pap. Ghôran* II, *BCH*, XXX (1906), 123–49; Ohly, *Stich. Unters.*, p. 50.

[34] The examples are collected by Ohly, *ibid.*, pp. 80–83. On marginal stichometries using neither letter labels nor the twenty-seven letter system, see Wendel, *Buchbeschreibung*, pp. 36–38.

[35] *Pap. Didot*; see Ohly, *Stich. Unters.*, pp. 50–52 (No. XXV).

[36] *POxy.* 445.

[37] Ohly, *Stich. Unters.*, pp. 83–84. On the stichometries of a tenth- and an eleventh-century manuscript of Acts and the Catholic and Pauline Epistles, see B. Hemmerdinger, *REG*, LXXVI (1963), 204–5. The other exception is the four-

Now D. Epp. 1–4 in codices **S** and **Q** exhibit both marginal sticho-metries in letter labels and total stichometries in acrophonic numer-als. Hitherto, only Epp. 3 and 5 possessed attestations from before the Christian era; now Epp. 1, 2, and 4 have equal claims to anti-quity. [38]

Yet more can be learned from the stichometries of the Demosthenic corpus. Since prose will not scan, some artificial accommodation had to be made when the hexameter line became the standard of measure-ment for prose works. Kurt Ohly has shown that the ancient scribes regarded the *stichoi* of prose works, like those of epic poetry, as aggregations the ultimate components of which were syllables, not letters.[39] An epic verse may have as few as twelve syllables or as many as seventeen. Ohly found that a prose *stichos* of 15 to 16 syllables established itself and became the rule throughout antiquity.[40] Even this degree of variability shows that different scribes would measure differently. The prose *stichos* in the Demosthenic corpus shows even wider variability; this fact suggests that those stichomet-ries may antedate the standardization of the unit demonstrated by Ohly.

The variability of the *stichos* within the Demosthenic corpus is not haphazard. Indeed, it suggests the activity of several different scribes.[41] F. Burger's researches have shown that the *Philippics* and

teenth-century Codex Laurentianus of Iamblichus (G. Vitelli, "Spicilegio fioren-tino," *Museo italiano di antichità classica*, I [1883], 4–5. In this case, the archaism may be due to Iamblichus himself or to the tendencies of the age of the Emperor Julian, who regarded the works of Plato and of Iamblichus with equal veneration. Since traces of stichometries in the Attic manner exist in the manuscript tradition of Plato (Ohly, *Stich. Unters.*, pp. 77–78), Julian or the Neoplatonic school of Athens may have felt that the works of Iamblichus deserved the same embellishments. None of the exceptional codices is reported to have marginal stichometry.

[38] Ep. 5, which is too short to have a marginal stichometry, does have a total stichometry; Ep. 6 has no stichometry whatever. The presence in Epp. 1–4 of both types of stichometry probably eliminates the possibility of an archaizing scribe (see the previous note). Moreover, stichometries to Demosthenes are attested by Dion. Hal. (above, n. 29); finally, one could wonder why an archaizing scribe would have left so many of the works of the Demosthenic corpus without stichometries.

[39] *Stich. Unters.*, pp. 22–30.

[40] *Ibid.*, pp. 4–22.

[41] Each scribe might adopt a different number of syllables for his standard *stichos*. Other factors to account for the variability would be individual scribal habits concerning elisions and individual means for reckoning the stichometries. Surely the scribes did not take the time to count individual syllables. They either droned out the words they wrote to a rhythmic syllabic sing-song or, knowing the average content of their written lines, simply counted those and converted the figure to *stichoi*.

the public orations (1–11, 13, 18–24), the *Prooemia*, and Epp. 1–5 consistently exhibit a longer *stichos* of 0.83 to 0.85 of a line of the Tauchnitz edition, while orations 14, 15, and 16, and the private orations, and the *Epitaphius* and the *Eroticus* exhibit a shorter one of 0.78 to 0.81 of a Tauchnitz line.[42] Burger did not know that the ultimate component of the *stichos* was not the letter but the syllable; nevertheless, the differences remain significant even when the count is based upon syllables rather than lines of print.[43] Burger's results, however, must be refined.[44] For the purposes of this study it is particularly important to note that Burger makes the *stichos* of Ep. 5 conform to that of Epp. 1–4 only by means of an emendation. But if the *stichos* of Epp. 1–4 was one of 15 syllables, that of Ep. 5 according to the actual stichometry was one of 16 syllables.[45] Both figures lie within the limits discovered by Ohly; hence Burger's emendation has no foundation. Thus we may see in the stichometry of Ep. 5 the hand of a scribe other than the one who reckoned the stichometries of Epp. 1-4. Although the designation may not be quite accurate, henceforth I shall refer to the *stichos* of the *Philippics*, public orations, *Prooemia*, and Epp. 1–4 as "the 15-syllable *stichos*."[46]

If the absence of the two letters of the marginal stichometry of

[42] *Stich. Unters. zu Dem. und Hdt.*, pp. 29–33.

[43] I have made the following trial counts of syllables, using the Oxford text of Rennie. Ep. 3 up to the alpha in the marginal stichometry contains 1,456 syllables; with elided letters restored, 1,492. Ep. 4 with a total of 101 *stichoi* contains 1,483 syllables; with elisions restored, 1,510. Restoring elisions, one thus gets a *stichos* of 15 syllables. On the other hand, D. 27 up to the alpha in the marginal stichometry contains 1,429 syllables; with the elisions restored, 1,474. The same oration between the alpha and the beta in the marginal stichometry contains 1,424 syllables; with the elisions restored, 1,471. Restoring elisions, one thus gets a *stichos* of 14.7 syllables.

[44] For an explanation of the anomalous stichometries of D. 59, and—in manuscripts of the family of **F**—of D. 19, see Drerup, *Philologus*, Suppl. VII, 536–37, n. 1. Drerup's solution of the problem of D. 59 leaves its stichometries based on a *stichos* of 0.75 of a Tauchnitz line. My count of the syllables between the beta and the gamma of the marginal stichometry yields 1,272 (1,280 with elisions restored). A *stichos* of 12.7–12.8 syllables still can be based upon the hexameter line. On the other hand, the marginal stichometry of D. 48 is either pure scribal guesswork or corrupt beyond repair. Burger's efforts (*Stich. Unters.*, p. 18) to restore it result in a *stichos* far shorter than a hexameter line.

[45] Burger emends the figure of the total stichometry from ΔΔΔΔ (40) to ΔΔΔΔΙΙΙ (43). Ep. 5 contains 626 syllables; with the elided syllables restored, 646. Using the original figure and restoring the elisions, one gets a *stichos* of exactly 16 syllables.

[46] See n. 43.

D. 1 and the total stichometry of D. 23 can be ascribed to accident, the collection of works with the 15-syllable *stichos* is distinguished throughout by possessing both marginal and total stichometries; whereas, for example, the three *symbouleutikoi* (D. 14–16) have no marginal stichometries. That these distinctions on the basis of stichometry are not fortuitous is confirmed by the fact that, unlike our entire manuscript tradition, they reflect the old arrangement of the orations which classified D. 13 with the *Philippics* rather than with the three *symbouleutikoi*. Didymus in the first century B.C. may have been the first to show that classification to be wrong, though he still based his commentary on an edition which included D. 13 among the *Philippics*.[47] The old order was known to Libanius[48] and the scholiast to D. 13.[49]

The works measured by the 15-syllable *stichos*, including the letters, are the best attested in the Demosthenic corpus and have always attracted the most interest.[50] Furthermore, three of the classified groupings of the manuscript tradition are measured by the 15-syllable *stichos*, but each has at its end works without stichometries. At the end of the *Philippics* in the families of **F** and **Y** appears the letter of Philip, which is certainly no speech of Demosthenes.

[47] Col. 13, lines 16 ff., Diels and Schubart, pp. 63–64; P. Foucart, *Étude sur Didymos*, pp. 3–7, 72–74.

[48] *Hypoth.* to D. 13.

[49] Schol. to p. 166, 1 Reiske in *Oratores Attici*, ed. Karl Müller, II, 573b.

[50] Dionysius of Halicarnassus touches upon many works of Demosthenes. In Dionysius' surviving writings, the works which have no stichometries or stichometries not measured by the 15-syllable *stichos* are hardly mentioned, except for the two *symbouleutikoi*, D. 14 and 15 (see the index at Dion. Hal. *Opuscula*, Vol. II 2, p. 415 U.-R.). At *Dem.* 57, Vol. I, p. 251 U.-R., he mentions D. 25, 26, and 59 only to say that they are spurious. At *Din.* 10, Vol. I, pp. 311–12 U.-R., he ascribes D. 58 to Dinarchus. At *Din.* 13, Vol. I, pp. 319–20 U.-R., he mentions D. 39 and 40 not as speeches of Demosthenes but at speeches wrongly ascribed to Dinarchus. Otherwise, he mentions only D. 54; Dionysius treats it as authentic and quotes from it (*Dem.* 12, Vol. I, p. 152 U.-R.). The papyri exhibit much the same proportions; see Pack, pp. 34–36: numbers 256–69, 274–323, 335–37, 339 from the collection measured by the 15-syllable *stichos*, and only numbers 270–73, 324–34 from the rest of the corpus. Fragments unavailable to Pack: A. E. Samuel, "*Beineke Inv. 4*, a New Fragment of Demosthenes," *Bulletin of the American Society of Papyrologists*, II(1964), 33–40, containing fragments of D. 19 and mentioning (p. 37) forthcoming publication of *P. Yalensis* I containing fragments of D. 19, D. 25, and D. 42; *POxy.* xxxi. 2548 (D. 24) and 2549 (Ep. 1). Harpocration, on the other hand, wanted all the surviving vocabulary of the Attic orators and cites from both groups without discrimination.

At the end of the public orations appear the two speeches against Aristogiton (and in **S** also D. 59, measured by a shorter *stichos*), all condemned as spurious by ancient authorities.[51] At the end of the letters in **F** and **Q** appear first Ep. 5, measured by a 16-syllable *stichos*, and then Ep. 6, which is absent from **S**, is nowhere else attested, and departs from the principles of Demosthenic style.[52]

The absence of stichometries cannot be attributed to the abuse suffered by material at the end of a volume, because the first oration against Aristogiton, as well as the second, lacks a stichometry. The suggestion is that the works measured by the 15-syllable *stichos* represent a collection assembled before the beginning of the Christian era, which excluded works considered to be spurious. To each of the sections of this collection the excluded works and Philip's letter[53] were later appended.[54] Clearly, then, this collection was already classified into the groupings found in our manuscript tradition. Its editor also probably compiled a list (*pinax*) of its component parts, establishing their order. This order may have left its trace in the medieval manuscripts. It was hard to preserve the order of the rolls of which a large corpus necessarily consisted in antiquity.[55] But Codex **S** of Demosthenes at least at its beginning goes back to a set wherein the rolls were numbered.[56] In **S** D. 13 no longer stands with the *Philippics*, and D. 25, 26, and 59 have been appended to the public orations; but otherwise only the *paragraphikoi*[57] interrupt the

[51] Dion. Hal. *Dem.* 57, Vol. I, p. 251 U.-R.; see also Blass, III 1, 56.

[52] The same phenomenon occurs in the group of *symbouleutikoi*; at its end, and without a stichometry, appears D. 17, condemned as spurious by ancient authorities. See Blass, III 1, 55–56. On the non-Demosthenic style of Ep. 6, see below, pp. 28–29.

[53] Philip's letter would naturally be appended in any case to D. 11. However, it did not appear in the edition used by Didymus, in which D. 13 immediately followed D. 11; hence, it was probably added to the Demosthenic corpus after D. 13 was removed from its position with the *Philippics*.

[54] Nothing of the sort appears in the other works of the Demosthenic corpus, apart from the *symbouleutikoi* (above, n. 52). Rather, in those other works the presence or absence of stichometries has no discernible pattern and can be ascribed, at least in part, to scribal carelessness. This is understandable, in view of the lesser interest of students in the private orations.

[55] See Appendix III.

[56] The scribe at the end of D. 7 notes the end of τόμος α′ containing six Philippic orations and gives its total stichometry.

[57] D. 32–38 (plus D. 45 and 46, appended to D. 36 because of their close relationship); see Drerup, Philologus, Suppl. VII, 534.

sequence of the works measured by the 15-syllable *stichos*. The interruption is not surprising, for the practice of ancient pinacographers was to place letters last and "hypomnematic" works like the *Prooemia* just before them.[58] Thus the *Prooemia* and Epp. 1–4 would tend to be relegated to the end of any collection of Demosthenic works, and their position in **S** may represent a stage wherein D. 25, 26, and 59, and the *paragraphikoi* had been added to the collection measured by the 15-syllable *stichos*. The position of the *Prooemia* and the letters at the very end of the Demosthenic corpus in **F**, **Q**, and **B** would then simply reflect the continued operation of the principle of the pinacographers.

These principles of classification and ordering go back to the very beginnings of Greek pinacographic activity in Alexandria or in fourth-century Athens.[59] How far back can the collection with the 15-syllable *stichos* be traced? Again with the help of the stichometries, the *terminus ante quem* may be pushed back to about 100 B.C., for the stichometries of *De Corona* were computed on a text which did not contain the spurious documents found in our manuscripts.[60] These documents were composed in the first half of the second century B.C. and were incorporated into the text no later than the beginning of the first century B.C.[61]

We may trace this collection back still farther, to the middle years of the third century B.C., when Callimachus was composing his *Pinakes*, a comprehensive bibliography of the works extant in his time.[62] Surviving fragments of Callimachus' list of Demosthenic works show that it contained D. 7 and D. 58. From this fact it can be deduced that Callimachus' list of Demosthenic works must have

[58] See Paul Moraux, *Les listes anciennes des ouvrages d'Aristote*, pp. 150–65.

[59] *Ibid.;* see also below, pp. 18–20.

[60] Christ, *Abh. d. philos.-philol. Cl. d. Königl. bayer. Akad. d. Wissensch.*, XVI, 192. There were texts of *De Corona* in antiquity containing even more fabricated documents than our manuscript tradition. Thus a Copenhagen papyrus of the first half of the second century A.D., containing fragments of pars. 217–23, has texts for the three documents mentioned there only by title in the medieval codices. See *Papyri Graecae Haunienses*, ed. Carsten Höeg, fasciculus primus: *Literarische Texte und Ptolemäische Urkunden*, ed. Tage Larsen (Copenhagen: Einar Munksgaard, 1942), pp. 14–37 (No. 5).

[61] P. Treves, "Les documents apocryphes du 'Pro corona,'" *Les études classiques* IX (1940), 138–74, esp. p. 140.

[62] See F. Schmidt, *Die Pinakes des Kallimachos*. Callimachus' death (between 246 and 221): Herter, "Kallimachos," *RE*, Suppl. V (1931), 395.

consisted substantially of our Demosthenic corpus;[63] thus, presumably, it included Epp. 1–5.

The presence of D. 7 and D. 58 in Callimachus' list is significant for another reason, for the collection measured by the 15-syllable *stichos* includes D. 7 and excludes the "private orations," D. 27–59. Hence the corpus which lay before Callimachus already contained both works from within and works from without the collection measured by the 15-syllable *stichos*. Furthermore, stichometries are known to have been included among the descriptive data which Callimachus gave for works listed in the *Pinakes*.[64] Our evidence indicates only that Callimachus compiled a vast bibliographical work which included a list of the writings ascribed to Demosthenes. It does not show that Callimachus or his associates or indeed any Alexandrian scholar was responsible for assembling the collection measured by the

[63] First by H. Sauppe in 1841, in his *Epistola Critica ad Godofredum Hermannum*, reprinted in his *Ausgewaehlte Schriften*, p. 110. All four manuscript families of our Demosthenic corpus contain D. 7, and only the fragmentary family of Y lacks D. 58. These two orations were known to be spurious even in later antiquity (Dion. Hal. *Din.* 10, pp. 311–12 U.-R.; Harpocration *s.vv. Hegesippos, Theokrines*, and *agraphiou;* Liban. *Hypoth.* to D. 7 and D. 58); see Blass, III 1, 498–500, and III 2, 137–46. But Dionysius of Halicarnassus quotes Callimachus' list as including both (*Dem.* 13, Vol. I, p. 157 U.-R.; *Din.* 10, Vol. I, pp. 311–12). The Demosthenic corpus does contain much that is not by Demosthenes, but with the exception of the spurious documents inserted into some of the orations (and possibly also of Ep. 6—see Appendix I), it contains nothing demonstrably later than the beginning of the third century B.C. Hence, if the collection of Demosthenic works which lay before Callimachus already included two of the wrongly ascribed orations of our corpus, one may infer that the rest of the corpus had been collected by that time. Furthermore, as Sauppe noted, Callimachus assigned to Dinarchus a speech ascribed by others to Demosthenes (Photius *Bibl.* Cod. 265, p. 491b Bekker), and that speech is absent from the extant corpus. Hence one may infer that Callimachus drew up his list with some critical judgment and that his judgment was sufficient to eliminate a work from our manuscript tradition. Naturally, later scholars exercised their own critical acumen on the works ascribed to Demosthenes, and at least one title in Callimachus' list was eliminated from the manuscript tradition (Harpocration *s.v. enepiskêmma*, p. 72 Bekker). There is, however, no evidence that any work not listed by Callimachus has found its way into the Demosthenic corpus, with the possible exception of Ep. 6.

[64] Athenaeus vi. 244a: "τοῦ Χαιρεφῶντος καὶ σύγγραμμα ἀναγράφει Καλλίμαχος ἐν τῷ τῶν παντοδαπῶν πίνακι γράφων οὕτως· '... στίχων τοε'''; xiii. 585b: "ἡ Γνάθαινα ... ἥτις καὶ νόμον συσσιτικὸν συνέγραψεν . . . ἀνέγραψε δ' αὐτὸν Καλλίμαχος ἐν τῷ τρίτῳ πίνακι τῶν Νόμων...'... στίχων τριακοσίων εἴκοσι τριῶν.'" Both works for which Callimachus is known to have given the stichometry are by Athenians of the second half of the fourth century B.C. On Chaerephon, see M. Wellmann, "Chairephon 4," *RE*, III[2] (1899), 2029; on Gnathaina, see Alfred Körte, *BPhW*, XXVI (1906), 901.

15-syllable *stichos* or even for assembling the Demosthenic corpus (though that is likely) or for originating its classified divisions and its stichometries.[65] Athenians of the third century B.C. were quite as capable of wrongly ascribing D. 7 and D. 58 to Demosthenes. Callimachus surely based the *Pinakes* upon the collections and catalogues of the Museum of Alexandria,[66] and these followed the patterns used already by Aristotle in fourth-century Athens. Aristotle may well have been not the only one in Athens to classify and catalogue his library.[67] The headings under which the Demosthenic corpus was classified and divided were native to the civic institutions and rhetorical theory of fourth-century Athens.[68] Moreover, there is no trace of alphabetical order in the transmitted arrangement of Demosthenic works. On the other hand, Callimachus seems to have arranged the works of an author in alphabetical order *except where another principle of arrangement had already established itself.*[69] Again, the combination of marginal stichometries in letter labels and total stichometries in acrophonic numerals represents the practice of fourth-century Athens.[70] It may not be an accident that neither of the surviving stichometric fragments of Callimachus' *Pinakes* uses acrophonic cardinals and that one of them uses the 27-letter system.[71] Indeed, if

[65] Cf. Drerup, *Philologus*, Suppl. VII, 546–50; Ohly, *Stich. Unters.*, pp. 101–2; Schmidt, pp. 85–86.

[66] Schmidt, p. 46; Wendel, *Buchbeschreibung*, p. 69.

[67] Strabo xiii. 1. 54; Wendel, *Buchbeschreibung*, pp. 24, 70–71 (traces of book classification in classical Athens), and Milkau-Leyh, III 1, 54–60. See also Regenbogen, *RE*, XX, 1415–19 (Aristotle's works in *pinax* form).

[68] See below, pp. 98–100, 117–18; on collections of prooemia, see Ludwig Radermacher, *Artium scriptores*, pp. 80, 119–20. On the bibliographic classification of prooemia as "hypomnematic" works, see above, p. 17.

[69] Wendel, *Buchbeschreibung*, pp. 69–70, and Milkau-Leyh, III 1, 71. Moraux, pp. 221–47, contrasts Callimachus' method of bibliographical arrangement with that used in the ancient list of Aristotelian works which he ascribes to Ariston of Ceos in Athens in the third century B.C. The classification scheme of that list resembles the scheme of the Demosthenic corpus. See, however, I. Düring, "Ariston or Hermippus," *Classica et Mediaevalia*, XVII (1956), 11–21.

[70] Above, pp. 9–11.

[71] It is possible that the fragments in Athenaeus simply represent transcriptions made from the *Pinakes* when acrophonic cardinals had passed out of use. In a huge bibliographical work, however, acrophonic cardinals probably would have been both too space-consuming and too liable to corruption. Callimachus may have preferred the more compact 27-letter system, certainly available to him, or the less-corruptible procedure of writing the numbers out in words. See *POxy.* xxi. 2294 (second century A.D.) and the stichometries given in the bibliographical lists of Diogenes

all the stichometries of the Demosthenic corpus had been done at once under the direction of an Alexandrian, one would expect a certain uniformity, perhaps somewhat disturbed by the accidents of text transmission. But in our manuscripts, D. 58, known to have been listed by Callimachus, has no stichometry whatever, although at its end it bears the scribal notation that the manuscript has been corrected. And in the orations which do have stichometries two slightly differing units of measurement have been used. The difference in the two standard *stichoi* can hardly represent simply a division of labor between two Alexandrians who were editing the entire Demosthenic corpus, for to discover that D. 13 did not belong among the *Philippics* hardly required the vast erudition of a Didymus. If the classification of the works measured by the 15-syllable *stichos* dated from the time when the entire Demosthenic corpus existed in Alexandria, one would expect to find D. 13 grouped with D. 14–17. The "misclassification" suggests rather that at the head of the collection measured by the 15-syllable *stichos* stood a group of Demosthenic speeches to the Assembly which took no notice of D. 14–17. Hence the collection measured by the 15-syllable *stichos* probably antedates both the compiling of the rest of the Demosthenic corpus and the activity of Callimachus. When the corpus was assembled, it incorporated that collection without disturbing its groupings, and a separate category was created to include D. 14–16 and possibly D. 17.

This inference can be supported by other considerations. We have seen that the combination of marginal stichometries in letter labels and total stichometries in acrophonic numerals can still be found in works written in the first century B.C. Outside the mathematical tradition and before the archaizing tendencies of the later Roman empire, however, the 27-letter system seems to have completely replaced letter labels for the numbering of the subdivisions of a work already in the third century B.C.[72] There are clear traces that the *Prooemia*, which are among the works measured by the 15-syllable *stichos*, were numbered by letter labels.[73] It is, indeed, conceivable

Laertius, iv. 14 (Xenocrates) and v. 50 (Theophrastus), all of which use the 27-letter system; and iv. 5 (Speusippus), iv. 24 (Crantor), v. 27 (Aristotle), ix. 111 (Timon), all written out in words. The list of the works of Theophrastus probably was compiled by Hermippus, a pupil of Callimachus; see Moraux, p. 246, n. 148.

[72] Below, Appendix IV.

[73] See Appendix V.

that these numbers were put in during the efflorescence of Demosthenic studies which began in the second century A.D.[74] Nevertheless, of all the surviving ancient literature, the combination of total stichometries in acrophonic numerals, marginal stichometries in letter labels, and divisions numbered by letter labels is found elsewhere only in manuscripts of Homer and Sappho.[75] The edition of the *Iliad* with stichometries and book divisions designated by letters took place no later than the first half of the third century B.C.,[76] and the edition of Sappho was probably earlier than that date.[77]

We enter the realm of conjecture when we try to discover the origin of the collection measured by the 15-syllable *stichos* and the purposes for which it was assembled. Nevertheless, on the basis of what this canon includes and excludes one can draw conclusions of considerable probability, conclusions which again suggest that it was assembled before the time of Callimachus. The collection does contain the acknowledged masterpieces of Demosthenes' eloquence, the works most studied by rhetoricians; it does contain the pieces most relevant to his political biography. But it omits the early speeches against the young orator's guardians, so interesting for a biographer of an orator hero; it omits the morally piquant pair of speeches, D. 36 and 45, so interesting for scandal-mongering Hellenistic literary critics and biographers;[78] it omits the other private orations with their complicated legal aspects and their emotional appeals, which surely were attractive as examples for rhetorical exercises. It omits indubitably authentic pieces like D. 14, 15, and 16, which an avid collector of Demosthenica would certainly have included.

However, every one of the pieces measured by the 15-syllable *stichos* serves at least one of three functions: (1) it may present Demosthenes in his great struggle to defend Athens' interests against

[74] Harpocration (*s.v. orrhôdein*) and Pollux (vi. 143) cite from the *Prooemia* without numbering them, and *POxy.* i. 26 (first or second century A.D.) has no letter label but only a *paragraphus* at the beginning of *Prooem.* 28. See Pasquali, p. 288.

[75] Ohly, *Stich. Unters.*, pp. 84–85; *POxy.* xxi. 2289, fr. 1(a); and Appendix IV.

[76] See Paul Mazon, *Introduction a l'Iliade* (Paris: Société d'édition "Les belles lettres," 1942), pp. 139–40.

[77] E. Lobel, Σαπφοῦς μέλη (Oxford: Clarendon Press, 1925), p. xiv; Aly, "Sappho," *RE*, I^A2 (1920), 2369.

[78] See Aesch. 2. 165; 3. 173; Plut. *Dem.* 15. 1.

21

the menaces from the north, the temporary one from Thrace[79] and the inexorable one from Macedonia;[80] (2) it may present Demosthenes expressing his views on sound domestic policy or exhorting his fellow-citizens to a high standard of political and moral conduct;[81] (3) it may present an explicit account of Demosthenes' good services to Athens and a defense (often with a counterattack) against the charges leveled by his detractors.[82]

The absence of D. 14, 15, and 16 and the presence of the *Prooemia* give hints as to the purpose of the collection. The three speeches deal primarily with foreign policy. All three address themselves to situations which soon changed, never to recur. Of the three, only D. 14 fits one of the above-mentioned categories; the suggested reform of the trierarchy was "sound domestic policy." The Athenians adopted neither the naval reform nor the policies advocated in D. 15 and 16. The lasting political principles contained in these speeches are found elsewhere, in the works measured by the 15-syllable *stichos*.[83] Hence the one who assembled that collection had no interest in preserving those three orations in their entirety.

Nevertheless, D. 14, 15, and 16 contain exhortations of "timeless moral value." A prime function of the prooemia of Athenian speeches to the Assembly was to impress the audience with the righteousness of the speaker and of his proposal;[84] hence Athenian prooemia usually consisted of moralizing commonplaces, though the speaker may have been completely sincere. Demosthenes, in particular, even when addressing himself to a transitory situation, would give expres-

[79] D. 23.

[80] D. 1–11; 18–19; *Prooem.* 21; Ep. 1; D. 23, too, belongs here (see pars. 107–9, 116, 121, 183).

[81] Especially D. 13; 20–24; and the *Prooemia*.

[82] D. 18, 19, 21, and Epp. 1–4. This may have been the reason for the preservation and publication of D. 21 (see Aesch. 3. 52, and cf. Dion. Hal. *Amm. I* 4; Blass, III 1, 328). Autobiographical details not found elsewhere in the works measured by the 15-syllable *stichos* occur at D. 21. 78–82; Demosthenes recounts his liturgies in pars. 13–17, 66–69, 78–80, 154–57. His only detailed reply to the charges brought against his early career is at D. 21. 103–22. Pars. 189–92 answer those who would use against Demosthenes the common Athenian prejudice against politicians who were too able.

[83] The notion (D. 15) that Athens in her foreign policy should support democracies: D. 13. 9; the principles of naval finance and organization: D. 18. 102–9, which unlike D. 14 recounts a program which succeeded; the theory of the "balance of power" in foreign policy (D. 16): D. 23. 102–6.

[84] Anax. 29.

sion to the timeless moral values concentrated in his prooemia. Is it an accident that the exordia of D. 14, 15, and 16, alone among the Demosthenic speeches, reappear in the *Prooemia* with differences so small that the text there can have no other origin than those very orations?[85] Rather it would appear that the collector intentionally preserved the "lasting moral values" of these speeches by including their prooemia among the works measured by the 15-syllable *stichos*. At least some of the other *Prooemia* may have had such an origin, as extracts of "lasting value" from complete speeches on transitory issues, rather than as fragments found among Demosthenes' papers after his death or interpolated by a "redactor."[86] In any case, the entire collection of *Prooemia* serves the purpose of displaying the moral attitude of Demosthenes in addressing the Assembly.[87]

Likewise suggestive are the probable sources from which the compiler took his Demosthenic material. He took works which Demosthenes himself had published – certain orations and Epp. 1–4,

[85] D. 14. 1–2=*Prooem.* 7; D. 15. 1–2=*Prooem.* 27; D. 16. 1–3=*Prooem.* 8. The first paragraph of *Prooem.* 1 is almost as close in its wording to D. 4. 1, but it is a commonplace usable on many occasions by a young man, and the rest of the prooemium is quite different from the oration, although it may have been written against the same background. *Prooem.* 3 bears a close resemblance to D. 1. 1, but the words are transposed far more drastically in the two versions than with D. 14, 15, and 16; moreover, the piece is a commonplace usable almost anytime, and Demosthenes may have used it more than once. Cf. Albert Rupprecht, "Die demosthenische Prooemiensammlung," *Philologus*, LXXXII (1927), 372–75, 379, 381–82, 398, 402; Friedrich Focke, "Demosthenesstudien," *Genethliakon Wilhelm Schmid*, pp. 33, 46–50. Both Focke and Rupprecht believe that the slight differences between D. 14, 15, and 16 and the respective *Prooemia* arise from the finishing touches which Demosthenes put on his orations when he published them, the text in the *Prooemia* being the unretouched original found among his papers by his heirs. The differences are so slight that they might even be unintentional scribal variants.

[86] See Rupprecht, *Philologus*, LXXXII, 365–410; Focke, *Genethliakon Schmid*, pp. 30–67; Wilhelm Nitsche, *Demosthenes und Anaximenes* (*Sonderabdruck aus der Zeitschrift für das Gymnasialwesen, Jahresberichte des Philologischen Vereins*, XXXII; Berlin: Weidmannsche Buchhandlung, 1906), pp. 137–39.

[87] This statement applies to *Prooem.* 54 as well, which may have been included to show Demosthenes actively participating in religious ritual. The miscellaneous assortment of gods should cause no difficulty. The Greek oracles, when asked by individuals or cities what gods to sacrifice to in order to secure a favorable issue of matters at hand, are known to have replied with such arrays of deities; see, e.g. D. 21. 52–53 and 43. 66; X. *Anab.* iii. 1. 6, *Vect.* 6. 2; *GHI* 158. Only the naming of Apollo without an epithet is strange. Cf. Focke, *Genethliakon Schmid*, pp. 33–35.

if authentic.[88] Where no manuscript of a famous speech was available, the compiler might take a rhetorical historian's published reconstruction, such as D. 11, which originally stood in book vii of the *Philippic Histories* of Anaximenes of Lampsacus;[89] or he might include another politician's speech which was known to have expressed Demosthenes' views (D. 7).[90] Finally, he drew on material of interest found among the orator's papers after his death (the *Prooemia* and perhaps D. 21).

We have, then, the following clues to the identity of the compiler of the collection measured by the 15-syllable *stichos*: he worked at or before the time of Callimachus; he had access to Demosthenes' papers; he wished to present defenses of Demosthenes' career and to portray him as hero, patriot, and moral example. Our evidence is much too scanty to allow positive identification, but there is one obvious possibility fitting this description: Demochares of Leuconoë,[91] Demosthenes' nephew and "political heir."[92] After a long and

[88] This is not the place to discuss the intricate problems of whether and how Demosthenes published his orations. Hermippus *apud* Plut. *Dem.* 11. 4 implies that Demosthenes did publish some of his speeches to the Assembly. One possible clue should be mentioned here. D. 1–11 are all equally Philippics and are designated as *Philippics* 1–11 by Didymus, Harpocration, and in papyri (e.g., POxy. xv. 1804, fr. 4, lines 16–17). This is the normal procedure to follow when one has the entire collection of Demosthenic speeches to the Assembly. Whence comes it that D. 4, 6, 9, and 10 are singled out in the manuscript tradition with the titles *First* to *Fourth Philippic*? Perhaps Demosthenes himself gave these four speeches their titles, perhaps publishing them all together. Thereafter, until the tradition became obscured by the passage of time, the title *Philippic* belonged exclusively to them; a different nomenclature had to be used to refer to D. 1–3, 5, 7–8, and 11, until later commentators extended the title *Philippic*—quite logically—to them.

Every one of our four *Philippics* bears the marks of editing for publication. On the editorial omissions and changes in D. 4 and 6, see W. Jaeger, *Demosthenes*, pp. 120–22, 164, 245. D. 9 exists in two versions—perhaps one was reedited by the orator for publication and the other is the original found among his papers after his death. The relationship between D. 8 and D. 10 has been taken to suggest that one was delivered before the Assembly and the other edited for publication as propaganda. See the references cited below, Chap. 8, n. 70.

[89] Didymus col. 11, p. 51 Diels-Schubart.

[90] Blass, III 2, 137–38; below, commentary to Ep. 2. 10.

[91] See below, pp. 33–34, and cf. Drerup, *Philologus*, Suppl. VII, 549–50; Focke *Genethliakon Schmid*, p. 38; Nitsche, pp. 135–48.

[92] See *F. Gr. Hist.* II, No. 75, and Hermann Bengtson, *Griechische Geschichte*, pp. 356–57. Demochares was both a historian (see below, Chap. 4, n. 16) and an ardent partisan of democracy. It is tempting to speculate that his hostility to the advocate of oligarchy and rival historian, Androtion, led Demochares to include in his collection D. 22 and 24. On Androtion, see F. Jacoby, *Atthis* (Oxford: Clarendon Press, 1949), pp. 74–79.

active political career in which he surely aimed to carry on his uncle's tradition, Demochares finally succeeded in 280/79 in getting the Athenians to pass a resolution publicly honoring the memory of Demosthenes. Demochares' petition and the inscription on the base of the statue of Demosthenes which the Athenians erected at his request serve the same functions we have noticed in the collection measured by the 15-syllable *stichos*. Demochares' own death occurred before 271/0 B.C., the year in which his son, Laches, petitioned that the memory of Demochares be similarly honored.[93] This date would stand as a *terminus ante quem* for the collection measured by the 15-syllable *stichos*. Moreover, whenever Demochares might have compiled the collection, he could hardly have published it in Athens before 286, as we shall see.[94]

The collection measured by the 15-syllable *stichos* contains at least two pieces that are certainly not by Demosthenes, Orations 7 and 11. Hence, by tracing the letters and that collection back to the third century B.C. and possibly to Demochares, we have not proved their authenticity. Other methods must now be brought to bear.

[93] Inscription: *Vit. X orat.* 847a; Plut. *Dem.* 30. 5. Petitions: *Vit. X orat.* 847d–e, 850f–51f; on the authenticity and interpretation of the texts of the petitions preserved in Pseudo-Plutarch, see Fr. Ladek, "Über die Echtheit zweier auf Demosthenes und Demochares bezüglichen Urkunden . . .," *Wiener Studien*, XIII (1891), 63–128.

[94] Below, pp. 92–94, esp. Chap. 6, n. 154.

CHAPTER 3

The Style of the Letters

THE DISSERTATIONS OF A. Neupert and H. Sachsenweger have summed up the work of all their predecessors on the style of the letters.[1] Neupert gathered every instance he could find in Epp. 1–6 of usages which did not conform to those in Demosthenes' authentic works; Sachsenweger took every one of Neupert's stylistic arguments against the authenticity of Epp. 2 and 3 and showed it to be false or inconclusive. The shortcomings in Sachsenweger's discussion can be made good,[2] so that the net result shows that Epp. 1–4 are written in good fourth-century Greek and in good Demosthenic style. Since we have traced the letters back to the time of Demochares, this is not surprising.

[1] Albert Neupert, *De Demosthenicarum quae feruntur epistularum fide et auctoritate*, pp. 46–76; Horst Sachsenweger, *De Demosthenis epistulis*, pp. 18–46.

[2] Sachsenweger had at his disposal indices to all the Attic orators except Isaeus. An index to Isaeus is now complete, compiled by W. A. Goligher and W. S. Maguinness. The use of this index leaves Sachsenweger's results unchanged. Additions and corrections to Sachsenweger: commentary to Ep. 3. 6, δημοτικὸν κτλ.; 3. 10, βουλεύεσθαι κτλ.; 3. 26, τοὺς βίους κτλ.; 3. 36; 2. 16, ὅ ... χρόνος; 2. 17; 2. 19. Unusual constructions which Sachsenweger did not discuss are treated in the commentary to Epp. 3. 22, 40; 2. 20, 21.

Sachsenweger did not treat Epp. 1 and 4 at all. In the commentary we show that all the *hapax legomena* and unusual constructions in those letters could have been used by Demosthenes. The *hapax legomena* are ἐπινοίας (Ep. 1. 1), εὐκατεργαστότερα (Ep. 1. 6), πικραίνεσθαι (Ep. 1. 6), ἠπιώτεροι (Ep. 1. 7), ἐπιστατῆσαι (Ep. 1. 11), διελυμάνθη (Ep. 1.' 12), μετάγνωσις (Ep. 1. 15), θεοφιλεστάτην (Ep. 4. 3), προσεπισφραγιζομένους (Ep. 4. 3), ἀγάλλεται (Ep. 4. 11), αἰσχρορρημοσύνη (Ep. 4. 11), and ἀφελής (Ep. 4. 11). κώπαις (Ep. 1. 8) has another example in the Demosthenic corpus only at D. 13. 14, and μείγνυμι (Ep. 1. 10), only at D. 60. 18. Both D. 13 and D. 60 are of disputed authenticity. The unusual constructions are τὸν ἔπειτα χρόνον and ἐπὶ νοῦν ἐλθεῖν (Ep. 1. 1), ὡς σὺν θεοῖς εἰρῆσθαι (Ep. 1. 3), σὺν πολλῇ σπουδῇ καὶ πόνῳ (Ep. 1. 12), and κατὰ τῶν νικητηρίων ... εὐξάμενοι (Ep. 1. 15).

Like all of Demosthenes' authentic works, Epp. 1–4 contain *hapax legomena* but no words which might render them suspect such as expressions with a political connotation opposed to Demosthenes' views or demonstrably later coinages.[3] The peculiarities of an author's style are often better revealed by his almost unconscious preferences in the use of grammatical constructions and particles than by his mere vocabulary. For example, in Greek syntax it is hardly possible to avoid entirely the type of construction examined by Benito Gaya Nuño:[4] a verb accompanied by a dependent complementary infinitive which itself is accompanied by a dependent complementary infinitive. Gaya's researches have shown that individual Attic authors[5] exhibit statistically significant preferences in their arrange-ment of such constructions, with Demosthenes outstanding for the spectacular variety of his usages. The application of Gaya's methods of analysis shows that Ep. 3 is an outstanding example of this aspect of Demosthenes' style; for the other letters, the results are inconclu sive.[6]

Again, prepositions and particles always have to be used, and here peculiarities are more a matter of unconscious usage than of conscious choice. The use of prepositions in the letters is entirely that of Demosthenes and his contemporaries.[7] The same is true of the use of connective particles.[8] Certain combinations of particles are peculiar to certain authors in the extant Greek literature. Two combinations

[3] The frequency of *hapax legomena* in the corpus of Demosthenic works regarded by Sachsenweger as authentic is 6.6–6.7 per hundred Teubner lines; for *De Corona* it is 9.9; for Ep. 1 it is 7.5 if both D. 13 and D. 60 are considered spurious; for Ep. 2, 5.3; for Ep. 3, 5.9; and for Ep. 4, 5.8. See Sachsenweger's Table II, p. 22.

[4] *Sobre un giro de la lengua de Demóstenes.*

[5] In addition to selected orations of Demosthenes, Gaya examines the works of Antiphon, Thucydides, Lysias, Andocides, Isocrates, Isaeus, Aeschines, Hyperides, and Lycurgus.

[6] See Appendix VI.

[7] Every prepositional usage in Epp. 1–4 has been considered in the light of L. Lutz, *Die Präpositionen bei den attischen Rednern.* The instances which might raise problems are treated in the commentary. See above, n. 2.

[8] The use of connective particles in Epp. 1–4 has been examined in the light of J. D. Denniston, *The Greek Particles.* Neupert's objection (pp. 74–75) to the fre-quent and repetitious use of γάρ probably depends on the view ascribed to Isocrates (*apud* Syrianus *Scholia in Hermog.*, Vol. I, p. 28 Rabe), that the use of the same connective particle twice in succession is to be avoided. However, frequent repeti-tion of a particle was not generally felt to be a defect in fourth-century Greek; see Denniston, pp. lxii–lxiv. See also Sachsenweger, pp. 43–44.

notably characteristic of Demosthenes occur in the letters,[9] and in the genuine speeches of Demosthenes the particle τοιγαροῦν (Ep. 4. 10) is found to the exclusion of its synonym τοιγάρτοι.[10] Only one combination of particles might excite suspicion, οὐ γὰρ δήπου ... γε, found at Ep. 3. 43 and elsewhere in the Demosthenic corpus only at the probably inauthentic D. 61. 42. However, the combination is well attested in fourth-century prose.[11] Perhaps after the harshness of Ep. 3. 42 Demosthenes would have felt οὐ γὰρ δή ... γε[12] too brusque; hence the softening enclitic.[13] The subordinate clauses of Epp. 1–4 offer no grounds for suspicion.[14]

Furthermore, Epp. 1–4 avoid hiatus exactly in the Demosthenic manner.[15] They also conform to Blass's law, the rule of style which distinguishes the work of Demosthenes from that of nearly every other known ancient author. Blass discovered that in the mature works of Demosthenes extraordinary care is taken to avoid accumulations of three or more short syllables. Two studies, one by C. D. Adams and the other by F. Vogel,[16] attempt to give a strict formulation to the rule; both show Epp. 1–4 to be good examples of Demosthenic style. According to Adams, the figures are as follows (accumulations per hundred Oxford lines):

Ep. 1	6.2	Ep. 4	3.75
Ep. 2	8.	Ep. 5	26.
Ep. 3	3.7	Ep. 6	31.

[9] οὐ μὴν ἀλλά (Epp. 1. 3, 3. 5), also common in Isocrates; ἀλλὰ μήν to mark the transition from a statement to the presentation of evidence in support of it (Ep. 3. 23), also common in Isaeus. See Denniston, pp. lxxx–lxxxi, 28–29, 346.

[10] Denniston, p. 567; the sole exceptions are D. 8. 66, where τοιγάρτοι is a manuscript variant for καὶ γάρ τοι, and D. 23. 203.

[11] Denniston, p. 268.

[12] D. 6. 12, 19. 120; Ep. 3. 41.

[13] Denniston, p. 267; see D. 20. 167 and 57. 65 (οὐ δήπου γε).

[14] Against Neupert, p. 74, see R. Kühner, *Ausführliche Grammatik der griechischen Sprache, zweiter Teil: Satzlehre*, II, 434–36; Lutz, pp. 104–116 (the use of ἐπί with the dative); and cf. Sachsenweger, pp. 41–42. Examples in Demosthenes of relative pronouns as connectives: D. 9. 54, 65; 18. 27, 49, and 295; of relative clauses with optative verbs: 18. 89, 290; 8. 51; 21. 209; 27. 67; relative clauses with imperative verbs: D. 1. 20; 18. 173; 20. 14.

[15] Blass, III 1, 448, 451, 453, n. 3; Neupert, pp. 72–73; Sachsenweger, pp. 45–46.

[16] Adams, "Demosthenes' Avoidance of Breves," *CP*, XII (1917), 271–94; Vogel, "Die Kurzenmeidung in der griechischen Prosa des IV Jahrhunderts," *Hermes*, LVIII (1923), 87–108.

Even Ep. 2 compares favorably with authentic speeches of Demosthenes (D. 9: 9.4; D. 14: 9.6; D. 16: 8.4) and is far removed from Epp. 5 and 6 and from Philip's letter (D. 12), which otherwise has the lowest incidence (33) among the non-Demosthenic works in the corpus.

According to Vogel, the figures are (accumulations per hundred Teubner lines):

Ep. 1	2.50	Ep. 4	3.33
Ep. 2	3.17	Ep. 5	5.40
Ep. 3	1.85	Ep. 6	22.94

The average for indubitably authentic speeches is 4.57. D. 16 has 8.37, and D. 59, which has the lowest figure of all the non-Demosthenic works in the corpus, has 17.05.

The inconsistent results for Ep. 5 are ascribable to differences in Adams' and Vogel's formulations of Blass's law and to the fact that Ep. 5 is too short to provide a valid statistical sample.

No ancient rhetorical text mentions Blass's law. Only Aelius Aristides is known to have observed it,[17] obviously imitating Demosthenes. If such imitation was possible in the second century A.D., one cannot deny that it was possible in the fourth century B.C. However, the one fourth-century work known to have been fabricated as a speech of Demosthenes is D. 11.[18] Already in 1881 Henri Weil observed that the speech could not be by Demosthenes, for in avoidance of hiatus and other respects it is in the style of Isocrates.[19] D. 11 does not conform to Blass's law.

Scholars have tried to prove Epp. 1–4 imitative fabrications by collecting the numerous parallels between passages and arguments in the letters and passages and arguments in the orations, particularly *De Corona*.[20] However, these examples speak equally well for or against Demosthenes' authorship of the letters. For the most part the parallels are not even literal. There may be a difference between the repetitions which a writer would allow himself throughout his works

---

[17] Vogel, *Hermes*, LVIII, 105.

[18] Didymus, col. 11, lines 10–14, p. 51 Diels-Schubart.

[19] Weil, *Les harangues de Démosthène* (2d ed.; Paris: Librairie Hachette, 1881), p. 420. Cf. Blass, III 1, 393.

[20] A. Schaefer, "Sind die demosthenischen Briefe echt oder nicht?" *NJb*, CXV (1877), 164; Neupert, pp. 25–29, 43–46; Wilhelm Nitsche, *Demosthenes und Anaximenes*, pp. 141–48.

and the copying done by an imitator, but it could only be that the imitator might parrot the words and ideas in a context which they did not fit. But all the examples collected from the letters are aptly expressed integral parts of the discussions in which they are found.[21]

As for the parallels to *De Corona*, since the letters share with that oration the aim of presenting a justification of Demosthenes' career, it is not surprising that the same arguments should occur in both. Demosthenes, like any politician, had a limited stock of striking proofs of his right to be considered a patriot and a great public benefactor, and favorite ways of expressing them. Doubtless he drew upon these many times during his career. Demosthenes does quote and paraphrase himself from oration to oration.[22]

The only letter in which such parallels arouse great suspicion is Ep. 4, for with its almost total silence on the historical situation of 323 B.C. it looks too much like a parroting of the discussion of Fortune in *De Corona*.[23] However, advances beyond the situation reflected in *De Corona* exist in Ep. 4.[24] Hence, the examination of the style of the letters reveals nothing that Demosthenes could not have written.

[21] See Blass, "Die demosthenischen Briefe," *NJb*, CXV (1877), 544; Sachsenweger, pp. 16–17.

[22] See Theon *Progym.*, Vol. I, pp. 155–56 Walz; Jaeger, *Demosthenes*, p. 64.

[23] D. 18. 253–54, 270–71.

[24] See below, pp. 74–76.

CHAPTER 4

The Alternatives to Authenticity

I F THE TRANSMISSION of the letters can be traced back to the third
century B.C. and the style is entirely that used by Demosthenes
in the fourth, the presumption is that the letters arose in that period.
This, however, does not prove that Demosthenes wrote them. Other
methods, those of historical and rhetorical analysis, must now be
used to seek a decision of the question of authenticity. Each letter
must be considered both in the context of the others in the collection
and on its own merits; every possible genre in which an ancient
author could have fabricated letters of Demosthenes in the fourth
century or the early Hellenistic period must be considered. There are
at least four of these genres.

1. Epp. 1–4 may be the work of a rhetorician treating the theme:
"What would Demosthenes have written to the Athenians from
exile?"[1] Rhetorical exhibitions on mythological themes are well
attested from pre-Hellenistic times,[2] but letters of Demosthenes in
the first half of the third century B.C. would be themes taken from
actual "modern" history.[3] Ancient sources preserve two traditions
on when this genre of themes from actual history arose. Quintilian[4]
transmits a report that it began in the time of Demetrius of Phalerum;
according to Philostratus,[5] it began with Aeschines' activity in exile
as a teacher of rhetoric in Caria and Rhodes. Though attempts have

[1] So A. Schaefer, NJb, CXV, 166; Neupert, pp. 34–42.
[2] Surviving examples are Gorgias' *Palamedes*, Alcidamas' *Odysseus*, and Antisthenes' *Ajax* and *Odysseus*.
[3] See E. Bickerman, "Lettres de Démosthène," RPh, 3d series, XI (1937), 55.
[4] ii. 4. 41–42.
[5] VS i. 481.

31

been made to trace the genre of themes taken from actual history back into the fourth century,[6] clear-cut evidence for it does not appear before Hellenistic times.[7] A papyrus of the third century B.C. does contain a rhetorical exercise on a theme involving Demosthenes.[8] This composition, however, falls under the forensic genus of oratory, whereas the letters belong to the deliberative genus.[9] The evidence for the early existence of exercises on deliberative themes is extremely flimsy.[10] Exercises in letter form, mentioned in the first century B.C., were in vogue in the years between Cicero and Hadrian.[11] Hence letters which existed already in the third century B.C. are less likely to be rhetorical exercises, but this argument from silence proves little where the sources are so fragmentary. Rhetorical exercises, however, often can be made to betray their identity.

The writers of these rhetorical exhibitions showed little or no concern for historical accuracy, being primarily interested in character portrayal.[12] Hence, if analysis shows that the letters exhibit a minute accuracy in their allusions to the events of 323, the presumption will be against their being rhetorical exercises, and particularly so if those allusions are such as to be understandable to Athenians in 323 but only irritating or incomprehensible to a later audience. The study of the rhetorical form of the letters as compared to that of the surviving ancient rhetorical exercises offers some hope of deciding the problem of authenticity.

2. Epp. 1–4 may have constituted all or part of a historical no.

[6] W. Hofrichter, *Studien zur Entwickelungsgeschichte der Deklamation*; cf. R. Kohl, *De scholasticarum declamationum argumentis ex historia petitis*, pp. 3–4.

[7] W. Kroll, "Melete 1," *RE*, XV¹ (1932), 496.

[8] *P. Berol.* 9781, in *Rhetorische Papyri*, ed. Karl Kunst ("Berliner Klassikertexte," Heft VII); see Hofrichter, pp. 59–63.

[9] See Chaps. 7–8.

[10] Hofrichter, pp. 80–82 (for his "demonstrativum," read "deliberativum"). Hofrichter assumes, without justification, that the pairs of opposing speeches used by Anaximenes as examples were school exercises. Suetonius (*De rhet.* 1), in writing of the beginnings of Roman rhetorical exercises on historical or contemporary themes, mentions only forensic, not deliberative compositions.

[11] Theon *Progym.* 10, Vol. II, p. 115 Spengel; Sykutris, "Epistolographie," *RE*, Suppl. V (1931), 211; date of Theon in the first century A.D.: Stegemann, "Theon 5," *RE*, V^A² (1934), 2037–38.

[12] See the examples collected by Kohl. Even *P. Berol.* 9781, of the third century B.C., a piece constructed with no mean skill and our earliest example of such an exercise, contains a serious chronological error; see A. Körte, "Literarische Texte," *Archiv für Papyrusforschung*, VII (1924), 227.

in the form of a collection of letters. Works in such a form are known to have existed in the second century B.C.[13] There is no evidence to show how much earlier they existed. Such a *"Briefroman"* is really a collection of rhetorically fabricated letters, and hence the criteria which we have suggested for rhetorical exercises also apply here.[14]

3. The letters may be the work of a rhetorical historian or biographer. Greek historians were expected to embellish their works with speeches and letters which they composed for the persons in their narratives. Apart from the fact that no trace exists of the historical narrative in which the letters might have been embedded, the mere length of the letters all but precludes this possibility even for a biography—certainly if all four are taken as a unit.[15] We reckon with it only for the sake of completeness. To judge from the extant works of the ancient historians, moreover, they took pride in writing such insertions in their own style. Certainly Anaximenes, who composed D. 11 as a part of his *Philippic Histories*, does not conform at all to the characteristics of Demosthenes' style. Possibly he was not even aware of them. Again one might assume, with some slight probability, that Demochares, a very rhetorical-minded historian who wrote a work on what happened in Athens in his own time,[16] might have included the letters in it. The remarks we have made about historical allusions in rhetorical exercises apply here also, except that a historian might be more accurate than the author of a rhetorical exhibition, though not necessarily so. Since ancient historians wrote their works with an eye to the rules of rhetoric, comparative study of the rhetorical forms used by them with the rhetorical form of the letters will also be useful.

4. Finally, Epp. 1–4 could be political propaganda composed after Demosthenes' death, as has often been suggested.[17] Persons in

[13] See R. Merkelbach, *Die Quellen des griechischen Alexanderromans* (München: C. H. Beck, 1954), pp. 32–40.

[14] See Merkelbach, p. 33, and Heinrich Dörrie's review of Merkelbach in *Gnomon*, XXVII (1955), 583–84.

[15] Compare the extant examples of letters inserted in the narratives of ancient historians, collected by Sykutris, *RE*, Suppl. V, 208–10.

[16] Cicero *Brut.* 286: "Demochares . . . et orationes scripsit aliquot et earum rerum historiam quae erant Athenis ipsius aetate gestae non tam historico quam oratorio genere perscripsit."

[17] Ulrich von Wilamowitz-Moellendorff, "Unechte Briefe," *Hermes*, XXXIII (1898), 496–98; Nitsche, pp. 139–48; Piero Treves, "Apocrifi demostenici" and "Epimetron arpalico-demostenico," *Athenaeum*, n.s., XIV (1936), 153–59, 233–51, 258–65; cf. Bickerman, *RPh*, 3d series, XI, 55–61.

Athens who had an interest in clearing the smirched reputation of Demosthenes or in reaffirming his policies might have followed such precedents as Plato's *Apology* or Isocrates' *Archidamus* to compose the letters. Demosthenes' heirs, and in particular Demochares, had such an interest, and they might well have known the stylistic secret of Blass's law.[18] Moreover, a propagandist who lived through the events which are the background of the letters could have produced compositions free of anachronisms.

However, unlike the writer of purely literary fictions who can simply indulge his imagination, a propagandist must write against a specific historical background. If the letters contain matter which Demosthenes would have had to include in defending himself in 324/3 but would have been useless in a defense of his career after his death there would be a presumption in favor of authenticity. If the letters contain matter which would have been not only useless but also embarrassing in a posthumous defense and advocate policies unsuitable for the period after Demosthenes' death, the possibility that they are propagandistic fabrications would be excluded. Furthermore, a propagandist writing after Demosthenes' death would hardly trouble himself to reflect accurately the stages in the changing political climate of several years before even if he knew them. To the extent that the letters can be shown to form a sequence reflecting a continuously developing political situation, the hypothesis that they are propagandistic fabrications becomes improbable. Finally, examples of Athenian political propaganda defending the reputation of persons living and dead have survived to give an indication of how such propaganda was written, so here again a comparative analysis of rhetorical form will be helpful.

[18] The extant fragments of Demochares' works show no observance of Blass's law; see J. Sykutris, "Der demosthenische Epitaphios," *Hermes*, LXIII (1928), 255, n. 4. However, Demon, son of Demosthenes' cousin, who proposed the resolution securing him his return from exile, is the probable author of D. 32, an oration which exhibits a far stricter compliance with Blass's law than the other falsely attributed works in the Demosthenic corpus. See Adams, *CP*, XII, 293; Vogel, *Hermes*, LVIII, 94. Other possibilities are the orator's cousin, Thymochares (see G. Mathieu, "Notes sur Athènes à la veille de la guerre lamiaque," *RPh*, 3d series, III [1929], 165) and the illegitimate sons whose existence was asserted by ancient gossip and may be implied by Dinarchus (Idomeneus *apud* Athenaeus xiii. 592e; Din. 1. 71; see Schaefer, III, 395).

PART 2

Historical Analysis

CHAPTER 5

The Historical Background

E PP. 1–4 ARE WRITTEN against the background of the Harpalus affair and the Lamian war. Because of the dearth of precise information, the chronology of these two episodes is very problematical. We must first give an outline of the course of the Harpalus affair as far as it can be established.[1]

On his unexpected return from India, Alexander in Carmania in late 325 began to proceed with great punitive ferocity against many of his high officials. The news was not long in reaching Harpalus, Alexander's treasurer, at Babylon. Having reason to fear the king's wrath,[2] Harpalus fled to the Mediterranean coast and embarked with a fleet of thirty ships, taking on board 6,000 mercenaries and 5,000 talents he had brought from Babylon. As one who had been granted Athenian citizenship for the aid he had given the city during the

[1] Bibliography on the chronology of the Harpalus affair: G. Glotz, P. Roussel, and R. Cohen, *Alexandre et l'hellénisation du monde antique, première partie: Alexandre et le démembrement de son empire*, pp. 185–86. Add: Treves, *Athenaeum*, n.s., XIV, 153–59, 233–51, 258–65; Bickerman, *RPh*, 3d series, XI, 52–61; G. Mathieu, "Quelques remarques sur Démosthène," *REA*, XXXIX (1937), 375–80; G. Colin (ed.), *Hypéride: discours*, pp. 37–51, 221–43; *F. Gr. Hist.*, Part IIIb (Supplement), Vol. I, pp. 539–41; E. Badian, "Harpalus," *JHS*, LXXXI (1961), 16–43. Still useful is the nearly complete resumé of the literary sources in A. Schaefer, *Demosthenes und seine Zeit* (2d ed.; Leipzig: B. G. Teubner, 1885–87), III, 304–50.

[2] Summary and chronology of Alexander's actions against the satraps: Badian, *JHS*, LXXXI, 16–23. According to the literary tradition, Alexander was punishing men guilty of maladministration. It may well be true that this explanation is merely the "official story," but there is no compelling reason to accept Badian's reconstructed pattern of court intrigue and royal vindictiveness (*ibid.*, pp. 19–25), however ingenious.

famine which lasted from 331 to 324,[3] Harpalus had reason to believe that he would be welcomed there, quite apart from the possibility of stirring up a new revolt against the Macedonian hegemony. Nevertheless, on his arrival at the Piraeus he was rebuffed. So large a force, if admitted, could have taken over the city; moreover, to admit Harpalus would have been to risk war with Alexander. Doubtless involking these counsels of prudence, Demosthenes proposed a decree forbidding him to land, which was passed by the *demos*. Philocles, who was *strategos* in charge of the Piraeus, undertook the charge of preventing Harpalus from sailing into the harbor.[4]

Rebuffed, Harpalus went with his fleet to Cape Taenarum.[5] Leaving there most of his squadron and treasure, he sailed again to Athens with three ships and seven hundred talents. This time he was admitted to the harbor by Philocles and came before the Athenian Assembly as a suppliant.[6]

Macedonian authorities were quick to demand that the Athenians extradite the fugitive; Antipater, Olympias, and Philoxenus are reported to have done so.[7] There was a formal legal basis for this demand, beside the threat of Macedonian power. Athens was a member of the League of Corinth, and Harpalus was a rebel against Alexander, the *hegemon* of the League. The member cities had sworn to aid the Macedonian kings against any who would subvert their kingdom.[8] Moreover, the League of Corinth, like other Greek

---

[3] See M. Rostovtzeff, *The Social and Economic History of the Hellenistic World*, I, 95; III, 1329, n. 29; and *GHI* 196.

[4] Sources up to this point: Schaefer, III, 304–8; role of Philocles, Din. 3. 1: "φάσκων κωλύσειν Ἅρπαλον εἰς τὸν Πειραιᾶ καταπλεῦσαι, στρατηγὸς ὑφ' ὑμῶν ἐπὶ τὴν Μουνιχίαν καὶ τὰ νεώρια κεχειροτονημένος." Dinarchus designates Philocles by his chief functions; see Arist. *Ath. Pol.* 61. 1, 42. 3. But in the inscriptions of this period, the title of the general who had charge of Munichia and the dockyards was στρατηγὸς ἐπὶ τῷ Πειραεῖ; see *IG*, II² 1631, lines 214–15; the inscription from the Amphiareion, below, Appendix VII; and Walter Schwahn, "Strategos," *RE*, Suppl. VI (1935), 1089. On the authenticity of Din. 3 see Appendix VII.

[5] On the status of Cape Taenarum at this time, see my remarks on Chares in the commentary to Ep. 3. 31–32.

[6] Schaefer, III, 307–8.

[7] Antipater and Olympias: Diod. xvii. 108. 4; Philoxenus: Hyp. *Dem.* 8, Paus. ii. 33. 4, Plut. *De vitioso pudore* 531a.

[8] *GHI* 177; cf. Ps.-D. 17.10. "League of Corinth" is an established term used here for convenience. On the true nature of the relations of the Greek states to Philip and Alexander see T. T. B. Ryder, *Koine Eirene* (London: Oxford University Press, 1965), pp. 150–62.

leagues and hegemonies, had regulations that traitors, subversives, and certain other offenders be outlawed as enemies (*polemioi*) and be subject to extradition or summary arrest (*agôgimoi*) throughout the territory of its members.[9] The Athenians may have bound themselves still more directly to honor demands by the Macedonian kings for extradition. Just before Philip was assassinated in 336, an Athenian delegation notified him that he had been voted the right of demanding the extradition of plotters against him.[10] The enactment may have been renewed by the Athenians in 336 for Alexander; Arrian reports that after the young king had cowed the rebellious Greeks by his prompt and forceful action, the Athenians granted him more honor than had been granted to Philip.[11]

Both Phocion and Demosthenes were opposed to handing Harpalus over, at least so long as no demand had come from Alexander himself. However, once again, Demosthenes seems to have followed the counsels of prudence. On his own proposal it was enacted that Harpalus be taken into custody and his money deposited on the Acropolis to be held for Alexander. The enactment was to be carried out the following day, but Harpalus was to declare the amount of his treasure immediately. This he did: seven hundred talents. Despite this precaution, however, Harpalus apparently made full use of his night of liberty, for when the money was brought to the Acropolis it amounted to only 350 talents. Though he had immediate knowledge of the discrepancy as one of those who watched the delivery, Demosthenes failed to make any report or to denounce the negligence of the guards. Soon afterward Harpalus himself escaped, only to be murdered by his friend Thibron. Once again, Demosthenes failed to take any action against the guards who had let such a thing happen.

---

[9] Such provisions are attested for the first and second Athenian leagues, the Spartan and Theban "hegemonies," the Delphic Amphictyony, and the League of Corinth. The sources are assembled and discussed in Paul Usteri, *Ächtung und Verbannung im griechischen Recht*, pp. 17–34, 41–52; G. Glotz, "Poena (Grèce)," *Dictionnaire des antiquités grecques et romaines*, ed. Daremberg and Saglio, IV, 536; cf. Bickerman, *RPh*, 3d series, XI, 59–60.

[10] Diod. xvi. 92. 2.

[11] *Anab.* i. 1. 2–3. The extraditions demanded in 335 (*ibid.*, 10. 4) may have come under this provision. According to Aesch. 3. 161, Demosthenes was to be tried before the "synhedrion of the Greeks," so it is more likely that if there was a legal basis for the demand, other than the victor's prerogatives, it was the statute of the League of Corinth. See, however, Schaefer, III, 216, n. 1.

Since Demosthenes was not a magistrate[12] and since any citizen could have brought charges against the negligent persons, from the strict standpoint of law these "lapses" meant nothing. Nevertheless, they were to become a good weapon in the hands of his accusers as circumstantial evidence that he had done things for which he must have been bribed.[13]

Harpalus' death soon after his escape would have meant that his sojourn in Athens was no longer a serious matter between the Athenians and the Macedonian king, but for a more important factor: 350 talents of the money brought by Harpalus had disappeared, and the disappearance was soon common knowledge. Surely Alexander would demand restitution. How was Athens to pay him?[14] Every Athenian knew that the money had gone into the hands of the professional politicians, who had thus placed the city in dire jeopardy.[15] Public opinion became aroused against the men who for personal gain would expose the city to the wrath of Alexander. In the scandal over the money of Harpalus, the People's indignant reaction seems to have been an example of a well-known pattern in democratic politics. When the ordinarily indifferent citizens of a democracy are suddenly stirred to anger against their "corrupt politicians" who have "injured them," their anger may take the form of a wholesale condemnation of the men prominent in political life. The public begins to suspect that all of them, of whatever faction, are corrupt, and that though publicly the politicians pretend to oppose one another, they have formed a "ring" to profit at the expense of the people.[16]

---

[12] He is called τὸν ὅλων πραγμάτων ἐπιστάτην at Hyp. *Dem.* 12, but that is no official title and may be an epithet invented by Hyperides to use Demosthenes' undeniable prominence to heighten the impression of his guilt. But cf. Badian, *JHS*, LXXXI, 32–33.

[13] See Hyp. *Dem.* 10–12; *Vit. X orat.* 846b–c.

[14] See Din. 1. 68–70.

[15] Din. 1. 3–4, 89–90; Hyp. *Dem.* 12, 15.

[16] "The very definition of a 'ring' is that it encircles enough influential men in the organization of each party to control the action of both party machines; men who in public push to extremes the abstract ideas of their respective parties, while they secretly join their hands in schemes for personal power and profit" (Samuel J. Tilden, *The New York City "Ring"* [New York: J. Polhemus, 1873], p. 11). Tilden, the author of this definition, was an active politician "who had occasion to watch the growth of the successive Tweed Rings and understood them as no other man on the outside of these corrupt bi-partisan combinations" (Denis Tilden Lynch, *"Boss" Tweed* [New York: Blue Ribbon Books, 1927], p.212); indeed, he was justly

As one of the most prominent politicians and as one who had been conspicuous in the city's dealings with Harpalus, Demosthenes could easily look to be the leading figure of a ring of corrupt politicians which had now endangered the city. To counter the suspicions against him, Demosthenes proposed and carried an enactment turning the investigation of the affair over to the Council of the Areopagus.[17] In proposing the decree, he added that if the Areopagus found him guilty of taking bribes, he would accept the penalty of death. Others under suspicion, including Philocles, joined Demosthenes in putting forward this proposal, which Dinarchus was to call "a proposal against oneself," with the same acceptance in advance of the death penalty.[18]

Temporarily, these maneuvers had the desired effect. The Areopagus, whether for lack of evidence or because of its own political preferences, prolonged its deliberations for six months.[19] However, the scandal with its dangerous potentialities had stirred the people beyond the ordinary; as is typical of such outbursts of indignation in a democracy, public opinion demanded that *someone* be punished. Finally, popular demand forced the Areopagus to produce a list of

suspected of not being entirely outside. William Marcy Tweed was a notorious practitioner of ring politics in the city of New York until public indignation broke his power in 1871 and led to his trial and imprisonment in 1873. On the Tweed Ring and on Tilden's involvement see Alexander B. Callow, Jr., *The Tweed Ring*.

Speakers in the Athenian courts found a receptive audience for descriptions portraying Demosthenes and his contemporary politicians in the same terms as Tilden used for the Tweed Rings; see Ps.-D. 58. 40–44, and D. *Prooemm.* 6 and 53, addressed to the Assembly. Dinarchus (1. 99–104) sums up the Harpalus affair in exactly the same manner: the politicians on trial—he mentions by name Demosthenes, Polyeuctus, and Demades—have formed a ring to exploit the Athenian people, though publicly they behave as antagonists. See Plut. *Dem.* 25.

[17] Din. 1. 4, 86; 2. 23, 3.5; Hyp. *Dem.* 1–2; Plut. *Dem.* 26. 1.

[18] Din. 1. 1, 8, 40; 3. 5. Dinarchus implies that the decree itself recommended the death penalty for anyone found guilty; nevertheless, clearly the court was not deprived by the decree of the right to decide between fining the convicted bribe-taker and condemning him to death.

In turning the case over to the Areopagus with such an acceptance of the death penalty, Demosthenes and Philocles were performing a standard maneuver for use before the Assembly by persons under suspicion. See Anax. 29, p. 68. 6–9 Hammer: "ἂν δ' ἐπίδοξος ἡ κρίσις ᾖ γενέσθαι, λεκτέον, ὡς ἕτοιμος εἶ περὶ τῶν διαβολῶν ἐν τοῖς καθημένοις ἤδη κρίνεσθαι, κἂν ἐλεγχθῇς τι τὴν πόλιν ἀδικῶν, ἀποθνήσκειν ὑποτιμᾷ." See Andoc. 1. 32, etc.

[19] Din. 1. 45.

men against whom the people could vent their wrath in the courts.[20] For each man named, the Areopagus' report (*apophasis*) consisted only of the amount of the bribe which he was accused of taking; no evidence was attached.[21] Demosthenes was charged with having received 20 talents;[22] Demades, 6,000 gold staters,[23] an equivalent sum; Aristogiton, 20 minas.[24] Philocles, who had already been suspended from his office as *kosmetes* of the ephebes was named,[25] as were Charicles,[26] Cephisophon,[27] Aristonicus,[28] Hagnonides,[29] and Polyeuctus.[30] These reports accounted for 64 of the missing 350 talents.[31] Among those appointed to prosecute Demosthenes were Stratocles,[32] Hyperides, Pytheas, Menesaechmus, Himeraeus, and Procles.[33] Demosthenes, as the first to be tried, faced the full force of

[20] Hyp. *Dem.* 5; compare the history of the downfall of the Tweed Ring (see above, n. 16). Tweed was able to delay his trial until long after the ring was exposed but could not escape conviction (Lynch, pp. 370–94). New York politicians understood how the public would demand that someone be punished: the culprits sought to find one of themselves to be the scapegoat (M. R. Werner, *Tammany Hall*, pp. 217–23), and the end result, agreeable to the politicians who controlled the victorious opposition to the ring, was that Tweed alone of the major figures became the scapegoat (Lynch, pp. 403–5; Callow, pp. 279–300). Compare the effort to use Erasinides as a scapegoat in 406 B.C., P. Cloché, "L'affaire des Arginuses," *Revue historique*, CXXX(1919), 40–42, 59–60.

[21] Hyp. *Dem.* 6.

[22] Din. 1. 6, 45, 53, 69, 89; Hyp. *Dem.* 2, 10; Plut. *Dem.* 25. 3. Hence the figure of 30 talents at *Vit. X. orat.* 846c cannot be correct.

[23] Din. 1. 89.

[24] Din. 2. 1. Cf. D. Ep. 3. 37, 42–43.

[25] Din. 3; D. Ep. 3. 31.

[26] Plut. *Praec. ger. reip.* 808a; *Phoc.* 21. 4.

[27] Din. 1. 44.

[28] Dion. Hal. *Din.* 10, Vol. I, p. 312 U.-R.

[29] *Ibid.*; cf. Hyp. *Dem.* 40.

[30] Din. 1. 100.

[31] Din. 1. 89 (reading of A corr.²; A pr. and N have "four hundred," and Thalheim suggests "two hundred").

[32] Din. 1. 1.

[33] *Vit. X orat.* 846c; Procles is the reading of the manuscripts—see Schaefer, III, 329, n. 1. We know very little of the political factions which existed in Athens at the time of the trials, but the prosecutors seem to have been a heterogeneous group, including the radical anti-Macedonian, Hyperides, and Menesaechmus, the bitter enemy of the anti-Macedonian Lycurgus (see below, p. 54–55, and Schaefer, *Dem.*, III, 326–29). Scholars have focused their attention on Demosthenes and have assumed that a strange coalition of pro-Macedonian and anti-Macedonian politicians here conspired to destroy him. Demosthenes' enemies, particularly those in the anti-Macedonian faction, may indeed have made use of the Harpalus affair to eliminate him from the political scene (see below, Chap. 6, n. 89), but Demosthenes was not

the people's indignation.[34] Before the trial he seems to have tried to parry some of the anger by admitting that he had taken the money for public purposes, not as a bribe. He must have found that this plea was bad tactics, for he abandoned it for an outright denial of the charges, a course which itself made his position vulnerable.[35] Convicted, he was sentenced to pay fifty talents[36] and was cast into prison.[37] Despairing of his situation,[38] he escaped into exile across the waters of the Saronic Gulf.[39]

Demosthenes' trial was followed by those of the other defendants. We are ill informed as to the order of the later trials. From Dinarchus' speech *Against Philocles* we can infer that several other defendants were tried before Philocles, that all of them were convicted,[40] and that Philocles was tried before Aristogiton.[41] From Dinarchus'

the only one suspected or brought to trial. Of only one political factor operating in the entire set of trials am I reasonably certain: the mass indignation against all "corrupt politicians." One of the prosecutors, Hyperides, is known to have been suspected of taking money from Harpalus (see below, n. 57). Very likely, the politicians not named by the Areopagus were eager to purge themselves of suspicion by acting as prosecutors. Cf. Lucian *Dem. Enc.* 31, where Hyperides' motive is said to have been "flattery of the populace." The constructions of Badian, *JHS*, LXXXI, 34–35, are unfounded. Harpocration *s.v. Aristion* does not prove that Hephaestion was a "protector of Demosthenes," and Diod. xviii. 48. 2 says nothing about relations between Demades and Antipater in 324/3, and Din. 1. 100–1 is no evidence of real friendship and collaboration between Demosthenes and Demades (see above, n. 16, and below, pp. 162–63).

34 Din. 1. 105–6, 113; Hyp. *Dem.* 6–7; see commentary to D. Ep. 2. 14.

35 Hyp. *Dem.* 12–13; see G. Colin, *Hypéride*, pp. 230–31, 251–52, and J. O. Burtt, *Minor Attic Orators, II,* p. 509; C. D. Adams, "The Harpalos Case," *TAPA,* XXXII (1901), 144–46; Badian, *JHS,* LXXXI, 38–39.

36 Plut. *Dem.* 26. 2, 27. 6; Syrianus *In Hermog.,* Vol. I, pp. 49–50 Rabe; cf. Zosimus *Vit. Dem.* in W. S. Dobson (ed.), *Oratores Attici,* Vol. V, p. ccliv. The figures given at *Vit. X orat.* 846c–d for the amount Demosthenes was accused of taking, for his fine, and for its fictitious payment are corrupt; see Schaefer, III, 343, n. 1.

37 D. Ep. 2. 17; Plut. *Dem.* 26. 2; Syrianus, Vol. I, p. 49 Rabe; Anonymous *Vit. Dem.* in Dobson, Vol. V, p. ccclx.

38 D. Ep. 2. 17; Plut. *Dem.* 26. 2.

39 See below, Chap. 6, n. 33. According to the anonymous *Vit. Dem.,* Vol. V, p. ccclx Dobson, Demosthenes was in prison five days, escaping on the sixth.

40 Din. 3. 14: "ὑμᾶς . . . δεῖ . . . ἔχειν πρὸς τὰς ὑπὸ τῆς βουλῆς γεγενημένας ἀποφάσεις . . . ἀκολούθως ταῖς πρότερον κεκριμέναις."

41 In Ep. 3. 37–43 the author belabors the fact that Aristogiton had been acquitted. Yet, had he been acquitted before the trial of Philocles, Dinarchus would never have said (3. 12) that the two were now on the same footing. Note how the author of Ep. 3. 37–43 turns the similar predicament of Demosthenes into an argument in his favor.

speech *Against Aristogiton* we learn that before Aristogiton came to trial Demades had been condemned[42] and none of the defendants had been acquitted.[43] Indeed, by that time, the public indignation roused by the Harpalus affair may have subsided. We hear of no more convictions. Demosthenes, however, was not allowed to return from exile. Then, on the evening of June 10, 323,[44] Alexander died at Babylon. On reaching Athens, the news became the signal for the Athenians to undertake a "Greek war of liberation," the "Lamian" war, to throw off the Macedonian domination. Later in the year, Demosthenes' volunteer diplomacy in support of the Athenian delegates who were trying to win allies in the Peloponnesus so pleased the Athenians that they recalled him from exile and acted to cancel his fine.[45]

Since Epp. 1–4 are written in the setting of Demosthenes' exile and the oncoming war, to prove them authentic we must be able to fit them into the absolute chronology of the events, which we now turn to establish as accurately as possible.

[42] 2. 15; E. Badian (*JHS*, LXXXI, 35) assumes that the ἕτερον τῶν τὴν πατρίδα λελυμασμένων at Din. 1. 29 is Demades and that Demades at once went into exile without awaiting trial; if so, he soon returned, for he was there when the news of Alexander's death arrived (Plut. *Phoc.* 22. 3; Demetrius *Eloc.* 283). See also below, n. 67, and commentary to Ep. 3. 38, ἃ τοῖς τολμῶσιν. In any case, Badian is probably wrong; the passage is better taken to refer to Philocrates, in view of Din. 1. 28 and the extensive borrowings of Dinarchus from the speeches of Aeschines.

[43] In Din. 2 no effort is made to explain away a previous acquittal in the series of trials. The lack of any mention of Philocles at Din. 2. 15 presents no difficulty; the speaker is content with the prominent examples of Demosthenes and Demades. The surprising thing in the passage is that after such violent denunciations of Demosthenes and Demades, Dinarchus can still write of them in so complimentary a manner.

[44] A. E. Samuel, *Ptolemaic Chronology*, p. 47, quotes a cuneiform astronomical diary to establish this, the exact date of Alexander's death. It agrees with the date Daesius 28 given by the *Ephemerides* as reported by Plutarch (*Alex.* 75. 4).

[45] Schaefer, III, 351–71. We learn from Plut. *Dem.* 27. 4–6 and from *Vit. X orat·* 846d that in order to remit the amount of Demosthenes' fine, the people assigned him the task of decorating the altar of Zeus Soter, for which he was paid that amount. Plutarch wrongly remarks that there was no direct means of canceling Demosthenes' fine (see below, n. 110). He is wrong, too, if he means that the legal fiction was invented *ad hoc* for Demosthenes. It had been used before and surely was known both to Demosthenes and to his audience. We know of two other instances. Such a fiction was used in the fifth century for Phormio (*F. Gr. Hist.* No. 324 [Androtion], F 8) and in the fourth century for helping Conon, the son of Timotheus, pay his late father's fine (Nepos *Timotheus* 4. 1). See *F. Gr. Hist.*, Part IIIb (suppl.), Vol. I, pp. 125–26; Lipsius, pp. 963–64.

The date of Harpalus' flight depends on the date of the executions of the satraps by Alexander. The news would have taken some time to reach Babylon, and the march to the coast with 6,000 men past the king's garrisons, still more.[46] In any case, Harpalus could hardly have set sail on his first journey to Athens before the opening of navigation (about March 10), for his large fleet of thirty ships would scarcely have ventured upon the sea during the winter season;[47] he may have reached the coast much later.

On the other hand, Hyperides remarks that on coming to Greece Harpalus found affairs in the Peloponnesus and the rest of the country in quite a stir because of the arrival of Nicanor bearing Alexander's orders to the Greeks.[48] Several months before, Alexander had decided to require the Greek cities to readmit those whom they had banished, and at the Olympic festival of 324 (July 31 to August 4), Nicanor officially issued Alexander's proclamation.[49] Nicanor must

[46] Connection of flight with executions: Diod. xvii. 108. 6; date of executions: late 325 or early 324. See Badian, *JHS*, LXXXI, 23–24; we have no way of knowing how soon the news reached Babylon.

[47] Harpalus' fleet: Curt. x. 2. 1; opening of navigation, Theophr. *Char.* 3. 3 (the sea open from the Great Dionysia); Vegetius iv. 39: "Ex die . . . tertio Idus Novembris usque in diem sextum Idus Martias maria clauduntur." On how absolute was the closing of navigation, see E. de Saint-Denis, "Mare Clausum," *REL*, XXV (1947), 196–214, and J. Rougé, "La navigation hivernale sous l'empire romain," *REA*, LIV (1952), 316–25.

[48] *Dem.* 18.

[49] Alexander's decree and the mission of Nicanor: Diod. xviii. 8; Bickerman, "La lettre d'Alexandre aux bannis grecs," *REA*, XLII (1940), 25–35; Badian, *JHS*, LXXXI, 25–31. The above date for the Olympic festival of 324 seems at last to be established; formerly many scholars wished to place it in September. See R. Sealey, *CR*, LXXIV (1960), 185–86. Even with the September dating, Hyp. *Dem.* 18 would not cause great chronological difficulty. According to Diod. xviii. 8. 5, twenty thousand exiles gathered at Olympia to hear the proclamations; hence Nicanor's mission must have been known in Greece well before the Olympic festival. The date and place of Alexander's decision are obscure, though Wilcken placed it during the king's stay at Susa, "Alexander der Grosse und der korinthische Bund," *Sitzungsberichte der Preussischen Akademie der Wissenschaften*, Philosophisch-historische Klasse, 1922, pp. 115–16.

Alexander's proclamation struck Athens a double blow. Beyond requiring the return of men whose property had been sold and the return of subversives, it included an order "returning Samos to the Samians" (*SIG*³ 312). Athens had held the island since 365; her cleruchs now faced dispossession. Demosthenes led an Athenian delegation to Olympia and had long talks with Nicanor, but Nicanor can hardly have been empowered to negotiate. The only recourse was to appeal to Alexander. Meanwhile the Athenians did not carry out the king's decree (sources assembled at Schaefer, III, 314–20). All this had a serious impact on Athenian politics; see commentary to Ep. 3. 34.

have arrived in Greece somewhat earlier, surely not several months, but perhaps several weeks; we have no way of knowing how many.[50] Since Harpalus hardly waited until July to get out of Alexander's reach, Hyperides here probably is deliberately confusing the fugitive's two arrivals at Athens and giving the date of the second.

For Harpalus' entry into Athens there is a probable *terminus ante quem*. Philocles, at that time *strategos* in charge of Munichia and the dockyards, was blamed for allowing Harpalus to enter the port.[51] Philocles probably left that office at the beginning of the new Attic year on Hekatombaion 1[52] (July 23) and soon after[53] probably became *kosmetes* of the ephebes for 324/3.[54] If so, Harpalus must have entered Athens before July 23.

All efforts to derive from our evidence a fairly precise date for Harpalus' escape rest on assumptions too shaky to be accepted,[55] and

---

[50] He may have come early to allow the thousands of exiles to assemble at Olympia (Diod. xviii. 8); see, however, Badian, *JHS*, LXXXI, 42–43.

[51] See above, n. 4.

[52] See Schaefer, III, 308, n. 1.

[53] On Boedromion 1 (September 20); see Ulrich Kahrstedt, *Untersuchungen zur Magistratur in Athen*, p. 73, n. 5. My Julian equivalents are based on Benjamin D. Meritt, *The Athenian Year*, pp. 102–12, 133. Meritt there shows that there is no evidence for significant tampering with the calendar during the period of the Harpalus affair and the Lamian war. See now Meritt, "Athenian Calendar Problems," *TAPA*, XCV (1964), 200–60. According to Pritchett and Neugebauer (Meritt, *TAPA*, XCV, 228), the Athenian month began with the first visibility of the crescent moon. In that case, Boedromion 1 would be September 19. The difference is insignificant for this study.

[54] See Appendix VII.

[55] On the basis of Hyp. *Dem.* 18 and Din. 1. 81–82, 103, scholars have argued that Harpalus must have escaped after Demosthenes' mission to Nicanor at Olympia, for the suspicions aroused by the escape would have prevented the orator's being sent, and Hyp. *Dem.* 12 and *Vit. X orat.* 846c imply that the escape occurred when Demosthenes was in the city (Treves, "Note sur la chronologie de l'affaire d'Harpale," *REA*, XXXVI [1934], 517; Badian, *JHS*, LXXXI, 43). But the expedient of turning the case over to the Areopagus and accepting in advance the death penalty if found guilty was an efficacious measure for disarming such suspicions, at least temporarily; indeed, Demosthenes continued to play a prominent role in politics after the escape of Harpalus (Din. 1. 94–95; Hyp. *Dem.* 31). See above, n. 18.

We cannot tell whether Alexander had heard of Harpalus' escape by the time of Dionysiac celebrations at Ecbatana (October, to judge by Diod. xvii. 110; autumn or early winter, to judge by Arrian vii. 14. 1, 8–10; 15. 1–3). Julius Beloch, *Griechische Geschichte*, IV 2, 434–36, held that the satyric drama *Agen* (Athenaeus xiii. 595e–96b) was performed at Ecbatana, but his theory is unfounded; see Bruno

this is unfortunate, for Dinarchus[56] tells us that six months elapsed before the Areopagus submitted the report which brought Demosthenes to trial. To help us in fixing the six-month period we have only the *terminus post quem* for the release of the Areopagus' report derivable from the fragment of Timocles' comedy, *Delos*.[57] The fragment pokes fun at Demosthenes, Moerocles, Demon, Callisthenes, and Hyperides for taking bribes from Harpalus. Hyperides, far from being a defendant, was one of the prosecutors. No other report says that Moerocles, Demon, and Callisthenes were implicated; Demon was in sufficiently good repute to propose and carry the enactment

Snell, *Scenes from Greek Drama*, pp. 113–17. Even a possibility that Athens would refuse Alexander's order to restore Samos to the Samians is sufficient to explain Gorgos' offer at Ecbatana of armor and catapults for besieging Athens (Ephippus *apud* Athenaeus xii. 538a–b; cf. *SIG*³ 312), without any reference to Harpalus. The occasion of the *Agen* is a problem. Athenaeus says it was presented "at the Dionysiac celebrations on the Hydaspes river." Snell holds that the Hydaspes in India is meant. But were Athens' relations with the Macedonian power so bad in 326 that her acceptance of grain from Harpalus might prove to be her ruin? On the other hand, Athenaeus surely would have mentioned Ecbatana by name (or Susa—if the correct reading is "the Choaspes river"; see Colin, *Hypéride*, p. 233). Perhaps Athenaeus' "Hydaspes" is a river in Carmania; see Kiessling, "Hydaspes 2," *RE*, IX (1916), 37–39, "Hydriakos," *ibid.*, cols. 78–79, and "Hyktanis," *ibid.*, cols. 101–6. Alexander is reported to have celebrated Dionysia in Carmania at about the same time as he began to proceed against his high officials (Diod. xvii. 106, Arrian vi. 27–28). Against Snell, see also H. Lloyd-Jones' review, *Gnomon*, XXXVIII (1966), 16–17.

Other attempts to get a more precise chronology have been based on the fact that the debate in Athens over granting the honors of a god to Alexander occurred during the six months of the investigation (Hyp. *Dem.* 31, Din. 1. 94). There is, however, no way of independently dating the debate. The attempts to connect the issue of divine honors with Nicanor's mission at Olympia or with the death of Hephaestion have no basis; see J. P. V. D. Balsdon, "The Divinity of Alexander," *Historia*, I (1950), 383–88; Bickerman, "Sur un passage d'Hypéride," *Athenaeum*, n.s., XLI (1963), 70–85.

[56] 1. 45.

[57] Athenaeus viii. 341e–42a: "Καὶ Ὑπερείδης δὲ ὁ ῥήτωρ ὀψοφάγος ἦν, ὥς φησι Τιμοκλῆς ὁ κωμικὸς ἐν Δήλῳ διηγούμενος τοὺς παρὰ Ἁρπάλου δωροδοκήσαντας. γράφει δὲ οὕτως·

A. Δημοσθένης τάλαντα πεντήκοντ᾽ ἔχει.

B. μακάριος εἴπερ μεταδίδωσι μηδενί.

A. καὶ Μοιροκλῆς εἴληφε χρυσίον πολύ.

B. ἀνόητος ὁ διδούς, εὐτυχὴς δ᾽ ὁ λαμβάνων.

A. εἴληφε καὶ Δήμων τι καὶ Καλλισθένης.

B. πένητες ἦσαν, ὥστε συγγνώμην ἔχω.

A. ὅ τ᾽ ἐν λόγοισι δεινὸς Ὑπερείδης ἔχει.

B. τοὺς ἰχθυοπώλας οὗτος ἡμῶν πλουτιεῖ·

ὀψοφάγος γὰρ ὥστε τοὺς λάρους εἶναι Σύρους."

which restored his kinsman, Demosthenes, from exile.[58] Hence, surely, when the *Delos* was produced ca. January 27 or ca. March 24-28, 323, the Areopagus had not yet released its report.

For the period of Demosthenes' exile down to the death of Alexander, there is no evidence independent of the letters on which to base the chronology; the accounts of the preparations for the Lamian war at Diodorus xviii. 8–9 and Justin xiii. 5 are too vague. If reliable, however, the letters have much to say. Ep. 3 purports to have been written by Demosthenes from exile[59] after the conviction and exile of Philocles[60] and the acquittal of Aristogiton.[61] Hitherto, a misconception of the temporal sequence of the letters has impeded the utilization of the information which they contain. Modern investigators have taken it for granted that the "earlier letter" mentioned in Ep. 3. 1 is Ep. 2.[62] This interpretation, however, is impossible. Ep. 3 gives some indication of the contents of that earlier letter and its background. From Ep.3. 39 it is clear that in the earlier message Demosthenes had thrown himself upon the mercy of the Athenians and begged for immunity from imprisonment until the end of the ninth prytany (the prescribed limit for the payment of fines in Athens, after which the debtor's property would be confiscated).[63] Only thus could he return and try to raise money to pay at least part of his penalty. Nothing of the sort is mentioned in Ep. 2. Nor can the specific words of Ep. 3. 39 be the clear expression of what is implied in Ep. 2. 2, 14–16, 21, 23, and 26, for then it is hard to see how the Athenians would reply, as at Ep. 3. 39, "Who in the world is stopping him from coming here and doing as he proposes?"[64] Indeed, Ep. 2

[58] See above, n. 45.

[59] Ep. 3. 1, 31, 35, 37–40.

[60] Ep. 3. 31; Mathieu (*RPh*, 3d series, III, 163; *REA*, XXXIX, 379) tries to interpret προῆσθε at Ep. 3. 31 to mean merely that the Athenians have "abandoned" Philocles to the extent of allowing him to be brought to trial on an unjust accusation. This interpretation is impossible. A requirement for entering Athenian politics was to place one's trust in the People and be willing to stand trial before it. On the other hand, the People should stand by their friends, but they have abandoned Philocles just as they have abandoned Charidemus and Demosthenes, driving them into exile and letting Alexander and malicious prosecutors have their way.

[61] Ep. 3. 37–38, 42–43.

[62] Blass, III 1, 440; Neupert, p. 15; Sachsenweger, p. 10; Treves, *Athenaeum*, n.s., XIV, 239.

[63] Lipsius, pp. 945–47. Blass, III 1, 441, recognized the reference to the end of the ninth prytany.

[64] Cf. Blass, III 1, 441.

is a direct request for exoneration, not a vague request that it be made easier to pay a fine. At the time of Ep. 3, the trials are presumably still in progress since only the conviction of Philocles and the acquittal of Aristogiton are mentioned.[65] Ep. 2, on the other hand, reflects a time when many, perhaps all, of the defendants have been tried. It plainly states that the first several defendants to come to trial were all found guilty, while those who came to trial later were acquitted;[66] indeed, the Athenians have been reconciled even to those who were convicted—to all except Demosthenes.[67] Even if the author is exaggerating, several of those convicted have been exonerated.

Again, we have seen how Ep. 3 purports to have been written before the end of the ninth prytany. Ep. 2. 2 suggests that Demosthenes' property has been confiscated and, hence, that the ninth prytany has passed.[68] Finally, at Ep. 3. 37, Demosthenes speaks of "a long letter, which you should expect to receive if I live, unless I get justice from you first," a letter in which he will detail his grievances. In 324/3 the ninth prytany ended June 6, 323, and Demosthenes did not get "justice" until long after the death of Alexander (June 10).[69] The "long letter" sounds rather like Ep. 2.

All these facts lead to the conclusion that the author envisioned the following sequence of letters: the earliest letter sent after Demosthenes' escape was not Ep. 2, but one answering the description at Ep. 3. 39, one which has been lost; next, and before the end of the ninth prytany, came Ep. 3, with Ep. 2 somewhat later.[70]

[65] See the remarks on Polyeuctus, commentary to Ep. 3. 31–32.

[66] Ep. 2. 1–2, 15, 16, 21, 26; the same initial series of consecutive convictions was inferred above, p.43–44, from Dinarchus.

[67] Ep. 2. 2, ". . . and not be the only one . . ."; 16; 22, "the same concessions . . . made for the rest." Although Demades was convicted and fined, he was not a fugitive in exile (above, n. 42). Moreover, his conviction was not solely on the basis of the Areopagus' report (aitia—see Ep. 2. 16) but also on the basis of his own confession (Din. 1. 104).

[68] "Deprived . . . of property"; however, in context, the words may simply describe Demosthenes' exile.

[69] 324/3 was an ordinary year; the last day of the ninth prytany was the 319th day of the year, Thargelion 24 (Meritt, p. 105). The 319th day of a year which began July 23, 324, is June 6; see above, n. 53. The Lamian war was well under way before Demosthenes was restored (Plut. Dem. 27; Vit. X orat. 846c–d; Justin xiii. 5. 1–11; cf. D. Ep. 1).

[70] The author of the spurious letters of Aeschines seems to have known the true order of Epp. 2 and 3, for his Ep. 3, which is the counterpart of D. Ep. 3, represents an earlier state of affairs than his Ep. 12, the counterpart of D. Ep. 2. See Appendix

49

This chronology can be made still more definite, for Ep. 3 has a *terminus post quem*. At Ep. 3. 30, Demosthenes complains to the Athenians that the "turncoat," Pytheas, "is offering on your behalf the ancestral sacrifices at Delphi." Bickerman believed these sacrifices to be those of the Pythaïs.[71] Indeed, a Delphic inscription probably of 106/5 calls the offerings of the Pythaïs "the ancestral sacrifices,"[72] and Aelius Aristides speaks of the celebration as "an ancestral rite peculiar to the Athenians."[73]

The Pythaïs was not celebrated every year, but only after the Pythaïstae had seen lightning strike an area in northwest Attica known as the *Harma* within one of three three-day periods which had been designated in three designated months.[74] Boëthius has shown[75] that the three months were Munichion, Thargelion, and Skirophorion and that the three-day periods probably lay around the seventh of each month.[76] Since Pytheas could not be spoken of as offering the sacrifices of the Pythaïs unless the lightning stroke had been observed, the letter would have to have been written after Munichion 7 (April 21) or possibly even after Thargelion 7 (May 20).

There is, however, no necessity to assume that "the ancestral sacrifices at Delphi" are those of the Pythaïs. "Ancestral sacrifices offered on behalf of the people" were a common feature of Athenian life.[77] Other Delphic inscriptions show that the words here can apply equally well to sacrifices offered at the amphictyonic meetings.[78]

II. Perhaps the second-century rhetor Hermogenes also knew the correct order, for he cites the two letters together, mentioning Ep. 3 before Ep. 2 (*Id.* ii. 8, Vol. III, p. 349 Walz); see also Syrianus *In Hermog.*, Vol. I, pp. 49–50 Rabe. In the papyrus, Ep. 3. 1–38 follows immediately the speech of Hyperides, *Against Philippides*.

[71] *RPh*, 3d series, XI, 55.

[72] *FD* III 2, 48 = *SIG*³ 711 L, 3–10.

[73] *Panathenaicus* 189, Vol. I, p. 308 Dindorf.

[74] Strabo ix. 2. 11, C. 404; see A. Boëthius, *Die Pythaïs: Studien zur Geschichte der Verbindungen zwischen Athen und Delphi*, pp. 1–2.

[75] *Ibid.*, pp. 13–25.

[76] For a discussion of the festal calendar, *IG* II² 1357b, used by Boëthius, in the light of new fragments of the inscription, see J. H. Oliver, "Greek Inscriptions," *Hesperia*, IV (1935), 21–30.

[77] See D. 59. 73.

[78] *FD* III 2, 86 = *SIG*³ 539 A [dated by Pomtow ca. 216/5] lines 12–21: "ἐπειδὴ Εὔδαμος Ἀπολλωνίου Ἀθηναῖος, παραγενόμενος ἐν Δελφούς, τάς τε θυσίας ἔθυσε τὰς πατρίους καλῶς καὶ φιλοτίμως . . . ἐπεμελήθη δὲ καὶ τῶν λοιπῶν ἀκολούθως τοῖς τε νόμοις καὶ τοῖς ψαφίσμασι τῶν Ἀμφικτιόνων, καὶ ἀξίως καὶ τοῦ θεοῦ καὶ τᾶς πόλιος τὰν ἐπιδαμίαν ἐποιήσατο

Since Ep. 3. 30 would be the only source for a Pythaïs in 323, it seems more likely that the words refer to rites at the spring amphictyonic session.[79] Pytheas then would have been one of the Athenian delegates, probably the hieromnemon, since the hieromnemones—never the pylagoroi—are the ones mentioned in connection with sacrifices at Delphi. Another possibility is that the Athenians sent "sacrificers" (*thyontes*) along with the hieromnemon to perform the religious rites.[80] A Delphic inscription bearing the names of the hieromnemones of 324/3 could help decide the issue, but no such list has as yet been found.[81]

The spring amphictyonic meeting took place in the Delphic month Endyspoitropios,[82] which corresponds to the Attic month Thargelion. Since, however, there is no assurance that intercalations of the year at Athens and Delphi coincided, Endyspoitropios could fall in Munichion or Skirophorion as well.[83] Thus the hypothesis that Pytheas participated in a sacrifice at the spring amphictyonic session can lead to practically the same *terminus post quem* for the letter as the hypothesis that he participated in the Pythaïs.

There is, however, one element of uncertainty. Although no one could be said to be an "offerer of the ancestral sacrifices" of the Pythaïs until after the prescribed omens had been observed, the hieromnemones could be so described throughout their year of office, which ran from Hekatombaion 1 to Hekatombaion 1.[84] If the parti-

μετὰ τῶν λοιπῶν ἱερομναμόνων κτλ." *FD* III 2, 67 = *SIG*³ 772 [of 26/5] has a parallel for the phrase ὑπὲρ ὑμῶν used at Ep. 3. 30: "ἐπειδὴ Θρασυκλῆς Ἀρχικλέος Ἀθηναῖος ἱερομναμο[νήσας καὶ ἐπιδα]μήσας ἐν τάν πόλιν ἁμῶν τὰς [τε] θυσίας τὰς ὑπὲρ τοῦ δάμου τοῦ Ἀθηναίων ἔθυσε κὰτ τὰ πάτρια κτλ."The words of the first passage cannot be made to refer to the Pythaïs since that rite was not observed in the third century (Boëthius, pp. 53–57). The discussion at Boëthius, pp. 21–22, of the second passage establishes that its words refer to sacrifices at the amphictyonic meeting.

[79] So Schaefer, III, 349, and Blass, III 2, 285; cf. Treves, *Athenaeum*, n.s., XIV, 243–44, 264–65.

[80] See Aesch. 3. 124.

[81] Theon was archon at Delphi in 323/2 (J. Pouilloux, "Nouveaux fragments d'un compte delphique," *BCH*, LXXV [1951], 296–301); correct accordingly P. de la Coste-Messelière, "Listes amphictyoniques du IVe siècle," *BCH*, LXXIII (1949), table facing p. 242.

[82] E. Bourguet, *L'administration financière du sanctuaire pythique au IVe siècle av. J.-C.*, pp. 141–44; Busolt-Swoboda, pp. 1303–4.

[83] G. Daux, *Delphes au IIe et au Ier siècle*, pp. 625–26; George Thomson, "The Greek Calendar," *JHS*, LXIII (1943), 57–59.

[84] D. 24. 150, Aesch. 3. 115. In 324/3 Hekatombaion 1 corresponds to July 23; see above, n. 53.

ciple, "offering sacrifices," here is used loosely as a synonym for "being hieromnemon," no *terminus post quem* can be derived. Nevertheless, since the context dwells on recent events in the life of Pytheas,[85] probably "offering sacrifices" is to be taken literally. In view of the general inability of ancient writers to achieve anything like chronological precision except when writing of the immediate present, the fact that the *termini* for Ep. 3 lie between fairly narrow limits argues for its authenticity.[86]

Recognition of the true chronological sequence of the letters allows us to trace by means of them a plausible sequence of events in Athens and of reactions to them by Demosthenes. Thus we may assume that Demosthenes, an accomplished writer of speeches for the Athenian courts, was not one to overlook arguments that could help his case. In pleading for leniency, he certainly would ask for the best treatment that he thought the Athenians would grant him. At the end of his trial, the utmost leniency which the Athenians would extend to him was to fine and imprison him rather than to sentence him to death. His situation looked so hopeless that he felt he had to escape into exile, for there he had at least a faint possibility of acting upon public opinion. Such precedents as the case of Andocides showed how one who had been deprived of civil rights could nevertheless communicate with the Council and the People from exile and even come before them to deliver a speech.[87] From the information given at Ep. 3. 1 and 39 we can infer that immediately upon reaching his place of refuge, Demosthenes wrote the first of a series of open letters to his countrymen, the one which has been lost. In it he exploited the talking points he had won through his escape, feeble though they were. If he refused to defy the verdict of the court but instead made an abject plea to be allowed to return and raise the money to pay his fine, such loyalty was sure to be appreciated by the Athenians, at least by those who were willing to overlook his escape from prison as being hardly unusual for the city.[88]

However, the hopes which the orator had built upon the shaky foundation of that lost earliest letter were doomed to disappointment. Such arguments were of little avail against an adverse public opinion

[85] See commentary to Ep. 3. 29–30.

[86] See E. Bickerman and J. Sykutris, "Speusipps Brief an König Philipp," *BVSAW*, Vol. LXXX (1928), Heft III, pp. 32–33.

[87] See Andoc. 2; Blass, *NJb*, CXV, 544, and *Att. Ber.*, III 1, 441.

[88] See Plato *Crito* 44–46; D. 25. 56; Hyp. *Dem.* 12; *Vit. X orat.* 846b.

directed by powerful men strongly opposed to his return. As a seasoned politician, Demosthenes knew better than to annoy so hostile a public by bombarding it with a series of ill-timed appeals. If he wished future letters to have any effect, he had to wait for the strategic moment and then compose his message with all the skill at his command.

At first the situation deteriorated. It had been bad enough when Demades' confession[89] and Demosthenes' conviction had confirmed the *apophases*. The public trust in the Areopagus was further strengthened and Demosthenes' political associates still further discredited by the conviction of Philocles.[90] To make matters even worse, Lycurgus had been posthumously convicted, doubtless on a charge of embezzlement in office, a charge prosecuted by the same Menesaechmus who had been one of the prosecutors of Demosthenes.[91] Lycurgus was the man who had filled Demosthenes' place as the spokesman of "patriotic policy" in the parlous times after Chaeroneia —the man whose reputation for probity as chief financial administrator of Athens had been a bulwark which the political opposition had assailed in vain. The principle of guilt by association was accepted by Athenian juries. If a person's associates were guilty of a crime, the presumption was that he was, too.[92] Athenians regarded embezzlement as closely related to bribe taking.[93] Surely, to Demosthenes this trend threatened to destroy whatever political following he still had. If there was any way in which he could make an effective protest, this was a time which required him to do so. Fortunately for him, other aspects of the rapidly changing scene gave him material to construct the stirring plea which is Ep. 3.

The acquittal of Aristogiton brought the first break in the series of convictions of the men named in the *apophases*. Since Aristogiton had been a vigorous political opponent of Demosthenes and his allies,[94] his acquittal at first sight confirmed their disgrace. But his

[89] Din. 1. 104.

[90] Ep. 3. 31.

[91] *Vit. X orat.* 842e–f, 846c.

[92] Anax. 7, p. 38. 12–16 Hammer: "τὸν αὐτὸν δὲ τρόπον καὶ ἐὰν τοὺς ἑταίρους αὐτοῦ δεικνύῃς τοιούτους ὄντας οἷον σὺ τοῦτον· καὶ γὰρ διὰ τὴν πρὸς ἐκείνους συνήθειαν δόξει τὰ αὐτὰ τοῖς φίλοις ἐπιτηδεύειν."

[93] See below, Chap. 6, n. 18.

[94] D. 25. 37 (p. 781. 6 Reiske) and scholium, *Oratores Attici* (Müller), II, 735b; Ps.-D. 26. 11; Hyp. fr. 27–39; *Vit. X orat.* 848f; *Suda, s.vv. Aristogeiton* and *Timarchos*. On the authenticity of D. 25, see below, Chap. 8, n. 163.

reputation as a notorious blackmailing prosecutor or "sycophant" was so unsavory[95] that even the prosecutors stressed that to acquit Aristogiton when Demosthenes and Demades had been sentenced would redound to the discredit of the *apophases*.[96]

Demosthenes could now also find a vulnerable target in Pytheas, who had been one of his accusers, for Pytheas had suddenly changed his political position and was now working with those who had been his bitter enemies when he had been active in politics in support of "the People's cause." Surely only the pay he had received for his *volte-face* had enabled him to afford his new profligacy and extravagance, so different from the difficult conditions he had known before. Pytheas had also just lost a lawsuit on account of which he had to pay a fine of five talents; possibly, this was the beginning of the troubles which eventually drove him to flee from Athens to Antipater.[97] Moreover, Demosthenes knew how to turn to effective propaganda use the very fact that his associates had been condemned. Hyperides in prosecuting him had dissociated other proponents of anti-Macedonian policy from Demosthenes' discredit.[98] After Chaeroneia and certainly after the destruction of Thebes, Demosthenes had not been particularly distinguished for resistance to Macedonia. As regards Philocles, however, the little which we know of him suggests that Hyperides and his circle, who had desired to form an alliance with Harpalus against Alexander, did not welcome the downfall of the man who had let Harpalus into the city.

Finally, Demosthenes could make good use of the circumstances of the condemnation of Lycurgus' children. Menesaechmus, Lycurgus' successor as chief financial administrator of Athens,[99] cherished the most bitter enmity toward his recently deceased predecessor. Lycurgus had prosecuted him successfully on a religious charge, possibly from political motives, especially if Menesaechmus had pro-Macedonian sympathies.[100]

---

[95] D. 25 and 26; Din. 2, 3. 12; Plut. *Phoc.* 10. 2.

[96] Din. 2. 15, 21.

[97] Ep. 3. 29–30; see commentary and *Suda s.v. Pytheas*, quoted below, n. 107.

[98] Hyp. *Dem.* 20–21.

[99] Dion. Hal. *Din.* 11, Vol. I, p. 316 U.-R.

[100] *Vit. X orat.* 843d. Four fragments of Lycurgus' speech against Menesaechmus survive. Pro-Macedonian sympathies might be inferred from Menesaechmus' later association with Thrasycles, who may be identical with the one at Aesch. 3. 115.

against him.[110] Probably, enough politicians of all factions were content to see Demosthenes remain the sole scapegoat in the recent scandal.[111] Hyperides had given him ample provocation and may have feared his vengeance. There was also Demosthenes' influence in favor of a policy, so odious to Hyperides, of avoiding open conflict with Alexander.[112]

Demosthenes probably felt that public opinion could be made to go in his favor, whatever the views of the politicians. In Ep. 2 he seems to have kept the promise at Ep. 3. 37 to send after the end of the ninth prytany a long "message of friendly reproof." He abandons the querulous tone of Ep. 3 for the more dignified manner of an injured person who believes that he has a strong case. And Demosthenes' argument now did rest on a solid foundation. Everything that had recently happened tended to vindicate the position he had taken at his trial, the position which his accusers had been at such pains to refute: that he had been framed by the Areopagus.[113] Whereas before only Aristogiton, a political opponent, had been cleared, now there had been a long series of acquittals. Philocles, who had been associated with Demosthenes and convicted of taking money from Harpalus, had now been exonerated. The exoneration of Lycurgus and his sons from the charge of embezzlement, which Athenian law treated on the same footing as bribe taking,[114] was a further valuable precedent. The turn of events could not help but discredit the reports of the Areopagus in the public eye.[115] The ninth prytany had passed,

[110] In Athens one who would propose so to override a conviction and sentence pronounced by a court had to secure beforehand the protection of a vote of immunity passed by an Assembly of at least six thousand. The proposal, too, had to be passed in the presence of such a quorum. Under such circumstances, a politician with a large following *might* be able to secure the exoneration of a person he wished to save, and *certainly* he could block the reinstatement of his condemned enemies. The number of six thousand was so high a proportion of the citizenry, and so many of the citizens lived outside the city, that only extraordinary interests or extraordinary pressure could bring such a quorum to the Pnyx, as in the case of the restoration of Alcibiades. See Lipsius, pp. 388–89, 963–64; Busolt-Swoboda, I, 446; II, 987, 989, 1001, 1167.

[111] Compare the plight of "Boss" Tweed. above, n. 20.

[112] Hyp. *Dem.* 17–20, 31.

[113] Hyp. *Dem.* 14; Din. 1. 5, 7, etc.

[114] Below, Chap. 6, n. 18.

[115] The prosecutors in the Harpalus affair recognized the vulnerability of the *apophases* should even one of the trials result in an acquittal. See Din. 2. 15, 21; Hyp. *Dem.* 5–7; and cf. Arist. *Rhet.* iii. 15. 6. 1416a 24–26; D. 51. 9; Lyc. *Leoc* 53–54.

but Demosthenes no longer cared. His case was now so strong it would have been foolish for him to make the same abject appeal. The charges against him were now clearly false; he would ask for nothing less than complete exoneration.[116]

Indeed, at the outset of Ep. 2, he has to explain away the content of his earlier letters. His earlier request, limited as it was to asking for temporary immunity so that he could try to pay his fine, was a recognition at least of the legal validity of his conviction, despite all his protests, and as such could have been an obstacle to his request for complete exoneration. Neither Demosthenes nor his heirs had any interest in preserving so incriminating a document as his earliest letter. His flight, too, must have looked to many like a tacit admission of guilt. Demosthenes is treating these two situations when he says that until recently he chose to "acquiesce." Far from rebelling against the Athenians by fleeing, he has merely made a realistic decision "patiently to submit to his fate." How could he make an effective protest when the Athenians themselves were allowing their democracy to be subverted by an oligarchical conspiracy? His struggle is thus identified with that of the people, and his enemies with the people's standard enemies, the "oligarchs."[117] Since few, if any, could find convincing the claim that Demosthenes' jailbreak was really "patient submission," the author had to return to deal with the problem in pars. 17–20. Hence those paragraphs do not imply that the letter was written immediately after the escape.

The political situation in Athens may be reflected in another aspect of the argument of Ep. 2. His enemies had accused him before the court of betraying his former principles after Chaeronea and of collaborating with the Macedonian order,[118] and now in the

---

[116] In the letters, "exonerate" and "exoneration" are expressed by *sôizein* and *sôtêria* (Ep. 2. 2, 3, 12, 15, 19, 23; Ep. 3. 25, 26, 27, 36, 43; Ep. 4. 2), "condemn," by *apollynai* (Ep. 2. 13, 24; Ep. 3. 35, 43); these common usages are not mentioned in the *Greek-English Lexicon*. See D. 19. 296, and for the exoneration of a person who has been convicted, D. 24. 84.

Although already at Ep. 3. 36 the writer speaks of *sôtêria* as his aim, he does not dare to ask directly for exoneration in Ep. 3. 37–45. At Ep. 3. 36 he is either expressing his wishful thinking or using *sôtêria* to mean only permission to return to Athens. If Aristogiton has gained *sôtêria* (exoneration), Demosthenes should be allowed at least immunity from imprisonment until the end of the ninth prytany.

[117] See commentary to Ep. 2. 1, τοὺς ὀμωμοκότας κτλ.

[118] See below, pp. 80–81.

months just before the outbreak of the Lamian war there was surely a rising tide of anti-Macedonian sentiment in Athens. Hence Demosthenes took care to deny that his avoidance of conflict with Alexander was treasonable collaborationism; rather it had been forced upon him and upon Athens by the baseness of the rest of the Greeks and by the blind favoritism of Fortune (Ep. 2. 4–6).

However strong Demosthenes may have thought his argument in Ep. 2, it did not lead the Athenians to grant him his restoration. The message which the author wishes to give to the people in Ep. 4 is that Athens is of all cities the most fortunate and the dearest to the gods. If Alexander were already dead, the author would certainly have used the fact as the most striking proof of the city's good fortune. Since there is no such mention, Ep. 4, if authentic, was written before the news of Alexander's death reached Athens, and hence it must be earlier than Ep. 1, in which Alexander is mentioned as dead. On the other hand, Ep. 3. 1 implies that only one message, the lost earliest letter, preceded Ep. 3. There are no other clues, however, by which we can decide whether Ep. 4 precedes or follows Ep. 2. The sole reference connecting Ep. 4 with the Harpalus affair and Demosthenes' exile is the clause, "If ever vindicated I return from exile" (Ep. 4. 2). Nevertheless, it may be possible to assign Ep. 4 to a definite stage in the developments which led to the Lamian war. Indeed, all four letters, if authentic, should reflect the agitation preceding the outbreak of the war and probably do. Ep. 3. 34 hints darkly at coming upheavals,[119] and the apprehensions at Ep. 2. 20 may arise from the same unstable situation. Ep. 1 gives directions how most expeditiously to begin the war.

Ep. 4 is written as a public reply to Theramenes, who, among other slanders, has called Demosthenes a carrier of dangerously contagious ill fortune. In American slang, such a bearer of ill fortune is called a jinx. The brevity of the term commends itself, and I shall use it henceforth even though it is slang. In Ep. 4 the author brings proof that Athens in fact enjoys good fortune, and that proof is made to imply as a corollary that Demosthenes is far from being a jinx. One might wonder, with Blass,[120] what possible interest a proof that Demosthenes was not a jinx could hold for the Council and the

[119] See commentary.
[120] III 1, 450–51.

People. But the argument of the letter may contain information of sufficient interest to the people to warrant their paying attention to the corollary.

The proposition which is the main burden of Ep. 4 is not merely something to flatter civic pride. In fourth-century Athens one of the prerequisites for recommending that the city go to war was to prove that it enjoyed better luck and more divine favor than the enemy. Indeed, in Anaximenes' practical handbook for Athenian politicians, it is listed even before the consideration of military superiority.[121]

There were two ways of fulfilling this prerequisite. First, the speaker could appeal to existing pronouncements of the oracles. Since the gods were known to be capricious, such oracles had to be recent. The speaker's exegesis of the oracular scripture would give a deductive proof of luck and divine favor. If it was a matter of actually declaring war, oracles were usually sought,[122] and, if recent omens seemed unfavorable, the speaker had to explain them away.[123] Second, the speaker would consider the recent luck of the city, trying to produce an inductive proof. Particularly where no recent oracles lent themselves to the purpose, and where the speaker felt that action was urgent, he would not risk the delay and uncertainty of seeking a fresh oracle. Thus we find that Demosthenes in his speeches advocating war with Philip used only inductive arguments to explain away past failures; the luck of the city, in fact, was not at fault. Where the Athenians had not spoiled it by their own stupidity, it had brought them success.[124]

A speech to the Assembly advocating something that might ultimately lead to war would also require such discussions. If the Athenians decided to continue to postpone implementing Alexander's decrees, they were risking war.[125] Against that background, Ep. 4 presents both the deductive and the inductive proof of good fortune, as matters deserving "not only to be heard but to be remembered." Hence, though Ep. 4 carefully avoids mentioning Alexander and

---

[121] Anax. 2, p. 25. 9–15 Hammer: "ὅταν μὲν οὖν ἐπὶ τὸ πολεμεῖν παρακαλῶμεν, . . . δεικτέον, ἐξ ὧν ἔστι περιγενέσθαι τῷ πολέμῳ, ὅτι τὰ πλεῖστα τούτων τοῖς παρακαλουμένοις ὑπάρχοντά ἐστι. περιγίνονται δὲ πάντες ἢ διὰ τὴν τῶν θεῶν εὔνοιαν, ἣν εὐτυχίαν προσαγορεύομεν, ἢ διὰ σωμάτων πλῆθος κτλ." Cf. D. 2. 22.

[122] See Th. i. 118. 3, 123. 1; viii. 1.

[123] Aesch. 3. 130–31.

[124] See D. 2. 22; 1. 10–11; 4. 45.

[125] Diod. xviii. 8. 4.

restricts itself to speaking about the past, it can be interpreted as encouraging the Athenians not to comply with the decrees. Their luck is sufficiently good to warrant the risk of temporizing.

First comes the proof from oracular "scripture." Recent oracles proclaimed that Good Fortune had her abode in Athens; to gainsay them was impious (paragraphs 3–4).[126] Next comes the inductive proof (paragraphs 5–9).[127] The policy which avoided open conflict with Macedonia and yielded minimal compliance had made Athens the most fortunate of the Greek commonwealths. In the spring of 323, when the embassies to Alexander had not yet returned with the news that the king demanded complete fulfilment of his orders,[128] that message would have been heartening.

Thus Demosthenes' argument that Good Fortune resided in Athens may have been encouragement to assume some risk of war; the suggestion is plausible but by no means certain. Everything else in Ep. 4 can serve only the interests of Demosthenes and his supporters. Both proofs of the good fortune of Athens are made to imply as a corollary that Demosthenes himself is not a jinx. If, as seems likely from Dinarchus,[129] the mere presence of such a jinx on Athenian soil was thought to be ruinous, Demosthenes could have had to write such a letter either before or after Ep. 2.

Fortune herself, according to the account in Diodorus,[130] brought the Athenians the opportunity actively to resist the return of the exiles and, at the same time, brought Demosthenes the occasion for Ep. 1, for on the evening of June 10[131] Alexander died. The letter purports to have been written after the news of the king's death reached Greece[132] and before the Athenians decided in favor of the Hellenic revolt. Here was a new situation that Demosthenes could turn to good use. Clearly reflected in Ep. 1. 5–9 are the difficulties faced by the war party in Athens on the eve of the Lamian war. They had to impose their will on a population that was rent by divisions. Many of the wealthier citizens, who would have had to pay much of the cost

[126] See commentary.

[127] See Arist. *Rhet.* i. 5. 17. 1361*b*39–1362*a*12.

[128] Arrian vii. 19. 1; Diod. xvii. 113. 2–4; Hyp. *Dem.* 19.

[129] 1. 77.

[130] xviii. 8. 7.

[131] See above, p. 44.

[132] Probably not before July. The ordinary ancient messenger could travel about 60 km. per day; the maximum for horse relays was 300 km. per day (Reincke, "*Nachrichtenwesen*," *RE*, XVI² [1935], 1537–41).

of the war, had compromised themselves and were regarded as collaborationists. They doubtless feared a reign of terror. Diodorus, too, reports the tensions and hesitations of the crisis, but says that those richer elements who were in favor of peace were simply outvoted.[133] But some of the propertied elements had to be won over if the war was to be paid for. Moreover, this problem was not peculiar to Athens. Throughout the Greek cities there were large numbers of influential people similarly compromised. There was one way to cut the knot: to sacrifice domestic animosities to the common weal by declaring an amnesty. Even those who had compromised themselves by seeming to collaborate with the Macedonian hegemony would find it to their interest to prevent the return of revolutionary exiles. At least one leading proponent of the war seems to have come to this conclusion. One of the Hibeh papyri,[134] most unlikely to be later than the reign of Ptolemy Philadelphus, contains fragments of a speech purporting to be by Leosthenes. Whether the speech actually was by Leosthenes, or whether it is the creation of a rhetorical historian to represent the discussions that took place during the crisis, it represents a reliable tradition.[135] The very first remnants of this speech contain an appeal for amnesty in order to expedite at home the decision to go to war and to win over willing allies.

Demosthenes knew the divisions of the Athenian citizenry. He saw that by adding the weight of his opinion to the proposal for an amnesty he could at once conciliate the war party and make a subtle plea for himself. He, too, had been condemned at least partly because he was looked upon as a collaborationist.[136] Both before and after putting forward the plea for an amnesty, Demosthenes artfully denies that the plea is for himself, a denial which only increased the emotional appeal (paragraphs 2, 10).

The curious phraseology at the beginning of paragraph 11 may reflect conditions at the time of writing. Demosthenes' forte in the *Philippics* had been to give well-organized instruction on the practical preparations (*paraskeuai*) required for war. But the practical preparations for the Lamian war were probably all but complete before the news of Alexander's death reached Greece.[137] Even so,

[133] xviii. 10.

[134] *The Hibeh Papyri*, ed. B. P. Grenfell and A. S. Hunt, I, 55–61, No. 15.

[135] See Mathieu, *RPh*, 3d series, III, 159–70.

[136] Hyp. *Dem.* 18–21. See below, pp. 80–81.

[137] Diod. xvii. 111, xviii. 8–9; Justin xiii. 5.

in a manner appropriate to a man past his prime, Demosthenes tries to use the language of the Demosthenes of old by speaking of the proposed amnesty as a *paraskeuê*.[138]

In paragraphs 11-16 he openly adds his voice to those advocating a new war. The customary discussion of Fortune and the favor of the gods follows. Characteristic of Demosthenes is the attitude that Luck helps those who help themselves. The issue of the prosecution of the war would not be decided with the vote to go to war. The Athenian democracy, like other democracies, was known for reposing its confidence in personalities rather than in policies. Thus, the people had elected Phocion to the post of *strategos* forty-five times.[139] To have appointed him to the command of the war might have been as disastrous as the appointment of Nicias to command the Sicilian expedition. Throughout his life Phocion had counseled peace with Macedonia, and he was outspoken in his opposition to the Lamian war.[140] That there was real danger Phocion might be selected is clear from the fact that his opponents found it necessary to resort to a political trick to prevent his being elected to replace Leosthenes when Leosthenes was killed.[141] Without invidiously naming names, Demosthenes foresees this danger and warns against it, doubtless here again trying to endear himself to the war party. Demosthenes concludes his letter on a ringing note, aiming to drown out any echo of his alleged collaborationism. Let every man do his duty! Let the Athenians follow the lead of Zeus of Dodona and the other gods— those whose oracles declared that Good Fortune herself dwelt in Athens. The letter ends with the call to liberty, the favorite Hellenic war slogan. Go forth to liberate the Greeks!

Stirring words in a letter were not enough. Demosthenes' belated endorsement of their cause may even have antagonized leading anti-Macedonian politicians like Hyperides, who, moreover, still had reason to fear the return of the man they had prosecuted. It was Demosthenes' voice in the Peloponnesus preaching a united Hellas to bring down the "New Macedonian Order" that brought him his restoration, perhaps by so impressing Athenian public opinion that the politicians could no longer prevent it.

[138] Cf. the use of *paraskeuê* at D. 14. 14-15.
[139] Plut. *Phoc.* 8. 1.
[140] Plut. *Phoc.* 23. 1.
[141] *Ibid.* 24. 1-2.

CHAPTER 6

Historical Analysis and the
Problem of Authenticity

B Y ANALYZING THE historical content of the letters and establishing their chronology, we have produced a good argument for
their authenticity. The lost letter and Epp. 3, 2, and 1 constitute a
series of messages which press the theme of Demosthenes' restoration, each according to the state of affairs at the moment. It is hard
to see how a propagandist or a literary artist would have had either
the interest or the knowledge to produce such a series. Much more
effective dramatic settings for a forged document could be imagined
—for example, the scene of Demosthenes' "martyrdom" at Calauria
in 322, when he committed suicide to avoid capture after the capitu-
lation of Athens to Antipater at the end of the Lamian war.[1] According to some reports of the event, he was indeed writing letters before
he took the poison.[2] A propagandist writing after the outcome might
still have taken the situation of Demosthenes' exile in 323 because the
orator at that time had the leisure to compose a detailed defense of
his career and rebuke the Athenian people for its mistakes. In that
case, however, he would hardly have written our series of letters. It
was the living Demosthenes who had to write messages like the abject
lost letter and Ep. 3 with its highly unpromising background. A
propagandist probably would have picked as the background for his
composition not the evolving setting of Epp. 1–4 but a single state of

---

[1] See below, p. 68. The setting of Demosthenes' suicide is used in Luc. *Dem.
Enc.*
[2] Plut. *Dem.* 29. 3, 30. 1; *Vit. X orat.* 847a–b.

64

affairs advantageous for his argument. Particularly embarrassing in posthumous apologetic propaganda would be the changing petitions of the orator in the letters. A later propagandist would have made Demosthenes ask immediately for exoneration. In each of the letters, however, the orator asks only for what the situation at the moment allows. In the lost letter and in Ep. 3, he does not ask for exoneration but only for the opportunity to return to Athens and raise the money to pay his fine. In Ep.2 he repeatedly asks for the "same exoneration already granted to others."[3] In Ep. 1. 6–10 he suggests that his restoration should come through the general amnesty which is the prerequisite for Athens' entry into the Greek war of liberation.

If written by Demosthenes in 324/3, the letters must not be in error on events important to the orator and his audience during that year. Piero Treves thought he had found such errors. First, Ep. 3. 31 implies that Philocles was convicted of bribe taking in the Harpalus scandal and probably also that he was driven into exile. Conviction certainly would have disqualified Philocles from public office.[4] Yet the ephebic inscription from Oropus shows Philocles in office as *kosmetes* at the end of 324/3 and being honored for his year of service.[5] Is Ep. 3. 31 contradicted by epigraphic evidence? It is not, for the conviction of Philocles can be inferred from Dinarchus,[6] and our established chronology of Epp. 1–4 allows us to deduce from Ep. 2 that Philocles was convicted but subsequently exonerated[7] and presumably reinstated as *kosmetes*.

Second, Treves tried to show that Epp. 1–4 presuppose an impossible chronology.[8] The words of Ep. 3 imply that Demosthenes had already written two letters from exile before the end of the ninth prytany (June 6, 323).[9] His trial and imprisonment, therefore, must

---

[3] See below, p. 78.

[4] Below, p. 68.

[5] See Appendix VII; Treves, *Athenaeum*, n.s., XIV, 239–40.

[6] Above, pp. 43–44.

[7] Above, pp. 48–49, 56. There is nothing to tell us what happened to the office of *kosmetes* in the interim. Was Philocles replaced? Or did the generals and the other ephebic officials take over his functions? Did his reinstatement mean the removal of a replacement? The sources bearing on the problem are collected at Busolt–Swoboda, pp. 1006–7, 1008, n. 4. The conviction need no more have barred his reinstatement than did Pericles' (Th. ii. 65).

[8] *Athenaeum*, n.s., XIV, 236–38.

[9] See above, pp. 48–49.

have occurred well before that date. According to Athenian law, persons who had not paid their fines by the end of the ninth prytany of the year were subject to imprisonment and a doubled fine.[10] If the letters are authentic, some other cause must be found for Demosthenes' imprisonment than the passing of the ninth prytany. Treves argued, moreover, that if the end of the ninth prytany had come after Demosthenes' conviction, his fine would have been doubled by the time of his return from exile; yet we know from Plutarch[11] that it had not been.

However, the account of Plutarch itself gives rise to difficulties.[12] In Athens, there were only two possible sentences for bribe taking, death or a tenfold fine.[13] Yet Plutarch reports a fine of only fifty talents, not two hundred. If Plutarch's figures are incorrect, no inference can be drawn from them.[14] On the other hand, Plutarch may be correct and our knowledge of Athenian law incomplete. Then, the otherwise unknown 250 per cent fine, like tenfold fines, might not have been doubled by the passing of the ninth prytany, only lesser fines being so doubled.[15]

Even so, the end of the ninth prytany would have had sufficient importance for Demosthenes for him to allude to it at Ep. 3. 39. It was the time when his name would be published on the tablets on the Acropolis as a debtor to the state and when his property would be confiscated and sold to cover the amount of his fine.[16]

As for the legal basis for the orator's imprisonment, there are several possibilities which raise no chronological difficulties for the letters. The court may have used discretion allowed it by the law to impose an additional punishment (*prostimêma*) irrespective of whether the guilty failed to pay his fine.[17] According to the law at

[10] Lipsius, pp. 945–47; imprisonment: *Hypoth.* 2. 4 to D. 24.

[11] *Dem.* 26. 1 and 27. 6.

[12] See Treves' own hesitation, *Athenaeum*, n.s., XIV, 237.

[13] Arist. *Ath. Pol.* 54. 2; Din. 1. 60, 2. 17; Lipsius, pp. 403–4.

[14] No better is the fivefold fine at *Vit. X orat.* 846c, otherwise unknown in Athenian law; see above Chap. 5, n. 36.

[15] Arist. *Ath. Pol.* 54. 2. Cf. Mathieu, *REA*, XXXIX, 378–79.

[16] See above, n. 10. The *atimia* imposed on embezzlers and bribe takers did not include the confiscation of their property (Andoc. 1. 74). When the speaker at Lys. 21. 25 fears that he will lose all his goods, he is referring to the vast amount of the tenfold fine. The only source which contradicts Andoc. 1. 74 is D. 21. 113, but that document is spurious. See Drerup, *NJb*, Suppl. XXIV (1898), 304–5.

[17] Lipsius, pp. 255–56; cf. Treves, *Athenaeum*, n.s., XIV, 236.

D. 24. 105, courts had such power to imprison common thieves; hence, surely also to imprison embezzlers, "thieves of public funds." Since Athenian law treated bribe taking and embezzlement under the same head,[18] surely the court had the power to impose on Demosthenes the additional sentence of imprisonment.

However, Ep. 3. 40–42 and *Vit. X orat.* 846c connect the orator's flight with his inability to pay his fine.[19] Imprisonment for non-payment of fines, even before the end of the ninth prytany, was known in Athenian law. We hear of a whole class of offenses for which courts were empowered or required by law to impose an additional sentence of "imprisonment until he shall pay."[20] Thus, although we do not possess the text of the law under which Demosthenes was imprisoned, we have clues as to its content.

If Demosthenes was imprisoned for failure to pay his fine, why did he not make use of the customary means to gain his release? Fifty talents was indeed a huge sum, but under normal conditions its magnitude would not have prevented him from winning his release, either through raising the money by turning his assets into cash and asking his friends for an emergency free loan[21] or through having them go surety for him.[22] We can understand, however, that as things were, Demosthenes' friends failed him, either because they were afraid or—like Hyperides—alienated; they, as well as the orator, would in any case have had difficulty in raising so large a sum in specie at short notice.[23] The background of the imprisonment of the sons of Lycurgus, which was soon to follow, was surely the same.[24] An instructive parallel is the plight of Miltiades more than one and a half centuries earlier. Imprisoned after being fined fifty talents, he died in prison before he could produce the liquid capital, although his wealth probably exceeded even the enormous fine, inasmuch as his son, Cimon, was able to pay it after his death.[25] Demades may

---

[18] Arist. *Ath. Pol.* 54. 2; Andoc. 1. 74; Lipsius, pp. 399–404; the speaker who at Lys. 21. 21 defends himself against a charge of bribe-taking speaks in terms of embezzlement at par. 16.

[19] See below, Chap. 8, rhetorical analysis of Ep. 3. 40–42.

[20] D. 24. 39, 63, 105 end; Arist. *Ath. Pol.* 63. 3; Lipsius, p. 946.

[21] *Eranos*; see commentary to Ep. 3. 38.

[22] D. 24. 39 and 144, but note the speaker's explanation in 145.

[23] See Ep. 3. 38–40; on Hyperides, see below, p. 80.

[24] See above, pp. 53–56.

[25] Plut. *Cimon* 4. 4, Hdt. vi. 136. 3; Obst, "Miltiades 2," *RE*, XV² (1932), 1704.

have found it possible to pay his fine and remain in Athens,[26] but Demosthenes could well have found his situation hopeless. Conviction on a charge of bribe taking carried with it loss of civil rights (*atimia*) for both the defendant and his descendants.[27] The *atimia* would remain even after payment of the fine and also made it very difficult to raise the money to pay it. An *atimos* could neither bring suit to collect debts owed him nor even enter the agora[28] on pain of immediate arrest by *apagôgê* or *endeixis* and severe punishment.[29] In such a situation of "ignominy, helplessness, and fear" (Ep. 3. 40), Demosthenes could well have thought that the only hope lay in flight.

Other attempts to point to historical errors in the letters are either inconclusive or rest on misinterpretations of the text.[30] We must, however, give special attention to the difficulty which has most often led scholars to declare the letters spurious: the possibility that Ep. 2. 20 contains a *vaticinium ex eventu*.[31] There, Demosthenes says that his fears for his safety have driven him to leave Troezen and take refuge at the temple of Poseidon on Calauria, and even in the temple he is afraid of what his powerful enemies can do. More than a year later, Demosthenes committed suicide at the same temple to escape capture.[32] Surely this looks like a prophesy after the fact! The sources leave room for doubt whether Demosthenes was at Calauria during his first exile.[33] What had he to fear among the pro-Athenian

[26] See above, Chap. 5, n. 42.

[27] Andoc. 1. 74; Lys. 21. 25; Aesch. 3. 232. G. Glotz, *La solidarité de la famille dans le droit criminel en Grèce*, pp. 500–5, tries to prove that the *atimia* was not hereditary in the fourth century, but see Lipsius, p. 404, n. 111.

[28] Lys. 6. 24; D. 21. 87; Busolt-Swoboda, p. 950.

[29] D. 24. 105; Lipsius, pp. 327–28, 331–32.

[30] Attempts of Schaefer and Neupert: below, Chap. 8, rhetorical analysis of Ep. 3. 24–27; commentary to Ep. 3. 19, 31 (on Charidemus). Attempts of Treves: above, Chap. 5, n. 101; commentary to Ep. 3. 29–30.

[31] A. Schaefer, "Sind die demosthenischen Briefe echt oder nicht?" *NJb*, CXV (1877), 163; Neupert, pp. 31–34; U. von Wilamowitz-Moellendorff, "Unechte Briefe," *Hermes*, XXXIII (1898), 497–98; Treves, *Athenaeum*, n.s., XIV, 245–46, 263–64.

[32] Plut. *Dem.* 28–30; *Vit. X orat.* 846f–47a.

[33] Several cities are mentioned as Demosthenes' places of refuge in 323. Troezen, then Calauria: D. Ep. 2. 19–20. Calauria: Pausanias i. 8. 2–3 and perhaps Philodemus *Volumina rhetorica*, Vol. II, p. 303 Sudhaus. Troezen: anonymous *Vita Demosthenis*, Vol. V, p. ccclx Dobson, and third biographical note at *Suda s.v. Demosthenes*. Troezen, then Argos: Syrianus *In Hermog.*, Vol. I, pp. 49–50 Rabe: ". . . ἀπῆλθε εἰς Τροιζῆνα κἀκεῖθεν εἰς Ἄργος· ὅθεν τῷ δήμῳ τὰς ἐπιστολὰς ἐπιστέλλει

people of Troezen who were to join the Hellenic alliance?[34] One would, indeed, expect such a *vaticinium ex eventu* in literary or rhetorical fictions or in propaganda written after the orator's death.

However, there is nothing to show that Demosthenes could not have stayed at Calauria in 323, and Demosthenes need have had no immediate cause for fear in order to use a stock rhetorical device for winning sympathy, that of pretending to be in danger.[35] To do so, he would have to believe that the pose would somehow be credible to the Athenians. Demosthenes' efforts to conciliate Alexander[36] and his cautious policy since 335 and his ambiguous treatment of Harpalus were used by his enemies to refute his claims to be in danger from Macedonia, but surely he made them anyhow at his trial,[37] and all the more could he make them in exile after an Athenian verdict declaring him the paid accomplice of Harpalus. At odds with the two chief powers of the Greek world, Macedonia and Athens, Demosthenes could feel his plight to be closely parallel to that of Themistocles, who could find no safety in Greece when pursued by the two great powers, Athens and Sparta.[38]

Moreover, Demosthenes could present his position under the existing international law as precarious. As Harpalus' convicted accomplice, Demosthenes was subject to extradition in all the states of the League of Corinth upon Alexander's demand; worse yet, he was

---

ταύτας συκοφαντουμένοις τε τοῖς Λυκούργου τοῦ ῥήτορος παισὶν ὑπὸ Μενεσαίχμου προθύμως ἐπικουρῶν καὶ τὴν ἑαυτοῦ κάθοδον πρυτανευόμενος· Ἀθηναίοις τε πρεσβευομένοις πρὸς Ἀργείους περὶ συμμαχίας ἄριστα συνεῖπεν οὐδεμίαν τῶν λυπησάντων φροντίδα ποιησάμενος." "For the most part" Aegina and Troezen: Plut. *Dem.* 26. 4. Aegina: Zosimus *Vit. Dem.*, Vol. V, p. cccliv Dobson. Megara: Justin xiii. 5. 9. Syrianus' statement that Ep. 2 was sent from Argos contradicts Ep. 2. 20 and is probably a lapse of memory· Perhaps Syrianus read in a lost history that Demosthenes in exile first lent his support at Argos to the Athenian embassy seeking Peloponnesian allies; see Diod. xviii. 11. 2 and Schaefer, III, 368, n. 2. Demosthenes may have stayed at all these places during his exile, except perhaps Megara, where he may have had dangerous enemies among the Athenian exiles (Din. 1. 58, 94). He was at Aegina when the trireme came to restore him to Athens (Plut. *Dem.* 27. 4). A brief stay by Demosthenes at Calauria may account for the failure of Plutarch and others to mention the island.

[34] See commentary to Ep. 2. 18–20.

[35] See below, Chap. 8, rhetorical analysis of Ep. 2. 18–19; cf. Bickerman, *RPh*, 3d series, XI, 61.

[36] Marsyas of Pella *apud* Harpocration *s.v. Aristion* (*F. Gr. Hist.*, No. 135, F 2); Aesch. 3. 162.

[37] See Hyp. *Dem.* 14; Din. 1. 102–3.

[38] Th. i. 135–37; Diod. xi. 54. 2–56. 3.

probably an outlaw whom anyone could kill with impunity.[39] The treaty with Alexander was unpopular, and the Greek cities probably would not honor these provisions without Macedonian prodding. Nevertheless, the provisions were legally binding,[40] and even before the Harpalus affair Alexander had enough grounds on which to call for the orator's extradition.[41] By the time of Ep. 2, preparations were well under way for the Lamian war, for which the money of Harpalus became the Athenian war chest. If Athens went to war with Alexander, it would be an open violation of the treaty of the League, and Demosthenes was sufficiently implicated for him to pretend that the king might then demand his extradition. Troezen, as a member of the League, would be bound as if by her own laws to comply. Nor would the sanctity of the temple of Poseidon necessarily protect Demosthenes. In Greece a suppliant seeking the protection of a god asked for the protection of the *laws*, and even the pious Lycurgus found it proper that Callistratus, who had been condemned to death and later returned to Athens from exile, was put to death though he had taken refuge at the altar of the twelve gods.[42] Thus, even in a friendly city, Demosthenes as an alien had no reason to hope for better treatment than he himself accorded Harpalus, a citizen of Athens. Surely, then, he could have thought it worth while to portray his peril to the Athenians.

Hence our sources do not prove that Ep. 2. 20 contains a *vaticinium ex eventu*. Moreover, let us consider the places elsewhere in the letters where a later author might have been strongly tempted to

[39] See above, pp. 38–39.

[40] The extant speeches of Demosthenes' prosecutors say nothing of the provisions of the League of Corinth but do stress the risk of war with Alexander should the orator be acquitted (Din. 1. 69; Hyp. *Dem.* 35–36). See, however, Paus. vii. 10. 10; Aesch. 3. 161, 254; D. 18. 322; Schaefer, III, 216. Again, there is a parallel in the case of Themistocles as related in Diod. xi. 54. 2–56. 3: the Lacedaemonians demanded that Themistocles be brought to trial before the general congress of the Hellenic League. Diodorus' account is generally rejected by modern writers but was current in fourth-century Athens.

[41] Even if Alexander had no evidence that Demosthenes had taken money from Harpalus (see Paus. ii. 33. 4) or was implicated in the preparations for the Lamian war, the Persian papers captured at Sardis in 334 showed that the orator had received Persian gold and was a traitor to the League (Plut. *Dem.* 20. 5). There were also the charges under which the king had demanded his extradition from Athens in 335 (see commentary to Ep. 3. 31–32).

[42] Bickerman, *RPh*, 3d series, XI, 57–61; Lyc. *Leoc.* 93.

endow Demosthenes with dramatic foresight. For example, Demosthenes expresses fears for his future also at Ep. 3. 41 and Ep. 2. 21–22. Yet nowhere does the author betray knowledge of the striking fact that the Athenians themselves caused Demosthenes' death. When Archias, Antipater's agent, came to arrest Demosthenes at Calauria, he was acting under the authority of the death sentence passed by the Athenians upon the fugitive politicians; officially, Antipater simply put his power at the Athenians' disposal.[43] A later writer would have before him the example of Plato's *Apology*, where Socrates warns the people that by putting him, their wise citizen, to death they will badly damage their reputation.[44] In the letters, however, there is no suggestion that the Athenians will be brought to cause the death of Demosthenes, their great patriot. At Ep. 2. 21–22 the meaning is that if the Harpalus scandal has rendered the Athenians permanently hostile to Demosthenes, they would have done him a favor at the end of his trial by choosing to sentence him to death. The passage is in the past tense; it contains no threat of suicide. Demosthenes' only fear is that the Athenians will not become reconciled to him, not their action, but their inaction. Similarly, at Ep. 3. 41 at worst Demosthenes will perish through the inaction and indifference of the Athenians.

A writer after the Lamian war might well have included another "prophesy." Hyperides, Aristonicus, and Himeraeus, the brother of Demetrius of Phalerum, joined Demosthenes in martyrdom.[45] Both Hyperides and Himeraeus prosecuted Demosthenes in 323. Why, then, no admonition to them by name in the letters?[46] The warning to patriotic politicians at Ep. 3. 34 is so vague that no one has ever suggested that it is a *vaticinium ex eventu*. Indeed, Demosthenes could be expected so to play upon the ever-present fear of subversion and revolution in the period of explosive uncertainty following Alexander's decrees on the return of the exiles. Furthermore, propaganda

---

[43] *F. Gr. Hist.*, No. 156 (Arrian), F 9, pars. 13–14; Plut. *Dem.* 28. 2–31. 4; *Vit. X orat.* 851c; and cf. *Suda s.v. Antipatros*. On the legal procedure by which the sentences were obtained, see G. de Sanctis, "I nomophylakes d'Atene," *Entaphia in memoria di Emilio Pozzi* (Torino: Fratelli Bocca, 1913), pp. 7–10.

[44] 38c.

[45] *F. Gr. Hist.* No. 156, F 9, par. 13; Plut. *Dem.* 28. 4.

[46] Luc. *Dem. Enc.* 31 dwells on the "poetic justice" of Hyperides' fate. Mention by name: see below, pp. 114–17.

written under the regime of Demetrius of Phalerum probably would allude to the fact of the martyrdom of his brother.

In Ep. 1 the author shows no fear that Athens will be deserted by her allies, as she was in 322; this is the optimism of a writer before the events.[47] Moreover, Ep. 1. 16 mentions by name only Zeus of Dodona and not the Pythian Apollo as a god to be taken as a leader (i.e., consulted). The normal procedure in fourth-century Athens was to seek oracles at both Dodona and Delphi before any weighty undertaking.[48] Demosthenes condemned the Delphic oracle for "Philippizing," just before Chaeroneia; later, the Delphians are reported to have announced dire omens against Thebes in 335.[49] Hence, one may infer that Ep. 1. 16 omits the Pythian Apollo as hostile to the Hellenic cause. Demosthenes would use a hostile witness to support his argument in Ep. 4. 3 but would not recommend Delphi's advice on matters of policy. Yet there is ample evidence that the Delphic Amphictyony as a body joined the Hellenic revolt.[50] Since the oracle usually marched in step with the attitude of the Amphictyony,[51] in all likelihood the Pythian Apollo thereupon became, to Demosthenes, a deity to be trusted. Surely, only Demosthenes, writing before the decision of the Amphictyony, could have omitted the most famous of Greek oracles.

Similarly, the unsympathetic mention of the Thessalians, Argives, and Arcadians at Ep. 4. 8 as those who brought evil and slavery upon the Greeks indicates that if that letter is propaganda it antedates the Lamian war (a writer of *literary* fiction might have borrowed the

[47] See below, pp. 90–92.

[48] *X. Vect.* 6. 2; cf. Plato *Lg.* v. 738b–c.

[49] Aesch. 3. 130; Diod. xvii. 10. 5; H. W. Parke and D. E. W. Wormell, *The Delphic Oracle*, I, 239–42.

[50] The list of the members of the anti-Macedonian alliance at Diod. xviii. 11. 1–2 includes those peoples of central Greece whose representatives commanded a majority of the Amphictyonic votes. The Amphictyony also turned its displeasure against "collaborationists," revoking honors previously granted to Aristotle (Aelianus *Var. hist.* xiv. 1 = fr. 666 in V. Rose, *Aristotelis qui ferebantur librorum fragmenta*). An Amphictyonic inscription also shows evidence of the decision; see J. Pouilloux, *BCH*, LXXV, 300.

[51] When the Amphictyony "Philippized," so did the oracle (D. 18. 151–52, 156; Aesch. 3. 130); see Parke and Wormell, I, 233–38. On the position of the Amphictyony and the oracle in the Persian wars, see Parke and Wormell, I, 165–78, and Hermann Bengtson, "Themistokles und die delphische Amphiktyonie," *Eranos,* XLIX (1951), 86–92.

theme from *De Corona*). In 324/3 the alliances of these peoples with Philip could still be held against them,[52] but the Hellenic revolt wiped out much if not all of the stain, especially for the Thessalians.

The Arcadians, although apparently swayed enough by Demosthenes' eloquence to become neutral,[53] played no active role in the Lamian war, but the Argives did take part.[54] The activity of the Thessalians in the revolt was most distinguished. Their cavalry defected from Antipater to Leosthenes, thus bringing about the victory at Thermopylae which drove Antipater to shut himself up in Lamia. Thereafter, the Thessalians contributed to every brilliant Hellenic success;[55] all Thessaly except Pelinna joined the revolt.[56] The defection from Antipater seems to have atoned completely for the ignominy mentioned at Ep. 4. 8. To Hyperides, the Thessalians hitherto had been unwilling victims of Macedonia.[57] No discredit attached to them for their separate peaces with Antipater after Crannon; the Hellenic army did nothing while Antipater besieged and took their cities.[58] In 321 with Aetolian help the Thessalians again revolted. Deserted by the Aetolians, the Thessalians under Menon faced Polyperchon's Macedonians but were defeated.[59] Thessaly thereafter remained passive, but after this brave effort a propagandist could hardly call them those who had brought slavery to Greece.[60]

So much for the problem of whether there are *vaticinia ex eventu* in Epp. 1–4. A case against the authenticity of Epp. 2 and 4, the letters in which the central motif is the defense of Demosthenes' career, could be based upon the great similarity of the arguments there to those in *De Corona*.[61] We have already noted[62] that there is nothing strange in a politician's repeated use of the same arguments to defend his career. Since the years after *De Corona* added little noteworthy to Demosthenes' positive achievements, the similarity

[52] See commentary to Ep. 4. 8.
[53] See below, n. 144.
[54] Diod. xviii. 11; Paus. i. 25. 4.
[55] Hyp. *Epit.* 12–13; Diod. xviii. 12–13, 15. 3–4, 17. 4.
[56] Diod. xviii. 11. 1.
[57] *Epit.* 13.
[58] Diod. xviii. 17. 7; Pharsalus taken by siege: *Vit. X orat.* 846e.
[59] Diod. xviii. 38.
[60] H. D. Westlake, *Thessaly in the Fourth Century B.C.*, pp. 229–36.
[61] Cf. Treves, *Athenaeum*, n. s., XIV, 248–50; Blass, III 1, 451.
[62] Above, Chap. 3, end.

is hardly surprising. To demonstrate how inconclusive these objections are, it is sufficient to show the differences from *De Corona*.

During the reign of Alexander, Demosthenes' conduct in connection with two cities put weapons into the hands of his enemies. Demosthenes had had a hand in the Theban revolt which led to the destruction of that city by Alexander.[63] His enemies ascribed the ruin of Thebes to Demosthenes' failure to use the Persian funds at his disposal to win the adherence of the Arcadians to the revolt; they blamed it on his avarice.[64] In addition, they portrayed Demosthenes as a jinx who brought ruin wherever he went.[65] Of this, Thebes was the most striking proof.

The revolt of the Spartans led by Agis against the Macedonian hegemony in 330 was an opportunity for the Greeks to join in casting off the Macedonian yoke, yet Athens stood aloof, and the revolt failed. Aeschines speaks of Demosthenes' efforts in favor of the Spartans as inept bombast.[66] The accusations with respect to both Thebes and Sparta recur in the speeches against Demosthenes in the Harpalus affair.[67]

There is a striking contrast between the treatment of these two themes in *De Corona* and in the letters. *De Corona*, Demosthenes' spectacularly successful defense of his career in 330, mentions the Thebans and their plight repeatedly but passes over the defeat of the Spartans in silence. In Epp. 2 and 4, on the other hand, the author is equally concerned with defending Demosthenes' career, and yet no mention is made of his most striking success, that of winning over Thebes to the alliance against Philip before the battle of Chaeroneia. The avoidance of the mention of Thebes is so striking that it must be intentional. As for the Spartans, the author of Ep. 4 does not hesitate at all to mention them and to claim by implication that Demosthenes' policy was not inept bombast but had left Athens far better off than the unfortunate Spartans, whose fate could not be blamed on him.

These differences between the letters and *De Corona* in themselves show that Epp. 2 and 4 are not mere imitations of the other work.

[63] Diod. xvii. 8. 5–6; Plut. *Dem.* 23. 1–2; *Vit. X orat.* 847c.

[64] See, e.g., Aesch. 3. 133, 134, 156, 157, 239–40.

[65] *Ibid.*, 157–58.

[66] *Ibid.*, 3. 165–67.

[67] Thebes: Hyp. *Dem.* 17; Din. 1. 10, 12, 18–21, 24–27, etc. Sparta: Din. 1. 34.

Indeed, the changed treatment of the fate of the two cities probably reflects changes in Athenian public opinion.

In 330, the majority of the public still was convinced that Demosthenes was an incorruptible Hellenic patriot who could not have been led by avarice to betray Thebes; his pro-Theban sympathies were well known. The people still had enough appreciation of Demosthenes' successes not to be convinced by the suggestion that Thebes had perished because she had been infected by Demosthenes' contagious ill fortune. After more years of Demosthenes' seeming collaborationism, however, the image of Demosthenes as an anti-Macedonian patriot began to fade. And then the scandal of 324/3 brought dangerous confirmation to all these charges against the orator. The august Council of the Areopagus now declared him to be a corrupt taker of bribes. His accusers drove home the inference that he must have been so all along; the stories about Thebes must be true![68] Demosthenes by taking the money of Harpalus had placed the city in a position which could bring upon it terrible ill fortune, just as his jinx had brought disaster to Thebes.[69] Dinarchus dwells upon the ruin of Thebes and upon Demosthenes' jinx at such length that it is clear he expected these arguments against the orator to carry great weight with the dicasts.[70] Hence, in 323, the ruin of Thebes probably was so sore a point that Demosthenes in writing his letters could not have risked reminding his audience of it.

The Spartans did not have so strong a claim on the gratitude of the Athenians as did the Thebans who had twice fought to keep the Macedonians from Attic soil. Thebes had been ruined; Sparta had at least not been destroyed. In 330 Demosthenes' inept policy toward Agis' revolt probably was a live enough issue to be embarrassing. But the most glorious period of Demosthenes' career was still fresh in memory. Demosthenes had enough material to produce a defense so impressive that this one embarrassing detail could be passed over in silence. Aeschines, in challenging Demosthenes to tell what effective action he had taken in connection with Agis' revolt, might have been provoking him to make statements for which he could be prosecuted as a rebel against the League of Corinth[71]—yet another reason

[68] Din. 1. 10, 18–21, 24–29; Hyp. *Dem.* 17.
[69] Din. 1. 64–77, 88; see Hyp. *Dem.* 39.
[70] See commentary to Ep. 4. 1, δυστυχίαν.
[71] Aesch. 3. 165; Blass, *Demosthenes Rede vom Kranze*, p. 9.

for passing it over in silence. Dinarchus does not dwell at length upon Demosthenes' failure to take advantage of Agis' revolt. In the perspective of 323 the cautious and ineffective sympathy shown by Demosthenes in 330 could look to be the part of wisdom and, as such, a part of Athens' good fortune in having the good advice of Demosthenes.

Moreover, if the letters are to be regarded as propaganda, the treatment of Thebes and Sparta in Epp. 2 and 4 suggests very early dates for their composition. At Ep. 4. 7 the misfortunes of the Spartans are mentioned. Yet a pro-Demosthenic propagandist would hardly have wasted sympathy on the Spartans after the Lamian war, for they did not rally to the cause of Greek liberty.[72]

On the other hand, the prospect of Thebes still ruined would have added weight to the arguments of those who saw in the disastrous end of the Lamian war more evidence of Demosthenes' jinx. There is, however, a *terminus ante quem* after which a propagandist might no longer have to avoid, in writing documents like Epp. 2 and 4, all reference to the ill-fated city, for in 316 Cassander provided for its restoration. The greater part of the wall was rebuilt through Athenian contributions.[73] In his petition of 280/79, Demochares both mentions the Theban alliance as one of Demosthenes' great achievements and proudly contradicts the charge that Demosthenes' avarice caused the fall of Thebes. Demosthenes "*prevented* the Peloponnesians from going to the aid of Alexander against Thebes, *giving money* and going in person as ambassador."[74]

Since Ep. 2 contains many allusions to events of the year 324/3, there is no need to point to other instances in it of advance beyond the situation reflected in *De Corona*. For Ep. 4 there is also the reference to the effects of Alexander's invasion of India in par. 7.[75]

Historical analysis can be most fruitful when brought to bear on the hypothesis that a propagandist fabricated Epp. 1–4. A writer of literary fiction can simply indulge his imagination. A propagandist necessarily writes against a specific historical background. All four letters contain arguments to defend Demosthenes' career, and Ep.

[72] Diod. xviii. 11.
[73] Diod. xix. 53–54.
[74] *Vit. X orat.* 851b.
[75] See commentary *ad. loc.* Another possible advance in Ep. 4 beyond *De Corona* is discussed in the commentary to Ep. 4. 3.

3 also contains a defense of the career of Lycurgus. Hence, if the letters were written as propaganda, they must have been written when the judgment to be placed upon Demosthenes' career was still an issue in Athens. In 280/79 Demochares successfully petitioned the Athenian people that in recognition of the excellence of Demosthenes' career a statue of him be set up and the eldest of his heirs be granted meals at the public table in the Prytaneum.[76] The text of the petition in Pseudo-Plutarch presents Demosthenes as one who was always ready to give his money in the service of the state and as one who nobly died on Calauria because of his devotion to the people. The inscription on the statue celebrated him as the hero of the resistance to Macedonia.[77] In effect, Demosthenes was thereby "canonized" as a "saint" of the Athenian Democracy and of Hellenic liberty. If the letters try to defend Demosthenes against charges of avaricious corruption, of collaborationism, and of being a jinx, they must have been written before the passage of the decree.[78]

Again, the defence of Lycurgus at the beginning of Ep. 3 could hardly have been written as propaganda after the passage of the similar decree in his honor proposed by Stratocles in 307/6.[79]

We have shown that Epp. 1–4 seek only what Demosthenes would have sought at each stage during the months of his exile. It may be possible to exclude the hypothesis that the letters are posthumous propaganda if we can show, in addition, that they fit Demosthenes' actual purposes in 323 and no others, and that they reply to the charges brought against him in 323 with only the arguments then available to him. The petition of Demochares will be a useful basis for comparison, inasmuch as it is an authentic piece of propaganda for Demosthenes written after his death.[80]

Taken in their proper sequence, Epp. 1–4 appear designed to serve Demosthenes' purposes in 323, for his appeal for restoration to Athens is the thread which unites the letters, trying even Ep. 4 into

[76] See above, Chap. 2, n. 93.

[77] Plut. *Dem.* 30. 5; *Vit. X orat.* 847a.

[78] Bickerman, *RPh*, 3d series, XI, 55; Treves, *Athenaeum*, n.s., XIV, 251.

[79] *Vit. X orat.* 843c, 851f–52e; *IG* II² 457 = *SIG*³ 326. The defense of Lycurgus, however sincere, is used in the letter as a subtle means of furthering Demosthenes' own cause (see below, Chap. 8, rhetorical analysis of Ep. 3. 1, 35–36). Hence one could argue that a propagandist was trying to vindicate Demosthenes by portraying him as sending a plea for an already vindicated patriot.

[80] See above, Chap. 2, n. 93.

the series.[81] For Demosthenes himself, all would be subordinated to restoration; he would not be interested in a vindication that would be merely posthumous.[82] On the other hand, for any other author the question of restoration could be the pretext for a letter, but would hardly be a burning issue, especially after Demosthenes' return and martyrdom. What a writer of literary or propagandistic fiction after Demosthenes' death would probably have done we can judge from the letters of Aeschines, literary fictions written as imitative counterparts of D. Epp. 1–4.[83]

Demosthenes' Ep. 2 is the one which takes as its entire subject the orator's return, and from beginning to end the audience is never allowed to forget it (Ep. 2. 1–3, 8, 12, 16, 21, 23, 26). By contrast, although the occasion for Aeschines' defense of his conduct in the spurious Ep. 12 is to seek a restoration from exile for his little children, and possibly for himself, this purpose or rather pretext for the letter is not even hinted at before paragraph 12 and is not explicitly stated until paragraph 15.

Similarly, in Ep. 3 Demosthenes places a reminder of his own affairs at the very outset and devotes the vehement conclusion (paragraphs 35–45) to a plea for restoration. The spurious counterpart, Ps.-Aesch. Ep. 3, expresses no interest in restoration at all. A similar difference can be shown to exist between D. Ep. 1 and Ps.-Aesch. Ep. 11.[84]

There is a strong request for restoration at Ps.-Aesch. Ep. 7. 4, whereas D. Ep. 4 merely attempts to remind the audience in passing of Demosthenes' plea. But the simulated Aeschines in the very next paragraph views the possible rejection of his request with equanimity.

Viewed as propaganda, Epp. 1–4 not only defend Demosthenes' career. They also advocate a number of policies: the achievements of Demosthenes and of Athens in the struggle against Philip should be remembered with grateful appreciation; gratitude should be shown to patriots like Lycurgus, Philocles, and Demosthenes; the Athenians should have confidence in the good fortune of their city; the prerequisite for taking full advantage of the death of Alexander and

---

[81] The author sees to it that the subject of restoration, though mentioned only in passing, is given a prominent position at Ep. 4. 2.

[82] See Ep. 3. 41.

[83] See Appendix II.

[84] See below, Chap. 8, end of rhetorical analysis of Ep. 1.

leading a Hellenic war of liberation is an amnesty for all seeming collaborators with the Macedonian order. All these policies serve Demosthenes' purposes in 323; since they are closely connected with Demosthenes' defenses against the charges against him, we must consider how these policies fit the purposes of posthumous apology. One must also consider the possibility that apology is only a dramatic pretext and that the policies are the real purpose of the letter. In that case, it is hard to find a parallel for the letters in ancient Greece.[85] Athenian propagandists did fabricate material pretending to come from the past in order to support policies for the present. There were false historical accounts, false references to the glorious ancestors, false texts of the "ancestral constitution." There may have been false decrees of the Council and the People. So far as we know, however, no one in fifth- or fourth-century Athens circulated a speech of Peisistratus' rival, Lycurgus, or a letter of Draco to support a policy, and no one composed an extra Philippic in the name of Demosthenes to stir the Greeks to fight against the Macedonian successors of Alexander.[86]

The charges against which the letters defend Demosthenes are the charges which his enemies used against him in 323 with telling effect. They are the following:

1. Demosthenes was a corrupt politician who repeatedly took bribes to betray the interests of Athens, first from the Persian king and later even from Philip and Alexander.[87] His conduct in the Harpalus affair was only the latest instance.

---

[85] In Plato's *Apology*, the defense of Socrates is the real purpose, not a dramatic pretext. The surviving examples of this propaganda genre are treated below, pp. 120–26.

[86] See Alexander Fuks, *The Ancestral Constitution* (London: Routledge and Paul 1953); E. Ruschenbusch, "*ΠΑΤΡΙΟΣ ΠΟΛΙΤΕΙΑ*," *Historia*, VII (1958), 398–424; Christian Habicht, "Falsche Urkunden zur Geschichte Athens in Zeitalter der Perserkriege," *Hermes*, LXXXIX (1961), 1–35. In the posthumous speech placed in his mouth (Plato Ep. 8. 355a–57d), Dion speaks directly of the events of the time of the letter, not of the events of his lifetime, just as Socrates in the *Menexenus* speaks of the events of the Corinthian war. In another era, in the fifteenth Christian century, Cardinal Bessarion did publish a Latin translation of the *First Olynthiac* to stir the western Christian princes against the Turks.

[87] The Persian king: Aesch. 3. 156, 173, 209, 239–40, 259; Din. 1. 10, 15, 70; Hyp. *Dem.* 25. Philip and Alexander: Aesch. 3. 85, 103, 146, 173; Din. 1. 28, 41–45; Hyp. *Dem.* 25. Defense at D. Epp. 3. 42; 2. 6–9, 14–16.

2. Demosthenes collaborated with the Macedonian order,[88] impeding efforts to liberate the Greeks. Aeschines had been unable to convince the court in 330 with this charge, but by 323 Hyperides used it with such bitterness against his former political ally as to suggest that he was taking advantage of the outburst of public indignation to remove Demosthenes from the political scene.[89] The speeches of both Dinarchus and Hyperides suggest that Demosthenes' conviction was due nearly as much to this charge as to the actual charge of taking money from Harpalus. Indeed, considerable circumstantial evidence lay behind it. In the years after Chaeroneia the orator had no great anti-Macedonian achievements to speak of, for he had avoided contending with the invincible Fortune and dangerous wrath of Philip and, after the destruction of Thebes, of Alexander.[90] Demosthenes' failures to take effective action during the rebellion of Thebes and the revolt of Agis — failures which his enemies eagerly exploited in their propaganda against him — were followed by years of quiet on the question of the Macedonian hegemony, even though Alexander

[88] Defense at Epp. 3. 4; 2. 4; 4. 7–9; 1. 8.

[89] Ettore Lepore in his "Leostene e le origini della guerra lamiaca," *La parola del passato*, X (1955), 176–85, shows how different Demosthenes' policy was from that of the more radical anti-Macedonians during the years after the destruction of Thebes and plausibly connects the condemnation of the orator in the Harpalus affair with the effort of the radicals to put him out of the way.

[90] Demosthenes' behavior from 338 on is succinctly summarized from his enemies' point of view at Din. 1. 96–97. See also Aesch. 3. 159–167; Din. 1. 17, 28–36, 91, 94–95; Hyp. *Dem.* 17–22, 30–31; Plut. *Dem.* 21. 3, 23. 2–3, 24. 1. The change in Demosthenes' policy was obvious, and at least in part accounts for Theopompus' statement (*apud* Plut. *Dem.* 13. 1), that Demosthenes was unable to remain true for long to the same policies or the same men. Demosthenes could not deny that his behavior had changed but insisted that his attitude had not; he spoke of the patriotic silence imposed upon him by the cruel blindness of Fortune (D. 18. 308, 320; see commentary to Ep. 2. 4, 5).

Since there is ample evidence for Demosthenes' fear of Philip's and Alexander's Fortune and some also for his fear of his own inherent bad luck (see commentary to Ep. 4. 1, δυστυχίαν), the colorless and form-bound character of D. 60 is no reason to declare that oration spurious, though critics ancient and modern have done so; see Blass, III 1, 404–6; Treves, *Athenaeum*, n.s., XIV, 153–74. The speech is just what one would expect of Demosthenes. He accepts the honor conferred upon him as a duty; now is no time to risk inflammatory statements. Intentionally, he keeps close to the traditional pattern of the funeral oration (par. 1), and where he refers directly to the contemporary situation, in pars. 18–24, he does express his hostility to the Macedonian victors and to fickle Fortune while avoiding inflammatory remarks. In 322 Hyperides could do otherwise in his *Epitaphius*, but with Alexander dead and a strong Hellenic army doing well, Fortune appeared to be on his side.

was far away. Only twice between 335 and 323 is Demosthenes known to have directly opposed Alexander. In the first case, he spoke against granting Athenian ships to Alexander because it was not clear whether or not he would use them against the city.[91] This advice was not necessarily more belligerent than Phocion's warning to the Athenians of the entangling consequences of joining Philip's Hellenic League.[92] At any rate, surely the Athenians supplied the ships. In the second case, after first opposing the deification of Alexander, Demosthenes reversed himself.[93] On the other hand, it was a matter of record that Demosthenes had made efforts to conciliate the Macedonian authorities.[94]

3. He was a jinx whose participation in the direction of affairs and perhaps whose mere presence brought disaster to cities and to individuals, including even his associates. Aeschines raised such accusations in 330; in 323 they are urged with great vehemence by Dinarchus.[95]

In addition, Demosthenes' enemies made charges against his character, charges which were not actionable or provocative of superstitious fear but were useful in portraying him as a hateful personality: he was guilty of sexual perversion, and he was a coward who failed in his military duties, leaving his post at Chaeroneia.[96] These two charges the letters answer with the merest allusion,[97] though a literary or propagandistic fabrication might be expected to devote considerable space to them.[98]

[91] *Vit. X orat.* 847c; for the date, see commentary to Ep. 3. 29–30.

[92] Plut. *Phoc.* 16. 4.

[93] Din. 1. 94; Hyp. *Dem.* 31–32.

[94] Aesch. 3. 162; Hyp. *Dem.* 20; cf. Din. 1. 81, 103.

[95] For a discussion of the texts, see commentary to Ep. 4. 1, δυστυχίαν. Defenses at D. Epp. 3. 31; 2. 5; 4; 1. 13.

[96] Sexual perversion: Aesch. 1. 131; 2. 99, 127, 154; 3. 162, 174; Pytheas *apud* Duris, *F. Gr. Hist.* No. 76, F 8. Cowardice and desertion: Aesch. 3. 148, 152, 155, 175, 187, 244, 253; Din. 1. 12, 71, 81; Pytheas *apud* Plut. *Dem.* 20. 2. If Demosthenes' conduct at Chaeroneia was actionable, by 323 he had long since been tried and acquitted; see E. Drerup, *Demosthenes im Urteile des Altertums*, pp. 33–34.

[97] Ep. 2. 25; see commentary to Ep. 2. 5, ἐξηταζόμην.

[98] Socrates' enemies had to try him on a charge of impiety (*graphê asebeias*). Among all known provisions of Athenian law, there is none under which Socrates could have been prosecuted on the other count of corrupting the young, even if it was a truer motive for the prosecution; see Lipsius, p. 363, n. 24, and A. E. Taylor, *Socrates* (New York: D. Appleton and Company, 1933), pp. 93–106. The strongest evidence for it, Socrates' association with Critias and Alcibiades, was excluded

One might think that Demosthenes' activity to advance the Hellenic revolt, his triumphant return to Athens, and his martyrdom would have been sufficient to put an end to the charges of corruption and collaborationism, if not to the charge of being a jinx. Nevertheless, all three chief accusations against Demosthenes probably did survive 322, so that posthumous apologies refuting them might have been fabricated for him. Thus, the orator was the *bête noire* of the pro-Macedonians; his behavior under Alexander need not have been forgotten by the anti-Macedonians; and the defeats of Chaeroneia and Crannon may have made his memory distasteful to the entire generation born before 350. His undependability as a soldier and his acceptance of Persian bribes were remembered against him, as is attested by Demetrius of Phalerum,[99] a biased observer, but still one who lived through the period between 322 and 283. Indeed, Demosthenes received "canonization" long after Lycurgus and even after Phocion.[100] In his petition, Demochares had to present a detailed list of Demosthenes' liturgies as part of the usual proofs of worthiness for

from consideration in court by the amnesty of 403. This second charge was used only to heighten the dicasts' hostility. But if the Socratic circle tried to defend the reputation of their founder and ideal after his death, the charge of corrupting the young was a stain which they could not allow to remain on his character. This unactionable charge constituted the chief burden of Polycrates' attack on the dead Socrates and the chief burden of the Socratic Xenophon's reply in defense; see Ivo Bruns, *Das literarische Porträt der Griechen*, pp. 193–96, 361–66; P. Treves, "Polykrates 7," *RE*, XXI² (1952), 1738–50. Similarly, in the polemical exchange over the figure of Alcibiades after his death, the speaker for the defense makes a lengthy reply (Isoc. 16. 22–35) to the accusations against Alcibiades' character at Lys. 14. 41; on these speeches of Isocrates and Lysias, see below, pp. 120–23.

The defects of Demosthenes' character were a favorite subject for later writers; see Drerup, *Demosthenes im Urteile des Altertums*, index *s.v. Unwürdigkeit zur Volksführung* (pp. 256–57). Characteristic is Panaetius' opinion of Demosthenes (Plut. *Dem.* 13. 4–5; Plutarch's quotation of Panaetius probably extends through the entire passage). For the Stoic Panaetius, the orator's fortune would in no case be a consideration. Significantly, however, Panaetius has no knowledge of Demosthenes' "collaborationism"; to him the orator's political policy was steadfast. Rather, he finds him wanting because he lacked "the bravery becoming to a warrior" and "purity in all his dealings."

[99] *Apud* Plut. *Dem.* 14. 2 (*F. Gr. Hist.* No. 228, F 19).

[100] Lycurgus: above, n. 79; Phocion: Plut. *Phoc.* 38. 1 and F. Robert, "La réhabilitation de Phocion," *Comptes rendus de l'Académie des inscriptions et belles lettres*, 1945, pp. 531–33. We cannot be entirely sure what was the opinion of Demosthenes held by the majority of the Athenian people during these years because they may have been compelled by factors beyond their control to refrain from honoring his memory; see below, n. 154.

public honors; nevertheless, he may also have included the list to dispel the suspicion that Demosthenes was a corrupt politician.[101] Demochares contradicts the charge that the orator's avarice and ill fortune were responsible for the fall of Thebes with a proud assertion that his generosity and his diplomacy *prevented* the Peloponnesians from going to Alexander's aid at Thebes. Demochares' entire petition, and especially its concluding paragraph,[102] can be read as an eloquent denial that Demosthenes was a collaborationist. And the inscription on Demosthenes' statue[103] implies that no fault and no "jinx" of his caused the Greeks to lose to the "big battalions" of Philip.

There is thus good evidence of efforts by Demochares to clear the reputation of Demosthenes. Demosthenes' heirs could well be expected to do so.[104] Propaganda to clear the reputation of the dead is always written to serve the purposes of the living; besides the motive of filial piety Demosthenes' heirs had the prospect of public maintenance as a posthumous reward to Demosthenes. It is hard, however, to see how any other group in Athens might feel pressed to defend Demosthenes' reputation. Hyperides did suggest that Demosthenes' downfall brought discredit on the entire group of anti-Macedonian politicians. This, however, is surely courtroom rhetoric.[105] A party is rarely brought into lasting discredit when individual members are convicted of corruption. Usually, at the very worst, it may be forced to disown the culprits as "men who have proved false to their trust."[106] Hyperides here readily disowns the "corrupt collaborationist," Demosthenes. Whatever anti-Macedonian party existed in Athens after 322 probably had no compelling reason to write apologetic propaganda for him.[107]

---

[101] Similarly, Cleochares' rhetorical contrast of Demosthenes' "poverty" with Philip's wealth may be a reply to the charges of avarice (quoted *apud* Herodianus Rhetor *Fig.*, Vol. VIII, p. 599 Walz). The sources on Cleochares' association with Demochares are collected by Drerup, *Demosthenes im Urteile des Altertums*, pp. 92–97.

[102] *Vit. X orat.* 851c.

[103] *Ibid.*, 847a; Plut. *Dem.* 30. 5.

[104] See above, Chap. 4, end.

[105] Hyp. *Dem.* 21; cf. Anax. 36, pp. 87–88 H. The embarrassing fact for Hyperides is his former friendship with Demosthenes.

[106] See above, Chap. 5, n. 20.

[107] Cf. Wilamowitz, *Hermes*, XXXIII, 497; Treves, *Athenaeum*, n.s., XIV, 249–51.

Since no citizen body would vote to honor the memory of a corrupt, ill-fortuned traitor, propaganda by Demosthenes' heirs would have to prove that Demosthenes never sold his country's interest, that he was always anti-Macedonian, perhaps also that he was never pro-Persian, and that he was not a jinx. How well do Epp. 1–4 serve these purposes of Demosthenes' heirs?

In reply to the charge of taking bribes to oppose the city's interests, the letters do contain many of the elements one would expect in propaganda written by Demosthenes' heirs. Ep. 3. 42 and Ep. 2. 15 deny his guilt outright. Nothing is said of Persian bribes, but in Ep. 2. 6–12 evidence is presented to show that never in his life did he succumb to bribery at the hands of Athens' enemies. There are, however, elements which one would hardly expect in propaganda written after the death of Demosthenes. When Ep. 2 attempts to prove Demosthenes' probity throughout his career, it does so for the purpose of proving his innocence in the affair of the money of Harpalus. In 323, this makes sense. His being implicated in the scandal had brought upon Demosthenes his condemnation and exile. But such an argument after the events of 322 would be contrary to the facts of democratic politics. Democracies always conduct their affairs through professional politicians who supplement their incomes and recoup their expenses by financial practices which are questionable but are not usually treated as crimes.[108] Such questionable practices occasionally excite public indignation, which, as we have seen, is almost always very brief.[109] If politician X, exposed to such indignation, can weather the temporary storm and somehow emerge vindicated, the episode becomes dead as a political issue, and few, if any, would be interested in hearing an outright denial that X did what the public knows practically all politicians do.[110] The indiscretions of Demos-

[108] *IG* II² 223 of 343/2 reveals the attitude of the Athenians towards the acceptance of money by politicians: the one who abstains from taking gifts is singled out for reward, but nothing is said against those who accept them. Cf. Arist. *Pol.* v. 8. 19. 1309a13–14; Hyp. *Dem.* 24–25.

[109] Above, p. 56.

[110] In the American presidential campaign of 1952, the Republican candidate for vice-president, Richard M. Nixon, was accused of possessing an "improper" fund to cover his political expenses, raised from his supporters. He weathered the temporary storm. Republicans won the election, and the political issue of the Nixon fund was dead. Few, if any, Americans afterwards could be interested in discussing it. Nixon went on to become the Republican candidate for president in 1960. For a good description of the political passions roused in such affairs, see Nixon's *Six Crises* (Garden City, New York: Doubleday, 1962), pp. 73–129.

thenes in the Harpalus affair were questionable acts. The court, in deciding that he had taken a bribe from Harpalus and against the interests of the city, turned those indiscretions into crimes. But the Athenians themselves eventually took over Harpalus' money as the chest for the Lamian war, and then they granted Demosthenes public vindication.[111] What segment of public opinion in Athens after this would be interested in reading the denials found in Epp. 2 and 3?

Perhaps, however, the concentration on the Harpalus affair was imposed on the hypothetical propagandist by his choice of Demosthenes' exile as setting. But there are further difficulties. The point upon which Epp. 2 and 3 dwell is not the *truth* of the charges of the Areopagus; indeed, Demosthenes even obliquely admits that he had been indiscreet.[112] Rather, the letters dwell on the vulnerable *procedure* of the Areopagus. This is what Demosthenes had to do. The legal basis for the condemnation of the politicians involved in the Harpalus affair was the statement of the Areopagus, which simply gave names and the amount of the bribes. There was no other proof, and the statement contained no argumentation. For this reason it was impossible for Demosthenes to argue against the statement of the Areopagus or to refute it. But since the evidence was the same against all the incriminated politicians, the acquittal of even one of them overthrew the basis of all the condemnations,[113] and this fundamental argument the letters urge repeatedly.[114] After Demosthenes' death, pointing to the vulnerability of the procedure of the Areopagus would have been superfluous and worse than useless. In a *post mortem* debate, the question is not whether the pronounced judgment followed due process but whether the man did commit the crime. No one asked after Socrates' death whether the court had voted according to all rules of Athenian criminal procedure. The verdict of the Athenian jury did not settle the question of the character of Socrates as a citizen, and the controversy over whether he had or had

---

[111] The method used (see above, Chap. 5, n. 45) could hardly have detracted from Demosthenes' vindication. But even if it did, a writer seeking a better vindication of the orator's posthumous figure would not have used the arguments in the letters; see the beginning of this chapter.

[112] See commentary to Ep. 2. 1, μηδὲν ὑμᾶς ἀδικῶν κτλ.

[113] See above, Chap. 5, n. 115.

[114] Ep. 3. 37, 43; Ep. 2. 2, 14–16, 21, 26.

not committed crimes continued after his death.[115] *Post mortem* the issue could be only whether Demosthenes had taken money, not whether Aristogiton had; the only right way to clear Demosthenes then would be to prove the falsity of the report of the Areopagus.

Thus the arguments of Epp. 2 and 3 against the charge of corruption have no meaning unless they were written to meet the situation of 323, when the indignation of the public against Demosthenes as a member of a supposed "ring" had not yet cooled. Epp. 1 and 4 are too loosely connected with the Harpalus affair and the charge of corruption to allow such inferences to be drawn concerning their authenticity. Let us therefore examine the way in which Epp. 1–4 reply to other accusations against Demosthenes.

The reply of the letters to the charge of collaborationism is equally damaging to the hypothesis that the author was writing posthumous propaganda. One would expect that a fabricator writing against the background of 323 would try to clear Demosthenes of the charge of collaborationism by presenting him as warning the Athenians against Alexander, condemning his deification, praising Leosthenes, and, in a word, using the themes of Hyperides' *Funeral Oration*. Moreover, whether his aim would be only to clear Demosthenes' reputation or also to advocate a policy for his own time,[116] he would

---

[115] See below, p. 120. Similarly, Isocrates (15. 129–39) does not try to prove that the judgment of the court against Timotheus was legally faulty; rather, he explains how Timotheus, though innocent, could have been convicted.

[116] See Nitsche, *Demosthenes and Anaximenes*, pp. 140–41, who suggests that Ep. 1 was fabricated as an expression of the policy of Demochares, decades after Demosthenes' death. This view is completely impossible. The war contemplated in Ep. 1 is a *Hellenic* war; the writer does not consider the possibility of getting "barbarian" allies. Demosthenes, where barbarian allies were available, was a thoroughgoing opportunist. He was quite willing to join forces with the Persian king in order to secure the ends of Hellenic Athens. But in 323 such allies were not available. There was no longer a Persian king; no longer was there any prospect of help from disaffected Macedonian satraps (Hyp. *Dem.* 19). Even the minor barbarian groups in the Balkan peninsula, who had an interest in curbing Macedonian power, made no significant contribution to the Hellenic revolt of 323/2 (Diod. xviii. 11. 1—Molossians, Illyrians, Thracians). In the period from Crannon down to 280/79, on the other hand, there was simply no occasion to suggest that Athens lead a Hellenic war against Macedonia. The city had enough troubles trying to maintain a semblance of independence. The vital question in Athenian foreign policy was whether to choose one or another of the warring *diadochoi* or adopt a policy of neutrality. Nothing indicates that Demochares preached a Hellenic war. Rather, his policy was shaped by the struggles of the *diadochoi*. He was hostile to Antigonus and Demetrius and sought, in the interests of Athens, the

wish to portray Demosthenes' policy as consistent and unwavering. The argument of the letters presents nothing of the kind.

Collaborationism is a live issue to the author of the letters, and he is quite defensive about it. At Ep. 2. 4 he apologizes for the abandonment of the once-glorious policy of resistance to Macedonia for one of avoidance of conflict: it is a necessary evil. At Ep. 4. 7–9, Demosthenes proudly proclaims the policy of avoiding conflict with Alexander to be the best policy. Even when, with the death of Alexander, the author turns from that "best policy" to advocate in Ep. 1 the risky project of leading a Hellenic war of liberation, he does not feel that this step in itself removes the odium of previous collaborationism but includes a defense of his earlier policy as having been adopted for the good of Athens.[117] In each of his separate appeals during his exile, Demosthenes would have to argue against the prejudices against him. The strongest proof that at heart he was still anti-Macedonian, his participation in the Lamian war, still lay in the future. But would a later propagandist so belabor the embarrassing point of collaborationism and make such a display of Demosthenes' changes of policy?

Furthermore, the absence in Epp. 1–4 of any hostile mention of Alexander is striking. Alexander must have had a very bad reputation among partisans of "Hellenic liberty" in the period between 322 and 279, even if it improved by comparison with Antipater's rigorous rule.[118] The caution exercised by the author of the letters, despite his need to show that Demosthenes' collaborationism was not from choice, strengthens the impression that he was the orator in exile, who did have something to fear from Alexander and his power over the Athenians.[119] In the letters purporting to be written before Alexander was known to be dead, the king is not mentioned at all, except at Ep. 3. 24–26, where Demosthenes adduces his successful intervention for Laches, the son of Melanopus, as a precedent for the

help of Lysimachus, Ptolemy, and Antipater, the son of Cassander (see Habicht, *Gottmenschentum*, pp. 55–57, 214–16; *Vit. X orat.* 851e). Barbarian allies were now both indispensable and available, and Demochares was willing to use them, whereas Ep. 1 makes not the vaguest suggestion that the Greeks should take advantage of possible rivalry among Alexander's successors.

[117] Ep. 1. 8.

[118] See Plut. *Phoc.* 29. 1.

[119] Demochares, in his petition for the "canonization" of Demosthenes, did not fail to mention an act of the orator in opposition to Alexander (*Vit. X orat.* 851b).

exoneration of Lycurgus' sons. In the passage he praises the Athenians for acceding to the request and expresses no hostility whatever toward Alexander. At Ep. 4. 7 Alexander has no brought grievous evil to the conquered peoples; somehow, the evil "happened" to them. Only Ep. 1 stands apart, with its call after Alexander's death to liberate the Hellenes, and even in Ep. 1 nothing evil is said of Alexander. Indeed, of all the dangers threatening the Athenians in 323, the letters mention by name only the machinations of Pytheas (Ep. 3. 29–30). In 323 Demosthenes was able to make good use of them in his argument,[120] but the deeds of Pytheas were of little interest to anyone in Athens after 323 and of no interest whatever after 318.[121]

The figure of Demosthenes which emerges from Epp. 2 and 4, of a man proud of having resisted Philip up to the defeat at Chaeroneia but also of one who after the destruction of Thebes avoided conflict with Alexander to the point of not mentioning his name — that figure is hardly a propagandist's fabrication; it is that of the living Demosthenes. Thus the treatment in the letters of the charge of collaborationism serves the interests of Demosthenes in 323 but not the purposes of Demosthenes' heirs or those of any conceivable political grouping after his death. Let us now consider how the treatment in the letters of the charge that Demosthenes was a jinx might serve the purposes of posthumous propaganda.

The disastrous end of the Lamian war to which Demosthenes had lent his support might well have confirmed the belief that he was a jinx. His martyrdom might have been taken as the conclusive proof, especially since it was shared by Hyperides and others who had joined

---

[120] See above, p. 54, and below, Chap. 8, rhetorical analysis of Ep. 3. 29–31.

[121] The Athenians fined and imprisoned Pytheas while Demosthenes was in exile. Pytheas and Callimedon fled to Macedonia and became agents of Antipater, traveling through Greece to dissuade the cities from joining in the Lamian war (*Suda s.v. Pytheas;* Plut. *Dem.* 27. 1–4). Pytheas later returned to Athens (*Suda s.v. Pytheas*), but unlike Callimedon, Pytheas is not mentioned in Plut. *Phoc.* 33–36 among the supporters of the regime who escaped or were executed after the revolution of 318. Plutarch implies that Pytheas was active in politics only as a young man (*An seni resp. ger.* 784c). So aggressive a politician would hardly have left the political arena willingly; hence by 318 Pytheas was probably dead (cf. D. Ep. 3. 30). It is difficult to believe that a pro-Demosthenic propagandist writing during the regime of Phocion or in 318 would take the trouble to protest the brief prosperity and distinction enjoyed by Pytheas in 323. After 318, Pytheas surely was not an issue.

him in preaching the Hellenic revolt.[122] A propagandist would have had to insist that no jinx of Demosthenes' caused either the defeat of the city or the martyrdom of her politicians. He would have to insist that the cause was the blind power of Fortune supporting the Macedonians,[123] an idea widely accepted at the close of the fourth century.[124]

The motif of Fortune runs through all four letters. At Ep. 3. 31 it is the Fortune that is the way of all flesh which has carried off the patriotic politicians associated with Demosthenes in the struggles against Philip and Alexander. At Ep. 2. 5 the blindness of Fortune and the baseness of the rest of the Greeks are to blame for the defeat at Chaeroneia. A propagandist writing after Demosthenes' death could have made both statements, using the earlier misfortunes to represent those of 322. One might, however, have expected a longer argument, not just the mentions in passing which the letters contain. It is harder to see how the argument of Ep. 4 would serve the purposes of a propagandist. For the living orator writing in 323 there was still some point in arguing that Athens was the most fortunate of all cities in having had the advice of Demosthenes. In Ep. 4. 5–9 the author argues inductively to prove that this is so: the city has fared best of all those that resisted the Macedonian hegemony and more nobly than those who collaborated with it. The implication is clear that the fortunate quality of Demosthenes' policy lay in avoiding both conflict with the invicible Fortune of Alexander and collaborationism beyond the minimum required. But in supporting the Hellenic revolt, Demosthenes himself abandoned that policy. The new policy with which he identified himself brought a result such that no one could say that Athens was the most fortunate of all cities. The allies of the Athenians who deserted them after the battle of Crannon surely received more favorable terms from Antipater.[125] Of the Athenians Antipater demanded unconditional surrender and dictated a peace under which the democracy was abolished, and citizenship restricted to those who had more than 2,000 drachmas. Many were driven into exile. A Macedonian garrison was placed in Munichia,

[122] Plut. *Dem.* 28. 2–4.

[123] Cf. Treves, *Athenaeum*, n.s., XIV, 248–50.

[124] Demetrius of Phalerum *apud* Polyb. xxix. 21. 1–6 (*F. Gr. Hist.* No. 228, F 39); Wilamowitz, *Der Glaube der Hellenen*, pp. 295–305.

[125] Plut. *Phoc.* 26. 1; Diod. xviii. 17. 7–8.

and the Athenians had to pay the costs of the war and a fine.[126] The new Athenian government condemned Demosthenes, Hyperides, and other anti-Macedonian politicians to death *in absentia*. The terms could have been worse,[127] but they caused great bitterness among the people, especially those disfranchised.[128] There was thus nothing glorious about the city in defeat. Whatever honor could be won among the Greeks for continuing to resist the Macedonian hegemony belonged to the Aetolians and, briefly, to the Thessalians.[129]

One would thus expect a propagandist to devote more of Ep. 4 to a somber disquisition on the blind favoritism of Fortune and on human helplessness, rather than to content himself with the brief statement in paragraphs 5 and 6. One could defend the cautious policy of Demosthenes between 338 and 323 as a very successful effort to make the best of a bad situation. But if the matter at issue is a posthumous judgment on whether Demosthenes as an adviser was a blessing or a jinx, the proud portrayal of a policy which the orator himself abandoned for one which had disastrous consequences would seem to be embarrassing for a propagandist.

The argument of Ep. 1 can be shown to contain matter even more inconvenient for posthumous propaganda. When Ep. 1 presents Demosthenes supporting the war of Hellenic liberation, he is made to safeguard himself and his Fortune against being blamed for the failure of the generals.[130] But in the letter there is no effort to protect him against a failure of the Hellenic alliance to hold together. Instead, the orator writes with optimism about liberating the Greeks, as if he expected their wholehearted support. The only advice which he offers for binding the loyalty of the allies is the proposal of an amnesty.[131] Fortune, too, will be with them if they invite her by pursuing a policy of unvacillating action.[132] It is at least doubtful that the war was lost because of poor generalship. We hear nothing of Athenian vacillation. Leosthenes was phenomenally successful in the opening stages until his death.[133] Antiphilus, who succeeded him, is judged to

[126] Plut. *Phoc.* 27. 3; Diod. xviii. 18. 3–5.

[127] Diod. xviii. 18. 6.

[128] Plut. *Phoc.* 29. 1.

[129] Diod. xviii. 24–25. On the Thessalians, see above, nn. 55–60.

[130] Pars. 11–14.

[131] Pars. 6–9.

[132] Pars. 13–16.

[133] Glotz-Roussel-Cohen, pp. 266–70.

have been a fine soldier,[134] and won a respectable victory over Leonnatus[135] before the defeat at Crannon. Even Phocion won a victory, repulsing a Macedonian attempt to land in Attica.[136] Moreover, as far as the strength of the Hellenic army was concerned, Crannon itself would not have been a serious defeat.[137] A more serious matter was the decisive defeat of the Athenian fleet, first at the Hellespont and finally at Amorgos.[138] There is no way of telling whether these defeats were due to incompetence. Their place in the narrative of Diodorus[139] implies that they occurred before the Battle of Crannon. The immediate cause of the crushing Athenian defeat was therefore the break-up of the Hellenic alliance after Crannon, when Antipater refused to deal with the alliance as a unit, insisting on treating with the members separately. The siege and capture of a few Thessalian towns as the Hellenic army stood by, unable to come to the rescue, brought a succession of separate peaces, and the Athenian and Aetolians were left without allies.[140] The Aetolians in their wild territory could continue to resist with some hope, but the Athenians, having lost naval supremacy, were left in hopeless isolation and had to surrender unconditionally to Antipater.[141]

The only attested activity of Demosthenes in the Lamian war is his diplomacy in building up the alliance.[142] Indeed, it won him his return from exile. Yet, if his enemies wished to depict him as at best misguided and at worst a jinx, the results of this activity easily lent themselves. The accounts in Plutarch and Pseudo-Plutarch[143] portray as his most striking success the way in which he bested the pro-Macedonian spokesmen in argument before the Arcadians – a success which seems to have been sterile, for the Arcadians apparently took no active part in the revolt.[144]

---

[134] Diod. xviii. 13. 6.

[135] *Ibid.* 15. 7.

[136] Plut. *Phoc.* 25.

[137] See Diod. xviii. 17. 5.

[138] Glotz-Roussel-Cohen, pp. 271–72.

[139] xviii. 15. 8–9.

[140] Diod. xviii. 17. 7–8.

[141] Diod. xviii. 18.

[142] See, however, Plut. *Dem. et Cic. Comp.* 3. 1; 4. 2.

[143] *Dem.* 27. 3; *Vit. X orat.* 846d.

[144] They are not mentioned in the lists of the allies at Diod. xviii. 11 and Paus. i. 25. 4. Pausanias (viii. 6. 2 and 27. 10) states explicitly that the Arcadians did not fight in the war. *Vit. X orat.* 846d may, indeed, mean only that Demosthenes persuaded the Arcadians to "violate their alliance" by remaining neutral.

The sources admittedly are scanty, but it would seem that the instability of the alliance was the point through which Demosthenes' enemies after his death would attack him as ill-advised and as a jinx. Since Ep. 1 in no way protects the orator against this failure, it is almost more conceivable that after the facts an enemy of Demosthenes fabricated such an expression of misguided optimism.[145] Yet a propagandist could easily have gone beyond the admonition (Ep. 1. 2) that the opportunity to declare war must not be missed. It was to his interest to add that in view of the well-known instability of Hellenic alliances the war must be prosecuted with vigor and brought to a quick conclusion. Indeed, Demosthenes may have thus expressed his apprehensions during the war.[146] Surely a later apologist would have welcomed an opportunity to display the statesmanlike prescience of Demosthenes by including such a statement. It would have been too slight a *vaticinium ex eventu* to be jarring; nevertheless, it does not appear in the letter. Thus the arguments of the letters against the charge of being a jinx fit the situation of Demosthenes writing in 323 but do not serve the purposes of a later propagandist.

Also incongruous with the hypothesis that Epp. 1–4 are propaganda written between 322 and 279 is the conciliatory spirit shown to the orator's opponents. Except for Pytheas, at no point in the letters does Demosthenes attack one of his prosecutors. At Ep. 2. 26 he even offers peace to them and excuses their action, declaring his willingness to regard it as having arisen from the (forgivable) ignorance of the Athenian people. And at Ep. 1. 6–8 he asks amnesty for all who have collaborated with the Macedonian order. This is natural in 323. It is hardly possible afterwards, for after the Lamian war the political climate of Athens was pervaded by the strife of bitterly opposed political factions.[147] In 322 Demosthenes' political opponents had him sentenced to death along with the politicians who had led in the

---

[145] The fragments of the speech of Leosthenes (see above, Chap. 5, n. 134) express the same sort of optimism—an indication that the speech is either authentic or not intended as posthumous propaganda to defend the reputation of Leosthenes.

[146] *Vit. X orat.* 846e; at Plut. *Phoc.* 23. 3, however, the same sentiments are attributed to Phocion. See Schaefer, III, 371, n. 5.

[147] Ep. 2. 26 would be particularly incongruous if Pytheas was included among those offered peace. Propaganda written after the Lamian war could not show a conciliatory spirit toward this agent of Antipater (Plut. *Dem.* 27. 2–4). However, by the time of Ep. 2, Pytheas may already have been fined and imprisoned so that the words of conciliation need not refer to him.

Hellenic revolt. Demochares carefully identifies them with the oligarchs, the enemies of the people, and declares that Demosthenes did not commit suicide but rather was carried away by the grace of the gods to escape the cruelty of the Macedonians.[148]

In the years that followed, the regime of Phocion aroused great bitterness, and his downfall in 318 was accompanied by a furious outburst of passion. Hagnonides, the leader of the restored democracy, was in turn condemned to death after the fall of Athens to Cassander in 317, and his associates killed.[149] Death sentences followed the fall of the regime of Demetrius of Phalerum in 307, though only against those who had fled.[150] The bitter passions certainly continued. This is the period of the angry clashes between Stratocles (one of the prosecutors of Demosthenes!) and Demochares, as a result of which Demochares was forced to go into exile from 303 to 286/5.[151] Surely Demochares would not express conciliatory sentiments toward Stratocles! The bitter strife continued into the third century. In the opening years of that century, Lachares, after considerable bloodshed, established a "tyranny" in Athens. Strong opposition sprang up in the Piraeus. Since Lachares was an adherent of Cassander, Demetrius Poliorcetes laid siege to the city ruled by his rival's ally. Lachares and his partisans in Athens resisted bitterly, but by 294 he was forced to flee.[152] The city fell into the hands of Demetrius, who garrisoned the city and held the strong points in Attica; he restored the exiled oligarchs and may have imposed constitutional changes. Eleusis seems to have been detached from Athens. All this roused angry resentment against Demetrius and his collaborators. By 286 the forces of Demetrius had been driven from Athens, but he still held the frontier forts, the Piraeus, and Eleusis.[153] Demochares by this time had returned from exile. He was active in recapturing Eleusis and in securing war funds from Lysimachus, but it took years of hard

---

[148] *Vit. X orat.* 851c; Plut. *Dem.* 30. 4.

[149] Plut. *Phoc.* 29–37; 38. 1.

[150] Philochorus, *F. Gr. Hist.* No. 328, F 66.

[151] Plut. *Demetr.* 24. 5; Athenaeus vi. 252f–53d. On the reliability of the report in Plutarch and on the dates, see Leonard C. Smith, "Demochares of Leuconoë and the Dates of His Exile," *Historia*, XI (1962), 114–18. Demochares' bitter attack on the philosophers (*Athenaeus* xi. 509) displays his spirit and the temper of the times.

[152] *F. Gr. Hist.* No. 257a and Jacoby's commentary *ad loc.*; Glotz-Roussel-Cohen, pp. 351–53.

[153] *Ibid.*, pp. 253, 363–64.

fighting and negotiation to free the entire Athenian territory.[154] How, then, can one expect a conciliatory spirit in propaganda written during these years for Demosthenes' heirs?

Totally out of keeping with the purposes of posthumous propaganda is the general figure of Demosthenes which emerges from the letters. Plutarch was struck by the unmanly temperament displayed by Demosthenes during his exile; the principal source of his information was surely the letters.[155] The "unmanliness" is easily explainable by the mental distress of the aging orator[156] and by the rhetorical postures one had to assume in laying a petition before the Athenian public.[157] But the figure actually presented by the later propagandists, Demochares and Cleochares,[158] and by the inscription on Demosthenes' statue[159] is, on the contrary, one of a hero fearless and unbending even in defeat.

We have shown that in none of Epp. 1–4 is there a historical error such as would prove it to be a fabrication composed after Demosthenes' death. Minute chronological precision such as might prove their authenticity is not present, either. Nevertheless, as far as we know, the historical allusions of the letters are accurate, and some are so obscure or so subtle that they suggest authenticity.[160] Moreover, we have found a considerable body of other evidence rendering any alternative to the authenticity of the letters improbable. Historical analysis thus gives strong reason to believe that Demosthenes himself wrote Epp. 1–4.

[154] *Ibid.*, p. 369; W. S. Ferguson, *Hellenistic Athens*, pp. 144 56. With the possible exception of the brief and harried democratic regime led by Hagnonides, no Athenian government down to the time of Demochares' return from exile would have tolerated a proposal to honor the memory of Demosthenes, the martyr to the cause of resistance to Macedonia. The memory of Lycurgus was not thus compromised; hence Stratocles could propose honors for Lycurgus without offending Macedonian Demetrius.

[155] See above, Chap. 2, n. 3.

[156] See Ep. 2. 17, 25.

[157] See below, Chap. 8. Note the contrary judgment of Anton Westermann (quoted at Neupert, p. 5): "Me ut ficticias arbitrer cum compositio movet minime Demosthenica, tum anilis auctoris verbositas, indigna tali viro mali immeriti licet perferendi inertia atque ignavia . . ."

[158] *Vit. X orat.* 850f–51c.

[159] See above, nn. 101, 103.

[160] See above, p. 32. The subtlety is illustrated by the general failure to recognize the correct sequence of Epp. 1–4, though this may in part be due to neglecting them as spurious.

PART 3

Rhetorical Analysis

CHAPTER 7

The Forms of Ancient Apology
and Polemic, Real and Fictitious

Historical analysis has established a strong case for the authenticity of Epp. 1–4. The fragmentary nature of our information, however, makes it desirable to study the problem of authenticity from still another point of view. Let us try to determine whether the letters are written in the form which the living Demosthenes would have used and conform to the rules of composition followed by writers in fourth-century Athens and by Demosthenes. If it can be shown that the letters throughout carefully include elements which were superfluous in a posthumous fabrication but were always included by Athenian orators addressing a plea to a real audience in order to win a favorable reception, the probability that they are authentic will be increased. In so far as it can be shown that the letters belong to a genre which at the time of their composition was not used for the purposes which a fabricator might have had in mind or which was even inconvenient for them, this probability would approach being a certainty.

Whether the letters had a spurious origin as propaganda or as rhetorical fictions, the aim of the author would be to present a defense of Demosthenes' career, a simulated self-apology.[1] For the

---

[1] See above, Chap. 4. On the strongly apologetic character of the fourth-century propaganda letter, see Sykutris, *RE*, Suppl. V, 201, 210–11; on the apologetic nature of rhetorical exercises in this form, *ibid.*, col. 212; and on the same in the *Briefroman*, *ibid.*, col. 214. That the letters are a form of self-apology is also clearly the underlying assumption of Schaefer, *NJb*, CXV, 162; Wilamowitz, *Hermes*, XXXIII, 497; and Treves, *Athenaeum*, n.s., XIV, 249, 251. See also Nitsche, *Demosthenes und Anaximenes*, p. 139, "Um sein Gedächtnis zu bewahren."

further course of our investigation we must have a clear definition of apology. A work can be called an apology provided its content throughout aims at presenting a defense in answer to accusations against a certain person or group of persons or at overcoming or preventing opinions adverse to them.[2] A favorable portrayal of a person where no accusation and no adverse opinion are contemplated is not an apology. Nor is a work an apology merely because its author seeks to set aside at the beginning his audience's preconceptions against him by means of the *captatio benevolentiae* of a rhetorical prooemium.[3]

The assumption that the letters are apology is obviously correct in large measure. They do answer most of the charges against Demosthenes' career made in the speeches of Dinarchus and Hyperides, and they surely preserve much of the orator's defense at his trial.[4] They are aimed at overcoming prejudices which were all the more in the public mind after his condemnation. This hypothesis of the meaning of the letters can explain why the orator's heirs took the trouble to preserve Epp. 1–4 but let the earliest letter perish since it contained no such defense of his career.[5]

The use of the form of the open letter is nothing unusual in self-apology. In fourth-century Athens it, like the published oration, was a favorite vehicle both for this and for other propagandistic purposes.[6] Moreover, except for Ep. 1, which is unusual in having a prayer before the formula of address and salutation,[7] all four letters consistently exhibit characteristics of epistolary style that were current around the time of Demosthenes.[8] The stability of epistolary form throughout Hellenistic and Roman times[9] renders this fact of but slight positive value in proving the authenticity of Epp. 1–4.

The ancient theory of epistolography would have classified the

---

[2] Anax. 4, p. 31. 4–6 Hammer: "τὸ δ' ἀπολογητικὸν ἁμαρτημάτων καὶ ἀδικημάτων κατηγορηθέντων ἢ καθυποπτευθέντων διάλυσις."

[3] See below, Chap. 8, rhetorical analysis of Ep. 3. 1.

[4] For details, see commentary, *passim*.

[5] Above, p. 52.

[6] See Sykutris, *RE*, Suppl. V, 200–2.

[7] See below, Chap. 8, rhetorical analysis of Ep. 1. 1.

[8] Formulas of address, salutation, and farewell: see F. X. J. Exler, *The Form of the Ancient Greek Letter*, pp. 60–77; H. Koskenniemi, *Studien zur Idee und Phraseologie des griechichen Briefes bis 400 n. Chr.*, pp. 151–67. See also commentary to Ep. 3. 1.

[9] Koskenniemi, pp. 155–57, 201–2.

letters under the category of *litterae negotiales*, which deal with weighty problems as opposed to the ordinary personal relations forming the content of *litterae familiares*. To the former, the rules of oratory rather than those of letter writing applied.[10] The special character of *litterae negotiales* addressed to cities and kings was already recognized in the teachings of the early Peripatetics presented by Demetrius.[11] Ancient literary critics judged the letter of Nicias in Thucydides and the letters of Plato under the canons of oratory.[12] Indeed, D. Epp. 1–4 are letters only because Demosthenes as an exile could not deliver them in person as orations.[13] Hence, if the author uses the style and locutions of an oration rather than those of a letter, there is no reason to think that he forgot that he was writing and not speaking, and still less to suspect the document of inauthenticity.[14]

Examination of Epp. 1–4 from the point of view of epistolary form thus leaves the question of authenticity open. Yet their mere character as open letters gives some positive indication in their favor. When later we shall examine the forms used in Athenian polemical literature, we shall see that the form used for the self-apology of one who had been worsted in court was not the open letter to the public, but the real or simulated law-court speech.[15] What we know of the ancient open letter, indeed, shows that it was almost always addressed to a foreigner or a citizen abroad, but not directly to the public. It was employed usually for airing views on general problems rather than on particular aspects of social and political life.[16] The only extant examples of open letters pleading the case of men defeated in

[10] Jul. Vict., p. 447 Halm: "Epistolarum species duplex est; sunt enim aut negotiales aut familiares. Negotiales sunt argumento negotioso et gravi. In hoc genere et sententiarum pondera et verborum lumina et figurarum insignia conpendii opera requiruntur atque omnia denique oratoria praecepta, una modo exceptione, ut aliquid de summis copiis detrahamus et orationem proprius sermo explicet." Cf. Quint. ix. 4. 19–20.

[11] *Eloc.* 234: "Ἐπεὶ δὲ καὶ πόλεσίν ποτε καὶ βασιλεῦσιν γράφομεν ἔστωσαν τοιαῦται αἱ ἐπιστολαὶ μικρὸν ἐξηρμέναι πως." On the early Peripatetic origins of the doctrines of Demetrius, see W. Kroll, "Rhetorik," *RE*, Suppl. VII (1940), 1077–80; Koskenniemi, pp. 24–27; G. M. A. Grube, *A Greek Critic: Demetrius on Style* (*The Phoenix*, Suppl. IV [1961]), pp. 22–56.

[12] Dion. Hal. *Thuc.* 42, Vol. I, p. 397 U.-R., and *Dem.* 23, Vol. I, p. 180 U.-R.

[13] Ep. 3. 1, 35; Ep. 1. 2–4.

[14] Cf. Schaefer, *NJb*, CXV, 166; Blass, *ibid.*, p. 542; Neupert, p. 42; Conrad Rüger, *PhW*, LVI, 292.

[15] See below, pp. 117–27.

[16] Sykutris, *RE*, Suppl. V, 201.

court are the letters of Demosthenes and the obvious imitation of them, the spurious letters of Aeschines.[17] This fact suggests that propagandists normally would not use the form; but Demosthenes, who wanted to appeal from exile for exoneration or at least a way to return safely to Athens, could hardly have used any other.

We must now go beyond the scanty remnants of ancient epistolographical theory to the abundant resources of ancient rhetorical theory and practice. A detailed treatise reflecting the usages of fourth-century Athens has survived, the so-called *Rhetorica ad Alexandrum*, now generally agreed to be the *Technê* of Anaximenes of Lampsacus.[18] Less important because of its more speculative and original character but still of great value is Aristotle's *Rhetoric*. Both these works present a classification of public oratory which divides it into genera based upon the peculiar institutions of Athenian society. That classification nevertheless remained almost unquestioned ever after in the theory and practice of ancient rhetoric.[19] The genera are:

1. The "deliberative" speech (*symbouleutikon, dêmêgorikon*) or *demegoria*, which lays before the public assembly information and advice on public issues.

2. The "forensic" speech (*dikanikon*), addressed to a panel of judges trying a case in court.

3. The "epideictic" speech, which seeks to eulogize or disparage the persons who are its subject, usually made not in order to fight a case but for display before an audience of mere spectators. Aristotle notes that it is primarily concerned with the present, that is, with fitting the mood of the occasion on which it is delivered.[20]

---

[17] On Isoc. Ep. 8, see below, Chap. 8, beginning, and rhetorical analysis of Ep. 3. 35–45.

[18] Kroll, *RE*, Suppl. VII, 1052–53, 1066; P. Wendland, *Anaximenes von Lampsakos*, pp. 62–63; see Philodemus *Rhet.*, Vol. II, p. 254. 20 ff. Sudhaus.

[19] Quint. iii. 4. 1; R. Volkmann, *Die Rhetorik der Griechen und Römer in systematischer Übersicht*, pp. 16–26.

[20] The genera and their species are systematically defined at Anax. 1–4 and Arist· *Rhet.* i. 3; see also Anax. 35, p. 80. 8–9 H., and Arist. *Rhet.* ii. 18. 1. 1391b8–20. Spengel's emended text of Anax. 1, p. 12. 14–15 H., and 17, p. 51. 20 H., would speak of only two genera, omitting the epideictic in order to conform to the descriptions of the work in Quintilian (iii. 4. 9: "Anaximenes iudicialem et contionalem generales partes esse voluit, septem autem species: hortandi, dehortandi' laudandi, vituperandi, accusandi, defendendi, exquirendi, quod ἐξεταστικόν dicit; quarum duae primae deliberativi, duae sequentes demonstrativi, tres ultimae

The address of the letters, "To the Council and the People," shows immediately that they are intended to be *demegoriae*. Ep. 1, which presents a political program for Athens' entry into the Hellenic revolt, patently belongs to that genus. But even with the more obviously apologetic of the letters, membership in the genus of the *demegoria* may be more than a mere matter of the body addressed. Aristotle notices that *demegoriae* may contain apologetic elements; at the same time, however, he implies that the form is not really adapted to apology. A *demegoria* may contain such elements, but "not in so far as it lays advice before the public," that is, not in so far as it fulfills the function for which it is designed.[21] Aristotle here may be merely referring to such things as the *captatio benevolentiae* of the prooemium.[22] Anaximenes, however, may have meant to imply that any of his seven species may be found in either of his two genera.[23] In any case he does give instructions for constructing *demegoriae* which aim at persuading the people "to come to the aid of the distressed, whether private individuals or city-states."[24] To win the sympathy of the people, it was often necessary to give the entire content of such a speech the character of an apology. Thus the source of Pseudo-Plutarch[25] naturally uses the verb *apologeomai* to refer to the action of Democles, the pupil of Theophrastus, to persuade the

iudicialis generis sunt partes.") and Syrianus (*In Hermog.*, Vol. II, p. 11. 17–21 Rabe: "'Ἀριστοτέλης δὲ δύο γένη φησὶν εἶναι τῶν πολιτικῶν λόγων, δικανικόν τε καὶ δημηγορικόν, εἴδη δὲ ἑπτά, προτρεπτικὸν κτλ."). See now M. Fuhrmann, *Untersuchungen zur Textgeschichte der pseudo-aristotelischen Alexander-Rhetorik* ("Abhandlungen der Akademie der Wissenschaften und der Literatur in Mainz, Geistesund sozialwissenschaftliche Klasse," 1964, nr. 7), pp. 143–58. Fuhrmann would regard all references in the text of Anaximenes to genera as spurious but then cannot explain the testimonia of Quintilian and Syrianus (see Fuhrmann, p. 157). For a possible explanation retaining the reference to genera at Anax. 1, p. 12. 14–15 H., see Appendix VIII.

[21] *Rhet.* iii. 13. 3. 1414b2–4.

[22] Thus, Alcibiades' defense of himself at Th. vi. 16–17. 1 clearly partakes of the nature of an apology. But Nicias' effort to discredit Alcibiades (*ibid.*, 12. 2–13. 1) is not intended to lead the people to take action against Alcibiades himself, but rather to encourage them to vote against his policy. In his reply Alcibiades goes into his personal affairs at such length that at the outset he is made to excuse his doing so. Nevertheless, the lengthy reply is but the usual prooemium required in a *demegoria* when the speaker has first to overcome prejudice against him before presenting his recommendations. The main burden of his speech is a matter of policy: Shall the Sicilian expedition be attempted?

[23] See Appendix VIII.

[24] Anax. 34, p. 76. 25–26 H.

[25] *Vit. X orat.* 842e.

Assembly to set aside the sentence against the sons of Lycurgus.[26] Anaximenes mentions another type of speech which might lay an apology before the Council or the Assembly: the report of an unsuccessful embassy.[27] The speaker must show that he was not at fault in the failure. Still other occasions for apologetic *demegoriae* presented themselves frequently in the Assembly. For example, the people had to decide whether to entrust or whether to continue to entrust the conduct of a military campaign to one or another *strategos*. Again, if a proposal to grant public honors to someone met with opposition, an apologetic *demegoria* was in order. Thus the apologetic *demegoria* was a known oratorical form in ancient Athens, even though the rhetorical texts may not give it that name.

Here may be the desired key to a proof of the authenticity of the letters by rhetorical analysis, in so far as the following can be demonstrated:

1. There are real distinctions among the three genera of speeches by which a speech in one can be distinguished from a speech in another.

2. In the time of Demosthenes, the *demegoria* as described by the rhetorical handbooks and as practiced by the leading politicians would have presented inconveniences for one whose purpose was self-apology or personal attack, whereas the forensic genus was designed for that purpose.

3. Because of the nature of Athenian institutions, the preferred arena for attack on both personal and political opponents was, in fact, the courts, and defense necessarily took place in the same arena. When, as often, Athenian brochures of polemical propaganda adopted one of the forms of public oratory, literary form followed real life, and the genus that was chosen was almost without exception the forensic genus.

4. The living Demosthenes, in order to lay a petition before the people, would have had to use the form of the *demegoria*.

5. The letters of Demosthenes conform to the rules and practices of fourth-century *demegoriae* even where these obstruct the purposes of apology.

[26] Alcibiades' defense of himself before the Council and Assembly on his return to Athens in 407 (X. *Hell.* i. 4. 20) is not a normal example classifiable under the categories of rhetorical teaching, Normal procedure was set aside for the returned exile, now a popular hero.

[27] Anax. 30, p. 71. 10–17 H.

First, then, it is necessary to determine what were the essential distinctions between compositions in the forensic and deliberative genus, for it is an easy matter to show that the letters do not fall into the epideictic classification. They are not intended to give the impression of mere display but of bitter controversy.[28] They are not organized as a systematic exposition of excellences or vices beginning with the subject's ancestry and upbringing and then considering his adult life under the heads of the cardinal virtues.[29] To differentiate between apologetic *demegoriae* and forensic apologies is a more difficult task. The body addressed is obviously not a sufficient criterion. A forensic speech could be delivered to the Council and to the Assembly on the occasions when those bodies exercised judicial competence.[30] Nor is the intention to advocate a policy sufficient to mark off a *demegoria*, for a forensic speech might do so as much as a *demegoria*.[31]

However, Anaximenes and especially Aristotle present differences between the two genera which should give rise to recognizable distinctions between forensic and *demegoric* apology. Aristotle remarks[32] that forensic speeches are primarily concerned with justice; and deliberative, with expediency. This, however, would be too subtle a difference, because pleas for action by the Assembly had also to make a strong appeal to justice.[33] More useful is Aristotle's remark[34] that *demegoriae* are concerned with the future, giving advice on the course to be adopted; whereas forensic speeches are concerned with the past, one party accusing, the other defending himself with reference to things already done.[35] However, here also an apologetic *demegoria* pleading for future action by the People would be difficult to distinguish from a forensic defense pleading for an equally future acquittal; moreover, a *demegoria* in order to give advice about the

---

[28] See Arist. *Rhet.* i. 3; Anax. 35, p. 80. 8–9 H.

[29] Arist. *Rhet.* i. 9; iii. 16. 1–3. 1416b16–29; Anax. 35; *Rhet. ad Herenn.* iii. 7. 13–8. 15.

[30] E.g., Lys. 28; see Lipsius, pp. 42–47, 176–219.

[31] E.g., D. 23; see W. Jaeger, *Demosthenes: the Origin and Growth of His Policy*, pp. 98–102.

[32] *Rhet.* i. 3. 5–6. 1358b20–37.

[33] See Quint. iii. 4. 16.

[34] *Rhet.* i. 3. 4. 1358b13–17.

[35] See D. 18. 192; *Prooem. 11.*

future often must give so much information derived from the past[36] that the distinction will be blurred.

Nevertheless, another statement of Aristotle makes of this generalization a fundamental distinction that can be used as a criterion. The law, he says, is the starting point for a forensic oration but not for a *demegoria*.[37] Thus the forensic genus, unlike the deliberative, is con-concerned with the past because every forensic speech takes as its basis the existence of a law which ordains punishment or redress if certain things have been done in the past. Theoretically, a forensic speech needs only to prove whether or not the actions described in the law have occurred.[38] Therefore, a speech containing accusation or defense which bases itself on the existence of such a law will be forensic, even if delivered before a normally deliberative body, and can be said to be concerned primarily with the past. A speech before the Council or Assembly which does not have such a law as its basis and wherein it is not even theoretically sufficient to prove that certain events have occurred in the past will be a *demegoria* and can be said to be concerned primarily with the course which the people should adopt in the future.[39]

This fundamental distinction is a helpful criterion, but if our use of it is not to be a rather subjective judgment of the general character of a work, we must find out how the differences between the genera were reflected in practice, and wherein the composition and organization of a complete forensic speech (as opposed to the freer and more fragmentary *deuterologiae* delivered by supporting speakers) differed from that of a *demegoria*.[40] Detailed schemata of organization were

[36] Arist. *Rhet.* iii. 17. 5. 1417*b*38–1418*a*3; iii. 16. 11. 1417*b*11–15.

[37] *Rhet.* iii. 17. 10. 1418*a*21–26.

[38] Arist. *Rhet.* i. 1. 6. 1354*a*26–28.

[39] Living institutions rarely conform to theoretical definitions. There are borderline cases which defy exact classification. E.g., in D. 20, the point at issue is whether the court should decide to annul a law as inexpedient. Since the suit was brought more than a year after the law was proposed, the proposer, Leptines, was no longer liable (Lipsius, pp. 385–86). With no question of punishment involved, the speech, as a discussion of public policy, resembles a *demegoria*. Nevertheless, the suit against the law of Leptines was based upon a law, and the nullification of Leptines' proposal can be considered analogous to redress. See par. 11 of the second *hypothesis* to D. 20.

[40] Aristotle also indicates stylistic differences between the two genera (*Rhet.* iii. 12. 5–6. 1414*a*7–18), but Demosthenes seems not to exemplify this. Quintilian (iii. 8. 65) found no differences in style between the *Philippics* and the forensic orations.

given by later teachers of rhetoric, but these can prove little when applied to works of the fourth century. In our analyses we must content ourselves with the less-detailed schemata of Anaximenes and Aristotle.

What were these differences in content and arrangement? Speeches in the two genera did have much in common. The techniques of the prooemia and of the epilogues are essentially the same for both,[41] but the fundamental distinction between them gives rise to differences in the narration (*diêgêsis*) and in the argument or proof (*pistis, bebaiôsis*).

In forensic speeches a detailed narrative of the events directly connected with the acts mentioned in the charge is almost always necessary, for the nature of what happened in the past is at issue. According to Aristotle, the defendant's narrative need not be as long as the prosecutor's, for, speaking second, he does not have to give in detail the points on which he agrees with his opponent. Nevertheless, both prosecutor or plaintiff and defendant must narrate fully whatever facts bear on the point at issue or can turn the judge's emotions in favor of the speaker.[42] On the other hand, the orator in the Assembly usually has no need to give a detailed account of past events and current affairs. Whatever extensive narrative may be present in *demegoriae* is organized not show that some particular action took place, but to remind the hearers of facts that will help them make a good decision. Hence the narrative of a forensic speech will be concentrated on the facts contained in the charges. The essential unity of such narratives leads to their commonly occurring as a distinct division of the speech, between the prooemium and the proof. The brief allusive narrative portions sporadically occurring in the argument of a *demegoria* are quite different from the kind of narrative described by Aristotle's contemporary rhetoricians; Aristotle ridicules them for making such detailed concentrated narrative an essential constituent of *demegoriae*.[43]

[41] Prooemia: Anax. 36, p. 85. 4–18 H.; Arist. *Rhet.* iii. 14. 12. 1415b32–37; *Rhet. ad Herenn.* i. 3. 5–7. 11, iii. 4. 7. Epilogues: Anax. 34, pp. 76. 25–77. 21, 78. 27–79. 18; 36, pp. 95. 11–97. 15 H.; *Rhet. ad Herenn.* iii. 5. 9 end.

[42] Arist. *Rhet.* iii. 16. 4–11. 1416b29–1417b11.

[43] *Ibid.*, iii. 13. 3. 1414a36–38; 16. 3. 1416b25–26, 11. 1417b11–15. See Dion. Hal. *Rhet.* x. 14, p. 369 U.-R., and Volkmann, p. 297. According to Anax. 30–31 and 36, p. 88. 11–14 H., narrative in both genera is handled in the same way. But given Aristotle's presupposition that the audience of a *demegoria* is fairly well informed about the past and the present, Anaximenes would agree that the only narrative normally required in a speech to the Assembly is a summary allusion attached to the prooemium. See below, Chap. 8, n. 9.

Treatment of the proofs in forensic defences and in deliberative orations differed greatly in fourth-century rhetorical teaching. Like forensic speeches, *demegoriae* sometimes had to prove facts before proceeding to advocate a policy,[44] but commonly the facts of a public matter were so well known that even narrative was hardly necessary, much less proof. In such cases, the characteristic issues for proof in deliberative orations could appear at the very outset of the argument.[45] Anaximenes reflects the prevailing practice in his classification of those issues under the heads of whether what is recommended is just, lawful, expedient, honorable, pleasant, easy of accomplishment, or – if difficult – possible and necessary to do.[46] Aristotle subordinates all other considerations to the expedient, but substantially presents the same description.[47] These heads were called by later rhetoricians the *telika kephalaia* and with small modifications are found throughout ancient rhetorical theory as the topics for the argument of *demegoriae*.[48] In a complete *demegoria*, unlike a forensic speech, it may not be necessary and it never is sufficient to prove whether a fact has occurred; the policy advocated must be shown to be describable by the *telika kephalaia*.

The dependence of forensic oratory on the provisions of law leads to a characteristic classification of the topics for the argument of forensic speeches. The nature of the issue depended on whether the defendant denied the fact that was the basis of the charge or admitted it but said that the law or at least its full rigor did not apply.[49] This classification of forensic issues, a natural consequence of their legal basis, eventually was systematized in ancient rhetoric in the theory ascribed to Hermagoras of the "status of the cause."[50]

A defendant who admitted the charges would turn in his proof to discussions of the just, the legal, the honorable, and the expedient.

---

[44] Anax. 32, p. 74. 7–24 H.

[45] *Ibid.*, pp. 74. 24–75. 4 H.: "ἐὰν δὲ πιστεύηται τὰ πράγματα εὐθέως ῥηθέντα, τὰς μὲν πίστεις παραλειπτέον, τῷ δὲ δικαίῳ καὶ τῷ νομίμῳ καὶ τῷ συμφέροντι καὶ τῷ καλῷ καὶ τῷ ἡδεῖ καὶ τῷ ῥᾳδίῳ καὶ τῷ δυνατῷ καὶ τῷ ἀναγκαίῳ τὰς προειρημένας πράξεις βεβαιωτέον."

[46] Anax. 1 and 6.

[47] *Rhet.* i. 3. 5. 1358b21–25; iii. 17. 4. 1417b34–36.

[48] Volkmann, pp. 299–314.

[49] Anax. 4, pp. 32. 18–33. 1 H.; 36, pp. 88. 15–89. 6, 91. 22–93. 10 H.; and Arist. *Rhet.* iii. 17. 1. 1417 b22–27.

[50] See *Rhet. ad Herenn.* i. 10. 18–15. 25; Volkmann, pp. 38–92; Navarre, pp. 259–71; Kroll, *RE*, Suppl. VII, 1091–95.

But if the defendant chose to deny them outright, his arguments had to be directed primarily toward factual proof of their falsity. Only then could he use the topics of the *telika kephalaia* by way of confirmation and amplification. The letters deny outright the charges against Demosthenes of bribe taking, collaborationism, and being a jinx. Hence, if the proof in a letter is organized around the issues of the *telika kephalaia* and the arguments directly refuting the substance of the charges do not occur first, we shall have before us an apologetic demegoria, not an analogue of a forensic defense which somehow happened to be delivered to a deliberative body.[51] The forensic apologies written by Plato and Xenophon for Socrates and by Isocrates for himself contain before the beginning of the main argument a statement of the accusations which are to be refuted.[52] If the letters of Demosthenes contain no such statements, that will be a sign that they do not belong to this tradition of propagandistic apology in forensic form.

Whereas Anaximenes[53] regards the *telika kephalaia* as most characteristic of the arguments of *demegoriae* and *pisteis*, that is to say, factual and deductive proofs, as most characteristic of forensic speeches, Aristotle[54] notes that deductive arguments by enthymemes are characteristic of forensic speeches, and examples from the past as a basis for predictions of the future, of *demegoriae*. Inasmuch as both Aristotle's types of argument may be found in either type of speech, the preponderance of examples over enthymemes or of enthymemes over examples will not be a clear criterion.

These differences stemming from the differences between the genera in subject matter are almost self-evident. Our sole reason for treating them at such length is to show that there can be a real distinction between an apologetic *demegoria* and a forensic defense. More interesting are the differences in composition arising from differences in the expectations and prejudices in the minds of the Athenian audiences. Here, indeed, we shall find the traits of the *demegoria* as practiced by Demosthenes and his contemporaries rendering it a strange and even inconvenient genre for self-apology. To some extent, these characteristics can be found or inferred from the

---

[51] See Anax. 6.
[52] Plato *Apol.* 19b, 24b; X. *Apol.* 10–11, 19, and cf. *Mem.* i. 1. 1; Isoc. *Antid.* 30–31.
[53] Anax. 6.
[54] *Rhet.* i. 9. 40. 1368a29–33; iii. 17. 5. 1418a1–5.

remarks of Anaximenes and Aristotle. However, since both authors take the institutions of the Athenian *polis* for granted, they leave much to be sought in other sources.

Aristotle calls attention to the central importance of the public interest for the argument of a *demegoria*; everything advocated must be connected with what is expedient for the state.[55] But this is not merely a principle which follows from the definition of a rhetorical genre; in its full extent it reflects the realities of the Athenian democracy. Where everyone theoretically could take part in politics and where the rewards for the selling of one's influence could be high, politicians were all the more subject to the perennial suspicion that they are corrupt. The Athenian critics of the democratic form of government were forever harping on this very theme, and even the politicians would admit on occasion that they profited from their public activity. Thus Hyperides, in order to avoid in prosecuting Demosthenes the retort that "the pot was calling the kettle black," declares that the city allows politicians to sell their services, provided that its interests are not injured thereby.[56] Demades seems to have openly avowed his venality.[57] In the Assembly, however, there was little room for such candor. Orators there were quick to deny that they had any motive other than the public interest and to accuse advocates of opposing views of acting for their own private gain if not actually in return for a bribe.[58] To have misled the public with bad advice for one's own profit was an offense punishable with great severity.[59] This standard pose of denial and accusation in the Assembly is observable throughout in the *demegoriae* of Demosthenes and Isocrates.[60]

On the other hand, clearing a man's reputation, particularly in ancient Athens, would require attention both to bygone political affairs no longer of public interest and to strictly personal matters such as his private life. To defend the reputation of someone else, calling upon the people to come to his rescue, was a recognized func-

---

[55] *Rhet.* i. 3. 5–6. 1358b20–37.

[56] *Dem.* 24–25.

[57] Din. i. 104.

[58] See the speech of Diodotus, Th. iii. 43.

[59] See commentary to Ep. 3. 3.

[60] The speech of Isocrates which exhibits this motif most is *De Pace*; but see also Isoc. 14. 3.

tion for a *demegoria*.[61] We can readily imagine defenders of Demosthenes reworking and publishing the dramatic appeal which Demochares is said to have made before the people, opposing the surrender of the anti-Macedonian politicians to Antipater at the end of the Lamian war.[62] But *self*-apology is inseparable from self-interest, and therefore for that purpose in Athens the *demegoria* was the most awkward possible form.[63]

Yet the subjects which were difficult if not impossible to introduce into a *demegoria* constituted an important component of both forensic[64] and epideictic speeches.[65] To an extent which astounds the modern reader, the Athenians not only allowed but demanded the assertion of private motives in forensic speeches, particularly those called "public" (*dêmosioi*), which were composed for suits in which the state took an interest (*graphai*), suits in which any citizen, not merely the injured party, could prosecute.[66] Private interests, when sufficiently free from the taint of avarice, served to show that the speaker was neither corrupt nor meddlesome. One who came before the courts to prosecute a public suit and hid behind the public interest without avowing any private motive usually aroused suspicions that he was a *sykophantês*, a scoundrel whose real aim was blackmail.[67] To speak for pay as an advocate (*synêgoros*) in support of someone else's cause was a crime, and advocates were careful to explain their action by friendship for the man whom they were aiding or by hatred for his opponent.[68]

Aristotle recognizes that Athenians imposed a more severe discipline on the *demegoria* than on the forensic speech. In the Assembly, he says, the citizens are deliberating over their own interests, and their suspicious regard for them holds in check the rhetorical trickery of the speakers there; whereas jurors in court, not being personally in-

[61] Anax. 34, p. 76. 25–26 H.

[62] *Vit. X orat.* 847d.

[63] Apsines 2, p. 226. 4–14 Hammer: "Γίνεται δὲ ἀντιπῖπτον καὶ ἀπὸ αἰτίας ... ὅταν ὑπὲρ ἑαυτοῦ δοκῇς σπουδάζειν καὶ μὴ τοῦ κοινῇ συμφέροντος, ὡς ἐπ' ἐκείνου· ἐξαιτοῦντος Φιλίππου τὸν Δημοσθένην μετὰ Χαιρώνειαν αὐτὸς Δημοσθένης ἐνίσταται. δοκεῖ γὰρ ὑπὲρ τῆς ἑαυτοῦ σωτηρίας, ἀλλ' οὐχὶ τοῦ κοινῇ συμφέροντος σπουδάζειν."

[64] Anax. 7, p. 37. 25–39. 21 H.; 36.

[65] Anax. 3 and 35.

[66] See Lipsius, pp. 238–46.

[67] See Navarre, pp. 235–39.

[68] Lipsius, p. 908; Anax. 36, pp. 87. 18–21, 94. 4–13 H.

volved in the proceedings, are all too ready to be entertained by dramatic pleas. This difference, Aristotle says, was so marked that the rhetorical teachers were not interested in treating the *demegoria*.[69] Quite apart from trickery, even to present a long discussion of the matter at hand was hard in a *demegoria*, for in this genus especially, length is prejudicial, as Anaximenes remarks.[70]

Moreover, Aristotle speaks of *demegoriae* as being more difficult than forensic speeches in offering less scope for digressions into one's own affairs or replies to one's opponents or appeals to the emotions.[71] The context shows that Aristotle here is referring to the task of find-ing what to say in a *demegoria*: it is difficult to construct arguments on the subjects dealt with in such a speech. But the statements about the prejudices which the writer of a *demegoria* must avoid suggest that such digressions, as well as detailed and lengthy narratives, were out of place in a *demegoria* not only because of the nature of the subject matter but also because of the prejudices of the audience. Neither Aristotle nor Anaximenes is interested in describing the attitudes and suspicions of the Athenians in the Assembly and the actual means by which they curbed the political spokesmen there. Hence we shall now have to seek information elsewhere.

An invaluable set of documents reflecting the effects of these res-trictions in the time of Demosthenes is the *Prooemia* in the Demos-thenic corpus. It has been questioned whether these short *demegoric* compositions are by Demosthenes, but it is now generally agreed that they reflect fourth-century rhetorical practice.[72] Thus they may be used to supplement the information derivable elsewhere.[73]

A speaker in the Athenian assembly had to await his turn, com-peting for possession of the floor with others of his fellow-citizens. Once he had gained it, so far as we know, there was no legally fixed time limit placed upon his speech, but neither was there a minimum

[69] *Rhet.* i. 1. 10. 1354b22–1355a3.

[70] 29, p. 70. 15–17 H.

[71] *Rhet.* iii. 17. 10. 1418a21–29.

[72] The authenticity of the entire collection is defended by A. Rupprecht, *Philologus*, LXXXII, 365–432. F. Focke, in *Genethliakon Wilhelm Schmid*, pp. 30–67, regards only *Prooemm.* 1–3, 7–9, 15, 16, 21-24, 27, 30, 32–36, 39–42, 45, 46, 48, 49–53 as authentic; on grounds which seem to me largely subjective he believes that the others were added by a redactor around 300 B.C.

[73] The material on the rules and conditions to which speakers in the Assembly had to conform is collected at Busolt-Swoboda, pp. 995–1000.

time during which he was entitled to hold the floor. The pressing order of public business, the impatience of rival orators waiting to speak, and the restlessness of the people who could and did shout a speaker down, refusing to listen to him,[74] all acted to limit the length of the *demegoria*. The prevalent attitude among the people toward listening to *demegoriae* can be gauged by the fact that in the fourth century, in order to assure the presence of a sufficient number of citizens, pay for attending the Assembly had to be instituted, raised to equal the three obols received by jurors, and finally pushed far beyond that sum to six and even nine obols.[75] Although an Assembly meeting might be so long that citizens had to bring lunches with them,[76] court sessions were not appreciably shorter.[77] The orators themselves speak of listening to *demegoriae* as a tedious duty.[78]

Moreover, the Athenians knew their own human tendency to delight in the more entertaining aspects of the activity on the Pnyx – the witty sallies and digressions and the attempts of rival politicians to assassinate one another's character. They were also aware that urgent business could be neglected with disastrous consequences if they allowed themselves that luxury. Thus, both when the audience was interested and when it was not, pertinent brevity was required of a *demegoria*. In the fifth century the Prytanes were empowered to deny the floor to a speaker whose utterances were not to the point at issue and even, if need be, to eject him forcibly.[79] In the fourth century seeing to orderly procedure in the Assembly was the responsibility of the Prohedroi,[80] but the people themselves had the power, if they wished, to force the speaker to be brief and stick to the point.[81] Some time before Aeschines wrote his speech *Against Timarchus* in 345, a law was passed giving system and precision to sanctions which surely had long been in use restricting the license of speakers in the Council and the Assembly. The document inserted in that

---

[74] Aristoph. *Ec.* 256, 399–402; Plato *Prt.* 319c; D. 2. 29–30, *Prooemm.* 21. 1, 36, 47; Isoc. 8. 3; Aesch. 1. 34, etc.

[75] Arist. *Ath. Pol.* 41. 3, 62. 2; Busolt-Swoboda, p. 921.

[76] Aristoph. *Ec.* 306–8.

[77] Arist. *Ath. Pol.* 67.

[78] D. *Prooemm.* 29. 3, 34. 2.

[79] Plato *Prt.* 319c; Aristoph. *Ach.* 54–60, *Ec.* 142–43, and (of a speaker before the Council) *Eq.* 665.

[80] Arist. *Ath. Pol.* 44. 3.

[81] D. *Prooem.* 56.

speech provides for not inconsiderable penalties to be levied against the orator who would speak on extraneous matters, fail to follow the order of the agenda, talk twice on the same subject in one day, or indulge in abuse or slander.[82] Doubtless the law was frequently honored in the breach,[83] but that does not mean that it was a dead letter. It was available for use whenever the Prohedroi saw fit. As a result, a good *demegoria* had to be made as brief as possible, and the speakers often call attention to their living up to that rule or say that they have talked only long enough to remind the people of their interests.[84] This is the background of Anaximenes' statement that length is prejudicial to *demegoriae*.

No such conditions operated to shorten speeches in the epideictic and forensic genera. Free from the worry that they were damaging their own personal interests, the Athenian jurors found the entertainment afforded by the courts so rewarding[85] that, unlike the pay for attendance at the Assembly, the three obols of the jurors did not have to be increased during the fourth century.[86] The period allotted to a speaker in the law courts for his speech was carefully measured, and during it he had the floor to himself, although the jurors might ask for clarifications and occasionally might give vent to an emotional outburst. A litigant during his allotted time could not be interrupted by his opponent, and even if unpopular was probably rarely if at all prevented by the juries from speaking his full piece.[87] In private suits the time limit could be quite short, and at least when Aristotle was writing the litigants were bound by oath to speak only on matters directly pertinent.[88] But no such oath is mentioned in connection with public suits, in which the speeches might last for three hours or more.[89] Indeed, whatever power the jurors may have had to keep

[82] Aesch. 1. 35 (cf. Isoc. 8. 52). E. Drerup, *NJb*, Suppl.-B. XXIV (1898), pp. 307–8, rejects the law as spurious, but on insufficient grounds. See Lipsius, p. 810, n. 23, and Busolt-Swoboda, p. 995, n. 2.

[83] Aesch. 3. 4, etc.

[84] E.g., D. 6. 37; 10. 75–76; 11. 23; 14. 14, 41; 15. 34–35; 17. 2; *Prooemm.* 4; 5. 2–3; 6. 2; 17; 19; 29. 3; 36. 2; 37; 56; Isoc. 6. 24, 40; 8. 145; 14. 3, 63.

[85] Hence comes the plot of Aristophanes' *Wasps*.

[86] Busolt–Swoboda, p. 921.

[87] See Lipsius, pp. 917–18; Busolt-Swoboda, p. 1162.

[88] *Ath. Pol.* 67. 1–2. If the oath was imposed earlier in the fourth century, litigants managed to ignore its force, as is abundantly evident from the surviving speeches. See Lipsius, pp. 918–19.

[89] Arist. *Ath. Pol.* 67. 3; Lipsius, pp. 912–16.

the speakers from introducing matter not pertinent to the case[90] was not effectively exercised.[91] Aristotle and Lycurgus[92] both praise the rule requiring that speeches in trials before the Areopagus be confined to the matter at issue, and there is evidence[93] that this rule applied to all trials for murder. But even there, so far as can be seen from the extant speeches, pleaders were not much restrained.[94]

Hence it is not surprising to find that all but one of the public forensic orations in the Demosthenic corpus are longer than the longest of the *demegoriae*.[95] So is Plato's *Apology*, counting only the defense speech itself (17a–35d). Similarly, Andocides' *De Mysteriis* is by far the longest of his extant orations. The *demegoriae* of Isocrates, as well as his only public forensic oration, the *Antidosis*, were never intended to be delivered, the oratorical form serving him as his mode of expression as the dialogue served Plato. Nevertheless, his *demegoriae*, though longer than those of Demosthenes, exhibit the same concern for brevity,[96] and the *Antidosis* is more than twice as long as any of them. Even if the "symbouleutic" orations that are not really *demegoriae*[97] are included, the disproportion with the *Antidosis* remains. The relative brevity of *demegoriae* is thus intentional and is ascribable to the rules and conditions affecting speakers in the Assembly. We may note that even the longest of Demosthenes' letters, Ep. 3, falls well within the limits of his *demegoriae*. Indeed, the defense speech in Plato's *Apology* is longer than Epp. 1–4 combined. This brevity argues already against all the theories of the inauthenticity of the letters, for we have seen that they assume that the main purpose of the letters is pure apology, and effective self-apology requires the ability to digress, to amplify, and to present extensively,

[90] See Aesch. 3. 205–6; 1. 175–76.

[91] Arist. *Rhet.* i. 1. 4–5. 1354a18–24; Lyc. *Leoc.* 11–12.

[92] *Ibid.*

[93] Antiph. 6. 9.

[94] See Ivo Bruns, *Das literarische Porträt*, pp. 484–88. On the law mentioned at Antiph. 6. 9, see Bruns, p. 486, n. 1., and Lipsius, p. 918.

[95] The only exception is Ps.-D. 26, a supporting speech written to be delivered after several other prosecutors have already spoken. Otherwise, the shortest public forensic oration in the corpus is Ps.-D. 58.

[96] See above, n. 84.

[97] Such are the *Philippus* and the half-epideictic *Panegyricus*, called a *demegoria* by Aristotle at *Rhet.* iii. 17. 10. 1418a31. See E. Buchner, *Der Panegyrikos des Isokrates*; Blass, II, 255–56.

in a light favorable to the writer, material much of which is common knowledge.

Moreover, if the person to be defended has been attacked from a definite quarter, for him the axiom that the best defense is a good offense applies. In Aristophanes' *Wasps*[98] Bdelycleon in defending Labes attacks the character of Cyon, the accuser. Socrates in the *Apology* undisguisedly impugns the motives and competence of Meletus and Anytus; Demosthenes in *De Corona*, those of Aeschines; and Isocrates in the *Antidosis* attacks his opponent Lysimachus. Both Hyperides and the client of Dinarchus expect Demosthenes to direct a personal attack against them,[99] and doubtless he fulfilled their expectation. The lack of restraint with which opponents in the Athenian courts attack each other can only mean that they could do so with impunity.[100]

There is, however, evidence that such unrestrained invective was not so indulgently received at deliberative meetings of the Assembly. Cleon's vituperative speech in the Assembly was exceptional in the fifth century, according to Aristotle; in Aristophanes' *Ecclesiazusae* the presiding officers have the means to eject abusive speakers.[101] At some time before 345 a law provided for considerable sanctions against abusive speech.[102] When the agenda called for discussions of policy, leading Athenian orators in the Assembly seem to have more than conformed to the regulation against abusiveness. Plutarch calls attention to the marked contrast between the abusive invective in Demosthenes' forensic speeches and its absence in the *Philippics*.[103] Blass[104] and Schaefer[105] call attention to the fact that Demosthenes

[98] 967–72.

[99] Hyp. *Dem.* 20–21; Din. 1. 48–54.

[100] Lys. 9. 6–10 alludes to a penalty for abusing a *magistrate* presiding in his own court. The law ascribed to Solon at Plut. *Solon* 21. 1, with its fine of five drachmas, would have been but a small deterrent in the fourth century. In that period a law did provide for a fine of five hundred drachmas for certain particularly grievous types of slander, but nowhere do we hear of a special penalty for abuse in court. See Lipsius, pp. 647–51, and cf. Plato *Lg.* xi. 935b. Indeed, in court, the absence of invective rather than its presence seems to have evoked astonishment; see Plato *Tht.* 174c and Bruns, p. 483.

[101] Arist. *Ath. Pol.* 28. 3; Aristoph. *Ec.* 142–43.

[102] See above, n. 82.

[103] *Praec. ger. reip.* 810d; cf. Plut. *Dem.* 11. 4–5, Arist. *Rhet.* ii. 1. 2–7. 1377b21–1378a20, and *Hypoth.* 2 to Ps.-D. 7.

[104] III 1, 391.

[105] II, 75, 305.

goes so far in conforming to the rule that he does not even mention the names of the citizens who were his opponents. Blass[106] observes the same practice in Demosthenes' contemporaries, the authors of Ps.-D.7 and 17, and he might have added Ps.-D.11, Andoc. 2–3, the *demegoriae* of Isocrates, the fragmentary Lys. 34, and the speech of Leosthenes,[107] and thus have included all the extant fourth-century Athenian *demegoriae*. The *demegoriae* of the same period reported in Xenophon and Diodorus are also free from abusiveness. The rule holds only for discussions of policy. The Athenian Council and Assembly also heard reports on the conduct of officials, and in such cases Demosthenes did not hesitate to accuse by name.[108]

The attitude of Demosthenes and surely of these other respectable and influential politicians toward abusiveness in the Assembly is set forth in the Demosthenic *Prooemia*. Vituperation, says the speaker, is out of place in a *demegoria*, which should not be made to resemble a law-court speech;[109] to indulge in abuse is to act contrary to the public interest and brings discredit on the speaker himself.[110] One may name a citizen and call attention to his past misdeeds, but only if the intent is not to attack him but to exhibit to the people their past mistakes and prevent a repetition of them.[111]

The exceptions in the *demegoriae* of these orators to the rule against assailing citizens by name are all easily explainable. Thus Demosthenes mentions in derogation a certain Callias at 2. 19, but the man is a discredited exile who has lost his citizenship. Hegesippus at Ps.-D. 7. 42–43 mentions Callippus as proposer of a decree favorable to Macedonia for which he had prosecuted him some fifteen years before, but he does not suggest that Callippus is now opposing him.[112] Hegesippus does not attack Callippus but calls the people's attention to past errors. Again, of all his enemies, Andocides in *De Reditu* mentions by name only Peisander, the condemned oligarch.[113] The treatment of Aristomedes at D.10. 70–75 will be discussed later.[114]

---

[106] III 1, 39.

[107] *Hibeh Papyri*, I, 55–61, No. 15.

[108] D. 19. 31–33.

[109] *Prooemm.* 11, 20, 31, 52, 53. 1–2.

[110] *Prooemm.* 6, 31, 53. 1–2.

[111] *Prooem.* 20. 3; cf. D. 6. 32–37, where the orator refuses to name the men he accuses.

[112] Blass, III 2, 136; Schaefer, I, 164, n. 2.

[113] Andoc. 2. 14.

[114] Below, Chap. 8, rhetorical analysis of Ep. 3. 16–18.

If a speaker before the Assembly is at a loss for a point of departure, Aristotle recommends following the example of Isocrates (and others). Isocrates attacked the Lacedaemonians in the *Panegyricus* and Chares in *De Pace*.[115] But the *Panegyricus* is not a real *demegoria*;[116] the attack on the Lacedaemonians, like the attack on the Thebans in the *Plataïcus*, is not abuse of Athenian citizens; and at *De Pace* 50 and 134 and throughout the speech, Isocrates abstains from naming Chares or any other proponent of the policies he is condemning.

Some modern writers have found it incredible that Demosthenes should have refrained so completely from attacking his opponents by name in *demegoriae* when he showed no such inhibition in court. These authors suggest that when the orator prepared his *demegoriae* for publication he removed the names.[117] But did all these orators or their redactors really expurgate the speeches? Surely the evidence just cited shows that here is a practice which was rooted in the facts of Athenian political life.

From the scanty evidence of the extant *demegoriae* it is impossible to tell how widely this self-restraint before the Assembly was practiced by Demosthenes' contemporaries and how far back in time it went.[118] Certainly, given the Athenian tradition of free speech, there must always have been some exchanges of abuse and recriminations in the Assembly. This is attested by Aristophanes[119] as well as by Demosthenes in his criticism of the Athenians for permitting such behavior.[120] Thus less responsible demagogues even of Demosthenes' time may often have found that the Athenians' appetite for lively invective made the regulations against abusiveness but a small deterrent.[121] But at least in the cases of Demosthenes and Isocrates, we

[115] *Rhet.* iii. 17. 10. 1418a29–32.

[116] See above, n. 97.

[117] C. D. Adams, "Speeches VIII and X of the Demosthenic Corpus," *CP*, XXXIII (1938), 136; R. Sealey, "Dionysius of Halicarnassus and Some Demosthenic Dates," *REG*, LXVIII (1955), 105; Stephen G. Daitz, "The Relationship of the *De Chersoneso* and the *Philippica quarta* of Demosthenes," *CP*, LII (1957), 145, 160.

[118] The survival of any authentic *demegoriae* at all is due to the few exceptional politicians who wrote them out. The *demegoria* was predominantly an extemporaneous oration. See H. Ll. Hudson-Williams, "Political Speeches in Athens," *CQ*, XLV (1951), 68–73.

[119] *Ec.* 248, 254, 434–39.

[120] D. 4. 44; 9. 54; 10. 75–76; and the *Prooemia* cited above.

[121] See Plut. *Praec. ger. reip.* 810d.

are entitled to use this avoidance of abusiveness as a necessary condition for the authenticity of *demegoriae* ascribed to them. Any unexplainable departures from the principle will show that the work is probably a forgery. D. Epp. 1 and 2 clearly pass this test. Epp. 3 and 4 require further study.[122]

We have now shown how the *demegoria* as practiced by Demosthenes and his contemporaries might indeed present inconveniences for anyone whose purpose was to write or fabricate self-apology. But our generalizations rest on scanty evidence; it is especially surprising that Aristotle and Anaximenes should say nothing about the avoidance of abuse in *demegoriae*. But is is still possible to show that the *demegoria* was a strange form for an Athenian to use for the purposes of personal polemics, even if it was not so inconvenient as we have described it.

No subtle analysis is required to show that the rhetorical form naturally adapted to personal attack and to self-apology is the forensic speech, which, indeed, includes them as species, according to the schemes of Aristotle and Anaximenes. Study of the avenues used by the Athenians to press their private and political antagonisms will show how even attacks on the reputation of dead men were deliberately put into the forensic arena and how purely propagandistic or rhetorical polemics almost inevitably chose the form of a speech to a court.

The ease with which a suit could be brought under the legal system of the Athenian democracy placed a powerful weapon in the hands of those who wished within the law not only to defame their private enemies or political opponents, but also to work them more tangible injury. In "private" suits (*dikai*), which could be brought only by the wronged party, the plaintiff usually ran no risk of penalty in pressing his case.[123] But even if no actionable private grievance could be found, a "public" suit (*graphê*) could be brought by

---

[122] See below, Chap. 8, rhetorical analysis of Ep. 3. 16–18, 29–31, and of Ep. 4. On the contrast between *demegoriae* and forensic speeches, see also Bruns, *Das literarische Porträt*, pp. 427–585, and Kramer, *De priore Demosthenis adversus Aristogitonem oratione*, pp. 12–39. Both studies show that invective, inherent anyhow in forensic speeches, with Demosthenes, Aeschines, and Dinarchus reaches surprising proportions, any legal restrictions upon it being ineffective. Meanwhile, in *demegoriae* there was an equally surprising absence of personal invective.

[123] On the *epobelia*, see Lipsius, pp. 937–39.

any Athenian citizen. The only deterrent lay in a fine of 1,000 drachmas and the loss of the privilege to bring such a suit again, should the prosecutor fail to obtain at least one-fifth of the votes.[124] There was no deterrent whatever to harassing those chosen for office at the obligatory scrutiny (*dokimasia*) before their tenure[125] and at the required audits after it (*euthynai*), both of which were forensic situations. If the object of hostility himself seemed unassailable, discredit and injury might be inflicted upon him by prosecuting members of his circle. The conviction of one vulnerable member could help discredit an entire faction. As a result, the judicial bodies became the favorite arena for such attacks. The Athenians became proverbial for their litigiousness. Mastery of the technique of speaking in the courts or the services of a speechwriter approached being a practical necessity for every citizen. The possibility of having to defend oneself in court always had to be anticipated.[126]

But especially in politics the courts were the favorite place for attack and the expected setting for defense.[127] Since all Athenian citizens were entitled to sit in the Assembly, one could not remove an opponent from the political scene by defeating him in an election. The efforts of politicians to defame one another before the Council or the Assembly tended to cancel out. Indeed, to voice a serious accusation before the Council or the Assembly rather than before a court[128] could arouse prejudice against the speaker himself, a possibility which Demosthenes took care to avoid.[129] The effective way to put an end to the influence of the opposition was through prosecutions in the courts. In the fifth century we hear of such a campaign against Pericles, beginning with suits against his entourage[130] and culminat-

[124] Lipsius, p. 940; *dikai* and *graphai: ibid.*, pp. 238–48.

[125] Lipsius, pp. 269–85.

[126] Plato *Grg.* 486a–b.

[127] See G. M. Calhoun, *Athenian Clubs in Politics and Litigation* ("Bulletin of the University of Texas," No. 262, January 8, 1913), pp. 98–107.

[128] On the Council and Assembly as courts themselves, see above, n. 30.

[129] E.g., D. 2. 4; the scholiast *ad loc.* remarks, "Λύσις τοῦ ἀντιπίπτοντος. ἀντέπιπτε γὰρ αὐτῷ, διὰ τί οὐ γράφεις καὶ κατηγορεῖς." See also the discussion of Demosthenes' avoidance of abusiveness above.

[130] Diod. xii. 38–39; Plut. *Per.* 31–32; F. Miltner, "Perikles 1," *RE*, XIX[1] (1937), 778–80. Doubt has been cast upon the reliability of the traditions presented by Plutarch and Diodorus; see F. E. Adcock in *Cambridge Ancient History*, V, 477–80. There is, however, no reason to doubt that Pericles' opponents did use the courts in this manner.

ing in his being convicted on a charge of embezzlement and fined.[131] Pericles was not alone in being the target of such politically motivated prosecutions.[132]

The courts were deliberately sought not only as an arena for attack but also for effective defense, as we learn from the agitation in the scandals on the eve of the Sicilian expedition. Alcibiades sought to stand trial for the accusations brought against him, for an acquittal would cut the ground from under the polemics assailing him. His enemies, on the other hand, sought to keep him from defending himself before a court only because they were looking for a more favorable opportunity to bring him to trial.[133]

After the Peloponnesian war, the disappearance of the procedure of ostracism and the decline of the political importance of officials like the *strategoi*, who could be unseated through political campaigns, made the courts all the more the preferred means for attacks on the political opposition. From the beginning to the end of the fourth century suits both public and private were used for such political purposes.[134] Demosthenes and his leading contemporaries must have faced a continual barrage of politically motivated law suits.[135] Demosthenes' downfall in the Harpalus affair probably was but one more example of this practice.

Hence the preferred setting for personal attacks both private and political was the courts. If the polemic was to be pursued outside the courts through the circulation of written propaganda, that propaganda, too, naturally took the form of a forensic speech or of a commentary on one. The remains of fourth-century Athenian literature provide us with a considerable collection of such compositions written

[131] Th. ii. 65. 3; Diod. xii. 45; Plut. *Per.* 35; Plato *Grg.* 516a–d.

[132] See Antiphon's speech *On the Choreutes*.

[133] Th. vi. 29.

[134] Private suits: Isoc. 16. 3. When Diodorus' authority, presumably Ephorus, has Pericles observe that the people in time of peace prosecute their able men out of "idleness and envy" (xii. 39. 3), he is surely reflecting the political prosecutions of his own century. On D. 20, 22, 24 as speeches written for such purposes, see W. Jaeger, *Demosthenes: the Origin and Growth of his Policy*, pp. 55–67. D. 23 can show the alacrity with which the young, still politically weak Demosthenes seized the opportunity to use a court instead of the Assembly to propose a policy which required him to make a violent personal attack against an Athenian citizen, Charidemus; see Jaeger, pp. 98–100.

[135] See D. 18. 249–51; Ep. 3. 6, 8; *Vit. X orat.* 842f; Aesch. 3. 194; Hyp. *Dem.* 28–29.

either for actual trials or as pure propaganda. Since we are concerned with the forms of political propaganda and literary fiction, speeches indubitably written to be delivered need not concern us here, although in fact they, too, are propaganda, and if anything, more effective as such than were mere written brochures.

The accusation of Socrates by Polycrates and the *Apologies* composed for him by Plato, Xenophon, and Lysias were all written after his death and are therefore pure propaganda.[136] All these compositions were in the form of forensic orations.[137] Xenophon's *Memorabilia* i–ii takes the form of commentary and criticism of the contents of the prosecution speeches. The forms here used can hardly be said to be the result of deliberate choice; they simply reflect the historical fact of Socrates' trial. Nevertheless, conceivably a propagandist could have used the *demegoria*. He might have set the dramatic date of his composition before the execution and composed an appeal to the People to set aside the sentence, or he might have written a proposal to set up a statue in honor of Socrates, as Stratocles did for Lycurgus or Demochares for Demosthenes. The latter alternative might have been suggested by Socrates' own proposal, as presented by Plato,[138] that his sentence be the reward of maintenance at the public table in the Prytaneum. There is no trace of any such composition in defense of Socrates.

If the speech *Against Andocides* in the Lysianic corpus[139] is indeed pure propaganda,[140] its form as a forensic oration, too, may simply reflect the fact of Andocides' trial in 399[141] and prove little about the choice of propaganda forms. But the polemics written around the person of Alcibiades are of great interest for our investigation. The purposes for which all three of them, Isoc. 16, Lys. 14, and Andoc. 4, were composed are a matter of controversy.

The speeches of Isocrates and Lysias are closely associated and must be considered together. Both purport to be written for trials in

---

[136] See Bruns, pp. 183–96.

[137] Quite likely, so was the *Apology of Socrates* by Demetrius of Phalerum, *F. Gr. Hist.* No. 228, F 40–45.

[138] *Apol.* 36d.

[139] Lys. 6.

[140] Bruns, pp. 521–24; L. Gernet and M. Bizos, *Lysias: discours*, I, 89–93. Blass, I, 562–70, regards it as a real forensic speech reworked after the trial. See also Plöbst, "Lysias," *RE*, XIII² (1927), 2451.

[141] See Andoc. 1.

which Alcibiades' son, the younger Alcibiades, was the defendant. The speech of Isocrates has been dated as early as 402, but it is now agreed that the trial which is its basis took place between 397 and 395. The form is that of the end of a defense speech spoken by the younger Alcibiades in a suit holding him responsible as his father's heir. The plaintiff charges that the elder Alcibiades wrongfully took as his own the plaintiff's team of horses and used it in winning his famous triumph at the Olympic games in 416. In the speech of Lysias, the younger Alcibiades is prosecuted on a charge of evasion of military duties; the trial is datable in 395/4.[142] The composition of Isocrates begins where the younger Alcibiades' defense in the actual matter at issue would end. Since it is generally agreed that Isocrates published the oration in the same fragmentary form,[143] it is clear that he was not interested in publishing the matter directly pertinent to the trial. This immediately suggests that the work as we have it is prepared for a special purpose, either propaganda or a display of the author's skill. This forensic epilogue is in fact an encomiastic defense of the elder Alcibiades and his career, displaying the epideictic scheme of organization.[144] As if in answer, the speech of Lysias, which has the form of a complete forensic oration, contains a lengthy attack on the elder Alcibiades.[145] There is a surprising mutual dependence between the two speeches, for each takes up and refutes the arguments of the other in such a manner as to suggest that the speeches were reedited for publication after the trials were over.[146]

For the purposes of our investigation, the opening paragraphs of the speech of Isocrates supply the key to understanding both the trials and the speeches: the younger Alcibiades complains bitterly that he has been the victim of continual harassment in the courts by men who, professedly for the benefit of the city, wish to destroy the

[142] See Münscher, "Isocrates 2," *RE*, IX² (1916), 2161; G. Mathieu and E. Brémond, *Isocrate: discours*, I, 48; P. Treves, "Note sulla guerra corinzia," *Riv. fil.*, LXV (1937) 113–17.

[143] See Blass, II, 225; Bruns, p. 496; Münscher, *RE*, IX, 2162; Mathieu and Brémond, I, 49.

[144] See above, p. 103.

[145] Lys. 14. 30–42.

[146] Bruns, pp. 494–95. There are many views on the relationship of Lys. 14 and Isoc. 16 to the speeches delivered in court. See Blass, I, 492–95, and II, 227–28; Bruns, 495–500; Münscher, *RE*, IX, 2161–64; Gernet and Bizos I, 222–23; Mathieu and Brémond, I, 49.

reputation of his father.[147] Evidently, in the Athenian politics of the 390s the figure of the martyred Alcibiades was a powerful symbol. The party identified with that figure strove to defend it and to increase its popularity; the opposition did its utmost to discredit the public image of Alcibiades.[148]

The speeches of Lysias and Isocrates show that the courts were deliberately chosen as the arena for these political polemics over the figure of Alcibiades. Upon his return from exile, Alcibiades had received practical exoneration from the charges against his earlier career. He was not again brought to trial. Whatever odium still attached to him in the eyes of the Athenian people was mitigated by his martyrdom. In the 390s he himself could no longer be brought to court, but the opponents of what he symbolized still sought an opportunity to use the most efficacious means for discrediting a figure in Athens. They found it in repeatedly bringing his son to trial. There had been other suits before the one on the team of horses, as the younger Alcibiades bitterly complains. The speeches of Lysias and Isocrates may have originally been written for the two most striking cases of this campaign in the courts. In the suit on the team of horses, the father's own wickedness could be made the issue. And the conviction of the son on a charge of evading military duty would contribute to the annihilation of the father's reputation.[149] Thus we learn that even when a dead man became the subject of political polemics in Athens, the partisans of both sides sought the arena of the

---

[147] Isoc. 16. 1–3.

[148] What the figure of Alcibiades symbolized is a subject which requires more extensive study than the present context allows. Some have suggested that it stood for an Athenian policy of active imperialism; so P. Treves, *Riv. fil.*, LXV, 115, and "Introduzione alla storia della guerra corinzia," *Athenaeum*, n.s., XVI (1938), 180–84; Gernet, "Notes sur Andocide," *RPh.* 3d series, V (1931), 318–19; Mathieu and Brémond, I, 49. Bruns (pp. 509–13) sees in these early stages of what he calls the "cult of Alcibiades" merely the recriminations of those policitians who supported and those who opposed the ambivalent genius in his lifetime. Perhaps most plausible is the suggestion that Alcibiades was the symbol of his class: the talented aristocrats, men who—despite their inherent disdain for democracy and the suspicions it incurred in the *demos*—wished to exercise their *aretê* by taking an active part in Athenian politics. Such men did face strong suspicion in the decade following the tyranny of the Thirty. See Claude Mossé, *La fin de la démocratie athénienne*, pp. 287–90.

[149] See Bruns. pp. 503–5.

court room. They were not content to cast aspersions upon him or upon one another at meetings of the Assembly. Surely we may also infer that Isocrates published his oration in its present form as propaganda, not as a mere rhetorical exhibition. Hence in the realms of both political action and published propaganda the polemics over the figure of Alcibiades were deliberately situated in the forensic arena.

The remaining work attacking Alcibiades, Andoc. 4, has a particular interest for this investigation, for among all the surviving pieces of this polemical literature, it alone seems to be addressed to the Assembly rather than to a court. But this is the "exception which proves the rule." The oration purports to be a speech delivered by the politician Phaeax on the occasion between the years 418 and 415 when the Athenians were about to use the procedure of ostracism for the last time and banish Hyperbolus. According to the speaker,[150] the possible victims of the ostracism are Alcibiades, Nicias, and himself.[151] The speaker wishes to show that not he himself but Alcibiades is guilty of misdeeds which make him worthy of ostracism. Since there was no deliberation in the Assembly as to who was to be ostracized – a fact which the speech itself admits[152] – scholars have ruled out if only for this reason the possibility that the oration was written for actual delivery before the Assembly. Most hold that it is but a rhetorical showpiece and try to discern in it the characteristic traits of such literature.[153] Others regard it as political propaganda of the period of the Corinthian war against the policies of which Alcibiades was the symbol.[154] Only Raubitschek[155] suggests that the speech is what it pretends to be, and he is forced to suggest that it was addressed

---

[150] Par. 2.

[151] See J. Carcopino, *L'ostracisme athénien*, pp. 191–232; A. E. Raubitschek, "The Case against Alcibiades (Andocides IV)," *TAPA*, LXXIX (1948), 192–93; C. Hignett, *A History of the Athenian Constitution* (Oxford: Clarendon Press, 1952), pp. 395–96.

[152] Par. 3.

[153] Blass, I, 332–39; Bruns, p. 514; Thalheim, "Andokides 1," *RE*, I² (1894), 2127; Carcopino, pp. 216–25; A. R. Burn, "A Biographical Source on Phaiax and Alkibiades?" *CQ*, XLVIII (1954), 138.

[154] L. Gernet, *RPh*, 3d series, V, 313–26; P. Treves, *Athenaeum*, n.s., XVI, 180, n. 1.

[155] *TAPA*, LXXIX, 191–210.

not to the Assembly but to an unofficial gathering of citizens before the vote on who was to be ostracized was held. One may remark that such a speech would then be pure propaganda, and it would make no difference whether it was actually delivered or merely circulated in writing.

Whichever of these views is taken, on closer examination Andoc. 4, far from being an example of the use of the *demegoria* for the purposes of polemical attack and defense, shows once again that in propaganda and in literature as in real life the forensic genus was preferred. Blass remarked[156] that although in form the speech was a *demegoria*, in reality it was a trial speech, as much a defense of the speaker as an accusation of Alcibiades. By the words "in form" Blass presumably meant that the speech was a *demegoria* in so far as it pretended to be addressed to the Assembly. If Raubitschek is correct in assuming that the Assembly is not contemplated as the audience, even this reason for calling the work a *demegoria* disappears.

The issue of Alcibiades' ostracism could have been presented primarily as a matter of public policy, showing that the interests of the city would be served by his removal and using his past behavior as supporting evidence. But it is not so presented. Rather, the obvious resemblances which ostracism bore to a sentence imposed by a court control the course of the argument. The speech, indeed, proclaims itself to be a forensic plea. Phaeax is made to regard his audience as in fact judges in a court, even though his complaint is that this court which decides on ostracism does not observe due process of law.[157] Most important, the speaker bases his entire argument on the assumption that there is a law of ostracism which—however badly formulated—exists to punish men like Alcibiades who are guilty of criminal conduct but are too insolent and powerful for the regular authorities to handle.[158] The argument is therefore concentrated on showing that Alcibiades, and not Phaeax, has done in the past the deeds which the law is designed to punish.[159] The oration is not primarily directed to showing, under the headings of the *telika kephalaia*, that the Athenians should pass an enactment for the future; those headings enter only in the peroration.[160] Therefore, the speech has every trait

[156] I, 334.　　　[157] Pars. 2–4.　　　[158] Pars. 4, 35.
[159] Par. 10.　　　[160] Pars. 32–42.

by which a forensic oration is distinguished from a *demegoria*.[161] Other details of the structure confirm this conclusion. Thus the prooemium[162] consists of courtroom commonplaces.[163] The preliminary discussion on the law affecting the case (pars. 3–6) is a feature peculiar to forensic oratory.[164]

Finally, when the author implies that the audience will next hear Alcibiades present a reply,[165] the maneuver is entirely that of a forensic speech. Even under Raubitschek's theory[166] it is difficult to believe that the same informal gathering that assembled to hear Phaeax would also grant a hearing to Alcibiades. Hence, one is led to the conclusion that the author, to make his composition as effective as possible, deliberately gave it the character of a forensic oration.

In sum, the author of Andoc. 4 has sought out and in part fabricated a situation where, as in court, an opponent can be portrayed as attacking Alcibiades with a severe penalty in the offing. The oratorical form used by propagandists or literary fabricators in writing personal polemics remains the forensic speech.

The most decisive example for our thesis in this literature of propaganda is Isocrates' *Antidosis*. The works dealing with Socrates, Alcibiades, and Andocides all have historical trials behind them. But Isocrates, when prejudice against him contributed to his defeat in a civil suit, wrote a defense of his career in the form of a reply to a fictitious capital accusation.[167] Isocrates frequently used the *demegoria* as a propaganda medium and repeatedly declared his preference for it over the forensic genus which he disparaged.[168] He might here have written a *demegoria* proposing to the people that their hostility toward him was detrimental to the best interests of the city and that, on the contrary, they ought to give honor and encouragement to such as he. But he does not even consider using that form. His choice of the forensic form was not just a slavish imitation of Plato's

---

[161] See above, pp. 103–7.

[162] Pars. 1–10.

[163] There are (1) the danger faced by the pleader (pars. 1–2; see Navarre, pp. 230–32); (2) the flattery of the judges (par. 2; see Anax. 36, p. 86. 2–4 H., and Navarre, pp. 218–22); (3) the appeal for a fair hearing (par. 7; Navarre, p. 216).

[164] Navarre, pp. 123–24.

[165] Par. 25.

[166] See *TAPA*, LXXIX, 197.

[167] Isoc. 15. 1–13.

[168] Isoc. 4. 188, 13. 19–20, etc.; see Dion. Hal. *Isoc.* 18, Vol. I, pp. 85–86 U.-R.

Apology. The preface of the *Antidosis* makes clear the reasons why he chose that genus. Had he used any other, he would have saddled himself with annoying inconveniences. To have used the epideictic genus would have brought upon him the inherent odium of a sustained piece of self-praise.[169] We may infer that to Isocrates the *demegoria* was out of the question in such a matter of obvious self-interest. Into the forensic form, however, he felt that he could introduce even matters which strictly speaking were not appropriate in a court.[170] He had done so before in placing a formal encomium of Alcibiades within a forensic speech. The example of Isocrates shows cogently that in Athens any literary effort to clear the reputation of a person who had been worsted in court (as opposed to an actual appeal for executive clemency) inevitably assumed the attitudes of the courtroom.

It is possible that the *Antidosis* was a model and a stimulus for Plato's Ep. 7. However, unlike Isocrates, Plato did not feel obliged to write in one of the forms of public oratory. In the *Seventh Epistle* he does present a defense of his own career in the course of giving advice to the adherents of the late Dion, but the work is not written as an oration. A "symbouleutic" composition it may be,[171] but it can hardly be said to be a *demegoria*, as Dionysius of Halicarnassus recognized.[172]

Like Socrates and Isocrates, Demosthenes had been worsted in court. If he himself had wanted to write apologetic propaganda rather than a direct appeal to the sovereign People for his restoration, he, too, probably would have chosen the forensic form. Certainly for a propagandist writing after his death, there was no dearth of situations around which to fabricate a forensic defense of his career. Since the orator and his heirs seem not to have preserved the defense-speech which he used without success at his trial, the speech entitled *Apologia dōrōn*, condemned as spurious by Dionysius of Halicarnassus,[173] may have been just such a piece of propaganda.

---

[169] Isoc. 15. 8.

[170] Isoc. 15. 10.

[171] See J. Klek, *Symbuleutici qui dicitur sermonis historia critica* ("Rhetorische Studien," 8 Heft; Paderborn: Ferdinand Schoeningh, 1919), pp. 64–69, 73–77.

[172] *Dem.* 23, Vol. I, p. 180. 1–6 U.-R. The *Seventh Epistle* is longer than any of Demosthenes' *demegoriae.*

[173] See commentary to Ep. 3. 42, οὐ μὴν οὐδὲ κτλ.

Moreover, there was already available a classic forensic defense of Demosthenes' career in *De Corona*. No better presentation of the stock arguments of Demosthenes' faction could be imagined. Although we have taken pains to point out the differences which make the letters far from a slavish reworking of the great reply to Aeschines,[174] the arguments in them in defense of Demosthenes' career are still substantially those of *De Corona*. After the trial, Demosthenes himself modified the text of that oration.[175] Surely the best method for a propagandist writing after his death would have been to publish an up-to-date edition of *De Corona*, perhaps substituting some other name for that of Aeschines, but in any case keeping to the forensic genus, not using the inconvenient form of a Demosthenic *demegoria*.[176]

If Epp. 1–4 prove formally to be *demegoriae*, it will also be unlikely that they are fictions produced by the rhetorical schools of the fourth or early third centuries. Whatever rhetorical exercises were practiced by students at that time must have been directed toward the needs of real public speaking.[177] An apologetic *demegoria* in letter form probably would have been too far-fetched a theme for the period. Surely the restrictions of the Demosthenic *demegoria* would have made it still less suitable in a historical novel or a rhetorical exhibition or school exercise, in all of which the goal was the most dramatic possible character portrayal. Even without the restrictions on invective and on discussion of personal interests, the dramatic attractions of a court setting and the traditions of polemic literature would make it surprising if any writer of fictional self-apology were to leave the forensic genus for the *demegoria*, although apologetic motifs may have been included in symbouleutic compositions which pretended to be addressed to powerful individuals like kings and dictators.[178] Whereever there were dramatic situations in history in which self-apologies

---

[174] Above, pp. 74–76.

[175] Schaefer, *Dem.* (1st ed.; Leipzig: B. G. Teubner, 1858), III 2, 72–81; Blass, III 1, 430–32.

[176] Self-apology remained in the forensic and epideictic genera down into the literature of the middle ages. See the poor dissertation of Fritz Loheit, *Untersuchungen zur antiken Selbstapologie*.

[177] See the words of Anaximenes quoted by Philodemus *Rhet.* Vol. II, p. 254 Sudhaus: "οὐκ ἄν ποτε προσῆσαν τοῖς ῥητορικοῖς ἀργύριον διδόντες εἰ μὴ τὸ δημηγορεῖν καὶ δικολογεῖν ἐκ τῆς τέχνης αὐτῶν περιεγίνετο τελείως."

[178] See Quint. iii. 8. 55.

were known to have been presented as *demegoriae*, the later rhetoricians did use them as themes for their compositions; the fact that the speeches themselves might be extant sometimes only called forth the emulation of the schoolmen, just as Aristides[179] produced a declamation on the theme of Demosthenes' *Against Leptines*. But in proposing themes, the schoolmen did not limit themselves, in general, to historical occasions where there was a record that a speech had been given. They enjoyed exercising great ingenuity in producing sheer historical fictions, distorting the facts to get the most advantageous setting for rhetorical display. If in such fictions self-apologetic *demegoriae* are extremely rare or absent, whereas forensic apologies abound, this will be an indication of how little a theme like that of Demosthenes' letters would have suggested itself to the mind of a rhetorical artist.

R. Kohl[180] has collected from the Greek and Latin rhetorical literature 429 themes based on historical situations which were to be used for rhetorical exercises. Among them are plenty of purely fictitious examples of self-apology classifiable in the forensic genus, but only a few themes that can be considered apologetic *demegoriae* and, of these, scarcely one that is a pure fiction.[181] One instance of a fictitious theme of self-apology worked out as a *demegoria* has survived, the four letters of Aeschines to the Council and the People. As we have shown, they are imitations of the letters of Demosthenes.[182] We have already used these spurious compositions for useful comparisons suggesting the authenticity of their model,[183] and we are shortly to use them for comparison again. But the isolation of the letters of Aeschines as apologetic *demegoriae* among the forms of ancient rhetorical fiction is in itself an important fact; it suggests that if the model had not existed, neither would the imitation have come into being. And there is no reason to believe that a model existed at the end of the fourth or the beginning of the third century which might have impelled a hypothetical fabricator of Demosthenes' letters to write apologies in the genus of the *demegoria*, even if such fictions were being written at the time.[184]

[179] *Or.* 53 Dindorf.
[180] See above, Chap. 4, n. 6.
[181] See Appendix IX.
[182] See Appendix II.
[183] Above, p. 78.
[184] See above, Chap. 4, beginning.

On the other hand, the theme of Demosthenes' defense speech at his trial in the Harpalus affair would be a setting at least as attractive for ancient novelists and rhetoricians as we have imagined it would have been for a propagandist, and there must have been many of these efforts in the regular forensic genre of self-apology.[185] This, rather than political propaganda, may have been the origin of the Demosthenic speech *Apologia dōrōn*.[186]

The apologetic *demegoria*, however, was precisely the form which the living Demosthenes would have had to use in making a succession of pleas for himself and for the sons of Lycurgus. All *judicial* proceedings were terminated by his and their conviction and sentence; there was no *court* of higher resort. Moreover, since all available proofs of innocence must already have been used at the trials, it was most unlikely that Demosthenes, now in exile, could find any new proofs, which were the necessary ingredients for a new forensic plea to be written as a propagandistic fiction. His only hope was to show the sovereign people that their interests demanded enacting the exonerations which he sought.

Therefore, the more the letters conform to the restrictions of the Demosthenic *demegoria*, the more likely is it that they are by Demosthenes. One might ask why even Demosthenes would have had so to hamper himself in writing open letters which were not actually speeches to the Assembly. An answer would be that the orator wanted his propaganda to give the same impression as real petitions or proposals. It is also possible to see here a hope of the writer that the letters would be read before the Council and the Assembly. That bodies like these did receive letters from private individuals and even private foreigners is clear not only from the fact that the early Peripatetics gave directions on how to write such letters[187] but also from the example of Isoc. Ep. 8.[188] Schaefer believed that since Demosthenes was a person without civil rights (*atimos*), he was worse off than a foreigner and could have had no hope of getting an official hearing for his messages.[189] Blass suggested that if the Athenians wished to give the letters a hearing, they surely could have, just as

---

[185] See Kohl, Nos. 323–25; No. 323 also appears at Philostratus *VS* i. 542.
[186] See above, p. 126.
[187] See above, n. 11.
[188] See below, Chap. 8, rhetorical analysis of Ep. 3. 35–36.
[189] Schaefer, *NJb*, CXV, 161; Neupert, p. 16.

they once granted a hearing to Andocides.[190] Indeed, the law at D. 24. 50 which forbids making appeals (*hiketeuein*) for people sentenced by a court before they had paid their penalties may not have applied here to prevent the orator's supporters from reading the letters to the Assembly. Perhaps the law applied only to the use of formal religious procedure of *hiketeia* mentioned at Aristotle *Ath. Pol.* 43. 6. In any case, as Schaefer and Neupert concede, Epp. 1–4 may be authentic as open propaganda letters even if they could not be read before the Assembly.

In sum, we can say that a "hybrid form" such as an apologetic *demegoria* would not be likely to suggest itself to any fabricator writing within the seventy years after Demosthenes' death, whether that fabricator was a propagandist or a littérateur. Isocrates readily used *demegoriae* placed in the mouths of Archidamus or the Plataeans to present the policies he favored.[191] Just as readily, he fabricated a forensic situation in writing his own defense and at least adapted one to defend Alcibiades. Similarly, the hybrid form of the deliberative forensic speech is hardly to be expected except where the writer has a polemic purpose; when the historians compose speeches to explain the policies that lay behind the course of events, they write *demegoriae*, not speeches like Demosthenes' *Against Aristocrates*.[192] Until the time that rhetoricians vied with one another in proposing far-fetched themes, such mixtures are a sign of creative adaptation of established forms to the exigencies of real life. And even the vogue of involved themes seems to have brought very few examples of rhetorical exercises in the form of apologetic *demegoriae*.

We have thus established what were the differences between the *demegoria* and the forensic speech in the time of Demosthenes. We have shown that any fabricator of apology would have found the *demegoria* a strange, even inconvenient form, whereas a man ap-

[190] *NJb*, CXV, 544; *Att. Ber.*, III 1, 441; see Sachsenweger, p. 11. On Andocides, see below, Chap. 8, end of rhetorical analysis of Ep. 2.

[191] Even if the *Archidamus* is merely a rhetorical exhibition, as now seems unlikely, it is still not a "hybrid form." On the *Archidamus*, see Münscher, *RE*, IX² (1916), 2200–2; E. Drerup (ed.), *Isocratis opera omnia*, I, cli–cliii; G. Mathieu, *Les idées politiques d'Isocrate* (Paris: Société d'édition "Les belles lettres," 1925), pp. 105–7; Mathieu and Brémond, II, 171–73. For the view that the work was composed as a rhetorical exercise, or at most, as a gift to be sent to Archidamus, see Blass, II, 288–89.

[192] See above, n. 134.

pealing for exoneration would have had to use it. To support our assumption of the authenticity of the letters by rhetorical analysis, we have only to show that the letters in fact do conform to the canons of the Demosthenic *demegoria*. In the process we shall achieve a better understanding of the unfolding of the argument of the letters.

To confirm the conclusions of our analysis, we are fortunate in that two useful bases for comparison have survived from antiquity. We have seen what a *rara avis* the self-apologetic *demegoria* must have been in ancient literature. In fact, only two significant examples have survived. Both reflect circumstances very similar to those of Demosthenes' exile. One is the spurious *Letters of Aeschines*; the other is a genuine appeal to the people by an exile for his restoration, Andocides' speech *De Reditu*. Comparison with these two examples will be an important means for confirming our conclusions. If the structure and tone of Ep. 2 resemble those of the speech of Andocides, our belief in its authenticity will be strengthened. The letters of Aeschines, on the other hand, will show how different the treatment would have been in a literary fiction. To be sure, when those spurious documents were written, the canons of the Athenian *demegoria* had long since fallen into disuse. Nevertheless, their author was imitating the letters of Demosthenes and probably had access to the rhetorical textbooks of fourth-century Athens. Hence, if this fabricator departs from the rules of the fourth-century *demegoria* and lapses into the more usual styles of apology and epistolography, the fact is not without significance, for it shows that a writer of such fictions would not confine himself to the rules of the *demegoria* even when he had a model. We may expect, therefore, that the hypothetical literary forger of Demosthenes' letters, who had no such compositions to imitate, would have done the same.

In preparation for these comparisons, we must note where the author of the letters of Aeschines did follow rhetorical style. Thus, Ps.-Aesch. Epp. 7, 11, and 12 exhibit a measure of avoidance of hiatus in accordance with their character as public orations in letter form, but not Ep. 3.[193] In writing Ps.-Aesch. Ep. 3, the fabricator fell completely out of the genres of public oratory into the genre of the private letter, both in tolerating hiatus and in presenting in a simple

---

[193] See E. Drerup (ed.), *Aeschinis quae feruntur epistolae*, pp. 37–38; his review of Schwegler in *Deutsche Literaturzeitung*, XXXVI (1915), 1282; K. Schwegler, *De Aeschinis quae feruntur epistolis*, p. 76.

epistolary style personal information of no political interest whatever.[194]

We are now ready to begin the rhetorical analysis of the letters. Our guides will be the textbooks of Aristotle and Anaximenes and the results of our investigation into the effects of the nature of Athenian political institutions on rhetorical form. We shall make occasional reference to later sources, but only when there is some reason to assume that they reflect the theory and practice of the time of Demosthenes.[195] By confining ourselves to the less-developed theories of Aristotle and Anaximenes, we shall most easily avoid overestimating the influence of the rigid schemata of the schools on Demosthenes and the other Attic orators, whose compositions responded more to the needs of the real situation confronting them.[196] Anaximenes and Aristotle themselves do not set forth rigid schemata. They indicate that the prooemium may be inseparable from the narrative,[197] the narrative from the proof, and the proof from the refutation.[198] With this flexible schematism, which represents the practice of the Attic orators, we shall still be able to see whether the letters conform to the practice of the fourth-century *demegoria*.

[194] See below, Chap. 8, end of rhetorical analysis of Ep. 3.

[195] Hence, in analyzing the long prooemium-narrative, Ep. 3. 1–10, we shall not call pars. 2–5 a *prokataskeue* between the prooemium and the narrative and proposition. The scholiast to D. 2. 5 (=p. 19. 9 Reiske; Vol. II, p. 540 Müller) speaks of a *prokataskeue* to D. 2, but this technical term appears first in Dion. Hal *Is.* 3, Vol. I, p. 95. 20 U.-R.; see Navarre, p. 123, n. 2.

[196] See W. Kroll, *RE*, Suppl. VII (1940), 1065–71; cf. Navarre, pp. 272–76, and Blass, III 1, 214–18.

[197] Anax. 31.

[198] Arist. *Rhet.* iii. 13 and 16. 11. 1417*b*10–11.

CHAPTER 8

Rhetorical Analysis of the Letters

W RITTEN IN THE FACE of extremely difficult conditions, Ep. 3 is a tour de force. Even the changing political situation lent itself more to the purposes of Demosthenes' enemies than to his. Nevertheless, the orator is able to begin with a tone of injured indignation and pass from humble suppliant to admonisher to undisguised accuser—a feat which his enemies had bitterly admired before[1] but which he had never accomplished under harder circumstances. Recognizing this unusually bold display of temperament by a petitioner, Hermogenes and Pseudo-Aristides take Epp. 2 and 3 as classic examples of the rhetorical "ideas" of "graveness" (*barytês*, the tone of injured indignation)[2] and "harshness" (*trachytês*, undisguised reproach of persons in a superior position).[3]

For Demosthenes, the sole exploitable avenue of protest was the plight of the sons of Lycurgus. The recognized patterns of the *demegoria* included one with the required function, the speech which aims at persuading the People "to come to the aid of the distressed."[4] An authentic example in letter form of this fourth-century rhetorical type has survived, Isoc. Ep. 8,[5] and will be useful for comparisons. At the outset, the orator could expect great difficulty in getting a hearing for his arguments. A condemned fugitive was about to plead for others condemned in court and ask for an extraordinary if not

---

[1] Aesch. 3. 193.

[2] Hermog. *Id.* ii. 8, Vol. III, p. 349 Walz; Ps.-Aristides *Rh.* i. 45, 47 Schmid, Vol. IX, pp. 360–61 Walz.

[3] Hermog. *Id.* i. 7, Vol. III, pp. 233–37 Walz.

[4] See above, p. 101.

[5] Authenticity: Münscher, *RE*, IX, 2212–13.

illegal act of exoneration. Surely, this condemned fugitive would turn to plead for himself! Indeed, he had already sent a letter begging for his own safe return. The Athenians, who had rejected the request, must have expected that the orator would continue to importune them. According to Apsines' scheme of classification, the situation was adverse in every possible way.[6]

Captatio benevolentiae, the task of winning the attention and good-will of the audience to the subject at hand despite such prejudicial conditions, is the function of the prooemium.[7] Since the facts of the career of Lycurgus and his posthumous trial were familiar to the Athenians, Demosthenes has only to summarize them.[8] The entire narrative in paragraphs 2–10 joins paragraph 1 in serving the function of the prooemium, in conformity with the recommendation of Anaximenes, that under such circumstances the narrative should be united with the prooemium.[9]

Demosthenes begins by removing the hostility of the Athenians, who expected him to send a renewed plea for himself. His first sentence seems to be an explicit denial of any such intention.[10] In fact, he goes farther, presenting himself as willingly submitting his fate to the will of the Athenians, a maneuver well calculated to win him sympathy.[11] Nevertheless, his statement is vague enough so that when

---

[6] Apsines 2, pp. 224. 13–17 and 225. 1–2, 11, 18–19 H.: "ἀντιπίπτει δὲ τὰ μὲν ἐκ προσώπου, τὰ δὲ ἐκ πράγματος, τὰ δὲ ἐξ αἰτίας. τὰ μὲν οὖν ἐκ προσώπου τριχῆ λαμβάνεται, ὅταν πρὸς ἔνδοξον πρόσωπον ἢ κατὰ ἐνδόξου προσώπου λέγῃς, οἷον στρατηγοῦ ἢ δημαγωγοῦ ἢ κατὰ πόλεως ἐνδόξου. . . . ἢ ὅταν τῶν μὴ σφόδρα πιστευομένων περὶ μεγάλων πραγμάτων εἰσίῃς. . . . γίνεται δὲ ἐκ πράγματος ἀντιπίπτον, . . . ὅταν ἐπαχθές τι δοκῇς λέγειν, ὡς ὁ ἀναιρεῖν νόμον γράφων." See Anax. 29, pp. 67. 13–70. 21 H. To appeal for the setting aside of a sentence was tantamount to asking for the repeal of a law; see Lipsius, pp. 963–64 and Navarre, pp. 221–22. For more of Apsines' discussion, see above, Chap. 7, n. 63.

[7] Anax. 29, p. 65. 12–18 H.; Arist. *Rhet*. iii. 14. 12. 1415*b*32–38; Apsines 2, p. 224. 10–13 H.

[8] See above, Chap. 7, n. 43.

[9] Anax. 31, p. 73. 12–15 H.: "ὅταν μὲν γὰρ ὦσιν ὀλίγα τὰ πράγματα, περὶ ὧν λέγομεν, καὶ γνώριμα τοῖς ἀκούουσι, τῷ προοιμίῳ συνάψομεν, ἵνα μὴ βραχὺ τοῦτο τὸ μέρος καθ' ἑαυτὸ τεθὲν γένηται." D. 5 has a similar narrative section (pars. 5–12) joined to the prooemium (pars. 1–4) and serving the functions of the prooemium by mitigating the orator's embarrassment over having to advocate peace with Philip after having been the chief advocate of resistance. See the Scholia to D. 5, pp. 68b–69a Baiter-Sauppe, and cf. D. 15. 1–8.

[10] Cf. Apsines 2, p. 226. 12–13 H.: "τοῦτο οὖν παντάπασιν ἀναιρήσει τὸ δοκεῖν ὑπὲρ ἑαυτοῦ λέγειν."

[11] See below, nn. 120, 126.

later he turns to argue for his own case there is no contradiction with the prooemium.[12]

Since here the ground has not yet been prepared, Demosthenes contents himself with describing his earlier pleas as "what I thought to be *just*." Having surprised and partially disarmed his audence, he can ask them to give what he has to say "a *just* hearing."[13] Demosthenes was writing to an impatient audience. He had to reveal the matter at issue immediately. Yet to do so would place him in the odious role of attacking the People—but for his use of the rhetorical device of putting the attack into the mouths of others[14] and presenting himself as the defender of the city's reputation. By so ascribing the reproof to foreigners, Demosthenes accomplishes yet another purpose: the subject of the letter appears not as something involving only the personal welfare of the orator and his circle, but as a weighty matter of the city's self-interest, the preservation of its prestige now under attack in foreign quarters.[15]

A *demegoria* had to ground its appeal thus in what was expedient for the city.[16] Anaximenes classified the consideration of prestige under "the honorable," rather than under "the expedient."[17] But the concept of prestige could easily be used in an appeal to expediency. Panhellenic prestige was frequently used as a motive to stir the Athenians in *demegoriae* and in speeches at trials important enough to attract Panhellenic attention,[18] and Athens was vitally concerned with her Panhellenic prestige in the months which saw the formation of the Hellenic alliance for the Lamian war.

Demosthenes could hardly have produced from exile a proof of Lycurgus' innocence, when pleaders on the spot had been unable to convince the court. Demosthenes could not deny his opponents'

[12] From par. 36; Nitsche, pp. 139–40, saw here the hand of a forger.

[13] See Anax. 29, pp. 65. 12–66. 2 H.; Arist. *Rhet.* iii. 14. 10–12. 1415b17–38.

[14] Arist. *Rhet.* iii. 17. 16. 1418b24–27. The device, *fictio personarum*, is a common one and was often used by Demosthenes in his *demegoriae*. See Tiberius *Fig.* 11, 12, Vol. VIII, pp. 537, 539 Walz; Blass, III 1, 179; Quint. ix. 2. 29–30; Volkmann, pp. 280–81, 489–90.

[15] See Arist. *Rhet.* iii. 14. 7. 1415b1–2; Anax. 29, p. 66. 3–10 H.; cf. Anax. 36, p. 87. 18–20 H; and Apsines, pp. 226. 13–14 and 233. 3–6 H.

[16] See above, Chap. 7, nn. 55, 58, 60.

[17] Anax. 1, p. 14. 18–20 H.

[18] D. 8. 34–37; Isoc. Ep. 8. 4–6; D. 18. 297; Aesch. 3. 56; see also Cic. *De inv.* ii. 51. 156, Quint. iii. 8. 1, *Rhet. ad Herenn.* iii. 2. 3.

claim that sentence had been passed on Lycurgus' heirs by due process of law; nor could he impugn the justice or expediency of enforcing sentences against convicted embezzlers.[19] Simply to assert that all the Greeks were shocked at the plight of Lycurgus' sons would hardly impress the audience. When confronted by such irrefutable claims, Demosthenes in his orations did not let his audience see his difficulty. He would dilate on matters reasonably pertinent until he had unobtrusively altered the original claim to one that was assailable. For example, in *Against Leptines* Demosthenes could not refute Leptines' assertion that many unworthy men enjoyed exemption from liturgies. Demosthenes subtly attaches to it the implication that therefore even public benefactors are to be deprived of their rewards and thus leaves the impression that he has refuted Leptines.[20]

Here, too, Demosthenes conceals his difficulty from the audience. Keeping far from the patterns of forensic oratory, he does not state the charges against Lycurgus.[21] Rather, his introduction continues with two narrative sections purporting to present the reasons he sent his letters, organized under the heads of justice (paragraphs 2–4) and expediency (paragraphs 5–10).[22] In both Demosthenes hammers on the fact of Lycurgus' renown as patriot and public servant, and what should have been a question of the correctness of a court decision becomes a question of whether in times like these the heirs of public benefactors should be made to suffer.

In paragraph 5 Demosthenes claims to be about to present arguments to justify Lycurgus and prove the decision of the court wrong. In fact, he does present evidence tending to prove his in-

---

[19] Demosthenes could refute his opponents neither *kat' enstasin* nor *kat' antiparastasin;* their claim was an *antithesis alytos.* See Hermog. *Inv.* iii. 6, Vol. III, pp. 120–21 Walz, pp. 136–38 Rabe; Apsines, pp. 268–72 H.; Volkmann, pp. 241–47.

[20] Maximus Περὶ ἀλύτων ἀντιθέσεων, Vol. I, pp. 578, 585 Walz: "Πάλιν ἐὰν ᾖ ἄλυτος, προστιθέναι τι αὐτῇ εὔλυτον ἵνα ἀπὸ τοῦ εὐλύτου ἀφορμὴ λύσεως γένηται. . . . Παραπλέκων δέ τι εὔλυτον τῇ ἀλύτῳ ἀντιθέσει δόξεις παρέχεσθαι λύσιν τὴν ἀφορμὴν ἀπὸ τοῦ συμπλεκομένου εὐλύτου λαμβάνων ὡς Δημοσθένης ἐν τῷ πρὸς Λεπτίνην πεποίηκεν κτλ." Schol. D. 2. 22: "εἴωθεν ὁ Δημοσθένης ἔνθα ἂν ἀπορῇ λύσεως πρὸς ἀντίθεσιν, μὴ ψιλὴν αὐτὴν τιθέναι, ἀλλὰ κατ' ὀλίγον πλατύνειν, ἕως ἂν λάθῃ τοιοῦτόν τι προσθείς, ἐξ οὗ λήψεται τὴν ἀφορμὴν τῆς λύσεως." See Apsines, p. 272 H.; Volkmann, p. 252.

[21] See above, pp. 106–7.

[22] Anax. 29, p. 66. 3–15 H., and cf. 36, p. 87. 18–21 H.; Isoc. 6. 34–37; Arist. iii. 17. 4. 1417b36 (placing justice first and then expediency).

nocence,[23] and the exposition does contain every element recommended by Cicero for a defense in court.[24] But the main proposition of the letter will avoid the question of fact to ask, "If nothing is said about whether this patriot was rightly convicted, is it wise or expedient to let the sentence against his children stand?" In a court the use of such evasive devices which in effect asked the jurors to ignore the law would be a vulnerable target for the prosecutors.[25] In the Assembly, where the main consideration was not what was the existing law but what measure should be taken for the future, the maneuver of discussing Lycurgus' case in the light of his patriotism and under the heads of the *telika kephalaia* had a greater claim to legitimacy.

Now let us consider more closely the content of the two sections which set before the audience the patriotism of Lycurgus. The just purpose of the letter, Demosthenes begins (paragraphs 2–4), is for him to show his gratitude toward Lycurgus and to urge the same just gratitude on the People.[26] In language reminiscent of honorific decrees,[27] Demosthenes sketches Lycurgus' public career. In view of the Athenians' perennial suspicions of the venality of their politicians, the allusion to Lycurgus' indifference to financial reward in having chosen the unremunerative "patriotic" side in politics (paragraph 3) is as strong a proof of Lycurgus' innocence as could be given in the absence of direct evidence in the orator's hands of the falsity of Menesaechmus' charges.[28] Alexander's demand for Lycurgus' extradition in 335 serves as the conclusive demonstration that he had been fearlessly active in the People's interest (paragraph 4).

The second narrative section (paragraphs 5–10) is divided into two parts. In the first (paragraphs 5–7), Demosthenes asserts that his purpose in sending the letter was to serve the interests of the Athenians. He appeals for the attention even of personal enemies of Ly-

---

[23]Hermog. *Inv.* iii. 21, Vol. III, p. 121 Walz, p. 138 Rabe: "τάξιν δὲ οὐκ ἀεὶ τὴν αὐτὴν ἔχει, τί πρῶτον θετέον, ἔνστασιν ἢ ἀντιπαράστασιν, ἀλλὰ τὸ παραδοξότερον αὐτῶν καὶ βιαιότερον δεύτερον τάττεται."

[24] *De inv.* ii. 11. 35–36.

[25] See Lys. 12. 38 and D. 25. 76.

[26] Compare the topics of gratitude used here with those listed at Arist. *Rhet.* ii. 7. 2. 1385a17–21.

[27] See commentary to Ep. 3. 3, 4, 9.

[28] See below, rhetorical analysis of Ep. 2. 7.

curgus.[29] Lycurgus had won many enemies by his implacable treatment of political rivals and even petty malefactors.[30] Enemies, too, should be concerned now, when the Athenians, who so extravagantly honored Lycurgus for his probity, have incurred severe reproach by condemning him after his death and punishing his innocent children. Throughout the plea for the sons of Lycurgus, which extends to paragraph 36, Demosthenes refrains from naming any of Lycurgus' enemies, in conformity with the principle of the avoidance of abusiveness in *demegoriae*. He speaks only in general terms of the charge against Lycurgus as having arisen from "malice" and of the accusers as "resenting something."[31] If he allowed himself to cast direct personal discredit on the accusers, he might have added force to his plea by portraying the charges as the vengeance of Menesaechmus, a man who had been convicted on a charge of impiety brought by Lycurgus.[32] The Assembly in 323 knew all about Menesaechmus' grudge, so Demosthenes could easily omit Menesaechmus' name. But why should a later propagandist spare the enemy of both Lycurgus and Demosthenes? Why should a writer of literary fiction lose an opportunity for vividness? The author of the letters of Aeschines has no such inhibitions.[33]

In a forensic speech the place for the arguments based on Lycurgus' reputation would be the *confirmatio*, where their insufficiency would be manifest to the Athenians, who had already rejected them once at the trial and were in any case perenially suspicious of politicians. Demosthenes' skill takes these weak proofs and places them in the introductory narrative of a *demegoria* as the background for a picture of the present situation which shows the citizens in an unfavorable light. He makes them credible enough to shame his audience into giving anxious attention. Again he has recourse to the rhetorical

[29] Forestalling opposition by the rhetorical technique of *praemunitio;* see Anax. 18, pp. 51. 23–52. 11 H. (*prokatalêpsis*); Volkmann, pp. 494–95.

[30] *Vit. X orat.* 841e; Diod. xvi. 88; Dürrbach, *Lycurgue*, pp. xli–l.

[31] "Those who for personal reasons are ill disposed to Lycurgus" (par. 5) may be a neutral expression, since there Demosthenes tries to conciliate his audience, but he may be implying that his opponents act only from private resentment, not from patriotic motives. Other pejorative terms for the opposition are found at pars. 6, 10, 11, 12, 15, 20, 28, 33, and 34.

[32] See above, Chap. 5, n. 100.

[33] See the discussions of Ps.-Aesch. Epp. 12 and 7 below, end of rhetorical analyses of D. Epp. 2 and 4.

device of *fictio personarum*, presenting the rebukes not as his own point of view but as that of "all the Greeks."[34] In a further bid for the Athenians' good will, Demosthenes presents himself as one who resented the aspersions cast upon his city and had replied to them as best he could. In fact, he says, he will not hurt his fellow citizens' feelings by transmitting the reproaches in their full bitterness but will present them in only the barest outline.[35]

After all this careful preparation, Demosthenes is able to present, in the second part of this section (paragraphs 8–10), the supposed content of those reproaches, at the outset seeming still to place them in the mouths of others. The language of the criticisms echoes the accepted slogans of Athenian political life to make it look as if the Athenians had violated their own precepts. The orator presents the reproaches as if they arose from an effort of foreigners to comprehend the strange behavior of the Athenians toward Lycurgus and his family. In paragraphs 8–9 it is found that the Athenians' action cannot be the result of ignorant error but can only suggest base motives. The perceptive Athenians cannot be ignorant of the inconsistency of their attitudes toward Lycurgus alive and Lycurgus dead. The citizens, who in honorific decrees repeatedly proclaim how they maintain gratitude toward deceased benefactors by honoring their heirs, only disgrace themselves by maltreating Lycurgus' children.[36]

The "foreigners' reasoning" is pushed farther in paragraph 10: the Athenians' behavior cannot be ascribed to regard for the public advantage or the public honor. Cleverly the author excludes the shameful possibility that the Athenians are "sycophants" who raise money by unjustly mulcting a wealth family.[37] He flatters them temporarily: they are too virtuous to do so. Their high-mindedness leads them even to sacrifice the public revenues in order to ransom captives.[38]

[34] Cf. D. 8. 34–37, and see above, n. 14.

[35] This type of *praemunitio* (see above, n. 29), is common. Any exile seeking his own restoration at the hands of his countrymen would naturally try to show that while in exile he had as far as possible worked for their benefit. See Ep. 2. 18–19; Andoc. 2. 10, 16, and the discussion of Andoc. 2 and Ps.-Aesch. Ep. 12 below, end of rhetorical analysis of Ep. 2.

[36] See commentary to Ep. 3. 9 10.

[37] Cf. Isoc. Ep. 8. 3.

[38] The ransom of captives was regarded as one of the highest civic duties and having done so was a strong point in favor of a defendant in court (Arist. *Rhet.* ii.

This argument based on slogans allows Demosthenes to be so sure of his audience that he no longer needs to use the device of using someone else's mouth. He dares to assert in the first person (paragraph 10) that the reproaches are basically true: there is no creditable way to explain the Athenians' behavior toward Lycurgus and his family. The opposition has been thus made to uphold a refutable thesis.

The prooemium-narrative concludes in paragraph 10 with the proposition (*prothesis*), of which paragraphs 11–34 are the proof or *confirmatio* (*bebaiôsis*).[39] The proposition is presented as a reluctant denunciation of the audience: the citizen's behavior can only reflect a bitter and factious attitude against the friends of the People which is neither right nor expedient for the city. The propagandistic skill of the author shows itself in the negative nature of this proposition. Throughout paragraphs 1–34, Demosthenes *never* directly advocates that the Athenians take any action. He will not ask them to take any extraordinary step; rather, he will convict *them* of violating established precedents, of going counter to justice and expediency in maintaining in force a sentence which resulted from their misplaced credence in a malicious accusation. This rancorous and factious attitude toward the friends of the People will be shown to be the outward manifestation of a subversive conspiracy which the citizens have allowed to flourish. Paragraphs 1–34, in reality a "persuasive *demegoria*" (*logos protreptikos*), are given the appearance of a "dissuasive" one (*apotreptikos*). Thus, not Demosthenes and Lycurgus, but the Athenians are put on the defensive.[40]

Furthermore, the proposition is patently that of a *demegoria*, not at all that of a defense speech; so is the *confirmatio* which follows.[41]

---

23. 23. 1400*a*21–22; Navarre, pp. 292–93). High-mindedness (*megalopsychia*) was a very important consideration in political propaganda, mentioned with liberty itself at D. 23. 205, and proudly asserted by Demosthenes for the Athenians over the Macedonians at D. 19. 235. Cf. D. 20. 142; Epp. 1. 9, 2. 11.

[39] See Anax. 29 end, pp. 70. 25–71. 5; 32, p. 74. 4–7 H.; Arist. *Rhet.* iii. 13. 1–4. 1414*a*30–1414*b*12; Volkmann, pp. 167–75.

[40] Arist. *Rhet.* iii. 17. 14. 1418*b*9–12: "ἂν δὲ πολύχους ᾖ ἡ ἐναντίωσις, πρότερον τὰ ἐναντία οἷον ἐποίησε Καλλίστρατος ἐν τῇ Μεσσηνιακῇ ἐκκλησίᾳ· ἃ γὰρ ἐροῦσι προανελὼν οὕτως τότε αὐτὸς εἶπεν." Demosthenes left the clearly implied positive conclusions to be inferred from his negative argument.

[41] Compare Anax. 1, p. 13. 6–18 H. with 4, pp. 32. 18–33. 25 H. See also Arist. *Rhet.* i. 3. 1–6. 1358*a*36–1358*b*37 and above, pp. 106–7.

Demosthenes did not expect anyone to deny that Lycurgus was a patriot. His letter is not organized under the heads of the theory of the "status of the cause," but as a *demegoria* proceeds directly to the *telika kephalaia*. The order of the proposition is followed in the proof: first, the "right" (*orthon*), which includes as subdivisions the "just" (*dikaion*) and the "honorable" (*kalon*), in paragraphs 11–22; then the "expedient" (*sympheron*) in paragraphs 23–34.[42] To give the impression that the Athenians' present course is so wrong as to defy explanation, Demosthenes introduces each of the two divisions of the *confirmatio* with the figure of simulated astonishment.[43]

Wherever possible, the argument from justice was placed first.[44] Demosthenes seems to have avoided doing so. Instead of the word "justly" (*dikaiôs*), the proposition has the vaguer word "rightly" (*orthôs*).[45] Thereby the orator may have gained several advantages. As was proper in a *demegoria*, he could view the plight of Lycurgus' sons as a matter of the Athenian's injudicious measures more than as a case of unjust judgment, for the word "right" is the one for describing a decision on policy.[46] Through the vague word Demosthenes could subsume the "honorable," the "fair" (*ison*), and the "just" under one head. Finally, through it he could avoid premature introduction of the word "just." By its very definition, the "just" implied the "legal" (*nomimon*) and the "equal" or "fair" or "uniform" (*ison*) application of the law.[47] A direct attack on the enforcement of a sentence imposed by due process of law on the grounds that such enforcement is unjust would have struck the hearer as absurd.

Where the audience was convinced that the case of his opponents was just, a speaker had to begin with another of the *telika kephalaia*.[48] Demosthenes turns to the "honorable" (*kalon*), which he had already touched upon in his long prooemium.[49] The Athenians' course, he

[42] See Anax. 32, pp. 74. 24–75. 4 H. (quoted above, Chap. 7, n. 45), and 34, pp. 77. 22–78. 27 H.

[43] See Quint. ix. 2. 26.

[44] Anax. 32, p. 75. 4–5 H. See also above, n. 22.

[45] Demosthenes uses the two words as synonyms; e.g., D. 18. 13, 15, 97, 216, 298, 303, 322.

[46] D. 18. 97, *Prooem.* 18.

[47] See Aristotle's definition of what is commonly meant by the "just," *EN* v. 1. 7–8. 1129*a*26–1129*b*1.

[48] Anax. 34, p. 78. 18–19 H.

[49] The "honorable" and the "just" were easily interchangeable; see D. *Prooem.* 22. 1.

says, is the reverse of honorable. Nevertheless, he refuses to concede even tacitly that justice is not on his side. By paragraph 12 he is able to use the word "just." Rhetorical teaching had a device for such situations: if the opposing case, taken as a unity, seems invulnerable, divide it up into several aspects and refute them piecemeal.[50] Demosthenes divides justice into its several aspects and shows the case of his opponents to be unjust.

Even here, there was difficulty. Demosthenes could not deny that justice implies legality and had to postpone discussion of the touchy point of legality to paragraphs 23–28.[51] But he was able to attack the claim that the present treatment of the sons of Lycurgus was simply fair and equal application of the law. Other definitions of the "just" were current—no one could deny that the "just" or its corrective extension, the "equitable" (epieikes),[52] implied respect for "worth" (axia), too.[53] Accordingly, Demosthenes reasons e minore ad maiorem from the magnanimity of Philip, the barbarian, after Chaeroneia to show that the highly civilized Athenians cannot excuse their neglect of the worth of Lycurgus' family by appealing to the principle of "equal" justice, for in so doing they show a disgraceful ignorance of the difference between mere affairs of weights and measures and the high interests of human society (paragraphs 11–15).[54] As Anaximenes prescribes,[55] this phase of the argument ends in relevant sententious statements and in an iteration of Demosthenes' thesis: the city's present policy can result only in the ruin of its patriotic statesmen.[56]

[50] Quint. v. 13. 13; Volkmann, pp. 250–51.

[51] No such subterfuges are needed at Isoc. Ep. 8. 3–4 or in D. Ep. 2. In both cases the writer has only to note that others no more deserving have recently been released from the very same punishment.

[52] See Arist. Rhet. i. 13. 11–19. 1374a18–1374b23; EN v. 10.

[53] Apsines 11, pp. 294. 15–295. 2 H.: "τὸ δίκαιον διχόθεν συνίσταται ἢ ἀπὸ προσώπου ἢ ἀπὸ πράγματος. ἀπο μὲν προσώπου· δίκαιον βοηθεῖν, ἀστυγείτονες γάρ, εἰ οὕτω τύχοι, ἢ ὁμογενεῖς ἢ φίλοι ἢ εὐεργέται· . . . ἀπὸ δὲ πράγματος ὅτι ἴσον, ὅτι πρὸς τὴν ἀξίαν, ὅτι καὶ πᾶσι τοῖς τὰ δίκαια φρονήσασιν οὕτως ἔδοξεν." See Anax. 1, pp. 13. 23–14. 1 H.; Rhet. ad Herenn. iii. 3. 4.

[54] Cf. Isoc. Ep. 8. 4–6.

[55] 32, p. 75. 12–16 H.

[56] The same thesis, that the city's present policy brings ruin to its patriotic statesmen and eventually to the city itself, reappears at the end of important subdivisions of the argument, at pars. 15, 18, 28, and 34; the use of an iteration (palillogia) to close each section of a speech: Anax. 20, p. 56. 7–9 H. Since this thesis is the foundation of Demosthenes' plea for exoneration, these iterations are an example of the figure commoratio (Rhet. ad Herenn. iv. 45. 58).

Demosthenes knew how vulnerable was his attack, however in-genious, on the principle of the equal application of the law. Rhetori-cal teaching required that he forestall his opponents' attack with an "anticipation" (*prokatalêpsis*) of their arguments.[57] This he does in paragraphs 16–18, but in a manner which requires explanation if Ep. 3 is to be considered authentic. At first sight, the section seems to be a personal invective against Moerocles, as if Moerocles had joined the enemies of Lycurgus;[58] Taureas, Pataecus, and Aristogiton are named as examples of blackguardism. Yet Demosthenes in his *demegoriae* avoids attacking by name the citizens whose views he opposes.

There is a partial explanation in the fact that those orators who observed the rule against abusiveness in *demegoriae* did permit themselves to name in a derogatory manner men who had been publicly discredited.[59] We know nothing of Taureas and Pataecus,[60] but Aristogiton's reputation was so bad[61] that Demosthenes might well have written of him as he does here and at paragraphs 37–43. Aristogiton did command a following,[62] but speeches from orators of diverse political tendencies concur in taking his bad reputation for granted.[63] Moerocles, too, may have had something of this sort of reputation.[64] Even so, Moerocles had been outstanding in Athens for his opposition to Alexander,[65] and Plutarch places him on a level with Demosthenes, Polyeuctus, and Hyperides.[66] Would Demosthe-nes mention Moerocles in the same breath as Aristogiton, the dangerous enemy of anti-Macedonian politicians after Chaeroneia?[67]

[57] Anax. 33.

[58] See Treves, *Athenaeum*, n.s., XIV, 242, 247; Neupert, pp. 22–23; Blass, III, 1, 445.

[59] Above, p. 115.

[60] See commentary to Ep. 3. 16.

[61] D. 25 and 26; Din. 2, 3. 12; Plut. *Phoc.* 10. 2.

[62] His influence in the Assembly: D. 25. 42, 64; ability to flout the law: D. 25. 4–12, 27; 26. 8, etc.; Din. 2. 12–14, 19; ability to threaten enemies with prosecu-tion: D. 25. 36–39, etc. Aristogiton, furthermore, was acquitted in the Harpalus trials.

[63] D. 25. 25, 26. 7; Din. 2. 15; Plut. *Phoc.* 10. 2.

[64] Arist. *Rhet.* iii. 10. 7. 1411a15–18; D. 19. 293; the fragment of Timocles' *Delos*, quoted above, Chap. 5, n. 57.

[65] See commentary to Ep. 3. 31–32.

[66] *Dem.* 13. 4; cf. Harpocration *s.v. Moiroklês*.

[67] Above, Chap. 5, n. 94.

If Moerocles had become a turncoat, why does the author not attack him for it explicitly, as he attacks Pytheas in paragraphs 29–30? The answer is that this passage is not a personal attack. Like Pytheas later, here Taureas, Pataecus, and Aristogiton are mentioned in an uncomplimentary manner not in order to accuse them but in order to show the Athenians their past errors, a procedure which was permitted in *demegoriae*.[68] The lenient treatment accorded these scoundrels makes a travesty of the claim that the punishment of Lycurgus' sons represented only the equal application of the law. As for Moerocles, Demosthenes does not really treat him here as one of his principal opponents. In the imprisonment of the children of Lycurgus, that politician surely played only the passive role of an administrative functionary.[69] It is barely possible that the mention of "blackguardism and shamelessness and deliberate wickedness" in paragraph 18 is not meant to refer to him but only to the other three. In that case, Moerocles may be mentioned to represent those citizens of unquestioned patriotism who have made the mistake of acquiescing in the punishment of Lycurgus' sons. Whatever the attitude toward Moerocles at this time, Demosthenes makes use of his name for a device found three times in the *demegoriae* of the Demosthenic corpus and described by Anaximenes. The other examples are the treatment of Theramenes in Ep. 4 and of Aristomedes at D. 10. 70–75.[70]

In these three cases Demosthenes attacks politicians with vulnerable reputations[71] who were certainly not his leading opponents; his important opponents were less vulnerable. In every case Demosthenes takes advantage of the fact that men of this stripe were numbered among his opponents. Moerocles was indeed one of the magistrates in charge of the imprisonment of Lycurgus' sons; Aristo-

---

[68] See above, p. 115.

[69] See above, Chap. 5, n. 101, and commentary to Ep. 3. 16–18.

[70] The authenticity of that speech, the *Fourth Philippic*, has been established once and for all by A. Körte's penetrating study, "Zu Didymos' Demosthenes-Commentar," *Rh. Mus.*, LX (1905), 388–410. Later writers have accepted Körte's proof of authenticity but have disputed both his espousal of Wilamowitz's theory that the speech was written not to be delivered but as a propaganda brochure and his analysis of its relationship to D. 8. See Jaeger, p. 258, n. 16; C. D. Adams, *CP*, XXXIII, 129–144; R. Sealey, *REG*, LXVIII, 104–10; S. G. Daitz, *CP*, LII, 145–62.

[71] Aristomedes: Körte, *Rh. Mus.*, LX, 398–401. Theramenes is known only from D. Ep. 4.

medes did oppose Demosthenes' recommendations; Theramenes did spread the stock calumny of Demosthenes' being a jinx. In treating these men as if they were the proponents of the views which he wished to refute, Demosthenes immediately discredits those views by association. For in each example, the history of the man himself contradicts what he advocates. Aristomedes, the reckless politician, nevertheless recommends to the city a policy of quiet passivity; Theramenes, whose life is the accursed one of an uncultured, un-filial, unrestrained pervert, dares to call Demosthenes a jinx and Athens unlucky; Moerocles, who even now benefits from laxity in the enforcement of the law,[72] advocates its rigorous application.

Anaximenes is unique[73] in classifying an orator's attempt to show a contradiction between what a man advocates and his mode of life under a separate species of oratory, the "oratory of exposure" (*exetastikon*).[74] An "exposé" may be an independent speech, but more usually it will be part of a composition belonging to another species of oratory;[75] exposés are especially useful for replying to an opponent's arguments.[76] Use of an exposé is inherently invidious; one must always present a good excuse for it.[77] Demosthenes by this point has long since taken care to secure the attention and good will of his audience; no more excuse is needed. Anaximenes recommends proceeding "not in a bitter but in a gentle spirit";[78] Demosthenes conforms by pretending that he could find no alternative to his bitter conclusion (paragraph 18).[79] In D. 10. 70–75 and in Ep. 4 Demosthenes carefully apologizes for the bitterness. Hence the three "exposés" were not considered abusive by a fourth-century audience and the rhetorical teaching of the time gave directions for including such passages in *demegoriae*.

---

[72] See commentary to Ep. 3. 16–18.

[73] Brzoska, "Anaximenes 3," *RE*, I (1894), 2088.

[74] I derive my renditions, "of exposure" and "exposé," from the definition at Anax. 5, p. 34. 1–6 H.: ". . . ἡ ἐξέτασίς ἐστι προαιρέσεων ἢ πράξεων ἢ λόγων πρὸς ἄλληλα ἢ πρὸς τὸν ἄλλον βίον ἐναντιουμένων ἐμφάνισις. δεῖ δὲ τὸν ἐξετάζοντα ζητεῖν, εἴ που ἢ ὁ λόγος, ὃν ἐξετάζει, ἢ αἱ πράξεις τοῦ ἐξεταζομένου ἢ αἱ προαιρέσεις ἐναντιοῦνται ἀλλήλαις."

[75] An exposé in a forensic apology: D. 18. 256–314. Note the use of the verb *exetazein* at D. 18. 256 and at Ep. 4. 10.

[76] Anax. 37, p. 97. 18–20 H.

[77] *Ibid.*, pp. 97. 24–98. 2 H.

[78] *Ibid.*, pp. 98. 21–99. 1 H.

[79] See below, n. 116.

An iteration of the main thesis once more drives home to the Athenians the message which Demosthenes wishes to set before them and brings this section of "anticipation" to a close.[80]

By now, the orator can write freely of justice. As he exposed to the Athenians their errors of commission in having destroyed the good name of Lycurgus and in having punished his children, so now he reveals their equally disgraceful errors of omission in failing to accord the late patriot and his descendants the privileges which have always been the just portion of public benefactors in Athens (paragraphs 19–22). The audience would have known very well that a respected politician could at the end of his career be discovered to have been an embezzler who deserved the hatred and contempt of the public. Hence Demosthenes does not even try to prove that the Athenians have unjustly failed to continue to honor Lycurgus himself after his death but passes over the delicate point as something to be taken for granted (paragraph 19).[81] Lycurgus' sons, however, unquestionably were the innocent descendants of a man who had done the city great service. Demosthenes proceeds to cite the many precedents for rewarding such descendants with privileges (paragraphs 19–20).[82] And yet, though Lycurgus' services were recent, the Athenians do not show his sons the mercy they would show to persons who had no claim to worth, but allow them to become the victims of unreasonable revenge (paragraphs 21–22). As Anaximenes recommends, the concluding portion of this section on the honorable and the just becomes an appeal for pity.[83] Demosthenes, however, maintains his pose of showing the Athenians that their present course is wrong. Even the pity for Lycurgus' sons is not asked for directly.

From the honorable and the just, Demosthenes turns to the expedient,[84] introducing this topic, too, with the figure of simulated astonishment, He will attempt to prove that the People's present course, far from being expedient, results from their blindness to a dangerous conspiracy against patriotic politicians; his own plight will be a pertinent example (paragraphs 23–34). Thus for the first

[80] See Anax. 33, p. 76. 21–22 H.; above, n. 56.

[81] See Anax. 36, p. 92. 4–6 H.; *Rhet. ad Herenn.* iv. 27. 37; Blass, III 1, 180–82.

[82] On the ineptness which scholars have found in these precedents, see commentary.

[83] Anax. 34.

[84] Anax. 32, p. 75. 21–25 H.; 34, p. 78. 7–14 H.

time he can inject a reference to his own case. Moreover, hitherto he has been unable to handle the topic of the "lawful." Yet he had to deal with it. His opponents were insisting that to set aside the duly imposed sentence against Lycurgus' sons would be to subvert the constitution.[85] In Athenian political rhetoric, legality could be treated as a topic separate from justice;[86] indeed, since law and justice were always understood to aim at the public interest (*sympheron*), legality could be brought under the head of the "expedient" (*sympheron*). Against his opponents' valid point of law, Demosthenes used the stock device of an appeal to the unwritten principles underlying the written laws and to expediency (paragraphs 23–38).[87]

By misconstruing the argument here, Neupert[88] found it too inept for Demosthenes. So it would be, if the author had presented Laches as an example of the prosperity of traitors[89] in contrast to the adversity of patriots, for then why should the writer cite the good fortune of the virtuous Mnesibulus in the same breath? However, the author here instead is presenting two precedents to prove that it can be both legal and expedient for the People to set aside a duly imposed sentence. He does not oppose the estimable Mnesibulus to the "traitor" Laches. Indeed, he describes both as "honest" (*chrêston*) men.[90] Laches is presented only as a citizen who has enjoyed the benefit of friendly ties with a foreign power. The example to prove that *traitors* fare better than patriots is Pytheas (paragraphs 29–30). The circumlocutions here used for "Alexander" are not forms of *heteros*, which might connote opposition to the Athenians,[91] but the

---

[85] See commentary to Ep. 3. 25; above, n. 6, and Chap. 5, n. 110.

[86] Anax. 2, p. 23. 15–26 H.; Arist. *EN* v. 1. 13. 1129*b*14–19.

[87] Anax. 36, pp. 89. 22–90. 8 H.: *"ἂν δ' ἡμῖν συμβαίνῃ τὸ παρὰ μοχθηροὺς δοκοῦντας εἶναι νόμους* [reading with E G Sp] *τὸ πρᾶγμα πεπρᾶχθαι, ῥητέον ὡς οὐ νόμος, ἀλλ' ἀνομία τὸ τοιοῦτόν ἐστιν· ὁ μὲν γὰρ νόμος ἐπὶ τῷ ὠφελεῖν τίθεται, οὗτος δὲ βλάπτει τὴν πόλιν. ῥητέον δὲ καὶ ὡς οὐ παρανομήσουσιν, ἂν τούτῳ τῷ νόμῳ ἐναντίαν ψῆφον θῶνται, ἀλλὰ νομο-θετήσουσιν, ὥστε μὴ χρῆσθαι δόγμασι πονηροῖς καὶ παρανόμοις. δεῖ δὲ καὶ τοῦτο συμβιβάζειν, ὡς οὐδεὶς νόμος κωλύει τὸ κοινὸν εὖ ποιεῖν, τοὺς δὲ φαύλους νόμους ἀκύρους ποιεῖν εὐεργετεῖν τὴν πόλιν ἐστίν."* See also Arist. *Rhet.* i. 13. 17–18. 1374*b*10–18 and 15. 4–7. 1375*a*27–1375*b*5.

[88] P. 36.

[89] Cf. par. 22, "those by whom you were wronged."

[90] Fourth-century rhetoric demanded as far as possible the use of reputable examples (Speusippus *Epp. Socrat.* 30. 10: *"καί φησι ... προσήκειν οἰκεῖα καὶ γνώριμα τὰ παραδείγματα φέρειν"*).

[91] See the forms of *heteros* as used at par. 10 and at Ep. 2. 13, 17, 20, 21; Ep. 1. 10; D. 18. 323; and D. 18. 320 with the commentary of Blass, *Demosthenes: Rede vom Kranze.*

neutral expressions *allēn* and *exōthen*. The word *heterous* enters only at paragraph 27, probably to express the dangerous potentialities for the *future:* if now it is safer to have "neutral" foreigners (*allous*) on one's side, eventually people will seek the friendship of foreigners who are opposed to the city (*heterous*). As usual after the fall of Thebes, Demosthenes here expresses no hostility toward Alexander.[92] Both Laches and Mnesibulus are honest men, but both are inferior to Lycurgus. Mnesibulus preferred to remain an unknown and avoid the risks of patriotic political activity,[93] and Laches did not place his sole reliance on the good will of the Athenian People. The conclusion follows logically: it is disgracefully contrary to the city's interest that the sentences of these men should be set aside while the sons of Lycurgus suffer the full rigor of the law (paragraphs 27–28). At this point the author feels able to assert that the claims of *justice* require the exoneration of a man like Lycurgus.

Throughout paragraphs 23–25, Demosthenes when speaking of being convicted by the courts uses euphemisms which put the blame on Fortune.[94] The repeated punning on *sympherein* and *symphora* which runs through paragraphs 23–28 is a rhetorical embellishment used elsewhere with great effect by Demosthenes.[95]

The precedents of Laches and Mnesibulus sufficed to dispose of the legal objections to the release of the sons of Lycurgus. For the larger theme of paragraphs 23–34, that the Athenians had been acting against their own interests, those precedents afforded only an argument that in the future men will prefer to pay court to opponents of the city rather than be known for serving the People. In the iteration of his main thesis at the end of the section on the "lawful," Demosthenes suggests that the Athenians' *present* conduct reflects a situation that is "disastrous for the entire city."[96] In paragraphs 29–34, Demosthenes tries to prove this. The case of Pytheas had no bearing on the legal problems, but it was so important for demonstrating the the Athenians' disastrous neglect of their own interests that the

[92] See above, pp. 80–81, 86–88.

[93] Cf. Th. ii. 40. 2. See also commentary to par. 26, σωφροσύνη.

[94] Anax. 36, pp. 92–93 H.: ["If the weakness of our legal position does not permit us to defend ourselves by appeal to legal considerations,] εἰς ἁμάρτημα ἢ ἀτύχημα καταφεύγοντας . . . συγγνώμης τυγχάνειν πειρατέον." See also Arist. *Rhet.* i. 13. 16. 1374*b*4–9.

[95] Blass, III 1, 162–65.

[96] On the *commoratio*, see above, n. 56.

orator "will not omit to mention it." Seen against the background of the ruin or death of one patriotic politician after another, the example of Pytheas proved that it was safer and more profitable to be a traitor than a patriot (paragraphs 29–31).

The uncomplimentary portrayal of Pytheas is no violation of the the rule against abuse in *demegoriae*. The unsavory reputation of Pytheas is well attested.[97] The letters throughout assume an audience hostile to the Macedonian hegemony though temporarily resigned to it. In the months before the outbreak of the Lamian war, Pytheas' new political stance, in so far as it looked to be one of active support of Macedonian interests, would further discredit him, as would his recent conviction in court. Although Pytheas had been one of the prosecutors of Demosthenes, he was surely not one of the orator's principal antagonists so as not to be mentioned by name. Indeed, the discussion of Pytheas is not primarily an attack on him, but an example to prove that the Athenians treat traitors better than patriots.[98]

At this point Demosthenes feels it possible to bring in his own example as a matter of public interest. The prosperity of Pytheas and the harsh fate of Demosthenes, Philocles, and other leading patriots threaten to deprive Athens of true patriots and encourage false ones to show their real colors (paragraphs 32–33). The citizens must awaken to the dangers of the present situation and stop yielding to the cruelty and spite of factious individuals. "Rancor" and "ill will" throughout have been Demosthenes' abstract designations for Lycurgus' enemies.[99] Here in paragraph 33, after the list of suffering patriots, Demosthenes' use of "rancor" invites the audience to think not only of Menesaechmus but of Hyperides also. Perhaps the orator, seeking a reconciliation with Hyperides, went on in paragraph 34 to mitigate this implicit attack on him by making the epithets inappropriate to Hyperides. Menesaechmus obviously was "indulging his rancor," perhaps even "selling his services to the People's enemies"; this description may not have suggested Hyperides to an Athenian audience in 323. If so, from paragraph 34 on, Hyperides is counted among the misguided loyal citizens who have heedlessly allowed patriots to be brought to ruin.[100]

[97] See commentary to pars. 29–30.
[98] Cf. D. *Prooem.* 20. 3.
[99] See above, n. 31.
[100] See also commentary to Ep. 3. 25.

The standard bugaboo to frighten the Athenian People was the threat of oligarchic revolution. The frequent use of it made it vulnerable to ridicule (*diasyrmos*).[101] Even in the troubled conditions of 323, Demosthenes takes care to avoid the possibility. At the beginning of paragraph 34 he seems to avoid the melodramatic term "revolution" (*nea pragmata*) and speaks only vaguely of the dangerous "circumstances" (*pragmata*). He then proceeds explicitly to anticipate the ridicule. Both he and his audience probably expected it to come from Hyperides, who was famous for *diasyrmos*.[102] If so, again Demosthenes ascribes an objection to one who can ill afford to make it. Hyperides, too, was identified with the "imperiled anti-Macedonian patriots" and may have narrowly escaped being implicated in the Harpalus scandal.[103] No sensible person, writes Demosthenes, could fail to view the present situation with alarm; the present symptoms are the same as those which preceded the revolutions of the Four Hundred and the Thirty, when the People were set at variance with their true spokesmen by the planted agents of foreign and oligarchic intrigue.[104]

The remainder of the letter (paragraphs 35-45) constitutes the epilogue. In a departure from the usual, Demosthenes turns the epilogue, which normally would be a plea for mercy (*commiseratio*, *eleou eisbolê*) for the sons of Lycurgus,[105] into a plea for himself. In this A. Schaefer saw a mark of inauthenticity,[106] but Neupert recognized the carefully executed transition, not unworthy of Demosthenes. In paragraphs 32-34 the orator had brought in his own example as an instance of the general ruin of Athenian patriots, and now the somewhat anomalous epilogue is introduced with well-formulated excuses (paragraphs 35-36).[107] The author in paragraphs 16-18 has even prepared the way for the use of the example of Aristogiton.

Demosthenes was doing nothing new in turning the epilogue of a plea for others into propaganda for himself. Isocrates did the same

---

[101] See commentary to Ep. 2. 2.

[102] See commentary to Ep. 3. 34, εἰ ... διασύρει.

[103] Above, Chap. 5, nn. 33, 57.

[104] See above, n. 56 (*commoratio*).

[105] Anax. 34; Arist. *Rhet.* iii. 19. 1-3. 1419b10-28; Volkmann, p. 295.

[106] *NJb*, CXV, 163; see Blass, *NJb*, CXV, 543.

[107] Neupert, p. 37; Sachensenweger, pp. 51-52.

in his Ep. 8,[108] written ostensibly to prove to the archons of Mytilene that is was both just and expedient to end the banishment of Agenor, the music teacher of the children of Isocrates' adopted son. At the outset Isocrates recognizes the awkwardness of presenting a petition to persons with whom he was unacquainted and with whom he had no influence (paragraph 1). He returns to deal with the situation in the epilogue: "Someone may say that those who bring petitions should not only praise what they wish granted, but show that they have a just claim to receive it" (paragraph 7). Isocrates proceeds to describe how, though leading a retired life, he deserves a favorable reception because of the great contributions of his writings and of his pupils to Panhellenic causes (paragraphs 8–9). By granting his request, the Mytilenaeans will be vindicating his chosen way of life. Isocrates uses almost half the letter in thus advertising himself.

Even more than Isocrates, Demosthenes as a convicted criminal was writing as a person of no influence. Even in a simple appeal for the children of Lycurgus with no plea for himself, he probably would have had to include a defense of the petitioner. Isocrates wrote his Ep. 8 to help Agenor but published it to advertise himself. Demosthenes had to be more devious; the main purpose of writing and publishing the letter was Demosthenes' restoration, and paragraphs 1–34 are a subtle introduction leading the audience to the orator's own plea in the epilogue.

In most respects, paragraphs 35–45 conform to the description of the epilogue in Anaximenes and Aristotle. Anaximenes does not give a detailed account of the epilogue in his discussion of this type of *demegoria* but says that his full description of the forensic epilogue also applies to *demegoriae*.[109] Beyond summarizing the speech for the audience, according to Anaximenes the speaker in the epilogue ought to dispose them to be favorable to himself and unfavorable to his opponents.[110] Aristotle assigned four functions to the forensic epilogue: (1) to make the audience well disposed toward oneself and ill disposed toward the opposition, (2) to amplify or minimize, (3) to excite the audience's emotions, and (4) to refresh their memory of

---

[108] See above, n. 5.
[109] Anax. 34, pp. 76. 25–77. 21 and 78. 27–79. 18 H.
[110] Anax. 36, p. 95. 11–21 H.

what has been said.[111] All four functions are served by Ep. 3. 35 -45.

A simple recapitulation (paragraph 35) ends the plea for Lycurgus and his sons; for their case there is no further need to amplify or minimize or excite emotions. Hence the orator summarizes the heads of the argument, first the two main divisions, the honorable and the expedient; then the just. There remains the function of rendering the audience well disposed to the speaker and ill disposed toward his opponents. His plea for Lycurgus and for the good name of Athens enables Demosthenes to pose as a fine gentleman who will rebuke the Athenians to save his friends and the city's reputation, caring as much for those good purposes as for his own exoneration. These considerations give him but a feeble claim on the audience's sympathy.[112] Nevertheless, the orator has put his audience on the defensive and means to keep them there. At this point his opponents are certain to attack his subterfuge of using a plea for Lycurgus' sons as a foundation for one for himself. Demosthenes anticipates them and makes the point himself, using it to present himself as a patriotic gentleman and to direct his audience's attention and pity to his own plight (paragraph 36).[113] Thus the orator makes the difficult transition to his own case without losing the offensive. "Enough of this," he writes, and turns to press his own interests.

The first of Aristotle's functions of the epilogue has still been only half fulfilled; Demosthenes has yet to render his audience unfavorably disposed toward his opponents. With good reason, for the audience themselves, the Athenians who refused to grant the plea of the earliest letter, were his opponents. Now he must rebuke them undisguisedly in his own interest.[114] Such was the situation giving rise to the "harshness" (*trachytês*) which Hermogenes found in Demosthenes' reproach of the Athenians for condemning him while acquitting Aristogiton. Hermogenes notes that the "harshness" at paragraph 37, as usual in Demosthenes, is mitigated by simulated

---

[111] *Rhet.* iii. 19. 1. 1419b10–13; see *Rhet. ad Herenn.* ii. 30. 47–31. 50, iii. 5. 9 end. Aristotle opposes both his predecessors and common practice in wishing to exclude the epilogue from the *demegoria qua demegoria* and even from some forensic speeches (*Rhet.* iii. 13. 3. 1414a36-1414b6).

[112] Andocides in *De Reditu* could present himself as the bringer of a convoy of food.

[113] See Anax. 36, p. 87. 7–10 H.

[114] See Apsines 2, p. 226. 4–14 H.; Navarre, pp. 221–22.

hesitation (*diaporêsis*).[115] But the reproach at paragraph 42 is formulated with unmitigated harshness, a phenomenon so rare in the Demosthenic corpus that Hermogenes prides himself on having collected all four examples.[116] The harsh passages here, however, are not to be taken in isolation from their context. Aside from preparing the way for them throughout the letter, Demosthenes has carefully introduced them at the beginning of paragraph 37 in a manner which at once mitigates the bitterness and maintains the offensive. For he writes that the reproach is being given "in a spirit of loyalty and friendship," as a "brief outline" of his grievances as long as he does not receive justice.[117]

Once again Demosthenes returns to a favorite theme. By acquitting Aristogiton of the same charge for which Demosthenes was driven into exile, the Athenians have again granted leniency to unscrupulous blackguards and denied it to a patriot (paragraph 38). In a bid for pity, the orator presents the content of his earlier letter: it was a very moderate request, to be allowed to fulfil in safety the obligations imposed upon him. He interrupts the sequence of reproaches to flatter the Athenians briefly for their traditional virtues,[118] only to remind them immediately that the "reasonable" request of a public benefactor has been rejected and that his humiliation is also their disgrace (paragraph 39).

To Demosthenes' pose of being a law-abiding citizen there was the obvious reply that he himself had made the decision to break the law by fleeing from prison into exile. As before, Demosthenes in paragraphs 39–41 forestalls the objection by making the point himself. He quotes the expected reply and turns it at once into a reproach of the Athenians for their callousness and into an opportunity again to speak of himself as a wronged public benefactor reduced to pitiable straits. His reference to his having been ruined financially because

---

[115] Ps.-Aristides *Rh.* i. 47 Schmid, Vol. IX, pp. 360–61 Walz, quotes "ὦ (τί . . .) λίαν ὀλίγωροι" of Ep. 3. 37 as an example of the "graveness" of rhetorical hesitation in a bitter complaint. See also *Rhet. ad Herenn.* iv. 29. 40, Quint. ix. 3. 88.

[116] Hermog. *Id.* i. 7, Vol. III, pp. 233–35 Walz; the other examples: Ps.-D. 7. 45; D. 3. 31, 10. 6. Ps.-Aristides *Rh.* i. 45 Schmid, Vol. IX, p. 360 Walz, uses Ep. 3. 42 as an example of the "graveness" which arises when one directs against his audience a reproach that is difficult to bear and then "sets it right" by saying that one can say nothing milder.

[117] See *Rhet. ad Herenn.* iv. 36. 48–37. 49 (on *licentia*).

[118] See *ibid.*, 37. 49.

he went surety for others reflects a favorite way of bidding for the sympathy of an Athenian audience.[119] The claim, that though in dire straits he would direct his plea to no one but the Athenians, is another commonplace, much used by Demosthenes.[120] The orator adds yet another commonplace for stirring pity: the Athenians will come to recognize how outrageously he has suffered, but only after he has perished through their inaction.[121]

Both he and the Athenians would lose by their tardy change of heart, he says. The Athenians would lose the money he could raise to pay his fine (paragraph 41 end), and he would lose the vindication due an innocent man (paragraphs 42–43). Demosthenes' enemies had countered his claims to have his sole refuge in the People by accusing him of residing in the Piraeus and even offshore and of keeping his capital liquid the better to be able to flee the wrath of his fellow citizens.[122] There may be some irony here when Demosthenes infers from the People's treatment of him that they do not believe his enemies. They think his only resources are his tangible property; since it would not cover his fine, they imprisoned him. He has more, however: the afore-mentioned claims on the men he had so virtuously helped. He now relinquishes title to his tangible property[123] and closes with an iteration of his request for temporary immunity to enable him to collect these funds and pay his fine.

Demosthenes turns to discuss his innocence (paragraphs 42–43). He repeats his objection that the accusations had never been proved.[124] Now he can add that the acquittal of Aristogiton has discredited the whole series of reports and put to shame those who condemned him. The thoughtless Athenians have increased his misfortune by leaving him to compare himself as a condemned criminal with the notorious Aristogiton who has won exoneration, a humiliating prospect.[125]

The orator has caught the offensive and held it, but he could not afford to leave his audience with that impression. On reflection they

[119] See Antiphon, *Tetral.* I 2. 12; D. 25. 86; Navarre, p. 292.

[120] Anax. 34, p. 77. 13–16 H.; *Rhet. ad. Herenn.* i. 5. 8; Din. 1. 102; Aesch. 3. 209; cf. D. Ep. 2. 21–23.

[121] Arist. *Rhet.* ii. 8. 11. 1386a13–16.

[122] Aesch. 3. 209; Din. 1. 69–71; Hyp. *Dem.* 17; see Anax. 34 end.

[123] See commentary to Ep. 3. 41.

[124] See commentary to Ep. 2. 1.

[125] See Din. 3. 12.

could only come to resent his attack on them. Hence he explains away his bitterly reasoned indignation as a relief of the emotions of a wronged person, similar to the groanings of one in pain (paragraph 44). He is not really angry at the Athenians; his loyalty to them remains undiminished in accordance with his resolve to behave with filial reverence toward the People. As in paragraphs 1 and 41, he solemnly declares that he willingly places his fate in their hands—a most efficacious means of stirring pity.[126] In this manner, without retracting a single one of his reproaches, he manages to leave the impression of being a loyal citizen who respects the people. Demosthenes usually ended his *demegoriae* on the calmest and most dignified note possible.[127] The letter conforms to the pattern, ending with the noble sentiment that Demosthenes, with all fair-minded persons, views his "filial submission" to the People as an honorable victory.

From the foregoing analysis it is easy to see that Ep. 3 is a real *demegoria*, not a forensic apology transferred to the Assembly. The only part of the letter which might indicate otherwise is the introductory narrative defense of Lycurgus in paragraphs 2–8. But we have seen that this defense is introduced at least as much to place the opposition in the indefensible position of upholding a policy of hostility to patriotic politicians as to show that Lycurgus is worthy of acquittal. If we are correct in saying that a forger's interest would be primarily apologetic, this passage hardly serves that purpose, for even a late author like Pseudo-Plutarch did not lack the facts to write a detailed apology for Lycurgus. Yet so little is it the intention of the author to write such an apology that Schaefer remarks[128] he can find more information on the career of Lycurgus in the one fragment of Hyperides than in all the paragraphs of Ep. 3. Demosthenes is interested in Lycurgus as a fellow patriot, not in the details of his achievements as financial administrator. And still less, in fact nothing, is mentioned of the actual charge against him. Moreover, the facts mentioned about Lycurgus in this introductory narrative are taken for granted. They do not become the issue of the *confirmatio*. In a *demegoria* which otherwise shows clearly that it is aimed at a particular situation, such narrative is only what is to be expected in

---

[126] *Rhet. ad Herenn.* iv. 29. 39; cf. Ep. 2. 21–22.

[127] Blass, III 1, 217.

[128] *NJb*, CXV, 163.

order that the audience be "reminded" before hearing the main argument.[129]

We have noted[130] that the topics for the main argument are the heads of the *telika kephalaia*, not those of the issues of the forensic speech. Moreover, Aristotle's generalization, that a *demegoria* concerns itself primarily with the future applies to Ep. 3. The entire main argument is taken up with proving not that certain actions have been done in the past but that the known course of events points to the existence of a developing conspiracy against patriotic politicians which menaces the future survival of the city's democratic institutions, with the implication that preventive measures must be taken. The argument of the epilogue where Demosthenes deals with his own case is also not concerned with proving assertions about the past, but with securing his future return.

Again, Ep. 3 bears out Aristotle's generalization that the most appropriate type of argument for *demegoriae* is from examples.[131] Each one of the sections of the *confirmatio* is built around an example; paragraphs 11–15, around Philip; 16–18, around Moerocles and the others; 19–22, around the descendants of Aristides, Thrasybulus, and Archinus; 23–28, around Laches and Mnesibulus; 29–35, around the successful turncoat Pytheas and the unfortunate patriots.

The invective, which might be an indication against authenticity, has been shown in every case not to go beyond the limits which Demosthenes seems to have set for himself in his *demegoriae*. The failure to attack leading opponents like Menesaechmus by name appears to be a striking forebearance to use a favorite device of self-apology, that of counterattack. Throughout, the letter shows a concern to dominate but not to antagonize the sensibilities of an audience in Athens in 323.

Thus, within the structure of a *demegoria*, the writer (1) uses an appeal for the sons of Lycurgus subtly to call attention to the possibility of setting aside "unjust" sentences, (2) builds the vicissitudes of Lycurgus, Pytheas, Philocles, Charidemus, and himself into proof of the existence of a dangerous conspiracy against patriotic politicians, and (3) uses the circumstance of Aristogiton's acquittal to

[129] Above, pp. 103–7.
[130] Above, rhetorical analysis of pars. 10–11.
[131] *Rhet.* i. 9. 40. 1368a29–33; iii. 17. 5. 1418a1–5.

evoke sympathy and create the impression of his own innocence—all this in a skillful effort to make a hostile public listen to rebuke and to an attempt to refute the credible charges of his opponents. One may say that this tortuous construction was not beyond the ability of an imitator. But the not altogether inept author of the letters of Aeschines made no attempt to fabricate a real counterpart. All that he does in his Ep. 3 is to have Aeschines cast an implicit reproach on Demosthenes' bitter indignation by proclaiming that unlike others he is himself properly reconciled to his exile. The content of this spurious letter could not have been of the slightest interest to the Council and the People, and unlike Demosthenes the author makes not the slightest effort to explain why he should receive a hearing. The devious argument of Demosthenes reflects closely the difficult political situation against which it was composed. The three bland paragraphs fabricated in the name of Aeschines reflect no definite political situation whatever.

Rhetorical analysis thus reveals that D. Ep. 3 is a creative adaptation of the form of the *demegoria* as practiced in fourth-century Athens and suggests that the author could be none other than Demosthenes.

Since the situation which Demosthenes faced markedly improved by the time he sent his promised "long letter," it is not surprising that the argument of Ep. 2 is far simpler. His case was now manageable enough for him to write a relatively straightforward composition which bears considerable resemblance to the ordinary forensic-epideictic genre of self-apology, doubtless repeating much of the defense which he had given at his trial.

The exoneration of the other defendants and the removal of the sentence against the sons of Lycurgus meant that the orator could no longer pretend to be warning the People against an "oligarchical conspiracy," but their continued hostility toward him alone could be depicted as anomalous. Philocles had been, if anything, more heavily compromised than Demosthenes. By exonerating Philocles, the People implied that Demosthenes, too, could have been guilty only of "moderate indiscretions," not of crimes. Unquestionably, Demosthenes had been indiscreet. The recommended course for one who had undeniably done things open to criticism was to admit them and convince the judges to forgive him.[132] However, at Ep. 3. 42 Demosthenes could not admit his mistakes; he had to proclaim his innocence of what his accusers presented as heinous crimes. In Ep. 2. 1-2 he can use a stock prooemium formula to assume immediately the indignant tone (*barytês*) of one who had been wronged, even while cautiously admitting his indiscretions.[133] His great contributions should far outweigh them.[134] To dispel the remaining prejudice arising from the court's verdict against him, Demosthenes turns, just as Anaximenes recommends,[135] to explain the verdict away as being based on illegal procedure and due to a now-frustrated political conspiracy. His flight from prison, which might have looked like rebellion or tacit confession of guilt, he excuses as sorrowful resignation. What could he do, when the People were blind to a pernicious conspiracy? The subject cannot be so easily dismissed, and Demosthenes will have to discuss it further in paragraphs 17-20. Nevertheless, here he can bid for the audience's good will by flattering them; the People did not acquiesce for long in the face of the plot. The orator still must tread carefully and avoid the odium of an attack on a decision of the People and the Areopagus.[136] He gives no precise designation of the "conspirators"; not the entire Areopagus, but only "certain members" of it were at fault.[137]

In paragraphs 1-2 Demosthenes takes advantage of nearly every pose mentioned by Isocrates as useful for stirring pity.[138] The victim of an oligarchic conspiracy, he was unjustly condemned to perilous exile, and even after the failure of the conspiracy he remains deprived of homeland, property, and friends, contrary to his deserts and contrary to his expectations.[139] Equal application of the law now was

---

[132] Indiscretion distinguished from crime: D. 18. 274; Arist. *Rhet.* i. 13. 16. 1374b4-10; *EN* v. 8. 6-12. 1135b11-1136a9. Demosthenes' indiscretions: above, pp. 39-40,43. Recommended course: Anax. 4. pp. 32. 22-33. 14; 36, p. 93. 1-10 H.; Arist. *Rhet.* iii. 15. 3. 1416a13-14.

[133] Stock formula: cf. Lys. 5. 2 and Isoc. 19. 1. Indignant tone: Hermog. *Id.* ii. 8, Vol. III, p. 349 Walz.

[134] See Cic. *De inv.* ii. 35. 106.

[135] 29, p. 68. 1-3 H.

[136] See above, n. 6.

[137] Cf. Hyp. *Dem.* 3; Din. 1. 5, etc.

[138] Isoc. 16. 48; placement of appeals for pity: Arist. *Rhet.* iii. 14. 11. 1415b26-27; Volkmann, pp. 276-77.

[139] "Contrary to deserts" and "contrary to expectations" in appeals for pity: Anax. 34. p. 77. 11-13 H.; Arist. *Rhet.* ii. 8. 2. 1385b13-14; Apsines, pp 308. 20-310. 7 H.

a principle which favored Demosthenes' plea: everyone else has been exonerated; Demosthenes, too, can receive justice if the Athenians but will it,[140] and justice now means not temporary immunity but complete exoneration. The argument is skillfully phrased in balanced diction.

With no need to elaborate on current events, Demosthenes proceeds from this brief prooemium to the proposition of the letter (paragraph 3): the Athenians have good reason to see to his exoneration. Justice demands that those who suffer outrage though innocent should be rescued; honor demands that the Athenians repair their prestige, injured by their maltreatment of a celebrated patriot. As in Ep. 3, the main argument is that of a *demegoria*; it says nothing of the charges against Demosthenes but asserts that the action now recommended to the People is just and honorable.[141]

The favorable portrayal of the orator's career in the *confirmatio* which follows could also be found in a forensic apology.[142] It does answer the charges of venality and of being a jinx, which the prosecution had pressed with vigor. But as in the introductory narrative of Ep. 3, the charges themselves are not mentioned. Indeed, in Ep. 2, the author nowhere even mentions the exact nature of the accusations against him, whereas in the apologies for Socrates and Alcibiades, in Isocrates' *Antidosis*, and generally in forensic apologies, care is taken to indicate what prejudices are being attacked. Moreover, the argument which has the most direct bearing on the actual charge of bribe taking occurs not here but only later, in the context of *commiseratio* at paragraph 14. This would be poor technique in a speech before a court or in a posthumous forensic apology, where the aim is to produce a concentrated refutation of the charges brought. It is not out of place in a *demegoria* where first justice and honor and then pity are used to motivate the audience to take action in favor of the speaker. We have seen[143] that legality, fairness, and respect for worth were essential components of the idea of justice. The exoneration of the other defendants in the Harpalus case made detailed argument on "legality" or "fairness" superfluous. It remained for Demosthenes to

---

[140] Cf. Anax. 34, p. 77. 13–20 H.

[141] On such arguments in forensic apology, see above, pp. 106–7.

[142] It corresponds exactly to the recommendations at Cic. *De inv.* ii. 11. 35–36.

[143] Above, rhetorical analysis of Ep. 3. 10–15.

reassert his worth and to connect his exoneration with the present interest of the city, for which purpose he raises, as in Ep. 3, the consideration of Athens' Panhellenic prestige.

As in Ep. 3, the argument of the *confirmatio* follows the heads laid down in the proposition. This time, however, the first head, that of justice, involves an assertion of innocence ("though innocent of any wrong toward you") which makes it more difficult to prove. Hence Demosthenes pretends to brush it aside in order to treat it later. The second head, the "honorable," is an advantageous way to begin the argument for several reasons. Demosthenes' achievements in the struggle against Philip were the foundation of his claim to public gratitude. Furthermore, he had to show how his continued exile was injuring the city and could point only to the loss of Panhellenic prestige incurred by mistreatment of a Panhellenic hero; to this one argument he returns repeatedly (paragraphs 3–4, 8, 19, 21).[144] Finally, this line of argument was to afford him an opportunity to refute the charges against him without any need to go on the defensive by mentioning them.

The section of the *confirmatio* devoted to the "honorable" begins with a forceful statement: the other Greeks cannot have forgotten, even if the Athenians have, Demosthenes' great contributions (paragraphs 3–4). Throughout the ensuing argument, however, the orator has to anticipate the hostile reactions of his audience (paragraphs 4–7 beginning). Self-praise is invidious;[145] Demosthenes stresses that all Athenians share the credit for his career. Hyperides had argued that Demosthenes' collaborationism deprived him of any claim to reward for previous services;[146] Demosthenes insists that the baseness of the other Greeks has forced not only himself but all Athenians to conduct unworthy of their former valor.[147] Athenians did not like being reminded of defeats;[148] Demosthenes blames the distressing course of events on the other Greeks and upon the thoughtlessness of Fortune. Though forced to speak so openly of his own achievements, he will limit himself to a modest fraction of what he could mention ("in sum").[149] Accordingly, a brief allusion

[144] *Commoratio*: see above, n. 56.
[145] D. 18. 3–4; Volkmann, p. 129.
[146] *Dem.* 20–22.
[147] Cf. D. 18. 20; 60. 18, 22.
[148] See Lys. 13. 43–44; Lyc. *Leoc.* 16.
[149] Cf. D. 18. 258.

suffices for his achievements down to Chaeroneia. For the majority of Athenians, who blamed the defeat on Fortune, the glory of them was an accepted fact after the trial on the crown.[150] A vigorous anaphora makes the most of Demosthenes' negative accomplishment in the years that followed, of having refrained from active support of the Macedonian hegemony despite powerful incentives.

One aspect of his Panhellenic career Demosthenes insists on singling out—a summary allusion is not enough: his incorruptibility in dealing with Philip (paragraph 7). He explains that it is the most striking example,[151] but his real purpose is to present a proof of his innocence in the Harpalus affair. In the Athenian courts, where it was easy to initiate a prosecution on slight evidence, prosecution and defense both tended to rely heavily on arguments from probability (to eikos).[152] The Areopagus had presented no evidence with its reports. The speeches of Dinarchus and Hyperides do not use any direct evidence to support the charges. Probably even Stratocles, who spoke first, relied almost entirely on arguments based on probability ("Would the Areopagus lie about a corrupt politician?").[153] Demosthenes here proceeds exactly as recommended by the rhetorical handbooks,[154] arguing *e maiore ad minorem*: if he had remained invulnerable to Philip's unparalleled skill at bribery, surely he had not succumbed to Harpalus' paltry twenty talents. By avoiding explicit mention of the Harpalus affair, the orator keeps from the posture of the defendant and maintains the attitude of the reprover. History has proved him to be an uncorruptible Panhellenic hero. He expresses the reproof as a self-evident principle: by maltreating "such a person," citizens do not convict him of turpitude but themselves of thoughtless ingratitude.[155] The Athenians are admonished to remove

[150] Nevertheless, there is an attempt to echo Aeschines' charges against Demosthenes' policy before Chaeroneia at Din. 1. 12–13, 28. See commentary to Ep. 2. 5, τῆς ἀναγκαίας κτλ.

[151] See Arist. *Rhet.* ii. 20. 9. 1394a9–18.

[152] Aesch. 1. 91; Antiph. 6. 30; Isoc. 18. 16; Lys. 19. 53; Hyp. fr. 195.

[153] See commentary to Ep. 2. 7–8.

[154] Arist. *Rhet.* i. 15. 17–18. 1376a17–29; Anax. 7, p. 38. 17–20 H. See Anax. 36, p. 92. 9–14 H., and Cic. *De inv.* ii. 11. 35–36.

[155] Athenians readily understood the meaning of "such a person." If Demosthenes had been more explicit, he would have lost the effect of a self-evident principle, as do the expanded explanations of the scholiasts to Hermogenes, Maximus Planudes, Vol. V, p. 495 Walz, and Joannes of Sicily, Vol. VI, p. 235 Walz.

their disgrace by changing their course. In voicing this reproach and admonition, Demosthenes has iterated his point of Athens' lost Panhellenic prestige and can bring the section to a close (paragraph 8).

So little has the orator gone on the defensive that Hermogenes regards this passage as a classical example of "harshness" (*trachytês*), while noticing that it is not one of Demosthenes' extremely rare instances of unmitigated harshness.[156] The orator did take care to mitigate it. He did not write that the Athenians' treatment of him was rank ingratitude, but only that it looked so to the rest of the Greeks; at the beginning of the letter he had placed the blame on "certain members of the Areopagus." A further mitigation was the use of the impersonal "such a person" instead of "me."[157] The use of the word "misfortune" (*symphora*) serves to places the blame partly on fickle Fortune. And in concluding, he bestows on the Athenians the flattering compliment of politely[158] asking them to save their own prestige and vindicate him.[159]

In Ep. 2, as in Ep. 3, Demosthenes was careful not to deal with the most difficult subjects until he felt he had convinced his audience that they were in the wrong. To the Athenian mind, the assertion that Demosthenes was suffering outrageous treatment though innocent contradicted what everyone knew from common sense (*to eikos*).[160] Surely anyone gifted with the power of persuasion would abuse his power for his own gain, especially a prominent politician.[161] Demosthenes' persuasive power was so universally recognized he could not use the stock maneuver of denying it but admitted it openly.[162] To counter suspicion of it, he had to prove his exceptional probity from the record of his conduct. Hence, throughout his career as a statesman, Demosthenes abstained as far as possible from appearing before the courts, wishing to show himself always as the "statesman-like counselor," never as the unscrupulous shyster.[163] This principle

[156] Hermog. *Id.* i. 7, Vol. III, p. 235 Walz.

[157] *Scholia minora* to Hermogenes, printed in apparatus, Vol. VII, p. 994 Walz.

[158] See commentary.

[159] Joannes of Sicily, Vol. VI, pp. 255–56 Walz; Maximus Planudes, Vol. V, pp. 495–96 Walz.

[160] Anax. 7, p. 36. 15–16 H.

[161] Navarre, pp. 222–30.

[162] D. 18. 277.

[163] The contrast: D. 18. 189, etc. Friend and foe alike attest Demosthenes' avoidance of the courts: D. 8. 68–71; 25. 13; 32. 31–32; Theopompus *apud* Plut.

he violated but rarely, and then for political reasons, as in his contests with Aeschines.

Accordingly, Demosthenes insists that his formidable skill as an advocate has never been used to further private against public interests. On the contrary, he has risen as advocate only when necessary to defend the Athenian People on trial. Once, in the presence of the whole Athenian assembly, he alone rose and successfully defended the Athenian case before a "jury" of Greeks against the accusations of Python.[164] Fewer Athenians witnessed his successful advocacy of Athens' cause as ambassador; he forbears to give details—to have mentioned them might have involved mention of ill-fated Thebes (paragraphs 9–10).[165]

The courts were not the only arena for corrupt and selfish interests. Politicians were notorious for selling their services in the the Assembly. Hence Demosthenes insists that in his political activity he has stood above faction, seeking only the glory of Athens and, unlike others,[166] sacrificing popularity to reprove the citizens for their errors. Finally, the orator adds a stock element from the epilogues of Athenian defense speeches, the description of his generosity in performing his liturgies.[167] The conclusion follows: so scrupulous, selfless, and generous a person could not have taken a bribe from Harpalus (paragraphs 11–12).

In the proposition (paragraph 3) Demosthenes set forth the topics of his innocence and his grievous suffering. He now gives the impression of passing from the former to the latter (paragraph 12 end–paragraph 13). In reality he continues to deal with the topic of innocence. As at Ep. 3. 42–43, so here, Demosthenes treats directly of the Harpalus affair only in a context strongly evocative of pity. Indeed, the motive of *commiseratio* pervades the remainder of the letter (paragraphs 13–26). Against the background of Demosthenes'

Dem. 14. 3(*F. Gr. Hist.* No. 115, F 327); Din. 1. 100–1 (described as a vice!). Cf. Th. viii. 68. 1–2; Anax. 36, pp. 93–94 H. D. 25 may well be by Demosthenes; see above, Chap. I, n. 8. Treves' objections, *Athenaeum*, n.s., XIV, 252–58, depend on his assessment of the character of Demosthenes; see above, Chap. 6, n. 90.

[164] See commentary.

[165] Contrast the detail at D. 18. 244, and see above, n. 81, and pp. 74–75.

[166] See commentary to par. 11.

[167] See Navarre, pp. 283–88. To avoid the impression of boasting of his benefactions, the orator introduces the subject of liturgies by *paraleipsis;* see above, n. 81, and cf. D. 18. 268–69.

meritorious career, the description of his present precarious and ignominious plight becomes a strong bid for pity according to the commonplaces of "contrary to deserts" and "contrary to expectation" (paragraph 13).[168] Now at last Demosthenes turns to give arguments bearing directly on his innocence in the Harpalus affair (paragraphs 14–15)—arguments which he would have had to place nearer the beginning of the *confirmatio* of a forensic apology.[169]

The arguments which the orator presents here he doubtless used before in court, but the march of events made them stronger. To judge by the speeches of Dinarchus and Hyperides, there had been no effective refutation of Demosthenes' argument that his behavior had not been that of a friend of Harpalus. The Macedonian authorities had not taken punitive action against Athens; hence Demosthenes could claim that enactments of his had preserved the city from blame. The undocumented reports of the Areopagus had become more vulnerable with each defendant to be acquitted, and those acquitted had no stronger defenses and claims to leniency than did Demosthenes. The disadvantage faced by the first of several defendants to go on trial on a single charge was a commonplace in Athens; now Demosthenes can blame that circumstance as the "piece of bad luck" reponsible for his conviction[170]—again, as in paragraph 8, harshness is mitigated by blaming luck. Though Demosthenes may have conceded in the prooemium that he had been indiscreet,[171] no one could prove him guilty as charged. To conciliate his audience at the end of these protestations of innocence, he pretends to be refraining from writing all he might have.[172] After another attempt to stir pity, by describing the mental anguish of a consciousness of helpless wronged innocence (paragraph 15, end), the *confirmatio* concludes with the usual iteration: Demosthenes, too, must be exonerated; his probity in his career should outweigh an unproved accusation and proves him to be no less deserving of vindication than the other defendants (paragraph 16).

When Demosthenes wrote of his "acquiescence" (paragraph 1), he surely knew he had to anticipate the rejoinder that his escape from

[168] See above, n. 139.

[169] See above, rhetorical analysis of pars. 3–4.

[170] See commentary to Ep. 2. 14 and to Ep. 2. 1, οὐδεμιᾶς κτλ., and Chap. 5, n.115 .

[171] See commentary to Ep. 2. 1, μηδὲν κτλ.

[172] See above, n. 149.

prison could not be so described. In paragraphs 17–20 he counters with several points in his favor the one point of his escape,[173] in a manner calculated to stir yet more pity: his motive was not desertion; how could the Athenians reasonably object to an aged and ailing patriot's escape from profitless costumely which was destroying him (paragraph 17)?[174]

He proceeds to prove that his motive was not desertion. His refuge is a city which in the past and at present has sympathized with the Athenians (paragraphs 18–19); while there he refuses to encourage criticism of the Athenians for their treatment of him. In a *demegoria* seeking the aid of the People, one evoked pity by portraying the dangers threatening the person to be rescued.[175] Demosthenes' prosecutors had mocked him for his claims to be in danger.[176] Here the orator describes how, as an exile, he is threatened by danger from "foreign quarters" (*heterois*),[177] and yet he has not gone to the most advantageous place but has picked as a his refuge a place from which every day he can gaze with loyalty and love upon his homeland.[178] Into this emotional passage Demosthenes weaves an allusive iteration of his plea for exoneration and thus ends this section of "anticipation" (*prokatalêpsis*).[179]

The epilogue (paragraphs 21–25) begins with an iteration of the appeal for exoneration on the grounds of justice, worth, and honor. The epilogue contains all the elements described by the rhetorical textbooks[180] and is given the most touching expression possible: the orator is in a pitiable plight; the Athenians, who have already released the others, can easily release him; dire consequences could follow if they do not; let them not force him to become a suppliant of their foreign opponents to their own disgrace. If no reconciliation is possible, the Athenians would have done him a favor had they sentenced him to death (paragraph 21). Indeed, he deliberately gave them the opportunity to sentence him to death when he proposed that the Areopagus investigate the Harpalus affair. He portrays this stock

[173] See Anax. 33, p. 76. 15–21 H.
[174] See Arist. *Rhet.* i. 13. 17. 1374b10–14; Cic. *De inv.* ii. 35. 106.
[175] Anax. 34, p. 77. 13–16 H.
[176] Din. i. 9; cf. Hyp. *Dem.* 14.
[177] See above, rhetorical analysis of Ep. 3. 23–27 and pp. 68–70.
[178] Cf. *Odyssey* i. 57–59.
[179] See Anax. 33, p. 76. 21–22 H.
[180] See above, rhetorical analysis of Ep. 3. 35.

maneuver, so heavily exploited by his accusers,[181] as a noble submission of his fate to the People's decision, right or wrong (paragraph 22).

More pathetic amplification follows. Good Fortune has saved the Athenians from an irrevocable mistake. Let them now vote Demosthenes, too, an enactment of exoneration worthy of him and them (paragraph 23). He summarizes the proof of his worth, and in so doing evokes more pity by the commonplace, "contrary to deserts" (paragraph 24). With its stronger case, Ep. 2 presents a tone of "indignation" or "graveness" (*barytês*) quite different from the querulous "harshness" (*trachytês*) of Ep. 3. Nevertheless, Plutarch[182] found the picture of the homesick sorrowing orator unmanly and unworthy. Demosthenes foresaw the same reaction. As at Ep. 3. 44, he excuses his emotionalism as the natural consequence of his suffering. In fairness, he insists, allowances must be made for that, and, if so, his present bearing is consonant with his behavior throughout his great career. Thus simultaneously he anticipates the objection and calls attention once more to his grievous suffering and his great worth (paragraph 25).

Probably the major factor blocking Demosthenes' restoration was the hold on the People of Hyperides and other politicians who feared Demosthenes' vengeance. Hence, in closing, Demosthenes pretends that the People are now his supporters and nobly forgives his opponents for sharing in the People's past misunderstandings, if only they will now join in rectifying their errors against him as they have for others. If the opponents remain obstinate, Demosthenes again places his reliance on the People and their gratitude. He thus ends auspiciously, identifying his cause with the People's virtue (paragraph 26).

The structure of the apologetic *demegoria* of Andocides is somewhat simpler, but allowing for the different circumstances and Demosthenes' greater skill, the two appeals are very similar. Hence Ep. 2 probably displays the typical pattern of this variety of *demegoria*.

Like Demosthenes, Andocides went into exile rather than suffer punitive disabilities. By his own confession he was implicated in the sacrileges of 415 which preceded the Sicilian expedition.[183] Although

---

[181] See above, Chap. 5, n. 18.
[182] *Dem.* 26. 4.
[183] Douglas MacDowell, *Andokides On the Mysteries*, pp. 3–4, 173–76.

he had confessed under a promise of immunity, he had been deprived of civil rights by a decree denying them to men who confessed to acts of impiety. The speech *De Reditu* was delivered bteween 410 and 405;[184] during a severe food shortage, Andocides contrived to bring a large grain fleet from Cyprus to Athens. Through negotiations with the Council, he secured the privilege of addressing the People though he was without civil rights.[185]

Andocides had left Athens voluntarily and committed no crime in returning, but his disabilities could be removed only by an act of the People. His appeal had to be a *demegoria*.[186] With his disgraced past, he could not make Demosthenes' plea on the grounds of worth, but he did have something more tangible than over-familiar Panhellenic laurels, food for a hungry city. Thus, against a possible rejection of his plea, he, too, can give his prooemium an indignant tone calculated to put his opponents on the defensive and avoid the odium of asking the People to revoke their own decree (paragraphs 1–5).[187]

Even if Andocides had had Demosthenes' power of compression, it is doubtful whether he could have reduced his *capatio benevolentiae* to two paragraphs. Whereas Andocides was a confessed criminal, events had all but vindicated Demosthenes, who could quickly dismiss most of the circumstances embarrassing to him. The ignominy which the earlier orator had incurred by his confession was too conspicuous to be thus glossed over. To hold his audience at all, Andocides had first to narrate that episode in his life and show that he had a claim on their sympathy for his "misfortune" (paragraphs 6–9). This narrative joined to the prooemium still remains but a bare allusion.[188] As in D. Ep. 2, the exact nature of the charge against the speaker is left unmentioned. Moreover, since Andocides was no fugitive from prison, he could, without having to add a justification later, speak of his going into exile as carrying out the will of the Athenians—indeed, as the beginning of a new career of service to them (paragraph 10). The mention of this new career of service implicitly constitutes the proposition of this apologetic *demegoria*: what Andocides has done and suffered since going into exile makes him

---

[184] MacDowell, p. 4, n. 9.

[185] Andoc. 2. 3, 21–22.

[186] See Blass, I, 322.

[187] See above, n. 6.

[188] See Anax. 29, pp. 67. 21–68. 6 H; above, p. 105.

worthy of restoration.[189] From that time, he, like Demosthenes, can point to a meritorious past. Able to contribute directly to the Athenians' present interest, unlike Demosthenes, he does not have to encumber his proposition with a *pis aller* like suggesting that his plight injures the Panhellenic prestige of the Athenians. With this exception, the argument of Andocides 2. 10–22 constitutes a part of the *confirmatio* which corresponds to D. Ep. 2. 4–15.

Andocides first outlines his services during the difficult period of the rule of the Four Hundred (paragraphs 11–12). The description in paragraphs 13–16 of the cruel and ungrateful treatment which he had received then at the hands of the oligarchs, whom his audience now recognized as public enemies, constitutes a bid for pity within the *confirmatio* comparable to that at D. Ep. 2. 13–15. The account of Andocides' refusal to be embittered in the face of such requital and of his efforts down to the time of the speech to confer the most tangible benefits on the city is simultaneously a proof of accumulated merit and of present loyalty (paragraphs 16–22).

Andocides' iteration of the proposition, in the form of a petition at paragraph 22, corresponds to D. Ep. 2. 16. A difference in the supplementary arguments required in the two works arises from the differing circumstances. Demosthenes does not have to argue for the legality of his proposal; a brief allusion to the fact that the other defendants have been exonerated is sufficient. But as a fugitive from prison, he does have to prove his present loyalty and does so in Ep. 2. 17–20; paragraphs 21–24, however, where he presses his petition, can be regarded more as part of the epilogue than as part of the *confirmatio*. On the other hand, Andocides' narrative of his recent services to the city was a straightforward demonstration of his loyalty, but the legality and justice of his petition had to be established in paragraphs 23–25, which are a necessary part of the *confirmatio*. One of his arguments is similar to that used by Demosthenes: the civil rights which the speaker seeks to have restored in consideration of his services have been so granted before even to slaves and foreigners.

Andocides' epilogue begins with a summary through which he strives to secure sympathy. He insists that his character has changed to that of the meritorious person that he should have been by

[189] See the explicit statement at Andoc. 2. 22.

heredity—a man who despite all bears no grudge against the citizens (paragraphs 26–27). Correspondingly, Demosthenes summarizes what he has written, presenting himself as a supremely worthy politician whose character has not changed, whose complaints are nothing disloyal or unmanly (Ep. 2. 25). Both orators close their compositions by identifying themselves with their audience, which has been duped into misunderstanding them but now should turn against the unworthy opposition.

The appeals of Demosthenes and Andocides are apology throughout and bear considerable resemblance to forensic speeches. Nevertheless, their structure differs significantly from that of a defense before a court. Except for the justification of the writer's present position of having gone into exile, there is no detailed discussion of the events which lay behind the accusations.[190] The exact nature of the accusations is nowhere stated, and the opposition is nowhere named. Neither work contains personal invective.[191] Andocides, having confessed, cannot refute the charges; Demosthenes, who can try to, postpones his proof of innocence to the context of *commiseratio* at the end of the speech. Both orators begin with argument under the heads of the *telika kephalaia*. Both appeals failed, for the opposition was too strong.

Quite different throughout is the spurious Ep. 12 of Aeschines. It begins with no prooemium at all. No reason whatever is given why the Athenians should pay any attention to the sender's presentation of his autobiography, which could hardly have been of interest to the Assembly. In a personal letter, such an omission would have been natural. In a public speech, however, even Aristotle, who scoffs at the mechanical inclusion of a prooemium, admits that a message like that of a discredited exile must have one.[192] Thus the author appears to have been so intent on character portrayal that he goes against the practical teaching of fourth-century rhetoric. Writing a mere piece of literature, he does not feel the inherent challenge to the writer of a real *demegoria* when faced by an impatient and inattentive audience.

Admittedly, the narrative which begins the letter does fulfill one of the functions of the prooemium. By refuting the charges made by

[190] See above, pp. 105–7.
[191] See above, pp. 114–17.
[192] *Rhet.* iii. 13. 3. 1414b1–3; 14. 12. 1415b32–36.

Demosthenes in *De Corona*, it attacks the prejudices which supposedly induced the Athenians to bring upon Aeschines the sentence of exile and thus works to win their good will. But even so, the interests of the portrayer of character as opposed to those of the author of a *demegoria* show themselves. Demosthenes at the outset speaks of the achievements of his political career from its beginning to the present as giving him a claim on the Athenians' gratitude. The simulated Aeschines apparently tries to improve on Demosthenes' summary reference. He will speak at the outset of the very beginning of his political career and of the activities which preceded it, but his age on entering politics and the nature of the roles which he played as an actor would have been of no effect whatever in winning the good will of an Athenian audience, to say nothing of gaining their attention to the words of a discredited exile. To a biographer, however, they are of supreme interest.

When Aeschines is made, without any real prooemium, to name Demosthenes as the source of the calumnies against him (paragraphs 1–2), no objection can be raised that this violates the rule of avoidance of abusiveness. At the time presupposed by the letter, Demosthenes was in exile as a condemned criminal. More questionable, however, is the propriety of the open attack on Ctesiphon (paragraph 3), wherein Aeschines is made to maintain the justice of his unsuccessful accusations against the politician. There is no evidence that Ctesiphon, if still alive in 323, was in disrepute, nor does Pseudo-Aeschines even suggest that he was.[193]

At the outset of the narrative it is by no means clear that Aeschines is seeking to refute all the accusations made against him by Demosthenes, although rhetorical precept requires that the subject be revealed quickly to the audience.[194] At last, in paragraph 4, he enunciates the propositions that the Athenians themselves thought well of his policy and that the accusations of Demosthenes were false. But the character of the discussion in these paragraphs is that of a forensic defense rather than of a *demegoria*, for they contain a statement and a direct denial of the charges, not an effort to convince the Athenians that justice and their own interests require them

[193] In Ps.-Aesch. Ep. 2, probably intended to reflect a time earlier than the Harpalus affair, Ctesiphon appears as a person of considerable political influence.

[194] See above, n. 13.

to take new action to rectify a wrongful situation.[195] Yet the real purpose of the letter—a purpose which is not even hinted at until paragraph 12—is to petition for such action.

In bringing proof of the propositions of paragraph 4, the simulated Aeschines takes no advantage of the circumstance that Demosthenes' condemnation in the Harpalus affair has vindicated the charges of corruption which he had made against the great orator. Nor does he allude to whatever of his own civic and Panhellenic services he might have cited. Instead he simply points to the Athenians' refusal to condemn him when he was prosecuted by Demosthenes for treason, declaring it to be a mark of their approval of his policy (paragraph 4).[196] Admittedly, Demosthenes' overwhelming victory in the trial on the crown created a presumption against Aeschines, but, says the letter, the defeated orator's conduct during the ensuing exile has proved his loyalty. Indeed, the author's desire is to portray Aeschines as outdoing Demosthenes' protestations of present loyalty.[197] It would not have been enough for Aeschines to have selected as his place of exile a city known to have been friendly to Athens. He is shown to have betaken himself far away, where no one will tempt him, as Demosthenes was tempted at Troezen, to take unpatriotic delight over hearing his fellow citizens censured for their ingratitude. On the mainland opposite Rhodes he lives in genteel poverty. If he had truly been the paid agent of the Macedonian king, who knew how to reward his partisans in Athens with munificence, surely his lot would have been otherwise (paragraphs 5–12).

The detailed description of his modest circumstances allows him to make mention of his children and pass at last to the real purpose of the letter, hitherto unmentioned—his children's return to Athens and quite likely his own (paragraphs 12–13).[198] Yet, with the favorable background of the release of the sons of Lycurgus and Demosthenes' continued disgrace on charges which he himself had pressed, Aeschines might well have made his purpose clear at the very outset, as did Demosthenes in Ep. 2. Furthermore, Pseudo-Aeschines alludes to only one thing in the state of affairs of 323, this exoneration

---

[195] See above, rhetorical analysis of Ep. 2. 3.
[196] Cf. D. Ep. 3. 6.
[197] D. Ep. 2. 17–20.
[198] See Appendix II.

of the sons of Lycurgus, and that he does with ostentatious specificity, whereas Demosthenes makes bare but recognizable allusions to this as well as other current events which were surely in the mind of every Athenian citizen.

The epilogue (paragraph 15–16) has the customary pathetic tone but sounds a jarring note for a *demegoria* in the direct attack on Melanopus, which acknowledges at the same time that he is a person of political influence. Demosthenes in his Ep. 2, on the other hand, takes such pains to avoid abusiveness that he speaks of his opponents only as a class and as misguided men who are to be forgiven if they will but rectify their error. The spurious letter thus lacks traits of the self-apologetic *demegoria* which mark both D. Ep. 2 and Andocides' *De Reditu*, even though the fabricator obviously took Demosthenes' composition as his model.

There is a striking feature of Ep. 2 which distinguishes it from both Andoc. 2 and Ps.-Aesch. Ep. 12: it contains two contrary motifs. In some passages Demosthenes appears as a weakling to be pitied; he is pathetically inconsolable—he weeps.[199] In others, he is arrogant, speaking like the Socrates of Plato's *Apology* translated into the language of demagogues: he is a model for the young, etc. He goes so far as to suggest that he has been the victim of rank ingratitude.[200]

Ancient rhetorical precept required the assumption of a pitiful mien by anyone who laid a petition before an audience to whom that petition might be offensive.[201] Hence this aspect of the letter fits the living Demosthenes or a rhetorical exhibition, though not posthumous propaganda.[202] On the other hand, rhetorical practice excluded in such cases any arrogant pose. Recitation of one's own virtues, as done by Demosthenes in Ep. 2, would only irritate the audience. It was also a rhetorical rule that the People and their courts are always just: if condemned, explain away the fact and do not reproach the judges.[203] We have seen how Demosthenes followed the rule; neverless, he dares to suggest that the People are ungrateful.

[199] Ep. 2. 13, 17, 20, 25; see Plut. *Dem.* 26. 4.
[200] Ep. 2. 1, 3–12, 14, 24; "rank ingratitude": par. 8, but see the rhetorical analysis of it.
[201] Navarre, pp. 314–20; Dion. Hal. *Thuc.* 45, Vol. I, pp. 400–1 U.-R.
[202] See above, Chap. 6, end.
[203] Navarre, pp. 221–22.

The care with which the arrogant passages are introduced is only a partial explanation. Andocides throughout maintains a humble conciliatory air; he makes excuses for himself and explains away the previous decision of the People. On the other hand, in posthumous apologies and in Isocrates' *Antidosis*, the author did not have to give his hero a humble stance. Socrates in the *Apologies*, Isocrates and Timotheus in the *Antidosis*, Alcibiades in *De Bigis*, Pericles at Thuc. ii. 60–64, and Aeschines in Ps.-Aesch. Ep. 12 all stand erect. The rhetorical tradition portrayed Demosthenes throughout as indomitable and unbending, never as pitiful.[204]

The strange combination in Ep. 2 is explainable by the peculiar conditions of 323. Demosthenes assumed, as he had to, the poses required of a petitioner, but he felt that the course of events had so vindicated him that the Athenian public needed only to be reminded of his worth to recognize the injustice of leaving him the only defendant still condemned. The orator was mistaken—probably the Athenians were antagonized by Ep. 2, but he had reason enough to make his attempt.

In general, the case for the authenticity of Ep. 4 is weaker than that of the other letters. This also holds true in what can be learned from the rhetorical analysis of it. The work is not the kind of *demegoria* concerning which Aristotle and Anaximenes give detailed directions, the type which advocates a policy for the future. In Ep. 4 no action is directly recommended, and the proof is the effort to demonstrate a fact. It is not based upon the heads of the just, the honorable, and the expedient. Indeed, Ep. 4 bears some resemblance to a forensic defense in being the reply to an accusation of being a jinx. The opponent is named and subjected to a violent counterattack. Nevertheless, it is noteworthy that the only charge which receives such treatment in the letters is one which can have a bearing on the Athenians' ability to act in the emergency caused by Alexander's decrees on Samos and on the return of the exiles.[205]

Anaximenes did give directions for one type of *demegoria* which might bring information without advocating a policy, the report of an embassy,[206] but Ep. 4 can hardly be regarded as analogous to that.

---

[204] Drerup, *Demosthenes im Urteile des Altertums*, pp. 89–113, 144–66.

[205] See above, pp. 59–61.

[206] Anax. 30, p. 71. 10–24 H.

Nor have any such *demegoriae* which do not directly advocate a policy survived, so that there is no useful basis for comparison. On the other hand, we have identified Ep. 4 as an example of what Anaximenes calls a "speech of exposure" before the Assembly, and Demosthenes did include invective like the attack on Theremenes in "exposés" to the Assembly,[207] even though scholars have used the invective to declare Ep. 4 spurious.[208] We can support our argument for authenticity by showing that Ep. 4 conforms to Anaximenes' rules for "exposés" and that it avoids offending a fourth-century deliberative audience, whereas the spurious counterpart, Ps.-Aesch. Ep. 7 does not.

The prooemium (paragraphs 1–2) even while it attacks Theramenes deftly removes from the writer the odium of engaging in an "exposé." Indeed, one of the devices recommended by Anaximenes for the prooemia of "exposés" is to begin *ek diabolês*, the speaker blaming the target of his "exposé" for having attacked him first.[209] Immediately after the salutation, Demosthenes sets the scene by mentioning Theramenes' slanders of him; no further narrative is needed. The orator's counterattack deftly associates the abusiveness with the low character of his opponent,[210] in whom it is not surprising.[211] Demosthenes and his audience, being "sane and fair-minded persons," are unaffected by it. Thus Demosthenes creates the impression that whatever derogatory remarks will appear in his *demegoria* against his named opponent will not be abuse, but just and true retribution.

Apparently, the orator felt the People were weary of receiving arguments for his exoneration. Hence in Ep. 4 he only attacks the propaganda of his opponents. His present circumstances and hopes for restoration receive only a brief allusion, to remind the Athenians and bid for their sympathetic attention. Having flattered his audience as "fair-minded" people, he now urges them to his side as fellow victims of Theramenes' "drunken abuse." In contrast to Theramenes, they will be able to grasp from the letter the views so im-

---

[207] Above, rhetorical analysis of Ep. 3. 16–18.

[208] Blass, III 1, 450; Neupert, p. 46.

[209] Anax. 37, p. 98. 2–5; prooemia *ek diabolês*: Arist. *Rhet.* iii. 14. 7. 1415*a*25–28, 14. 12. 1415*b*32–37, and Volkmann, pp. 131–32.

[210] Cf. *Rhet. ad Herenn.* i. 5. 8.

[211] "I am not surprised . . ." in prooemia *ek diabolês:* Apsines 1, pp. 221. 6–222.

2 H.

portant to the public interest and so worthy of being remembered which Demosthenes is about to impart (paragraphs 1–2).

Having connected his message with the public interest, Demosthenes maintains the pose of speaking on a public issue by not speaking of himself. In the prooemium he had suggested that Theramenes' slander of Demosthenes was also slander of the city for her ill fortune. Now Demosthenes turns in paragraph 3 to enunciate a proposition gratifying to patriotic Athenians: the city has been and is the most fortunate and the dearest to the gods. Only when Demosthenes has proved this proposition does he mention himself again. His own unblemished Fortune follows as a corollary, and the appearance of writing to protect the public interest is preserved.

The structure and content of the *confirmatio* of Ep. 4 and their relationship to the historical setting have already been treated.[212] It remains only to describe how the orator exploits his two proofs of the city's good fortune to defend his own reputation. The transition is easy, since the policies of the city, for ill or for good, were directed by him. The proof from "oracular scripture" (paragraphs 3–4) allows Demosthenes to describe his opponent as a shameless reckless fool who contradicts the expressed opinion of the gods. The proof from "history" (paragraphs 5–9) allows the orator to give the flattering suggestion that in the eyes of the Greeks the lot of the Athenians is glorious.

Theramenes probably was but the straw man whom Demosthenes chose to represent those who insisted that he was a jinx. In the epilogue (paragraphs 10–11) the orator completes his attack on the slander by demolishing the straw man.[213] The gods, he writes, have already begun to punish Theramenes for his slanders by allowing him to be the sort of person he is. Demosthenes follows a favorite practice of Athenian orators in alleging that Theramenes has been guilty of unfilial behavior and of sexual deviation.[214]

As required in an "exposé," Demosthenes in paragraph 12 denies that he himself has been guilty of intemperate abuse. He has exercised the utmost restraint, giving only hints of the vices of which

[212] Above, pp. 59–61, 74–76.

[213] See Anax. 37, p. 98. 17–21 H.; Arist. *Rhet.* iii. 19. 1. 1419b14–17.

[214] See Navarre, pp. 297, 299–301; examples of "unfilial behavior": D. 24. 200, 203; 25. 54–55; Din. 2. 8, 18; of "sexual deviation": Aesch. 1, 3. 162, 174; D. 22. 21–32; Hyp. *apud* Rutil. Lup. ii. 6.

Theramenes stands self-convicted. The last sentence, even while excusing Demosthenes' invective, summarizes it to fix it in the minds of his audience.[215]

The spurious imitation, Ps.-Aesch. Ep. 7, is superficially similar. But where Demosthenes in giving a fairly elaborate defense of his career seeks the appearance of writing in the public interest and of putting off until his return any direct rebuke of Theramenes, the simulated Aeschines after a very brief defense of himself addresses a bitter personal attack to Melanopus which was of no interest whatever to the public—without giving the slightest excuse. The author did not have to conform to the proprieties which Athenians expected of an orator addressing the Assembly. Nowhere in the letter, including the ironic appeal for restoration at its end, is any effort made to connect Aeschines' interests with those of the public as must be done in a *demegoria*.[216]

D. Ep. 1 is patently a *demegoria*, but we have uncovered its subtly concealed apologetic character.[217] We have disposed of the alleged absence of historical detail and the alleged commonplace nature of the recommendations.[218] Rhetorical analysis can now help explain the peculiarities which impelled scholars to regard Ep. 1 as an authentic incomplete sketch,[219] a forgery,[220] or a piece of allegorical political propaganda written by Anaximenes for Demochares.[221]

Ep. 1 as it stands in our manuscripts differs strikingly from other ancient letters: the formula, "Demosthenes to the Council and the People, greeting," appears only after paragraph 1, not at the very beginning, and paragraph 1 has the unusual form of a prayer. The anomalous paragraph cannot be removed as an interpolated introduction to the letters as a collection or as an intrusion from the collection of prooemia wrongly placed with the letters.[222] The passage

---

[215] See Anax. 37, pp. 98. 21–99. 4 H.
[216] See above, p. 108.
[217] Above, pp. 62,87.
[218] Above, pp. 61–63; see also Anax. 2, p. 23. 15–22 H.
[219] Blass, III 1, 451–54.
[220] Neupert, pp. 42–45.
[221] Nitsche, *Demosthenes und Anaximenes*, pp. 140–41.
[222] The passage uses the vocabulary of a letter (*grapsai, epistellō*).

obeys Blass's law[223] and is included in the total stichometry.[224] On the other hand, the passage was intended to precede the epistolary formula of address and salutation, for it ends with the statement that the writer is sending "the following letter" (*tad' epistellô*).[225]

Consideration of Greek pious usages, however, makes Ep. 1. 1 into just the sort of beginning that Demosthenes could have chosen in the situation. The message of Ep. 1 is a weighty one, and the author, following age-old Greek practice, feels that at the outset of such an undertaking one must turn to the gods.[226] In fifth- and fourth-century Athens speakers in all sorts of situations would show their piety and would lend force and solemnity to their words by prefixing the same sort of formula as Ep. 1. 1.[227] The famous double prayer at the beginning of *De Corona* is only the best-known example of such formulas in speeches to the Athenian courts.[228] Introductory prayers were common, too, in *demegoriae*;[229] there are two Demosthenic instances besides Ep. 1. 1.[230]

[223] There is only one accumulation of three short syllables (*men epi*). Blass eliminated even that by changing the word order to agree with the order at *Prooem.* 25. 3.

[224] Without paragraph 1, the *stichos* measuring Ep. 1 would be 7 per cent shorter than that measuring Epp. 2–4. Moreover, the misplacement of the marginal stichometry of Ep. 1 would be aggravated. See F. Burger, *Stichometrische Untersuchungen*, pp. 13, 19, 28. Incidentally, the marginal letter is not an alpha but a beta.

[225] The reason Ep. 1 stands first in all the medieval manuscripts of Demosthenes' letters probably is that the scribe or editor did view the prayer as a good introduction to the entire collection.

[226] Early Greek bards would begin their performances "from the gods," uttering words of praise to a deity or group of deities; the collection of *Homeric Hymns* consists of such prooemia. Cf. Hesiod *Theog.* 1, 36, and Pindar *N.* 5. 25–26. Along with the praise the bard often would utter a prayer for the success of his song as in *Hymns* 10 and 25.

[227] In Aristoph. *Ra.* 871–94 Dionysus, Aeschylus, Euripides, and the chorus all utter prayers for inspiration in the weighty trial of poetic skill. In Plato's *Timaeus* (27b–d) Socrates expects that Timaeus will begin his discourse on cosmogony *kata nomon*, by calling upon the gods, and Timaeus proceeds to utter substantially the same introductory sentiments and prayer as appear in D. Ep. 1. 1. See also V· Ehrenberg, *The People of Aristophanes* (3d ed.; New York: Schocken, 1962), p. 257, and X. *Oec.* 6. 1, 7. 7.

[228] D. 18. 1 and 8; Lyc. *Leoc.* 1; Polyxenus *apud* Gregorius Corinthius, Vol. VII, p. 1272 Walz (Baiter and Sauppe, Vol. II, p. 344); the speech *Diadikasia Athmoneusi* cited by Dion. Hal. (*Din.* 11, p. 314 U.-R.) as wrongly attributed to Dinarchus, its date being too early; cf. Aristoph. *V.* 844–46.

[229] Aristoph. *Eccl.* 171–72, *Eq.* 763-72; Plut. *Per.* 8. 4. Cf. Plato Ep. 8. 352e–53a.

[230] *Prooemm.* 25. 3 and 50. 1. D. 3. 18 speaks of the necessity of including prayers in *demegoriae*.

Most of these examples place the "beginning from the gods" in the body of the speech, within or after the sentence which contains the formula of address, *ô andres Athênaioi*. There are, however, parallels for the unusual position of Ep. 1. 1 before the body of the letter and the formula of greeting. In the *Knights* of Aristophanes, the sausage-seller utters his prayer *before* bursting through the lattice gate and addressing the Council.[231] Plutarch reports that Pericles habitually uttered such a prayer *while mounting* the platform to address the Assembly.[232] Furthermore, in Athens each meeting of the Council and of the Assembly was just such a "weighty undertaking" which should "take its beginning from the gods."[233] The herald would open the proceedings with a prayer of which the language, as preserved in Aristophanes parody,[234] strongly resembles all the prayer formulas just cited.[235] Inasmuch as he was in exile, Demosthenes could not take part in these rites of the meeting at which he hoped his letter would be read. Hence he may have felt all the more obliged to prefix his own prayer to make up for the omission.

Another peculiarity with which Blass[236] and Neupert [237] found fault is what they regarded as an overlong sequence of four vague, commonplace, and poorly connected introductory paragraphs. We have justified the presence of paragraph 1, which stands *outside* the body of the letter. The three paragraphs which follow are in fact indispensable for one in Demosthenes' position. Still a discredited exile, he was about to preach amnesty to a populace thirsty for revenge on supporters of the "old regime." In the light of his need to secure the good will of his audience at this crucial moment, a long *captatio benevolentiae* is just what one would expect.[238] The strong tendency

[231] Lines 634-44.

[232] *Per.* 8. 4.

[233] Busolt-Swoboda, p. 518.

[234] *Thesm.* 295-310.

[235] Important classes of Athenian inscriptions (treaties, honorary decrees, official documents of religious content) begin with the invocation *theoi* (W. Larfeld, *Handbuch der griechischen Epigraphik*, II, 591).

[236] III 1, 452-53.

[237] Pp. 43-44.

[238] Of the 25 paragraphs of D. 5, the first four are pure prooemium; and since the source of the orator's embarrassment is his former belligerent policy, one may include the introductory narrative, D. 5. 5-12, in the prooemium. The proportions of Ep. 1 are much the same and arise from similar embarrassment. See the Scholia to D. 5, pp. 68b-69a Baiter-Sauppe; Schol. D. 2. 1-5, pp. 54b-55b Baiter-Sauppe; and Volkmann, pp. 141-43.

of Athenian prooemia to be stereotypes has been known from ancient times[239] and renders the commonplace nature of the paragraphs irrelevant to the question of authenticity.

First, as in Ep. 3. 1, Demosthenes must recognize his status as an exile and explain why he should have a hearing. He takes note of his status by the noble gesture of forgoing a fresh appeal for restoration, thus at once turning a cause for hostility into one for admiration and reminding the Athenians of his plight. He deserves a hearing because his subject is an urgent matter of public interest which cannot bear delay: how to seize the opportunity brought by the death of Alexander (paragraph 2).

Immediately, he has serious obstacles. The normal way to lay such ideas before the Athenians was to deliver a speech before the Assembly, yet Demosthenes cannot do so. An unfriendly critic might have even asked why, if Demosthenes thought that his advice was so valuable, he did not bring it to Athens in person.[240] To meet this awkward situation, Demosthenes presents it as a handicap which gives him an even greater claim on the Athenians' indulgent attention. If the people will but listen to his letter, they will receive advice of great value and will see the extent of Demosthenes' patriotism (paragraph 3). The maneuver was frequently used in Athenian propaganda.[241]

Demosthenes' effort to embrace the popular cause of Hellenic liberation after having ruined the opportunity for revolt brought by Harpalus was certain to evoke the hostility of the leading anti-Macedonian politicians. To conciliate them, the orator has to avoid giving the impression that he is competing with them for the public favor; rather, he poses as their loyal assistant who wishes only to facilitate the realization of their own projects. Hence, paragraph 4 is indispensable.

The remarks on generalship and Fortune (paragraphs 11–16) serve as an anticipation of objections based on the bitter lessons of past failures. [242] The advice of Demosthenes, he insists, was not at fault, but the inept commanders to whom its execution was entrusted.[243] The writer summarizes his message and concludes the

---

[239] Navarre, p. 239.

[240] Cf. Ep. 3. 39.

[241] Isoc. 5. 24–29, Ep. 1. 2–3; cf. Alcidamas *Soph.* 22–23; Plato *Phaedrus* 275d–e.

[242] Anax. 33; Blass, III 1, 452, regards the section as an ineptly long epilogue.

[243] Cf. D. 18. 244–47, 300–3.

letter with a stirring epilogue, exhorting the Athenians not to repeat past mistakes but to go forth with the help of the gods to victory.

Ps.-Aesch. Ep. 11, the spurious counterpart to D. Ep. 1, is the most successful of the fabricator's efforts. Except for the flagrant anachronism in paragraph 3, wherein the king of Persia is said to be still ruling in 323, the content of the letter is remarkably appropriate for its intended setting.[244] Nevertheless, the more natural way in which Demosthenes' letter, far more than its counterpart, derives from and reflects the historical situation argues strongly for the authenticity of the one and even suggests the spuriousness of the other.

Ps.-Aesch. Ep. 11 does conform to the rule of avoidance of abusiveness, for Demosthenes in exile was fair game for attacks in a *demegoria*. Furthermore, Aeschines is made to give a defense of his conduct and his career in paragraphs 1–3. This, however, does not mean that the fabricator has composed an apologetic *demegoria* according to fourth-century Athenian practice. Unlike D. Ep. 1, neither overtly nor covertly does Ps.-Aesch. Ep. 11 aim at Aeschines' restoration, nor does the writer treat the clearing of Aeschines' reputation as an end in itself. Rather, his aim is to contradict the arguments of those who wished to precipitate the Hellenic revolt. Here, for once, the author recognized the obstacles to be faced by a discredited exile trying to gain a hearing. More than Demosthenes, Aeschines would have been suspect as a treasonable collaborationist. An elaborate prooemium is devised to overcome this suspicion.

Rhetorical analysis and study of the forms of Athenian polemics thus further confirm the authenticity of each of the letters. All four have been shown to be *demegoriae* which conform to fourth-century rhetorical practice, whereas the reverse has been shown of the spurious letters of Aeschines. Only Epp. 3 and 4 appeared not to observe the Demosthenic rule of avoidance of invective; the invective in Ep. 3 has been shown to lie within the hypothetical limits, and some justification has been found for Ep. 4. In Epp. 1 and 3 the form and content of the *demegoria* overshadow the apologetic interests which would have been the primary aim of a fabricator. The thoroughly apologetic Ep. 2 differs significantly from forensic apology and closely resembles the authentic *demegoria* of Andocides.

[244] See Blass, III 2, 186.

One can hardly ever prove authenticity, especially in the absence of adequate information in the sources. One can only answer objections and show that the works in question can be better understood if we suppose them authentic. Our studies of text transmission, style, historical content, and rhetorical form concur in establishing a strong presumption in favor of the authenticity of Demosthenes' four letters. The case is strongest for Epp. 1–3, but much can be said even for Ep. 4.

PART 4

Translation

EPISTLE 3

Concerning the Sons of Lycurgus

DEMOSTHENES TO THE Council and the People, greeting.   1
My own interests, the concessions I thought it just that I should
get from you, were the subject of the earlier letter I sent you. On
those matters you will take favorable action when it pleases you. But
the subject of my present letter is something I would not have you
disregard. Please do not listen in a spirit of contentiousness, but give
it a just hearing. For, though now out of the country, I hear many
persons reproaching you for what is happening in the affair of the
sons of Lycurgus.

Now, I would have written this letter anyhow out of consideration   2
for what Lycurgus accomplished during his lifetime. If you want to
do what is fitting, you would all feel a just sense of gratitude, as I do,
for what he achieved. For Lycurgus began his career in a post in the
financial sector of political life. He had had no experience in drawing
up proposals to deal with Hellenic affairs and with the problems of
military alliances. Nevertheless, at the very time when most of those
who even pretended to be devoted to the People were deserting you,
he attached himself to the People's cause. He did so, not because of   3
the rewards and profits which were to be had from that course—all
such inducements were coming from the opposite direction; nor
because he saw it was the safer choice—it involved many and obvious
dangers which one who chose to speak in the interests of the People
had to face. Rather, he did so because he was devoted to the People
and by nature a good citizen.

Indeed, he saw with his own eyes how the turn of events had   4
weakened those who would have aided the People and strengthened

185

those who were opposing you. Yet even so he chose the policy he
believed was to the interest of the People; from then on he was
conspicuous as one who performed his duty in word and deed. The
direct result was that the surrender of his person was demanded, as
everyone knows.

5   Now, as I said at the outset, I should have written this letter anyhow
out of gratitude to him. Nevertheless, because I also thought that it
was to your interest to know of the reproaches being uttered abroad,
I felt a much greater urge to send this letter. I beg those who for
personal reasons are ill disposed toward Lycurgus to listen with
patience to the true and just pleas which can be made in his behalf.
Make no mistake, gentlemen of Athens, the reputation of the city
is suffering from what has been happening in the affair of his sons.

6   All Greece knows the great lengths you went in honoring Lycurgus
during his lifetime. Many were the accusations raised by those who
bore him ill will, but you never found a one to be true. Indeed, so far
did you trust him and believe him, beyond anyone else, to be devoted
to the People, that you were in the habit of deciding many points of
justice on Lycurgus' mere word, and this was enough for you. For
the matter would not have been vouched for by him if it did not
accord with your own views.

7   So now, all who hear that Lycurgus' sons are in chains feel pity
for the deceased and sympathetic indignation for his children, whose
sufferings they believe to be undeserved. You, however, they reproach with a bitterness which I cannot bring myself to put into
writing. I feel indignant at what they say, and, as far as I can, I reply
in your defense. I think you ought to know just enough of what is
being said to show you how people in large numbers are voicing their
disapproval. That much I have written. To go through everything
in detail would, in my judgment, be offensive. Excluding mere abuse,

8   however, I shall report from what is being said the things which I
think you ought to hear.

No one believes that you really have acted in ignorance and that
the truth about Lycurgus himself has eluded you. Two considerations give good reason to rule out the plea of ignorance: first, the
length of time throughout which Lycurgus was under your scrutiny
without ever being found guilty of any thought or act that did you
wrong; and second, the fact that no man has ever found you guilty

of obtuseness in anything else. One possibility remains, what every- 9
one would call the conduct of base fellows: as long as you are using a
man you pretend to care, but afterwards you take no further thought
of him. Now, in what other way is one to expect that you will show
gratitude to a man who is dead, when one observes that the reverse
of gratitude befalls the children and the good name of the deceased?
The only thing about which everyone is concerned even on his death
bed is the security of his children and of his good name!

Again, even to let it seem that you are doing this for money is not 10
the part of honorable men, for it would be regarded as out of keeping
with your generous spirit and the rest of your character. If you had
to ransom persons out of the hands of others by paying the same sum
from the public revenues, I think you would all be eager to do it.
Now, when I see your reluctance to remit a fine which arose from the
mere words of a malicious accusation, I do not know what charge to
make, if not that in dealing with men who are devoted to the People
you have taken the thoroughly rancorous and factious course. If so,
your decision is neither right nor expedient.

I am surprised none of you notices that there is something dis- 11
graceful here: the Athenian People which has the reputation of excel-
ling all others in its sense of what is right and in its cultivation, the
People which has always offered a refuge to the victims of misfortune,
proves to be more callous than Philip! And Philip, one may say with
reason, was a man untouched by moral instruction, brought up as he
was with the power to do as he pleased. Yet when he stood at the 12
very height of his fortunes, even then he thought it necessary to present himself to the world acting at his most humane. He had been
risking everything against the men who had opposed him in the line
of battle, yet he did not venture to chain them, for he had assayed
their mettle and that of their ancestors.[1] Unlike some of your politicians, it appears, he believed that it was neither just nor seemly to
deal with everyone on the same footing. Rather, in such decisions
he took account of the additional consideration of worth.

You, however, are Athenians. You live in an atmosphere of free 13
speech, which is supposed to be able to render even obtuse people
endurable. Yet first, and most callous of all, you keep the sons in
chains because of accusations which certain persons bring against the

[1] See commentary.

father; and then you say that to do such things represents equality before the law, as if you were considering the equality of weights and measures and not discussing the principles and political conduct of
14 men. In an assay of principles and political conduct, if the acts of Lycurgus prove to have been serviceable and directed by devotion to the People and by good will, justice requires that his children should meet with no evil at your hands, but rather with everything good. And if the reverse proves to be true, Lycurgus should have been punished in his lifetime; and even then, his children should not have been made to feel your anger for charges brought by someone against their father. Every man's accountability for his errors ends with his death.

15 Is this your intention, that persons bearing a grudge against statesmen who support the People's cause should not lay aside their hostility even when those statesmen are dead but should persist in directing it against their children? And that the People, whose struggle each devoted citizen makes his own, should be mindful of their debt of gratitude only as long as they enjoy his services but thereafter should take no interest?[2] If so, nothing will be more wretched than to choose to defend the People's cause.

16 If Moerocles answers that all this is too subtle for him, that he himself put them in chains to prevent their escape, ask him about the times when Taureas and Pataecus and Aristogiton and he himself were consigned to the prison. Not only were they not chained, they continued to speak before the People. Why in the world did he not take notice of this point of law then?

17 Will he say that he was not then in office? As far as the law is concerned, he does not have the right now even to make a speech. I ask you, how is it equality before the law when some persons, who are not even entitled to speak, hold office, while others, whose father
18 did you many services, are in chains? For my part, I cannot figure it out, unless you wish to show in the name of the People that black-guardism and shamelessness and deliberate wickedness have the upper hand in the city, that the greater hope for security lies with them, and that whenever their adherents get into difficulties there is always a way out, whereas the decision to live a life marked by honest

---

[2] The rhetorical question is not so expressed in the Greek, but I know no better means of rendering the complicated Greek protasis in English.

intentions and scrupulosity and devotion to the People is full of pitfalls—one false step, and there will be no escape.

There is more to be said. I am going to pass over all such considerations as the injustice of your reversing the opinion which you held of Lycurgus in his lifetime, and the justice of holding those who have passed away in higher respect than those who are still with us. I assume that these are matters on which everyone agrees. But I would be glad to see you recall all those other persons, the public services of whose ancestors you do bear in mind. For example, there are the descendants of Aristides and of Thrasybulus and of Archinus and of many others. I do not make reference to these reproachfully. So far am I from doing so that I judge such examples to be of the highest advantage to the city. Thereby you invite all to devote themselves to the People, for they see that even if during their own lifetime malice stands in the way of their deserved honors, their children will still be able to get the deserved rewards from you. 19

Is there not something here which defies explanation? Or rather, is it not truly disgraceful? Certain other persons did you services in times long past. You have your notion of their services by hearsay from that distant past, not through your own observation. Nevertheless, toward those others you keep alive the good will owed to them. Moreover, hitherto you were always ready to show pity and human kindness even to persons of no distinction and even to men who wronged you. For Lycurgus, however, whose public career and whose passing are so recent, you do not show yourselves ready to go even that far, though the punishment is being inflicted on his children, whom even an enemy, provided he was moderate and reasonable, would pity. 20 21 22

Furthermore, I am astonished that any of you fails to perceive yet another thing, inasmuch as it, too, makes its appearance to the detriment of the republic: those who possess a foreign friend get more than their deserts in every respect when things are going their way, and even when they suffer adversity, they have easy avenues of escape; whereas those who pin their hopes on the People are not only to get less than their deserts in other respects, but they alone of all persons have misfortunes which prove enduring. Surely it is easy to show that is what is happening. Who among you does not know what happened to Laches, the son of Melanopus, how he was convicted 23 24 in court in the same way as the sons of Lycurgus now, yet had his entire fine remitted when Alexander sent a letter? Or how, again, Mnesibulus of Acharnae was convicted and sentenced by the court like the children of Lycurgus, but was let off, and deservedly, for he was a worthy man.

25 On those occasions none of those who are now raising an uproar said that the laws were being subverted. With good reason, for they were not being subverted—if, indeed, all laws are made for the purpose of justice and for the vindication of honest men, and if there is something to be gained by not making endless the calamities of persons struck by ill fortune, and if there is something to be gained by

26 not showing yourselves ungrateful. But surely if something is to be gained thus, as we should admit, not only were you not subverting the laws when you let those men off; in letting Laches off as a favor in response to the request of Alexander and in exonerating Mnesibulus because of the temperate character of his life, you were also preserving the intentions[3] of the men who established our laws.

27 So stop showing that it is more advantageous to possess a foreign friend than to place one's trust in the People and that it is better to be without distinction than to be known for taking part in politics in the interests of you, the People. The man who rises in the Assembly with a program to present and the man who holds public office cannot please everyone. Nevertheless, if from loyalty a man makes the People's concerns his own, he has a just claim to your clemency. Otherwise, you will teach everyone to pay court to foreigners rather than to the People and to avoid the reputation of serving your inter-

28 ests. In sum, gentlemen of Athens, everyone shares in the disgrace and the entire city suffers a grievous blow when malice is seen to have more influence among you than gratitude for public services, although malice is a plague and Gratitude[4] is numbered among the gods.

29 I certainly will not fail to speak of Pytheas, a fellow devoted to the People so long as he was on his way up and afterwards ready to do anything against you. Everyone knows that when he was making his way into public life in the role of your supporter, he was hounded like a slave and prosecuted on a charge of usurping the rights of a

---

[3] The text here is surely corrupt. See commentary.
[4] Literally, "the Graces," whose name in Greek (*Charites*) also means "thanks."

citizen. He was almost sold into slavery by the same persons whom he just now was serving as a writer of speeches against me. Everyone 30 knows that he is so well off doing the things for which he once procecuted others that he keeps two mistresses—women who have performed the good service of escorting him down the path to death from consumption. Fined five talents, he paid them more easily than he could produce five drachmas before. What is more, not only does he have from you, the People, a share in the rights of a citizen—a fact which is to the common disgrace of all; he also offers on your behalf the ancestral sacrifices at Delphi.

When such striking examples are there for everyone to see, by 31 which anyone can discern the profitable course, I am afraid that a time is coming when you will be bereft of men who will be spokesmen for your interests, especially when time and fortune and our common destiny have been carrying off some of the men devoted to the People, such as Nausicles, Chares, Diotimus, Menestheus, and Eudoxus, as well as Euthydicus, Ephialtes, and Lycurgus, and you yourselves have cast away others, such as Charidemus, Philocles, and me. Even 32 you consider these men second to none in loyalty. If you consider some to be their equals, I do not mind. On the contrary, I wish there would be ever so many of them, provided that you will deal justly with them and provided that they will not suffer our fate. But when, as now, you exhibit such examples, who is there who will honestly consent to put himself in this position for you? Surely you will never 33 lack men who are ready to pretend to do so, for you never have in the past. May we never come to see such pretenders put to the test and found wanting like those others who feel neither fear nor shame before any of you as they openly pursue in public affairs policies which they formerly disavowed.

Gentlemen of Athens, you must take all this into account. You must not disregard your loyal citizens. You must not listen to those who are leading the city into rancor and cruelty. The present circum- 34 stances call much rather for good will and humane consideration than for strife and ill will. Certain persons, indulging an excess of those vices, are selling their services to oppose your interests in anticipation of circumstances to come. May they be disappointed in their calculations! The man among you who tries to ridicule these warnings of mine is being very foolish. He knows that the unexpected has happened in the past. Does he think that what happened before, when the People was set against the spokesman for its interests by suborned subversives, could not happen now? If so, how can he be in his right mind?

35 All this, if I were present among you, I would explain to you by word of mouth. Now, however, I am in such circumstances as I would wish upon whoever told the lies which brought my condemnation, and so I have put all this in writing and sent a letter. In so doing, I have as my first and most important consideration your honor and advantage. Second, I think it my duty to continue to display toward Lycurgus' sons the same good will I had for him in his lifetime.

36 If it has occurred to anyone that I have abundant troubles of my own, I should not hesitate to tell him that I am as anxious to look to your interests and to keep from failing my friends as to achieve my own vindication. So it is not because of my own abundant troubles that I do this; rather, out of the same zeal and devotion I work single-mindedly for the one and for the other. And yet my abundant troubles are of the sort I should wish in abundance on those who have evil designs against you. But enough of this.

37 I should like, however, in a spirit of good will and friendship to take you to task, briefly for the present, but soon (unless I get justice from you first) you may expect to get a long letter. You—what can I say, without either giving the wrong impression or lying?—you all too heedless men. You are not ashamed to display to others and to your own consciences the spectacle of having acquitted Aristogiton on the same charge for which you have driven Demosthenes into

38 exile. Others can have what you do not grant to me, though they have the gall not to care a whit for you, and even though they get it without your leave. I refer to the means whereby I might, if able, collect the debts owed me and call upon my friends for contributions and thus fulfil my obligations to you. Then no longer would I be seen, wandering about on foreign soil, a reproach to all who have wronged me, with old age in exile as reward for my labors on your

39 behalf. Now my wish is that your gratitude and high-mindedness should procure me my return home and put an end to the defamation which has unjustly befallen me. All I ask now is immunity for as long a period as you have allowed for the payment of a fine, and that you refuse to grant. Instead you ask, so I have been told, "Who in the

world is stopping him from coming here and doing as he proposes?"
It is, gentlemen of Athens, because I know how to feel shame. It is 40
because I am in a plight which is unworthy of my political services
on your behalf. It is because I have lost my fortune through being
induced by certain persons to underwrite in advance the payment
of their installments, in order that they should not have to pay
double a sum which they could not pay as it was. Once back with the
help of your good will, I could probably recover part, if not all, of
that money, so as not to be reduced to unseemly destitution for the
rest of my life. But if I return in the manner in which the persons
who asked those questions think I should, I shall become a prisoner
of ignominy and helplessness and fear.

You, however, take none of this into account but will stand idly 41
by, if it comes to that, begrudging me mere words of human consideration as I perish because of you, for I would not appeal to anyone
else. There will be a time, I am sure, when you will say that I have
been outrageously treated – when it will do neither you nor me any
good. Clearly you do not think that I have resources apart from
my tangible property, to which I relinquish title. My other assets,
too, I now wish to collect, if only you will treat me with humanity
instead of enmity and allow me to apply myself to that task in safety.

Nor will you ever show that I took anything from Harpalus. 42
Neither was the case against me proved, nor did I take anything. If
you look to the conspicuous prestige of the Council or to the Hill of
Ares, remember the trial of Aristogiton and hide your faces in shame.
I have nothing milder to tell those who have done me such wrong.
Surely you are not going to say that it is right for him to be acquitted 43
and me to be condemned when he was indicted by the very same
Council as I, and in the very same words. You are not that unreasonable. This is not my due; I do not deserve it; I am not worse than he
though I do admit that because of you I am the victim of ill luck.
What else can you call it but "ill luck" when, in addition to my other
misfortunes, it is my fate to be comparing myself with Aristogiton,
and, worse yet, as one condemned with one who has obtained
exoneration?

Do not suppose that when I say this I feel anger. I could not feel 44
that towards you. But wronged men find a sort of relief in speaking
of their suffering, just as those who are in pain do in groaning. As

for good will, I feel as much toward you as I could wish you to feel toward me. I have shown this in all my actions and shall continue to do so. From the beginning I recognized that every person who took part in public life had the duty, in so far as he was a good citizen, to be disposed toward the entire citizenry in the same way as children should be toward their parents: he should pray to find them as considerate as possible, but he must in a good spirit bear with them as they are. Submission in such matters among fair-minded people is regarded as an honorable and fitting victory. Farewell.

45

EPISTLE 2

Concerning His Own Restoration

DEMOSTHENES TO THE Council and the People, greeting. 1
I used to believe, in view of my record throughout my political
career, not only that I should be spared such suffering as this if I remained innocent of any wrong toward you, but also that I should
meet with forgiveness even if, as was possible, I should be guilty
to some extent of mistakes. When things took their present turn,
however, I decided upon patient submission. As long as I saw you
voting to condemn all the defendants on the basis of what the Council
had drawn up in secret and was presenting without any evident
demonstration and without any proof, I thought that you were
surrendering something no less important than the things of which I
was being deprived. In fact, for the sworn judges to have agreed to
whatever the Council said when no proof had been presented was a
surrender of the constitution.

Now, however, you have done the right thing; you have come to 2
perceive the oligarchic power which certain members of the Council
were contriving to arrogate to themselves. Judging the trials in the
light of the proofs given, you now find reprehensible what these men
drew up in secrecy. Therefore, I think – subject of course to your
approval – that I, who faced the same charges, should now meet with
the same exoneration as the other defendants and not be the only one
deprived, on a false charge, of country, property, and the company
of his nearest and dearest.

Indeed, you would have reason, gentlemen of Athens, to care about 3
my exoneration, not only in view of the outrageous treatment that I
have suffered though innocent of any wrong towards you, but also

for the sake of your good name among other people. If no one reminds you of the times and occasions in which I was of the greatest service
4 to the city, do not think that the other Greeks do not know, or that they have forgotten the things accomplished by me in your behalf. There are two reasons why I hesitate now to write of these things in detail: first, because I am afraid of envy, in the face of which there is no use telling the truth; second, because we are now compelled, on account of the baseness of the other Greeks, to do much that is unworthy of those services of mine.

5 In sum, however, the way in which I rose to the occasions on your behalf brought you universal admiration and brought me the expectation that I could look forward to the greatest rewards from you. And when Fortune, as inexorable as she was callous, decided the struggle which you yourselves carried on for the freedom of the Greeks, not
6 as was right but as she pleased, I did not retreat from my loyalty to you even in the period which followed, nor did I take anything in exchange for it, not favor, not splendid prospects, not wealth, not power, not security. And yet I saw that all these were coming to the persons who were willing to take part in public affairs against your interests.

7 Although there are many important things which give me good reason to be outspoken, there is one which I consider most important; and I shall not hesitate to mention it here. Throughout the ages, Philip stands as the cleverest in the history of the human race both at using the art of conversation to persuade people to pay heed to his wishes and at using money to corrupt the leading citizens in each of
8 the Greek cities; and I alone was worsted by neither of these methods – a fact which is to your credit, too. I had many meetings and discussions with Philip concerning the affairs for which you used to send me as your ambassador, and yet I refused the many bribes which he continually offered. Many are still alive who can testify to that. Just consider what opinion they are likely to have of you! That you have treated such a person in the way you have may, I know, be construed as my misfortune, but not all at as my disgrace; certainly, however, as your lack of appreciation. Please remove this impression by changing your course.

9 All of the afore-mentioned I consider less important than the continuous record of my everyday political conduct, wherein I

showed myself in public life to be one who never lent his support to resentment or to ill will or to any grasping at unjust gain, whether public or private. I never hounded anyone with lawsuits, whether citizen or alien, nor did I use my talents against you for private interests; rather, whenever necessary I came forward in your behalf and in the public interest. The older people would know – indeed, 10 you ought to tell those who are too young to know – about the meeting of the Assembly when Python of Byzantium came bringing ambassadors from the Greeks, before whom he intended to prove our city guilty of wrongdoing. He left after meeting with the reverse of his expectations, when I alone of all who were then your spokesmen presented your side of the case. And I say nothing of all the embassies on which I served in your behalf, in which you never got the worst of it in any respect.

In my actions throughout my political career, gentlemen of Athens, 11 I was not looking for ways in which you might get the better of one another, nor was I spurring the city against itself, but doing what I thought would bring you glory and pride. It is for these considerations that all, especially the young, should give their admiration. You ought to look not only for the man who, to curry favor, will stoop in his political conduct to every form of subservience (for there can never be a lack of him) but also for the man who out of loyalty will take you to task for your errors of judgment.

Furthermore, I am leaving unmentioned many things on the 12 strength of which another person, even if he had no other service to his credit, would have a just claim to receive exoneration: paying for the equipment of choruses and triremes and donations of money to the state in every crisis. In all this you will notice that I have not only been the first to come forward myself, but I have also successfully urged others to do so. Gentlemen of Athens, consider these one by one and see how little I deserve the misfortune which has come upon me.

The troubles surrounding me are so numerous, I do not know 13 which to deplore first. Shall it be the age at which I am driven, contrary to usage and contrary to my deserts, to undergo a perilous exile? Shall it be the shameful charge under which I stand condemned although convicted without any demonstration or proof? Shall it be my dashed hopes, my woes which should have fallen to the lot of

14 others? My political record in the past gives no grounds why I should be punished, nor have the charges on which I was tried been proved. Indeed, I shall never be shown to have been one of the friends of Harpalus; of all the proposals put forward to deal with Harpalus, only those drawn up by me kept the city above reproach. From all this it is clear that I have been the victim of circumstances and not of my own wrongdoing; namely, as the first to come before the court, I was unjustly exposed to the anger directed against all those who

15 were accused. For which of the pleas that won exoneration for those tried later did I not advance? Or what proof did the Council present against me? Or what proof could it present now? In fact there is none, for it is impossible to make things to have happened that never happened. But on this subject I shall write no more, although I have much that I could add. To have the consciousness of being innocent is, I have found, a feeble help, but the most painful means of all for increasing my distress.

16 Now, however, that you have done the right thing and become reconciled to the other defendants, grant me that reconciliation, too, gentlemen of Athens. For I have never wronged you, as the gods and heroes may be my witnesses (indeed, testifying for me is the entire period which has gone by up to now, and it has a more just claim on your belief than the unproved accusation which was brought so recently). Nor shall I be made out to be the worst and most faithless of the accused.

17 Moreover, there is no good reason why my departure should arouse your anger. I did not leave because I had despaired of you or because I was looking in any other direction. I left, first, because mentally it was hard for me to bear the shame of being in prison, and, second, because physically I would not be able to endure the maltreatment, on account of my age. Again, I thought that you, too, would not object to my getting beyond the reach of contumely which was doing you no good and was destroying me.

18 In fact, you can see many indications that you were in my thoughts and no one else. In the first place, I did not go to a city in which I myself would have the greatest prospects but to one where I knew our forefathers had gone when the Persian menace was overtaking them, and to one where I was certain that there was the most good

19 will toward you. That city is Troezen. My first hope is that all the

gods may show good will toward her citizens in return for their good will toward you and their kindness to me; and my second hope is that, vindicated by you, I may myself be able to repay them my debt of gratitude. Moreover, when some persons in that city, thinking to please me, tried to cast reproach upon you for your mistaken conduct toward me, I, for my part, displayed all due reticence. This, I believe, was the chief reason why they all admired me and accorded me honor in the name of the city.

However, when I saw that great as was the good will of these men, 20 their power to deal with the present situation was very inadequate, I left and have taken asylum in Calauria at the temple of Poseidon.[5] I have done so not only for the safety which, with the help of the god, I hope is mine (indeed, I am not sure of it, for the power of others to do whatever they choose renders the safety of a person in jeopardy frail and unpredictable) but also because from here every day I see my country, toward which I feel in myself as much good will as I pray to obtain from you.

Therefore, gentlemen of Athens, in order that I should no longer 21 be kept in my present straits, enact for me what you have already voted for others, so that nothing unworthy of you may befall me and so that I may not be forced to become a suppliant eleswhere – for that would be to your discredit as much as mine. Indeed, if my differences with you really are irreconcilable, it would have been better for me to have been put to death. You would have good 22 reason to believe that I am so minded and am not now making an idle bluff. I even put myself in your power and did not run away before my trial. In so doing, I wished to keep from betraying the truth; I wished none of you to lose his power over me; I wished you to deal with me in whatever way you pleased. I thought that those from whom I had received all honor and distinction should have the power even to commit a blunder against me if they wished. But now 23 that the just Fortune has rightly prevailed over the unjust and allowed you to deliberate twice on the same questions since there is nothing irreparable about the verdict in my case, grant me exoneration, gentlemen of Athens, and pass a vote worthy both of yourselves and of me. On the score of none of my previous acts will you find me 24

[5] Alternative translation: "Resorting to the temple of Poseidon, I have taken asylum in Calauria."

guilty of any wrong or deserving to be disfranchised or condemned. On the contrary, you will find me as loyal to you, the People, as anyone – to write nothing invidious; you will find me to be a man who, among those living today, has accomplished most on your behalf, one who, for his part, can present the greatest tokens of his good will toward you.

25 Let none of you suppose, gentlemen of Athens, that when I express my grief throughout this letter I do so either from unmanliness or from any other base motive. Everyone ungrudgingly indulges his present sorrows, and those which are present to me (would they had never come to pass!), pain and tears and longing for my country and for you, and the thought of what I have suffered, all lead me to express my grief. If you give all these things fair consideration, you will find as little unmanly weakness attaching to me now as in my previous political activity on your behalf.

26 So much for what I have to say to all of you. I wish, however, to have a special word in your presence with those who are at odds with me. In so far as they acted to serve your mistaken judgments, let it be granted that they acted on your account, and I make no complaint. Now, however, that you have come to recognize those mistakes for what they are, if these men will grant me the same concessions that they made for the rest, they will be doing what is right. But if they venture to act spitefully, I call upon all of you to come to my assistance. Do not let me find their enmity stronger than your gratitude. Farewell.

EPISTLE 4

Concerning the Slanders of Theramenes

DEMOSTHENES TO THE Council and the People, greeting. I hear that Theramenes, among other slanderous things which he has said about me, is charging me with being a carrier of ill fortune. Clearly, the fellow does not know that abuse which fails to convict its victim of turpitude has no weight with fair-minded people. I am not surprised. After all, his manner of life is insolent; he is no citizen by nature; from childhood he was brought up in a brothel.[6] It is harder to understand how he would have any inkling of such truths than how he could fail to have knowledge of them.

Now, as for Theramenes, if ever vindicated I return from exile, I shall undertake to speak with the fellow concerning his drunken abuse both of you and of me. I think, even though he is entirely lacking in a sense of shame, that I shall bring him around to be more reasonable. To you, however, I should like in the public interest to present in a letter the thoughts I have on this subject. Please listen, giving your full attention, for I think they are worthy not only of being heard, but of being remembered.

In my opinion, your city of all cities is the most fortunate and the dearest to the gods. Indeed, I know that Zeus of Dodona and Dione and the Pythian Apollo continually say so in their oracles and confirm it by their seals: that Good Fortune has her abode with you in the city. When the gods make revelations concerning things to come, obviously they are making predictions. But whenever they confer a name which has reference to the past, they do so in consideration of developments which have come to pass.

[6] The word translated "brothel" is ambiguous and perhaps would better be rendered "workshop." See commentary.

4   Admittedly, the things which I accomplished among you in my political career are included among those developments that have already come to pass, referring to which the gods have given you the name of "fortunate." If those who have been persuaded get a name for their good fortune, wherein is it right that the one who persuaded them should acquire a name for the contrary? There is only one thing to say: whereas the common good fortune, brought about through my advice, is attested by gods who cannot lie, the personal slander directed against me by Theramenes has been uttered by an insolent, shameless, absolutely brainless man.

5   Furthermore, the oracles sent by the gods are not the only means by which you will be led to the conclusion that your fortune has been good, but also a look at the facts themselves, provided you examine them in the right way. If you choose to look at things the way human beings should, you will find that the city has been most fortunate as a result of my advice. If, however, you are going to demand that you get what belongs to the gods alone, you are reaching for the impossible.

6   What is the special privilege of the gods, impossible for man? That, having control over all blessings, they are able both to keep them for themselves and to confer them on others, and that throughout the ages they never suffer any humiliation or face the prospect of it. Once you have accepted these assumptions, as you ought, consider your own circumstances as compared to those of the rest of the human race.

7   No one is so unreasonable as to say that the fate which has come upon the Lacedaemonians, who were not advised by me, or upon the Persians, whom I never even visited, is preferable to your present circumstances. I say nothing of the Cappadocians and Syrians and the people who live in India on out to the farthest regions of the earth, upon all of whom has come much terrible and grievous suffering.

8   "That is all very well," someone will say. "Everyone will grant that you are better off than these; but you are worse off than the Thessalians, the Argives, and the Arcadians, or others whose lot it was to become Philip's allies." In fact, however, you have come off better than they, and by far. It is not only that you have not been reduced to subservience – and yet what else counts as much as that?

It is also that they are all thought of as bearing responsibility for the evils which have come upon the Greeks through Philip and through their subservience to him; for that, they are hated, and with reason. Whereas you are observed to have committed yourselves, your money, 9 your city, your land, your all to the struggle of the Greeks, in return for which there is good reason that glory should be yours along with the undying gratitude of all whose wish is to do what is right. Surely then, my advice has turned out to have brought the city the best fortune among those which resisted as well as the advantage of a nobler reputation than the cities which collaborated.

These, then, are the reasons the gods have given you favorable 10 oracles and are bringing the unjust slander down upon the head of the one who utters it, as anyone would know if he chose to examine the pursuits in which Theramenes spends his life. For he does by 11 preference the things which one would wish upon him in a curse: he is an enemy to his parents, but a friend to Pausanias, the catamite. He swaggers like a man, but allows himself to be used like a woman. He lords it over his father, but is a slave to degeneracy. His mind takes pride in habits for which he is the object of everyone's detestation: his foul language and his way of dwelling on things which bring pain to the hearers. Yet he goes on talking, as if he were a good-natured soul just bursting with frankness.

I would not have written even this had I not wished to stir your 12 minds to remember the evils that lodge with him. For there are things which anyone would hesitate to say and would avoid putting into writing and, as I think, would also be disgusted to hear. Reminded of those by what I have written, each of you is aware of all the shockingly disgraceful qualities that lodge with this man, so that without my having said anything indecent the fellow whenever seen serves as a reminder to everyone of the evils that belong to him. Farewell.

EPISTLE 1

On Concord

1   IN BEGINNING ANY weighty undertaking, whether in word or in deed, one should, I believe, first take his beginning from the gods. Therefore, I pray to all the gods and goddesses that whatever is best, both now and for the future, for the Athenian People and for those who wish them well, will occur to my mind to write and to the minds of the Athenians gathered in the Assembly to adopt. Having offered this prayer, and with the hope of good inspiration from the gods, I send the following letter.

2   DEMOSTHENES TO THE Council and the People, greeting.
    The subject of my return home, I think, is something about which you will all be able to deliberate at any time, and for this reason I am writing nothing about it now. I see, however, that the present opportunity can at one stroke win glory, security, and liberty, not only for you but for all the rest of the Greeks, provided you adopt the necessary measures; if you fail to recognize it or if you are misled, it will not be easy to get the same opportunity again. Therefore, I felt that I had to put before the public the opinion which I myself hold on this subject.

3   Now it is, to be sure, difficult for advice read from a letter to hold its own, for you have a way of opposing many a speaker without waiting to learn what he has to say. Of course, it is easy for one who is making a speech to sense your mood and set right any misunderstandings, but a written page has no such recourse against hecklers. Nevertheless, if you consent to listen quietly and wait to learn everything that I have to say, I think (in so far as I may speak with the

favor of the gods) that although my message is brief, you will find me doing my duty by you in all loyalty and revealing to you where your interests lie.

It is not because I thought you were in need of political speakers 4 or of persons who without reflecting will glibly say whatever comes to mind that I decided to send this letter. Rather, I wished, by revealing whatever knowledge I happen to have acquired from experience and from having kept close track of public affairs, to give those who choose to speak plenty of starting points for discussing what I believe is to your advantage, while making it easy for the People to make the best decisions. These, then, are the reasons why it occurred to me to write this letter.

First of all, gentlemen of Athens, you must establish concord 5 among yourselves for the sake of the common interest of the city and lay aside the disputes of past meetings of the Assembly. Second, you must all give your united and ardent support to your resolutions once passed. Indeed, failure to act unanimously and wholeheartedly is not only beneath you and ignoble; it is fraught with the greatest danger.

There is something else, too, which you must not forget; though 6 by itself not sufficient for mastery in affairs of state, when added to your military resources, it will make everything much easier of accomplishment for you. To what do I refer? To refraining from feeling bitterness or harboring a grudge against any city or against any of the men in any city who have collaborated with the existing order.

The fear of such animosity makes ardent collaborationists of those 7 persons who know that they themselves are bound to the existing order and that they are in obvious danger. Released from that fear, they will all become more tractable, and this is of no small benefit. To proclaim this policy publicly to the various cities is naive or, rather, not even in the realm of possibility. But the way you show yourselves dealing among yourselves will determine the sort of expectations you will inspire in everyone's mind as to your way of dealing with others.

So I say that you must not cast any blame or censure whatsoever 8 upon anyone, whether general, politician, or private citizen, who up to now has given the appearance of collaborating with the existing order. Rather, you must grant that everyone in the city has done his duty as a citizen, now that the gods have been so good as to deliver the city and give you the opportunity to consider afresh whatever you may want to do. You must think that just as on a ship for getting through safely some may recommend the sail and others the oars, so everything said on both sides has had the aim of deliverance, but its utility has been determined by the course of events as willed by the gods.

9   If you make that sort of resolution about what is past, you will be trusted by everyone; your actions will be the actions of honorable men; and you will have conferred no small benefit on your enterprise. Either you will cause all your opponents in the cities to change their minds, or you will bring it about that a very few of them, and those the guilty ones, will be left. Accordingly, pursue the common interest as befits high-minded men and good citizens, and forget your private grudges.

10   I advocate this policy though personally I have not met with such humane consideration at the hands of certain persons but have been unjustly and factiously sacrificed to please persons in other quarters, as thoughtlessly as one makes a gift in a drinking bout. But it is my opinion that I must not hurt the public interest by satisfying my private resentment, nor do I mix a drop of my private hatred into matters of the public interest. On the contrary, what I advocate for others I believe I should be the first to practice myself.

11   The preparatory steps and the things which must be avoided and the measures by which, within the limits of human reckoning, one can come closest to success have been pretty well set forth by me. To manage day-to-day affairs and to handle unexpected develop-

12 ments correctly and to know the right time for everything and to decide which objectives can be won by negotiation and which require the application of force – all these are the task of the commanding generals. For that reason one who gives you advice puts himself into a most difficult position. Plans correctly thought out and weighed with much trouble and effort have often been spoiled when the commanders carried them out otherwise.

13   This time, however, I hope that everything will go well. For, indeed, if anyone believes that Alexander had good fortune in that he succeeded in everything, let him take into this account, that Alexander enjoyed his good fortune by doing and toiling and daring,

not by sitting around. So now that he is dead, Fortune is looking for people to be with; those people must be you.

As the commanders by whom the enterprise must be effected, 14 appoint over your forces the very most loyal. And whatever each one of you personally will be able and willing to do, let him make that his command to himself and promise to fulfill it. Let him not prove false to it or shrink from it, saying that he was deceived or misled, for you will not find anyone to make up for the deficiency where you 15 yourselves fall short. Frequent changes of mind with respect to matters in which it is in your power to do as you please do not run the same danger as such changes in matters which involve war; in fact, a change of mind in the latter case means a defeat of your project. So do not do anything of that kind, but vote for that program which you will carry out with a noble and resolute spirit. And once you have passed 16 it, take as your supreme commanders Zeus of Dodona and the other gods, who have returned you many admirable and true oracles; call upon them, making vows to all of them of the prizes of victory. And then, with Good Fortune on your side, liberate the Greeks! Farewell.

PART 5

Commentary

EPISTLE 3*

Concerning the Sons of Lycurgus

TITLE. Περὶ τῶν Λυκούργου παίδων. Harpocration (s. vv. ἐρανίζοντες and φθόη) and Hermogenes (*Id.* ii. 8, p. 364 Rabe, Vol. III, p. 349 Walz) cite Ep. 3 under the same title (on Hermogenes' change of the the preposition to ὑπέρ, see below, on paragraph 1). Maximus Planudes, *Scholia in Hermog. Id. i*, Vol. V, p. 495 Walz, gives the letter the title Περὶ ἀφέσεως, *On Absolution*. Note the use of the verb ἀφίημι at paragraphs 10, 24, 26, 37, and 43; it reflects legal terminology. The anonymous *Scholia in Hermog. Id. i*, Vol. VII, p. 993 Walz, quote both titles. No title appears in the papyrus. Probably *On the Sons of Lycurgus* is the earlier title, though *On Absolution* is more appropriate, since Demosthenes is also pleading for himself. Compare Dionysius of Halicarnassus' proposal of the more appropriate *In Reply to the Letter and Ambassadors from Philip* for D. 7 instead of Callimachus' title, *On Halonnesus* (Dion. Hal. *Dem.* 13, Vol. I, p. 157 U.-R.; cf. Libanius *Hypoth.* to D. 7).

The principal sources on Lycurgus are *Vit. X orat.* 841–44 and the decree of Stratocles of 307/6, preserved in two versions, *Vit. X orat.* 851f–852e and *IG* II² 457 (fragmentary). A brief article in the *Suda* gives a list of his speeches. The best modern treatments are F. Dürrbach (ed.), *Lycurgue: Contre Léocrate*, pp. 1–22 and *L'orateur Lycurgue* (Paris: Ernest Thorin, 1889); and Glotz-Roussel-Cohen, pp. 198–202.

Lycurgus' earliest known political activity was his participation with Demosthenes in the embassies to win support against Philip in 342 B.C. (D. 9. 72—vulg., not **SFYO**; cf. *Vit. X orat.* 841e; Schaefer,

*For the historical background of Ep. 3, see above. pp. 52–56.

II, 427, n. 2). Shortly after the battle of Chaeroneia he was elected chief financial administrator of Athens with the title ὁ ἐπὶ τῇ διοικήσει (Hyp. *Dem.* 28; *Vit. X orat.* 852b; B. D. Meritt, "Greek Inscriptions," *Hesperia*, XXIX[1960], 2–4; Glotz-Roussel-Cohen, p. 199). In this post he handled large sums of money, became famous for his incorruptibility, and several times was publicly rewarded with a crown (*IG* II² 457, 13–14; *Vit. X orat.* 841b, d; 852b, d).

After Chaeroneia he also became a leading anti-Macedonian politician. In 335 the Athenians refused to comply with Alexander's demand for the surrender of Lycurgus' person (*Vit. X orat.* 841e, 852d; *IG* II² 457, 17–19; see below, paragraph 31). He was still alive in 324 to oppose the granting of divine honors to Alexander (*Vit. X orat.* 842d). For his last days and the trial which resulted in the imprisonment of his sons, see above, pp. 53–56.

An imprecation tablet cursing both Demosthenes and Lycurgus for participating in a prosecution: E. Ziebarth, "Neue attische Fluchtafeln," *Nachrichten von der Königl. Gesellschaft der Wissenschaften zu Göttingen, phil.-hist. Klasse,* 1899, p. 108.

PARAGRAPH 1. περὶ μὲν ... ἐπέσταλκα. In Athenian inscriptions of this time which record decrees of the Council and Assembly, when a speaker proposes amendments to proposals of others, his amendments are introduced by περὶ ὧν λέγει ὁ δεῖνα; and, if the earlier proposal came from abroad by letter, by περὶ ὧν ἐπιστέλλει κτλ· (e.g., *IG* II² 212, 213, both of 347/6). In this usage, περί begins to be replaced by ὑπέρ already in 307/6 and entirely disappears after the middle of the third century; see W. Larfeld, *Handbuch*, II, 682, and cf. Moraux, p. 37, n. 53, and Schwegler, p. 71. Hence we derive one more argument for an early date for Ep. 3.

In papyrus letters of the Ptolemaic period, sentences beginning with the phrase περί τινος are frequently used to call attention to the subject to be discussed. Serving the function of titles, these phrases are often included with no regard for the structure of the rest of the sentence, often, as here, serving as direct object (of "disregard" and "give a hearing"). See E. Mayser, *Grammatik der griechischen Papyri aus der Ptolemäerzeit*, II², 449–50.

On Demosthenes' "earlier letter," see above, pp. 48–49, 52. The perfect tense of ἐπέσταλκα is the regular usage in epistolary style (Mayser, II¹, 183; Kühner-Gerth, I, 168, n. 6). Epistolary perfects occur also at Ep. 3. 35 and at Ep. 1. 2, 3.

PARAGRAPH 1. ἐπιτιμώντων ὑμῖν τοῖς ... γιγνομένοις. This verb recurs with a double dative at Ep. 2. 19 but nowhere else in the Attic orators nor in Thucydides, Xenophon, Plato, and Aristotle; see Neupert, p. 59, and Sachsenweger, pp. 28–29. Nevertheless, both the dative of the person and the dative of the thing reproved are normal with this verb. Except at Aesch. 2. 79 the accusative is used with this verb only as a cognate accusative, usually a pronoun (so at Ep. 3. 19), which properly represents the content of the reproof, not the thing reproved.

PARAGRAPH 2. ἐκεῖνος ... προσένειμεν ἑαυτόν. Demosthenes' fondness for comparing political with military activity is the key to translating this passage (see also on Ep. 2. 5, ἐξηταζόμην). I have followed the unambiguous syntax of the similar military figure at D. 15. 31–33 in construing τῆς πολιτείας with μέρει; it might also be construed with τὸ κατ'ἀρχάς with the translation, "during the first stages of his political career." See 18. 62. The word μέρος here is probably also military; see 18. 292 and μερίς at 18. 63–64, 176. Finally, when Lycurgus is said at the end of the paragraph to have "attached himself" to the People's cause, the verb again is probably military idiom; see D. 14. 22 and 60. 11.

PARAGRAPH 2. περὶ τῶν ... γράφειν. In this field of politics, Lycurgus needed and used the help of others; and, lacking the aptitude for extemporaneous speaking necessary for success before the Assembly he constantly practiced to improve himself (*Vit. X orat.* 842c).

PARAGRAPH 3. Demosthenes says much the same of himself at Ep. 2. 6 as of Lycurgus here.

PARAGRAPH 3. πολλοὺς ... κινδύνους. The dangers lay not only in the power of Macedonia. In Athens, politicians could easily find means to prosecute their opponents. The constitution afforded many opportunities to attack a spokesman in the Assembly or an executive or administrative official who dared to take a position on a controversial issue. See Arist. *Ath. Pol.* 43. 4, 45. 2, 61. 2; D. 18. 189, 246, 249–250, 282, 322; 20. 100, 135; 23. 97; *Prooemm.* 25, 26. 2-3; Hyp. *Dem.* 28-29, *Eux.* 7-8; Lipsius, pp. 180–81, 286–96, 381–82.

PARAGRAPH 3. τὸν ... προαιρούμενον. This is the sort of language used in honorific decrees. Cf. the description of Lycurgus in Stratocles' decree of 307/6, *Vit. X orat.* 852d. Other examples of such vocabulary occur below in paragraphs 4 and 9.

PARAGRAPH 4. With τοὺς ... ἀσθενεῖς, cf. D. 18. 320. The vocabulary of honorific decrees appears again in εἴλεθ’ ... προσῆκεν; cf. *IG* II² 223, 11–12, and the formulas quoted at Aesch. 2. 49–50 and Hyp. fr. 76 Kenyon. The imperfect ἐξητεῖτο is used because the demand was not carried out (Kühner-Gerth, Vol. I, p. 144). Everyone knew that after the fall of Thebes in 335 Alexander also demanded the surrender of Demosthenes' person (D. 18. 41; see commentary to Ep. 3. 31–32). Having dismissed his own problems in paragraph 1, the orator refrains from mentioning himself here. Would a person not concerned with holding the attention of a hostile audience have passed up the opportunity?

PARAGRAPH 6. ζῶντα Λυκ. κτλ. See above, *Title*.

PARAGRAPH 6. δημοτικὸν παρὰ πάντας ἡγεῖσθε. "Believe him, beyond anyone else, . . ." here is paralleled by D. 19. 239, "care, beyond anything else, for . . ." Hence the author here does not "undemosthenically substitute positive adjective plus prepositional phrase for superlative adjective" (so Neupert, p. 59; cf. Sachsenweger, p. 29; comparative of this adjective: D. 22. 67, 24. 174; superlative: Lys. 25. 23; Isoc. 7. 16, 59; Hyp. *Dem.* 5, *Ath.* 21; Aesch. 3. 194).

PARAGRAPH 6. τῷ φῆσαι Λυκοῦργον. At *Vit. X orat.* 841f, Pseudo-Plutarch, obviously drawing on this passage, uses the same striking phrase: ὥστε καὶ ἐν τοῖς δικαστηρίοις τὸ φῆσαι Λυκ. ἐδόκει βοήθημα εἶναι τῷ συναγορευομένῳ. Cf. the fragment attributed to Demosthenes at Rutilius Lupus ii.4: "Atque ego illum, iudices, arbitror Lycurgum laudatorem producturum, scilicet qui sit testis eius pudori ac probitati. Sed ego Lycurgum vobis praesentibus hoc unum interrogabo, velitne se similem esse illius factis et moribus. Quod si negarit, satis factum vobis esse de veritate nostra debebit."

PARAGRAPH 6. οὐ γὰρ ἂν ἦν [Q Pap. ut vid.: ἄν καὶ F: ἦν S] τοιοῦτον μὴ δοκοῦν ὑμῖν. The ambiguous, elliptic, if not corrupt Greek has given considerable difficulty. Dindorf assumed a lacuna after ἦν, but the papyrus supports the reading of Q. τοιοῦτον has been construed as masculine and as part of the participial phrase: "All this could not have happened unless Lycurgus appeared to you to be that sort of person," or "And it would not have been [*sc.* sufficient] had you not had such an opinion of him" (Hieronymus Wolf; C. R. Kennedy; and the scholiast, *Oratores Attici* [Müller], II, 738). So complicated an impersonal construction with δοκεῖν is most unlikely. One would expect a genitive absolute as in the scholium and at D. 18. 228.

I have therefore preferred to construe τοιοῦτον as neuter, placing a comma after it to separate it from the participial phrase. "τοιοῦτόν ἐστι" means the same as "οὕτως ἔχει"; cf. D. 22. 6, 23. 193, 29. 38–39. The translation adopted is similar to that of J. Tate, Review of *Demosthenes VII*, by N. W. and N. J. DeWitt, *CR*, LXV (1951), 20–21. One might also translate, "All this could not have been so without your approval."

PARAGRAPH 7. δεδέσθαι. The verb here and at paragraphs 12 and 13 probably means not only "imprison" but "chain," for at paragraph 12 the lot of the sons of Lycurgus is compared to the lot of prisoners of war.

PARAGRAPH 8. ἐξεταζόμενος. The "scrutiny" includes not only the regular rendering of the accounts of his office (*euthynai;* cf. 18. 246) but also all those occasions on which Lycurgus had to defend his conduct (see paragraph 6). The same verb apparently was used by Lycurgus' enemy and successor Menesaechmus, to refer to the lawsuits in which his own conduct in office was challenged (Dion. Hal. *Din.* 11, Vol. I, p. 316 U.-R.). There is no trace here of the military connotation (see on Ep. 2. 5, ἐξηταζόμην).

PARAGRAPH 9. τῷ τετελευτηκότι κτλ. Athenian honorific inscriptions mention the citizens' intention of publicizing their gratitude to their benefactors (examples collected: Larfeld, *Handbuch*, II², 763–65). The point of civic gratitude also to the children of benefactors: *SIG*³ 317, 47–50 (318/7 B.C.); the decree of Stratocles, *Vit. X orat.* 852d (307/6 B.C.); and D. 20. 46, 72. To this strong point the author returns in paragraphs 15 and 19 below, another example of *commoratio* in Ep. 3 (see above, Chap. 8, n. 56).

PARAGRAPH 10. βουλεύεσθαι ἐγνώκατε codd.: βουλεύεσθε Pap.: ἐγνώκατε Blass. My translation renders any one of these readings. The reading of the papyrus has the merit for Demosthenes of suggesting that the Athenians' decision is not yet final. Though the hiatus exhibited by the reading of the manuscripts might be admissible (see Sachsenweger, pp. 45–46), the over-full reading of the manuscripts is probably a conflate. ἐγνώκατε may have been introduced or substituted for the reading of the papyrus under the influence of the perfect tense of the preceding clause, "You have taken the . . . course."

PARAGRAPHS 11–12. Like so many moralists, to goad his fellow-citizens to emulation, Demosthenes often praised the enemy while disparaging them; cf. 18. 67–68. On *synesis* and *paideia*, cf. D. 18. 127=Aesch. 3. 260. The contrast between the Athenians, possessors of these two virtues, and Philip, "a man untouched by moral instruction" (especially by the rebukes of free-speaking equals) and "brought up with the power to do as he pleased," reflects the view prevalent in Athens of the moral deficiency of a monarch when compared to a free citizen (Isoc. 2. 2–4; Plato *Lg.* iii. 694d–96a, Ep. 7. 332c–d). No matter what was the effect on Philip of his years as a hostage in Thebes (Diod. xvi. 2. 2–3; Justin vi. 9. 6; Plut. *Pel.* 26; F. Geyer, "Philippos 7," *RE*, XIX² [1938], 2266), an Athenian audience would readily accept this description of Philip (cf. H. Wolf in *Oratores Attici* [Dobson], VIII, 509; Neupert, p. 35). For the commonplace, Athens as a refuge, see Aesch. 3. 134; D. 57. 6; Isoc. 4. 52, 8. 138; *X. Hell.* vi. 5. 45; Apsines, Vol. IX, p. 581 Walz.

Although Philip kept the prerogatives of a victor (Paus. i. 25. 3), his leniency after the battle of Chaeroneia came as an unhoped for piece of good fortune to the Athenians. Even Demosthenes could do no more than question Philip's motives (D. 18. 231, 60. 20; Aesch. 3. 131).

With the portrayal here of Philip as undisciplined barbarian and sober statesman, cf. Diod. xvi. 87; Plut. *Dem.* 20; *Vit. X orat.* 849a.

PARAGRAPH 12. οὐκ ἐτόλμησε . . . ἐξετάσας. Since Demosthenes stresses immediately that Philip reckoned with the additional factor of worth, it would be wrong to take οὐκ as negating the participle as well and to translate, "He did not venture to chain them nor to ask whose sons they were and who they were." The point that Lycurgus' sons are being made to suffer for what their father was alleged to have done is not made until paragraphs 13–14.

In my translation I have tried to use the same English root to translate ἐξετάζειν here and at paragraph 14. The verb does mean to test the purity of metal (see the *Greek-English Lexicon*), and, in the opening stages of the battle of Chaeroneia, the Athenians did give a good account of themselves as descendants of the heroes of Marathon and Salamis.

PARAGRAPH 12. τῆς ἀξίας. The third-century A.D. Antiatticist lexicographer in *Anecdota Graeca*, ed. Immanuel Bekker, I, 77–116, gives articles for ἀξία here and for ἐργολάβος at Ep. 3. 34 (where not the noun but the related verb occurs). In both places he identifies Ep. 3

not by title but by incipit. He also has articles for ὁμιλία (Ep. 1. 12) and πικραίνεσθαι (Ep. 1. 6), each time identifying the source as "Demosthenes in a letter." Date of the Antiatticist: Kurt Latte, "Zur Zeitbestimmung des Antiatticista," *Hermes*, L (1915), 373–94; Tolkiehn, "Lexikographie," *RE*, XII² (1925), 2461.

ἀξία also appears in Hesychius, and ἐργολάβος in the *Etymologicum magnum* and in the *Suda*, which ascribes it to Demosthenes ἐν τῇ πρὸς τὴν βουλὴν καὶ τὸν δῆμον ἐπιστολῇ.

PARAGRAPH 13. ὄντες Ἀθηναῖοι. The papyrus omits this common oratorical mannerism of Demosthenes (cf. 18. 68; 15. 23; 23. 109; 32. 23).

PARAGRAPH 13. ἐν παρρησίᾳ ζῶντες Pap.: παιδείας μετέχοντες codd. The reading of the manuscripts may have been influenced by the mention of "cultivation" in paragraph 11; moreover, if "obtuse" here means absolutely stupid, the manuscript reading hardly makes sense. On the other hand, both "cultivation" and "free speech" were possessions on which the Athenians prided themselves and could be used almost interchangeably in contexts like the present one; cf. Isoc. 2. 2–4 and D. 60. 26–27.

PARAGRAPH 13. ἀνεκτούς. Neupert, pp. 55–56, objects that elsewhere in Demosthenes this word is always used with a negative. However, it is used affirmatively at Isoc. 8. 65 and 15. 48 and Aesch. 1. 34 (see Sachsenweger, p. 29).

PARAGRAPH 14. ἐν οἷς ἐξεταζομένοις. For the construction, cf. Lyc. *Leoc.* 30 and D. 18. 57.

PARAGRAPH 14. πᾶσι . . . τελευτή. The principle of not holding the children liable for the crimes of their fathers was the exception in antiquity, but it was well established in fourth-century Athens. The development by which the doctrine of personal responsibility replaced that of the collective responsibility of the family is traced in G. Glotz, *La solidarité de la famille dans le droit criminel en Grèce*, pp. 225–608.

Pecuniary obligations, however, were necessarily an exception. Thus the case against Lycurgus could still be pressed against his sons. The idea of the death of a parent as a limit for initiating actions against his irregularities was used by defendants in the Athenian courts at this time. See D. 57. 27.

PARAGRAPH 15. See on paragraph 9.

PARAGRAPH 15. μέχρι . . . χρῆσθαι. For the construction, cf. D. 19. 13.

PARAGRAPH 15. οὐδέν . . . αἱρεῖσθαι. Cf. D. 18. 138.

PARAGRAPHS 16–18. The sources on Moerocles have been treated above, Chap. 5, nn. 57, 101; Chap. 8, rhetorical analysis of Ep. 3. 16–18; and below, commentary to paragraph 31. Some further aspects of Moerocles' position as one of the Eleven remain to be considered.

The Eleven were responsible for preventing escapes from prison (Din. 2. 14). The unauthorized release of a prisoner was punishable by death (Isaeus 4. 28, but cf. P. Roussel [ed.], *Isée: discours*, p. 81, n. 1). Hence Moerocles could claim that in chaining Lycurgus' sons to prevent their escape he was merely doing his duty. In practice, however, the Eleven were not always strictly held to their duty (cf. Plato *Apol.* 37c, *Phaedo* 59e), as Demosthenes is quick to complain. On the other hand, the Eleven may have been rigorous now for fear of Menesaechmus (see above, p. 54–55). Moerocles, who had been suspected of taking money from Harpalus (see above, Chap. 5, n. 57), may have felt particularly vulnerable to prosecution.

The letter itself presents Moerocles' position as precarious. Paragraphs 16–17 imply that he had once incurred loss of his civil rights (*atimia*) and that the penalty, though never enforced, had never been revoked. Despite these disabilities, Moerocles had addressed the Assembly and now held office, crimes open to prosecution by the procedure of *endeixis* and punishable by death (D. 20. 156; Lipsius, 336–37).

Simple indifference and political realities at which we can only guess would explain why Moerocles had not been prosecuted. Perhaps he and Pytheas (paragraphs 29–30) had political connections powerful enough to deter or buy off anyone who would prosecute or to nullify the effect of any conviction. In practice the Athenians did ignore obscure facts which legally would involve *atimia* until they were invoked in grudge suits (Ps.-D. 58; D. 22. 21–24, 29, 33–34; 25. 85–91). Even then, the charge of violation of *atimia* might not secure a conviction; despite the charges of D. 22, Androtion was acquitted (*F. Gr. Hist.*, Part III b [Supplement], Vol. I, pp. 89, 93–95). As a dutiful official, Moerocles, too, may have had little to fear.

Political realities certainly prevailed over legal requirements in Aristogiton's case. Lycurgus proceeded against him by *endeixis* for prosecuting while *atimos* (*Hypoth.* to D. 25; D. 25 and 26), but only after waiting two years for a propitious moment (D. 25. 38); even the lodging of the *endeixis* did not deter him from inveighing against officials before his trial (D. 25. 64). Though Aristogiton was then convicted, the Eleven still failed to impose upon him the full measure of his disabilities (Din. 2. 13–14). Eventually, the Athenians executed Aristogiton (*Suda s.v. Aristogeiton*), perhaps for violating the disabilities of *atimia*. On Aristogiton, see also Chap. 8, rhetorical analysis of Ep. 3. 16–18, and *Pros. Att.*, No. 1775; possible identifications of Taureas and Pataecus: *ibid.*, Nos. 13430 and 11677–78.

The pairing of the words, "blackguardism" and "shamelessness" (paragraph 18), or of the cognate adjectives appears in the Attic orators only in Demosthenes (8. 68; 19. 175, 206; 21. 107, 151; 25. 27; fragment *apud* Philodemus *Peri rhêt.* col. 40, Vol. I, pp. 241–42 Sudhaus); cf., however, Aesch. 1. 105, 189.

PARAGRAPH 19. On the Athenians' treatment of the descendants of Aristides, see D. 20. 115 and Plut. *Arist.* 27. 1–3. Plutarch's citation from Demetrius of Phalerum there shows that descendants of Aristides were still receiving grants of public maintenance at the time of the letters.

Thrasybulus and Archinus were leaders in the movement which overthrew the Thirty Tyrants in 404–3 and in the restored democracy thereafter (*Pros. Att.*, Nos. 7310 and 2526). The city honored "the men who came from Phyle and restored the exiled democracy" with the modest rewards of willow crowns and money for sacrifices and other offerings to the gods (Aesch. 3. 187; *GHI* 100). According to Nepos *Thrasyb.* 4. 3, Thrasybulus was content with that; but the People, either then or later in his career, may have voted further honors to him and his descendants.

Demosthenes himself provides our only sources on how the city treated the descendants of Thrasybulus and Archinus (D. 19. 280–81; 24. 133–36); he says that descendants of Thrasybulus and Archinus received not rewards but harsh treatment. Is the letter then a forgery? (So Schaefer, *NJb*, CXV, 164; Neupert, p. 24; Blass, *NJb*, CXV, 543, gives the lame defense of suggesting that between the two orations and Demosthenes' exile the treatment of the descendants had changed.)

A correct interpretation of the passages vindicates Ep. 3. At 19.

280–81 Demosthenes reinforces his argument for the condemnation of Aeschines. Aeschines has been shown to have committed crimes and to be of worthless descent. The descendants of great benefactors of the people enjoy very real privileges accorded by a grateful citizenry. Nevertheless, when one of these descendants *himself* becomes guilty of a crime, his privileges do not protect him from being punished. How much less should Aeschines escape! Similarly, at 24. 133–36 famous examples are invoked to show that worthy men and their privileged descendants have been punished when they were *themselves* found guilty of crime. All the more are the wicked Androtion and his associates to be punished! Thus in both these passages the existence of privileges for the *law-abiding* descendants of the heroes of Phyle is confirmed. At this point of his argument, Demosthenes takes Lycurgus' patriotism as proved; moreover, everyone would admit that the children of Lycurgus themselves had committed no crime. Accordingly, the orator equates the children of the patriot Lycurgus with the *law-abiding* descendants of the patriots Aristides, Thrasybulus, and Archinus to show the Athenians the disgraceful inconsistency of their giving Lycurgus' sons dishonor and punishment as their heritage, instead of honor and privilege.

PARAGRAPH 22. The construction ἕτοιμος εἰς recurs in Demosthenes only at 18. 161 and Ep. 3. 29; it does not occur in the other Attic orators or in Aristotle, Plato, Thucydides, or Xenophon.

The papyrus confirms the reading of the generalizing optative, ἀδικοῖσθε (Kühner-Gerth, II, 427).

The expression λογισμὸν ἔχων does not occur elsewhere in the Attic orators. It is synonymous with the common νοῦν ἔχων (D. 18. 256; 19. 53; etc.), and a close enough parallel exists at Isoc. 12. 69, λογισμὸς ἐνῆν αὐτοῖς (cf. also Isoc. 15. 149; Plato *Lg.* vii. 805a).

PARAGRAPH 23. ἀγνοεῖ, ὡς κτλ. The ὡς-clause is adverbial (cf. D. 1. 3, 28; 2. 2; etc.). Only at Ps.-D. 40. 21 in the Demosthenic corpus does this verb govern an object clause introduced by ὡς instead of ὅτι.

PARAGRAPH 23. τῇ πολιτείᾳ. I have deliberately translated this word by the ambiguous "republic." An important connotation of the word in this context, where Demosthenes replies to legal objections to the release of Lycurgus' sons, is "the constitution." See above, Chap. 8, rhetorical analysis of Ep. 3. 23–28.

PARAGRAPH 23. ἀλλὰ μήν. See above, Chap. 3, n. 9.

PARAGRAPH 24. Laches, the son of Melanopus, was a member of a prominent Athenian family (stemma: *Pros. Att.*, No. 9019). See *Pros. Att.*, No. 9020; Berve, Vol. II, No. 465. Other intercessions by Alexander: Photius *Bibl.*, Cod. 176, p. 120b Bekker (for Theopompus); cf. Ps.-D. 17. 12 and Plut. *Alex.* 29. 5. A monument possibly set up by Laches to commemorate his exoneration: B. D. Meritt, "Greek Inscriptions," *Hesperia*, XVI (1947), 152, No. 44.

Mnesibulus of Acharnae is know only from here (*Pros. Att.*, No. 10268; Fritz Geyer, "Mnesibulus 2," *RE*, XV² [1930], 2274).

καλῶς ποιῶν is a common idiom for expressing approval. Where someone is praised for his action, it can be rendered "He did the right thing in . . .-ing," but in other contexts, as here, the idiom must be rendered "fortunately," "deservedly," etc.; another instance of the idiom with a passive verb: Aristoph. *Pl.* 863. See C. Rehdantz, *Demosthenes' neun philippische Reden*, Vol. II 2: *Indices*, pp. 120–21. καλῶς ποιήσεις as apodosis to a conditional participle or clause (as at Ep. 2. 26) is a formula of request, "please," or "be so good as to . . ."; it is common in papyrus letters from the very earliest (Mayser, II 1, 173–74; II 3, 62–63). The seven occurrences of this expression in the letters (Ep. 3. 24, 30; Ep. 2. 2, 16, 23, 26; Ep. 1. 8) should arouse no suspicion (cf. Neupert, p. 70). Elsewhere in the Demosthenic corpus it occurs twelve times, twice in one paragraph at D. 10. 38 and thrice in the short compass of D. 20. 110–49 (D. 1. 28; 10. 38; 18. 231, 314; 20. 110, 133, 149; 21. 2, 212; 25. 97; 57. 6; *Prooem.* 36. 1).

PARAGRAPH 25. τῶν νῦν βοώντων. There was already vociferous opposition to efforts to set aside the sentence imposed on Lycurgus' sons, according to these words. The author is not writing against a mere anticipated objection but meeting a real situation. Neupert, p. 42, viewed the words as a careless slip: the author forgot he was writing a letter and lapsed into oratorical language! (See p. 99.)

Since Demosthenes here alludes to efforts on behalf of Lycurgus' sons, Treves is not justified in complaining that Ep. 3 does not refer to Hyperides' efforts for them whereas Demosthenes himself would have used every means to reconcile his estranged ally (*Athenaeum*, n.s., XIV, 248). There are two possible reconstructions of the background of the letter. Either Hyperides early rose to the defense of the sons of Lycurgus, and Demosthenes here seconds his efforts; or

Hyperides at first did not oppose Menesaechmus, and Demosthenes here tries to rouse him to action.

From the surviving fragment of Hyperides' speech on behalf of Lycurgus' sons (*apud* Apsines, pp. 301-2 H.; Hyp. fr. 118), one cannot tell whether it was delivered to the court which condemned them and deplores the possibility that they will be imprisoned, or whether it was delivered to the Assembly to plead for their exoneration and release (so Schaefer, III, 349-50; Blass, III 2, 15). At *Vit. X orat.* 842e, Democles, the pupil of Theophrastus is the one who spoke, evidently before the Assembly, for the release of Lycurgus' sons; Hyperides is not mentioned.

Perhaps Hyperides at first was hostile to Lycurgus' sons. Lycurgus may have shared Demosthenes' views on how to deal with Harpalus (Philodemus *Peri rhêt.* vii, Vol. I, p. 359 Sudhaus: "Δημοσθένους καὶ Λυκούργου περὶ τῶν Ἁρπαλείων ψευδῆ πειράσονται δεικνύειν, (ἐκ) δέ τῶν μάλιστα πεπιστευμένων ἱστοριογράφων γράφειν, ἅ φησιν λέγειν, καὶ πάντως ἀσημότατον εἶναι διατενοῦνται καὶ δυσμενῆ καὶ τὸ πέρας ἀναιδείας"). Indeed, *Vit. X orat.* 848f suggests that Hyperides' friendship for Lycurgus cooled as much as his friendship for Demosthenes. Having been suspected of taking money from Harpalus (see above, Chap. 5, n. 57), Hyperides may have had reason to fear prosecution by Menesaechmus if he stood in the way of Menesaechmus' revenge.

Hyperides probably did rise to the defense from the first, joining Menesaechmus only to prosecute Demosthenes. Demosthenes here would not have singled out Hyperides' efforts for praise; thus far, they had been unsuccessful, and were but a half-way measure against the "general conspiracy against patriotic citizens," the existence of which Demosthenes seeks to prove. See the remarks on Hyperides below, to Ep. 3. 34. If *Vit. X orat.* 848f means that Hyperides grew hostile to Lycurgus, it is strange to find no mention there of a failure to defend Lycurgus' sons.

PARAGRAPH 26. τοὺς βίους ἐσώζετε. All manuscripts and the papyrus read βίους. Rendering it as "lives" leads to nonsense (Neupert, p. 36; Schaefer, *NJb*, CXV, 166). Greek usage forbids rendering it with the DeWitts as the "life-work" of the men who enacted the laws. It is barely possible that the word means "way of life" and has been corrupted from singular to plural under the influence of the genitive plural which follows; cf. Arist. *Pol.* iv. 11. 3. 1295a40-41. More likely, the presence of βίου and the verb "to save" led to the corruption of some other word into βίους, and that word referred to some aspect of the laws (cf. Plato *Lg.* vi. 769d–70c; Th. viii. 76. 6). Rennie's text has the mere conjecture λογισμούς. On the basis of Arist. *Rhet.* i. 13. 17. 1374*b*10 ff., I suggest τὴν διάνοιαν.

PARAGRAPH 26. σωφροσύνη. This untranslatable word denotes one of the four cardinal virtues of the Greeks (Plato *R.* iv. 430c–32a; cf. D. 18. 215, 26. 25). It was an important catchword in Athenian political life. To have this virtue meant to have the good sense which keeps one within the bounds of both expediency and morality (D. 2. 22, *Prooem.* 43; Th. i. 84. 1–3). Possession of it throughout life gave one a claim on the mercy of the court (D. 25. 77; cf. 24. 126). In paragraph 27, Demosthenes stresses that Mnesibulus was "unknown" to Athenian political life; hence the word here may carry the connotation of refusal to be drawn by ambition into the hazards of politics, despite the usual limitation of its scope to bodily pleasures (Lys. 21. 19; Arist. *EN* iii. 10. 1117*b*23 ff.; *Rhet.* i. 9. 9. 1366*b*13–15; but cf. Arist. *EN* iv. 4. 1125*b*11–13). Cf. Aesch. 3. 218 and Demosthenes' reply at 18. 263.

PARAGRAPH 27. Cf. D. 18. 138. Demosthenes sharply distinguishes the activity of the συμβουλεύων, the citizen who uses his right to suggest a course of action to the Assembly, from that of ὁ τὰ κοινὰ πράττων, the man who seeks and receives from the People a position of public trust such as general, ambassador, or treasurer (D. 19. 99; 23. 205–209; 26. 22; sharp distinction: 18. 212, 245–46, Ep. 1. 11–12). See above on paragraph 3.

PARAGRAPH 28. The personification here of gratitude (*charites*) as the Graces was probably so commonplace that neither the author nor his audience was conscious of a pun; cf. Arist. *EN* v. 5. 7. 1133*a*3–5 and S. Gsell, "Gratiae," *Dictionnaire des antiquités grecques et romaines*, ed. Daremberg and Saglio, II 2 (1896), 1661a–1662a, 1664a. Nevertheless, scholars have taken exception to the figure as undemosthenic, expecially in a *demegoria* (Schaefer, *NJb*, CXV, 166; Neupert, pp. 36–37; Blass, III 1, 449; see also Rehdantz, *Indices*, pp. 37–38). Far more violent personifications of abstractions as deities are found at D. 25. 11, 33–35, 52, which I believe to be authentic (see above, Chap. 8, n. 163). In Demosthenes' *demegoriae* Fortune is certainly so treated (2. 2, 22; 4. 45), and note especially

Demosthenes' characterization of the Athenians' folly as an "evil genius" at 9. 54. If Demosthenes intended a pun here, one may compare the use of μηχάνημα at D. 9. 17–18 with the double sense of "subterfuge to evade the terms of the treaty" and "siege engine"; see also Blass, III 1, 165–66.

PARAGRAPHS 29–30. The information on Pytheas here is in harmony with the surviving ancient anecdotes; see Hans Gärtner, "Pytheas 3," *RE*, XXIV(1963), 366–69; *Pros. Att.*, No. 12342; above, Chap. 5, n. 107; Chap. 6, n. 121. However, the words μέχρι τῆς παρόδου must be correctly understood (cf. the difficulty at Hdt. vii. 143. 1, W. W. How and J. Wells, *A Commentary on Herodotus* [Oxford: Clarendon Press, 1928], II, 184–85).

According to Plut. *Phoc.* 21. 1, Pytheas at the beginning of his political career came forward to oppose complying with Alexander's request for ships. The earliest of such requests from Alexander came with the raising of the Hellenic fleet in 335/4 before his invasion of Asia Minor (Berve, Vol. II, p. 338, and Vol. I, pp. 159–60). The fleet of Hegelochus of 333 (Arrian ii. 2. 3; Curt. iii. 1. 19–20; Berve, I, 160–61; Schaefer, III, 173–74) is the last fleet mentioned as being raised for Alexander among the Greeks. After the defeat of Agis in 331, the Macedonians no longer needed ships from Athens. Hence, by 324/3, Pytheas' entrance into Athenian politics was long past.

When Pytheas reappears in our sources in 324, he is still holding an anti-Macedonian position, opposing the grant of divine honors to Alexander (Plut. *Praec. ger. reip.* 804b). The letter here speaks of Pytheas' sudden change from the appearance of being a patriot to unabashed espousal of the opposite course (cf. paragraph 33) as having happened recently. Hence, μέχρι τῆς παρόδου, if the letter is correct, must refer to a lengthy period during which Pytheas "maintained the appearance of being on the People's side"; it cannot be rendered with Neupert (p. 53), Pabst, Kennedy, and the DeWitts by "Donec accederet ad rempublicam." Demosthenes would not have called a man δημοτικός who had not yet entered public life (cf. D. 18. 122). Nor can one render with H. Wolf and Auger, "Pro suggesto duntaxat," for Pytheas is not said to have changed on leaving the speaker's platform but upon entering the service of those whom he formerly opposed.

The key to a correct translation can be found in L. Radermacher's study of the word πάροδος and the related verbs ("Der neue Äschylos," *Zeitschrift für die österreichischen Gymnasien*, LXVII [1916], 590–94). The basic meanings of the word are "a going past" (Th. i. 126. 11) or "a way past," from which developed the sense of "the one path connecting two points." Radermacher says that the use of it to refer to the coming forward of a speaker to address the public occurs already "in altattischer Prosa"; I know no earlier instance of it than the one here in the letter. See also the use of the verb παριέναι for "come forward to address the Assembly" (D. 18. 170, etc.) and of its participle for "orators, politicians" (D. 2. 31, etc.).

Hence πάροδος here does not have to mean "political debut." If the word refers to a definite event, it is best taken as referring to Pytheas' participation in the prosecution of Demosthenes, and one would translate, "until the [notorious recent] appearance on the speaker's platform." But would Demosthenes have left the bracketed words unexpressed? Rather, the imperfect tense of παρῄει in the next sentence suggests that both verb there and noun here refer to no one event but to the entire first stage of Pytheas' political career down to his *volte-face* of 323. He waited until he felt sure of his place as an accepted and established politician before "selling his services." One might translate, "as long as he was still on the road to political eminence."

On the use of these idioms in Athenian politics see Sachsenweger, pp. 19–20, against Neupert, p. 53. Perhaps Demosthenes here exploits the theatrical connotations of the noun: Pytheas' apparent patriotism was mere play-acting; cf. paragraph 33, the invective against the ex-actor Aeschines at 18. 209, and Plut. *Praec. ger. reip.* 805d.

PARAGRAPH 29. μετὰ ταῦτα ... πάντα. Pytheas may well have become a pro-Macedonian speaker by the time of Ep. 3; but, in the propagandistic context here, all that can be inferred is that Demosthenes believed many Athenians could be brought to view Pytheas' recent conduct (including his prosecution of Demosthenes) as such a change of policy. For the bearing of the question on the authenticity of Ep. 3, see below on paragraphs 29–30.

On the construction ἕτοιμος εἰς see on paragraph 22.

PARAGRAPH 29. ὡς δοῦλον κτλ. Early in his political career, Pytheas barely escaped conviction on a charge of illegally exercising the rights of a citizen (Plut. *Phoc.* 21. 1). As the letter suggests, the suit probably was politically motivated. Dion. Hal. *Din.* 11, Vol. I, p. 311 U.-R., lists two speeches against Pytheas among the authentic public orations of Dinarchus, one of them written for a γραφὴ ξενίας (fragments: Baiter and Sauppe, *Oratores Attici*, II, 327–29). The defendant found guilty in such a suit suffered confiscation of his property and was sold as a slave; see Lipsius, pp. 412–16.

PARAGRAPH 29. οἷς . . . ἔγραφεν. At first sight these words imply that Pytheas had written speeches for Demosthenes' accusers to use against him at his trial. But Pytheas himself was one of the accusers (*Vit. X orat.* 846c) and delivered his own speech (fragments: Baiter and Sauppe, II, 311–12). Therefore, it is strange that the letter attacks Pytheas only for what he has written, not for what he has spoken. Perhaps Demosthenes' use of the verb "to write" is meant to cover both Pytheas' own speech and others he may have written for fellow prosecutors. The plural λόγους and the imperfect tense of the verb "to write" suggests that Pytheas wrote not only a speech or speeches for the trial but also propaganda brochures (λόγους) against Demosthenes; cf. *Suda s.v. Pytheas*: "ἔγραψε λόγους δημηγορικοὺς καὶ δικανικοὺς καὶ ἄλλα τινά."

Treves maintains that if Pytheas was so popular as to be chosen along with Hyperides as one of the prosecutors, he must have been an ardent anti-Macedonian (*Athenaeum*, n.s., XIV, 243, n. 1). However, our fragmentary and ambiguous sources give no evidence for Pytheas' political orientation at the time of the trial; cf. Colin, *REG*, XXXIX, 55. The same groups who later vigorously opposed entry into the Lamian war (Diod. xviii. 10. 1, 4) surely could have secured the appointment of a "pro-Macedonian" prosecutor. See above on μετὰ ταῦτα κτλ.

PARAGRAPH 30. ἐπειδὴ . . . πράττει. Cf. D. 18. 261.

PARAGRAPH 30. φθόης (Φυλῆς Pap.]. The scribe of the papyrus was familiar with the geography of Attica but failed to recognize the rare word φθόη (*pace* Blass III 2, 285, n. 4). Harpocration cites the word from here, ἐρανίσας (*s.v.* ἐρανίζοντες) from Ep. 3. 38, and Καλαύρεια from Ep. 2. 20, thus giving one more proof that Epp. 2 and 3 were known in the second century A.D. Moreover, he identifies them by their present titles. On the date of Harpocration, see B. Hemmerdinger, "Deux notes papyrologiques," *REG*, LXXII(1959), 107–9.

Moeris, p. 294 Pierson, has an entry φθόην, τὴν φθίσιν, Ἀττικῶς, without giving any reference (the word is also used by Plato, Isocrates, and Plato Comicus). φθόη also appears in Hesychius, Photius (who ascribes it to Demosthenes), the *Etymologicum magnum*, and the *Etymologicum Gudianum*. ἐρανίσας is ascribed to Demosthenes by Photius and the *Suda*.

As for the expression καλῶς ποιοῦσαι, see on paragraph 24, καλῶς ποιοῦντι.

PARAGRAPH 30. πέντε . . . ὀφλόντα. See above, p. 54.

PARAGRAPH 30. Θύονθ᾽ . . . Δελφοῖς. See above, pp. 50–52. Here again, as with the allusion to Pytheas' activity as prosecutor in paragraph 29, Treves held that no "pro-Macedonian" could have been permitted to serve as Athenian delegate to Delphi in 323 (*Athenaeum*, n.s., XIV, 243–45, to be corrected by his "Epimetron," *ibid.*, pp. 264–65). See my comments above on the problem in paragraph 29. More can be said here.

If Pytheas here is described as participating in a Pythaïs, nothing tells us how the various participants were chosen in the fourth century. Boëthius, p. 24, n. 3, conjectures that membership in the college of Pythaïstae was a prerogative of certain aristocratic families. In the attested practice of the second century B.C., the Pythaïstae and *theôroi* are members of aristocratic families (Boëthius, pp. 59, 68, 101–2), and other Pythaïstae are mentioned as chosen by lot (Boëthius, p. 104); none, then, had to be politically popular. As for the *hieropoioi*, since Lycurgus and Demades served together in that capacity in a Pythaïs between 331 and 324 (*SIG*³ 296; the date: Boëthius, p. 29, n. 1, and Daux, *Delphes*, pp. 529–30), they were probably elected, but a "pro-Macedonian" political orientation was no obstacle.

If Pytheas here is described as participating in an amphictyonic sacrifice, he probably was the hieromnemon (see p. 51), and the hieromnemones were picked by lot before the beginning of the Attic year, long before the *volte-face* here ascribed to Pytheas (D. 24. 150; Aristoph. *Nubes* 623–24 and scholia; Aesch. 3. 115; Busolt-Swoboda, p. 1304). Demosthenes might deplore the fact that in the spring of 323 no one had induced the Athenians to take the extraordinary step of deposing the hieromnemon. Even if Pytheas was one of the three elected pylagori (D. 18. 149; Aesch. 3. 114–15, 126; Busolt-Swoboda,

p. 1102), the fact of his election would again prove nothing about his attitude toward Macedonia; cf. D. 18. 149. On the other hand, there is no evidence that hostility to Alexander was a crime which might have barred Pytheas from attending amphictyonic meetings; cf. Treves, *Athenaeum*, n.s., XIV, 244. Crimes on which the Amphictyony was competent to pass judgment: Busolt-Swoboda, pp. 1302–3.

PARAGRAPHS 31–32. ἄλλως τε καὶ ... γενέσθαι. The passage shows a minute knowledge of the affairs of the time, recognized already by A. Boeckh, *Urkunden über das Seewesen des attischen Staates*, pp. 236, 244. As far as can be determined, the men "carried off by death" are listed in the chronological order of their deaths, the most recent being first. The only exception is Lycurgus, probably the last to die (324/3; see above, *Title*); perhaps his name appears last for emphasis. Nausicles was trierarch with his son in 326/5 (*IG* II² 1628, 100–2) but was dead, as were Diotimus and Menestheus, before the inscribing in 325/4 of the naval accounts which speak of their heirs (Nausicles: *IG* II² 1629, 707–8, and cf. *Vit. X orat.* 848f, where Schaefer, II, 330, n. 4, reads "Nausicles" for "Lysicles"; Diotimus: *IG* II² 1629, 539–41; Menestheus: *ibid.*, 486–88). Chares' death is reported only here, but we shall see below that it probably belongs to the same period. Nothing is known about the death of Eudoxus. Ephialtes died in battle at Halicarnassus in 334 (Diod. xvii. 27. 3). Din. 1. 33–34 mentions Euthydicus' death between that of Ephialtes and the defeat of Agis at Megalopolis in 331.

Darius executed Charidemus in 333 (Diod. xvii. 30; Curt. iii. 2. 10–19). To prove to the Athenians that they had cast patriots away, Demosthenes had to present examples of patriots who were not implicated in the Harpalus affair. Merely to point to his own case and that of Philocles would have been futile. Hence, he includes Charidemus among those cast away and not among those carried off by death. Charidemus had in fact been exiled from Athens, whereas Chares and Ephialtes left of their own free will (Arrian i. 10. 6). There is neither ineptitude in the argument nor a gross historical error of presenting Charidemus as still alive in 323 (cf. Neupert, p. 25; Schaefer, *NJb*, CXV, 164; Blass, *ibid.*, p. 542; *Att. Ber.*, III 1, 446). On Philocles' fate, see above, pp. 43–44, 65, and Chap. 5, n. 60.

It is instructive to compare the list here with other ancient lists of Demosthenes' associates. According to *Vit. X orat.* 844f and 848f, his chief supporters in the struggle against Philip were Hyperides, Polyeuctus, Nausicles, and Diotimus. The sources vary in their lists of the men whose surrender, along with Demosthenes, Alexander demanded of Athens in 335 (Arrian i. 10. 4; Plut. *Phoc.* 17. 2, *Dem.* 23. 3; Diod. xvii. 15. 1; *Suda s.v. Antipatros*). Arrian, Plut. *Dem.*, and the *Suda*, the sources purporting to give the full list, mention Polyeuctus. Plut. *Dem.* 23. 3 omits Hyperides, but *Phoc.* 17. 2 includes him. In any case Hyperides surely was anti-Macedonian in 335 as in 324. Schaefer, III, 137–40, reads "Moerocles" for "Patrocles" in the *Suda*; if so, Moerocles' name appears in every full version of the list.

How were the survivors faring at the time of Ep. 3? Polyeuctus apparently was a defendant in the Harpalus affair (Din. 1. 100). Demosthenes may have omitted his name because his trial was still pending (Demosthenes' opinion of Polyeuctus: D. 9. 72). Ep. 3. 32, "If you consider some to be their equals, etc.," may be a veiled plea for Polyeuctus and other defendants still untried. Ep. 2 implies that Polyeuctus was acquitted (see p. 49); later in the year he was an ambassador to the Peloponnesus (*Vit. X orat.* 846d). If Polyeuctus had already been acquitted, surely Ep. 3 would have exploited the fact. We have no information on Thrasybulus (listed by the *Suda*). Moerocles, Hyperides, and Demon and Callisthenes (listed at Plut. *Dem.* 23. 2) may all have been suspected of taking money from Harpalus (see above, Chap. 5, n. 57); Moerocles may have been otherwise insecure (see on paragraphs 16–18). The letter can be read as a warning to the surviving anti-Macedonian leaders; see below on paragraphs 33–34.

Probably Demosthenes here also replies to the charge (Din. 1. 31–33) that he had fatally infected Charidemus, Ephialtes, and Euthydicus with his contagious ill fortune. See on Ep. 4. 1.

The date of Chares' death remains to be determined. He is last mentioned alive leading a group of mercenaries at Taenarum, under the hire of Athens (*Vit. X orat.* 848e). The date of this activity is obscure. As a piece of Lacedaemonian territory, Taenarum probably became a gathering place for drifting mercenaries only after Sparta was weakened by the defeat of Agis in 331 (cf. Badian, *JHS*, LXXXI, 25–28). A date for Chares' activity before 324/3 is suggested by Diodorus' failure to mention Chares in his account of the mercenaries at Taenarum during and after 325/4 (xvii. 111. 1–3; xviii. 9.

1-5). Diodorus mentions only Leosthenes as their Athenian com-
mander. Berve (II, 404) plausibly dates Chares' activity at Taenarum
during or after Alexander's campaigns in India. In the years 327-325
even Alexander's satraps believed the king had disappeared forever
(Diod. xvii. 108. 4); Antipater with meager financial resources held
a Macedonia drained of manpower. Hence the Athenians might not
have hesitated to hire a mercenary force. Thus what evidence there is
for the date of Chares' death is consistent with placing it near the
death of Nausicles and of Diotimus.

Collected information on all the men mentioned here (except
Euthydicus) can be found in the respective articles in *Pros. Att.* and
(except Eudoxus) in the respective articles in *RE.* On Lycurgus, see
above, *Title;* on Philocles, above, pp. 38,41-42,46,65, and below,
Appendix VII.

PARAGRAPHS 32-33. ἀλλ' ὅταν ... αἰσχύνονται. Cf. D. 19. 232.
Pytheas is not alone; others like him may abandon their shallow
patriotism for "treason." Hyperides was so consistently anti-
Macedonian that Demosthenes could hardly have expected his
audience to think of him here, but the description of Hyperides at
Luc. *Dem. Enc.* 31 may be based on this passage and on Ep. 2. 11.

PARAGRAPH 33. μὴ ... ἰδεῖν. For the construction, cf. D. 22. 11,
Prooem. 19.

PARAGRAPH 34. The vague allusions here reflect the apprehensions
of the Athenians in the months before the outbreak of the Lamian
war (see above, Chap. 5, n. 49, and pp. 58-63). They had to choose
between readmitting a dangerous mass of subversives and dispos-
sessed (Curt. x. 2. 4-7; Justin xiii. 5. 2-4; cf. Diod. xviii. 8. 2) or
facing the wrath of Alexander, acting through his deputy Antipater
(Diod. xviii. 8. 4). Meanwhile, the exiles and their friends in the city
surely were not idle. During the weeks before his trial Demosthenes
denounced Callimedon for consorting with the exiles in Megara and
brought information before the People of a plot threatening the dockyards (Din. 1. 94-95). Callimedon soon proved to be a bitter enemy
of the Athenian democracy (Plut. *Dem.* 27. 2; *Phoc.* 27. 5, 33. 3, 35.
1-2).

PARAGRAPH 34. τινες ... λογισμός. Cf. D. 18. 89, and see above on
paragraph 12, τῆς ἀξίας.

For the meaning of εἰς ὑποδοχήν, cf. Th. vii. 74. 2 and especially
Ps.-D. 7. 13 in conjunction with the use of προλαβεῖν at 7. 9.

PARAGRAPH 34. εἰ . . . διασύρει. In these words Demosthenes may have wanted his audience to think of Hyperides, who was famous for his skill at *diasyrmos*, the ridicule by *reductio ad absurdum* of arguments upon which his opponent had laid solemn stress. Alex. *De Fig.* 26, Vol. VIII, pp. 457–58 Walz, in defining *diasyrmos* takes two examples from Hyperides, *Dem.* 3 and the fragment "Why is she [Phryne] to blame if a stone hangs over the head of Tantalus?" Other examples in the extant speeches of Hyperides: *Lyc.* 5–8, *Eux.* 1–3. At Longinus *De sublim.* 34. 2, Hyperides' adroit *diasyrmos* is one of the qualities which make him the most versatile of orators. The verb was part of the rhetorical vocabulary of Demosthenes' time (Anax. 33, p. 76. 1–15; 36, p. 89. 9–11 H.; D. 18. 27 with Aesch. 3. 82; D. 18. 126 with Aesch. 3. 166–67; D. 18. 299 with Aesch. 3. 236), so that Athenian connoisseurs of oratory might well have thought of Hyperides. See also above, pp. 55–57, and Chap. 8, rhetorical analysis of Ep. 3. 32–34.

PARAGRAPH 35. ἐπέσταλκα. See above on paragraph 1, περὶ κτλ.

PARAGRAPH 36. ἐκ τοῦ περιόντος. The correct interpretation of this phrase, "out of the abundance of my troubles," removes the objection of Neupert (p. 53; cf. Sachsenweger, p. 31) that the expression is unparalleled in Demosthenes. See the DeWitts' translation, *Demosthenes: VII*, pp. 248–49 and footnote. Demosthenes anticipates the suspicions of his audience that his plea is for himself (see above, Chap. 8, rhetorical anlysis of Ep. 3. 35–36). To forestall objections, he admits that he has an abundance of troubles of his own. The Greek is unimpeachable (cf. D. 21. 17 and 12. 7). When the abundance of troubles, alluded to before in a clause, is summarily referred to by the participle, the construction is as commonplace as is the use of ἐκ to express cause.

PARAGRAPH 37. On the "long letter" to be sent later, see above, p. 49. For the rhetorical hesitation over what to call the Athenians, cf. D. 18. 22.

PARAGRAPH 38. ἃ τοῖς τολμῶσιν κτλ. Blass (III 1, 440) saw here an allusion to Demades (cf. Din. 1. 104): Demades, though convicted found it possible to remain in Athens (see above, Chap. 5, n. 42). However, surely Demosthenes continues here to refer to Aristogiton. Aristogiton's "lack of respect for any in the city" was notorious, whereas Demades' reputation was not nearly so bad (D. 25. 49–50;

Din. 2. 15). μηδὲ λαβοῦσι παρ' ὑμῶν probably means that although Aristogiton never got the Athenians' permission to ignore the disabilities imposed by law on debtors to the state he does so anyway; cf. paragraph 16 and Din. 2. 12–13.

PARAGRAPH 38. τοὺς φίλους ἐρανίσας. To pay a fine or meet other emergencies, Athenians would call upon friends for an interest-free loan (*eranos*). The construction of the verb with the prospective contributors in the accusative is found only here in Attic. See Lipsius, pp. 729–34, and T. Reinach, "Eranos," *Dictionnaire des antiquités grecques et romaines*, ed. Daremberg and Saglio, II¹ (1892), 805–8. See also on paragraph 30, αἳ μέχρι φθόης.

PARAGRAPH 39. See above, pp. 48–49, 52.

PARAGRAPH 40. ἵνα . . . καταβολάς. *IG* II² 1628–31, the naval accounts of 326/5–323/2, use the same technical vocabulary and cast considerable light on this passage (cf. Blass, III 1, 446–47). There, too, delinquent trierarchs have their obligations doubled, and "underwriting" appears as a means of discharging the debt; see Boeckh, *Urkunden über das Seewesen*, pp. 225–30. "Underwriting" in the inscriptions means the deduction of a person's previous donations from his own or someone else's debts to the state, whereas here it implies the assumption of an obligation. Even so, the inscriptions let us know that at this time of naval construction debts to the state were being collected with considerable rigor, and yet the state allowed certain devices by which persons could aid their friends to discharge their obligations. Among those affected by these exactions appear Demosthenes and his associates. Demosthenes: *IG* II² 1629, 526; Hegesippus: *ibid.*, line 543; the family of Diotimus: *ibid.*, lines 539–40. Hegesippus, an associate of Demosthenes: D. 9. 72, 19. 331, *Pros. Att.*, No. 6351; Diotimus: see on paragraph 31.

καταθῶνται here surely means "pay." However, I have found no parallel for the middle voice with that meaning before *BGU* 1059. 22 (first century B.C.). Perhaps the middle is used when the sum is paid the payer's own money or is regarded as such. The similar context at D. 24. 115 uses the active, but there the law deals with single or double restitution of stolen property; the sum paid is not regarded as the payer's own money, for the undoubled sum is certainly not his.

PARAGRAPH 40. ⟨πρὸς⟩ τὴν ἀρχήν. Blass's inserted preposition probably improves the passage. Translate, "in the presence of the board," or "in the presence of the magistrate," instead of "in advance." Cf. *IG* II² 1629, 609–12 and *IG* XII (7) 3, 33–38 (from Arcesine on Amorgos).

PARAGRAPH 41. On the "prediction" here, see above, p. 71. "Tangible property" (φανερά) was property possession of which could not be concealed. Only against such property were *eisphorai* and liturgies assessed. Besides real estate, it included slaves, cattle, furniture, etc. "Intangible" (ἀφανής) property included invested capital and sometimes even cash. See Lipsius, p. 677.

A debtor in Athens unable to pay his debts would go into bankruptcy, abandoning his property to his creditors (ἐξίστασθαι τῶν ὄντων); see Lipsius, p. 734. Demosthenes here uses the related word ἀφίσταμαι, which means to relinquish title, whether voluntarily (D.19. 147; 35· 4, 44; 38. 7; 42. 19) or under compulsion (D. 21. 181).

PARAGRAPH 42. οὐ μὴν οὐδὲ κτλ. The denial here does not necessarily conflict with Hyp. *Dem.* 12–13. As quoted there by Hyperides, Demosthenes may have used λαμβάνειν to mean that he had *received* money from Harpalus, but on behalf of the city; at Ep. 3. 42 he may be using the verb to deny the charge that he had *taken* it as a bribe; cf. Colin, *Hypéride*, p. 230, n. 1. See, however, Ep. 2. 15.

Pausanias (ii. 33· 3) mentions Demosthenes' own denials of his guilt in the Harpalus affair, perhaps alluding to this passage and to Ep. 2. 14–15. He may, however, have been alluding to the lost speech Ἀπολογία δώρων, condemned as spurious by Dion. Hal., *Dem.*, Vol. I, pp. 250–51 U.-R., and probably identical with Περὶ χρυσίου mentioned at Athenaeus xiii. 592e.

See also above, pp. 84–85.

PARAGRAPH 42. τὸ περιφανὲς . . . (ἢ τὸν Ἄρειον πάγον). Except in the salutations to the Council and the People, throughout the letters "Council" means the Council of the Areopagus; in the historical context the audience would not think of the Council of Five Hundred (cf. Hyp. *Dem.* 3; Din. 1. 5, etc.). Demosthenes calls the Council of the Areopagus ἡ βουλὴ ἡ ἐξ Ἀρείου πάγου (18. 133, 134), ἡ β. ἡ ἐν Ἀρείῳ πάγῳ (20. 157), and τὸ ἐν Ἀ. π. δικαστήριον (23. 65). Hence, if the bracketed words, present in all manuscripts and in the quotations by Hermogenes and Pseudo-Aristides, are to be maintained in the text, they must be understood as the place where the Council of the Areopagus met; cf. Isoc. 7. 38; Din. 1. 47, 85. The translation "Hill of Ares" avoids the confusion which would be caused by the English use of "Areopagus" to refer to the council itself. Reiske, however, may have been right in bracketing the words as a gloss. If so, the glossator appears to have known that this is the first occurrence in the letters of *boulê* to refer to the Areopagus; hence, he would have known that Ep. 3 is dated earlier than Ep. 2.

The passage is quoted at Hermog. *Id.* i. 7, Vol. III, pp. 233-35 Walz, and at Ps.-Aristides *Rh.* i. 45 Schmid, Vol. IX, p. 360 Walz, with the reading περιφανές; the manuscripts of Demosthenes have ἀφανές. Unless the reading of the rhetors is a learned correction, the shorter adjectives of the manuscripts could hardly have given rise to it. Elsewhere in the Demosthenic corpus περιφανής always has a derogatory and polemic connotation ("flagrant" or "notorious"), being applied to crimes or to proofs that one's opponent is lying. In the Attic orators, ἀξίωμα always means "prestige" or "reputation," never "decision"; cf. also Plut. *Cimon* 15. 3. The reading of the rhetors, as a grudging admission of the Areopagus' prestige, fits the situation. The reading of the manuscripts can be translated "the dubious prestige." I hardly think it could be contrasting the "invisible" (but real) prestige of the Areopagus with the Hill of Ares, visible to the assembled Athenians; such expression seems out of character for Demosthenes—even Plato would probably have used ἀόρατον (but cf. Plato *Soph.* 232c).

The attitude of the Athenian public to the Areopagus at this time was ambiguous. Orators frequently appealed to its prestige (cf. D. 23. 65-66), and Dinarchus does so to support the vulnerable indictment (1. 6-9, 66, 86-87). Demosthenes in reply exploits the unpopularity of this "oligarchical" institution; the people might be led to believe that body had framed him, a democratic patriot (Din. 1. 62; Hyp. *Dem.* 14; D. Ep. 2. 1-2). See commentary to Ep. 2. 1. Lycurgus (*Leoc.* 52), when praising the Areopagus in 330, has to ask that the audience refrain from making an uproar.

PARAGRAPH 43. οὐ γὰρ δήπου ... γε. See above, p. 28.

PARAGRAPH 44. ἀλλ' ἔχει ... τὸ στένειν. Stobaeus quotes this passage, giving the source as Δημοσθένους ἐξ ἐπιστολῶν (Vol. IV, p. 124 Meineke).

PARAGRAPH 45. ὥσπερ οἱ παῖδες κτλ. Cf. D. 10. 41; Plato *Prt.* 346a-b, Ep. 7. 331b-d; Epicurus *Sententiae Vaticanae* 62; Livy xxvii. 34. 15.

PARAGRAPH 45. ἡ γὰρ ... κρίνεται. See above, Chap. 2, n. 6.

EPISTLE 2

Concerning His Own Restoration

PARAGRAPH I. ἀφ᾽ ὧν ἐπολιτευόμην. "ἀφ᾽ ὧν" in Demosthenes is always causal (18. 218; Ep. 4. 5, 9, etc.), not temporal. He expresses "from the time that" by ἀφ᾽οὗ or ἀφ᾽ ἧς (ἡμέρας). The causal sense is required here, for Demosthenes is protesting against treatment contrary to his deserts; cf. Hermog. *Id.* ii. 8, Vol. III, p. 349 Walz.

Demosthenes probably repeats in Ep. 2 the arguments he used at his trial. He surely asked for acquittal by pleading the greatness of his career, whereas his accusers sought his condemnation by representing his career as despicable (Hyp. *Dem.* 16–26; Din. 1. 12–36; see below on paragraphs 3–8). Dinarchus (1. 70–71) tries to show that Demosthenes himself had no confidence in his political record (cf. Aesch. 3. 209, Hyp. *Dem.* 17).

PARAGRAPH I. μηδὲν ὑμᾶς ἀδικῶν κτλ. Demosthenes here concedes, as obliquely as possible, that he may have been indiscreet. The participles are both conditional; hence μηδέν here, and οὐδέν in par. 3, where the denial is stated as a fact. καὶ μέτρι᾽ ἄν, the reading of all the manuscripts, may be a nuance which Demosthenes used to hedge his concession. Blass read κἄν to avoid hiatus and a tribrach; Rennie deleted ἄν. If the particle is retained, the participle ἐξαμαρτών represents the optative. The potential optative is found in protases in Demosthenes; the construction asserts the possibility or likelihood of the condition. See Kühner-Gerth, Vol. II, pp. 481–82; A. J. Aken, *Die Grundzüge der Lehre von Tempus und Modus im Griechischen*, pp. 166–73. On the other hand, I know no parallel for a participle in

* For the historical background of Ep. 2, see above, pp. 56–59.

such a construction (see Kühner-Gerth, Vol. I, p. 242, Anmerk. 1), and the only parallel for a potential optative protasis with a future apodosis is the variant reading from Hermogenes accepted by Blass at D. 4. 18.

Contrast the efforts of the prosecutors to magnify Demosthenes' "crimes": Din. 1. 22–26, 60, 68–71, 88, 93; Hyp. *Dem.* 11, 15, 24–26, 34–36.

PARAGRAPH 1. οὐδεμιᾶς . . . ἀπάντων. At the trial the only evidence presented of Demosthenes' guilt was the report (*apophasis*; see Lipsius, p.801) of the Areopagus (see above, p.42). Accordingly, the standing of that report as evidence became a major issue. The argument of the prosecutors and of Demosthenes at Ep. 3. 42 and Ep. 2. 1, 13–15 revolves around the words *apodeixis* and *elenchos*, which designate prerequisites for a legal conviction. *Elenchos* in these contexts means "proof of guilt"; cf. D. 22. 21–22 and Anax. 13, p.46. 5–9 H. Dinarchus begins by insisting that a clear *elenchos* has been established against Demosthenes (1. 1). Prosecution and defense may have differed in their interpretations of *apodeixis*. To Demosthenes as quoted at Hyp. *Dem.* 3, 6, *apodeixis* seems to mean the detailed statement of particulars which he did not find in the Areopagus' report (cf. Th. i. 97. 2; the title of the missing document at D. 4. 29; and the use of the related verb at Hyp. *Dem.* 9). On the other hand, in the restored text of Hyp. *Dem.* 38 the related verb seems to mean "denounce" (cf. Lyc. *Leoc.* 4; Andoc. 1. 47). Dinarchus insists that the Areopagus has made "just and true *apodeixeis*" (statements in explanation?) concerning its reports (1. 1). One can infer the strength of Demosthenes' interpretation from the way the prosecutors avoid considering the point on its merits (Din. 1. 84 ff. — appeal to the prestige of the Areopagus; Hyp. *Dem.* 3 — *reductio ad absurdum*).

PARAGRAPH 1. ἀπόρρητα. Probably Demosthenes chose this word as a substitute for the official designation of the Areopagus' report (*apophasis*, "disclosure") on account of its identical prefix and its opposite connotation ("the secret, the unmentionable"). The word sometimes refers to official or state secrets (D. 1. 4; Plut. *Per.* 23. 1; etc.); the privileged secrecy of deliberations of the Areopagus: D. 25. 23. Ironic use of the adjective: D. 21. 149. As a technical legal term, it means "actionable slander" (D. 58. 40; cf. 18. 123, and see Lipsius, pp. 648–51).

Throughout Epp. 2 and 3 Demosthenes refuses to use the word *apophasis*. The indictment is "the Council's say-so" a "false" or "unproved" accusation, "the slander which has unjustly come upon me" (Ep. 2. 1, 2, 16; Ep. 3. 39). The men indicted are "the accused" (Ep. 2. 14, 16). Only at Ep. 3. 43 does Demosthenes use the cognate verb, and there to discredit the indictments: even though the despicable Aristogiton was among the indicted, the People have acquitted him.

PARAGRAPH 1. καταψηφιζομένους . . . ἀποστερεῖσθαι. Construe ἁπάντων with καταψηφιζομένους, not with the infinitives; the point is that all the earlier defendants were condemned, not that the Athenians were surrendering everything as much as Demosthenes was being deprived of everything. Blass was probably correct in changing ἔλαττον to ἐλαττόνων, because in the orators this verb "surrender" is always accompanied by a genitive except where it means "yield the floor." (The verb does take a cognate accusative pronoun at Arist. *De Anima* 410b25.)

PARAGRAPH 1. τοὺς ὀμωμοκότας κτλ. The orators frequently allude to clauses of the heliastic oath which was taken by the Athenian jurors. The one text purporting to be the entire oath is D. 24. 149–151, but its authenticity has been disputed. Some, while admitting that the clauses of D. 24. 149–151 did occur in the heliastic oath at one time or another, have held that a clause like the one to protect the constitution against oligarchic change could not have still been in the oath at the time of D. 24, so long after the fall of the Thirty Tyrants. See R. J. Bonner and G. Smith, *The Administration of Justice from Homer to Aristotle*, II, 152–156, and for a good defense of D. 24. 149–151 against these doubts, see David Asheri, "Gli impegni politici nel giuramento degli eliasti ateniesi," *Rendiconti delle sedute dell'Accademia nazionale dei Lincei*, 8th series, XIX (1964), 281–93.

Ep. 2. 1–2 has not yet been used for its evidence on the question. Demosthenes accuses the jurors of "surrendering the constitution despite their oath." (Since only the defendants' rights were being surrendered, τῆς πολιτείας means "the constitution," not "the jurors' rights as citizens.") Below, in par. 2, Demosthenes asserts that when the jurors who had taken the oath surrendered the constitution by accepting the Areopagus' say-so without proof, they bowed to "oligarchic designs of certain Areopagites." Hence one may infer that a clause to protect the democratic constitution stood in the Heliastic Oath in 323. The Athenians seem to have feared such usurpation of power by the Areopagus after the battle of Chaeroneia. See Martin Ostwald, "The Athenian Legislation against Tyranny and Subversion," *TAPA*, LXXXVI (1955), 103–28; on the unpopularity of the Areopagus, see commentary to Ep. 3. 42, τὸ περιφανὲς κτλ·

PARAGRAPH 2. καλῶς ποιοῦντες. See on Ep. 3. 24.

PARAGRAPH 2. τὴν δυναστείαν. The prosecutors had ridiculed Demosthenes' charges that the Areopagus had formed an oligarchic plot against him to please Alexander (Din. 1. 62, Hyp. *Dem.* 14). Demosthenes himself had accepted its judgment (Hyp. *Dem.* 1–2), and the Areopagus, on the contrary, had honestly braved Demosthenes' power (Din. 1. 5, 7).

PARAGRAPH 2. μὴ μόνος. See above, pp.49, 56–58; Chap. 5, n. 20.

PARAGRAPH 2. ἐὰν καὶ ὑμῖν βουλομένοις ᾖ. For the construction, cf. D. 18. 11.

PARAGRAPH 2. τῶν ὄντων ἀποστερηθῆναι. See above, Chap. 5, n. 68.

PARAGRAPH 3. οὐδὲν ὑμᾶς ἀδικῶν. See on paragraph 1, μηδὲν κτλ. and on Ep. 3. 42, οὐ μὴν οὐδὲ κτλ.

PARAGRAPH 4. On the "unworthy" actions "forced upon" Demosthenes and the Athenians, see above, pp.58–61, 80–81, 87–88, and Chap. 8, rhetorical analysis of Ep. 2. 4–5.

PARAGRAPH 5–6. Dinarchus attacked Demosthenes' claim that his policy down to the battle of Chaeroneia was glorious even in defeat and thereafter was one of uncorrupted loyalty; rather, it was corrupt throughout and brought discredit and ill fortune to all Greece (Din. 1. 12–13, 30–33). As a former ally, Hyperides can attack only Demosthenes' later career (*Dem.* 17–21, 30–31).

PARAGRAPH 5. ἐξηταζόμην. The use of this word here and at paragraphs 9 and 12 is a metaphor borrowed from military parlance. Before troops went into battle a "mustering" (*exetasis*) was held to assign each contingent its duties and call for volunteers; cf. Th. vi. 96. 3. The verb thus means "present oneself at an *exetasis*," "volunteer," "come forward"; cf. W. W. Goodwin, *Demosthenes on the Crown* (Cambridge: at the University Press, 1901), to D. 18. 173, lines 4–5, and schol. D. Ep. 2. 12: ἐξητασμένος· ἠριθμημένος, παραγενόμενος. Other instances: D. 18. 277, 310, 320 21. 161–62. Hence the verb here does not mean "pass scrutiny" (cf. D. 18. 246; Ep. 3. 8), especially in view of the context, "on your behalf."

Though military metaphors were common (cf. Aesch. 3. 7), the figure here and in *De Corona* may be a reaction to the repeated charges of cowardice (Aesch. 3. 159; Din. 1. 12; Demetrius of Phalerum *apud* Plut. *Dem.* 14. 2). Reference to Demosthenes' military service is conspicuous by its absence from the letters and *De Corona* (contrast Aesch. 2. 167–71); see Navarre, pp.288–89.

PARAGRAPH 5. ἐλπίδα προσδοκᾶσθαι. The expression does not recur in the Demosthenic corpus; Reiske considered it bad Greek (quoted at Neupert, p.51). Sachsenweger, p.25, found a parallel in D. 5. 10, where the antecedent of ταῦτ' is ἐλπίδας κτλ. The combination here might seem redundant, but there is nothing unusual in Greek in making what would have been a cognate accusative with an active verb into the subject of a passive verb. Finally, the construction here may not be redundant at all. Probably the phrase ὑπὸ πάντων modifying the preceding infinitive is to be understood here, too. Then the "hope" of the noun belongs to Demosthenes; and the "expectation" of the infinitive to "all the Greeks."

PARAGRAPH 5. τῆς δ' ἀναγκαίας κτλ. The anti-Macedonian leaders and the common citizens who had followed them did not take the battle of Chaeroneia as a refutation; they ascribed the defeat to the blindness of Fortune. See Hyp. *Dem.* 28–30; Plut. *Dem.* 21. 1; and below on Ep. 4. 3. Cf. Demetrius of Phalerum *apud* Polyb. xxix. 21. On Fortune (*tyche, daimon*) in Greece at this period, see M. P. Nilsson, *Geschichte der griechischen Religion*, II, 201–12.

PARAGRAPH 6. Cf. D. 6. 10; 18. 297–98, 320; Ep. 3. 2–4. The construction ἀνταλλάτομαι ἀντί recurs in Demosthenes only at 16. 5, where the object of the preposition is not things but persons; but that is surely no objection to the usage here. Cf. Neupert, p.48; Sachsenweger, pp.25–26.

PARAGRAPHS 7–8. Demosthenes surely used these arguments from probability at his trial. The prosecutors, too, follow the course recommended by Anax. 7, pp.37. 25–38. 8 H., insisting that avarice has been the leading motive of Demosthenes' career (Din. 1. 18–28, 41–47, 70, 108; Hyp. *Dem.* 14, 17, 25).

As is only to be expected, Demosthenes by speaking of "many meetings" and by using the imperfect tense and present participle rhetorically exaggerates the number of his missions to Philip. Actually, there were only the two embassies of 346. Nevertheless, in his account of the second embassy, Demosthenes implies that he had more discussions with Philip than the official audiences (Demosthenes' role in the audience granted the first embassy: Aesch. 2. 22–24, 34–35, 38, 48, 52, and D. 19. 253–54; in that granted the second: Aesch. 2. 108–14). There were Philip's secret attempts to bribe (D. 19. 167–n.b. the imperfect tense and present participles; 222) and apparently also the negotiations on release of prisoners (D. 19. 166— again an imperfect tense and present infinitives; 168). Demosthenes may also be claiming to have refused bribes from Philip offered by intermediaries on other occasions than the two embassies to Pella.

PARAGRAPH 8. λύσαιτε. The better manuscripts of Hermogenes *Id.* i. 7 quote the passage with this reading, which is probably the reading which lay before Hermogenes. He describes the passage not as "harsh" but as "having a touch of harshness." This description excludes the imperative of the inferior manuscripts of Hermogenes— Hermogenes calls the imperative the harshest of forms (*ibid.*, Vol. III, p.237 Walz). The future of the manuscripts of Demosthenes might be inept overconfidence, though it could be taken also as a complimentary expression of trust. As a polite weakened imperative, the independent optative has Hermogenes' "touch of harshness."

PARAGRAPHS 9–12. The counterarguments of Dinarchus and Hyperides: above on paragraphs 7–8; Chap. 6, n. 90. Python's embassy: Ps.–D. 7. 18–23; Schaefer, II, 376–80; Bickerman and Sykutris, *BVSAW*, Vol. LXXX, Heft III, pp.39–41.

Both in language and in the allusion to the embassy of Python, paragraphs 9–11 are closely parallel to D. 18. 136, 244, 277–79. But the use of the material in the letter is strikingly different from that in *De Corona*. In *De Corona* Demosthenes' point is the contrast between himself and Aeschines as orator and politician. Both Python and the other ambassadors at D. 18. 136 enter as emissaries sent by Philip to convince the Athenians of their own wrongdoings. In so far as a court is envisioned, the judges are the assembled Athenians (cf. Ps.-D. 7. 23). In the face of Python's formidable advocacy of Philip's cause, Demosthenes so forcefully advocates Athens' cause that Philip's other spokesmen, who are his own allies, take the floor to agree – and still Athenian Aeschines speaks as Philip's advocate!

Instead of the explicit contrast with Aeschines, Ep. 2 presents an implicit contrast with the figure of Demosthenes as viewed by his opponents, as a typical corrupt politician and rhetorical trickster. Demosthenes, the writer insists, has stayed out of the courts, the favorite arena for self-seeking rhetorical trickery; his rhetorical skill has been used only to defend the community of his fellow citizens. Here Demosthenes needs an example wherein he successfully defended Athens before a "court." No Athenian would regard Philip or his "lackeys" as a court competent to try the city. But a condemnation of the city by Greeks would be a serious matter, particularly to an Athenian in 323. Hence here in Ep. 2 nothing is said of Philip. The ambassadors are not from Philip's allies but from "the Greeks," and Python and they are not on the same footing. The entire action is Python's: he *brings* the ambassadors as a court before whom to convict Athens but is foiled by Demosthenes' oratory. Philip, indeed, intended Python's mission to be so regarded, and the Athenians knew it; see Ps.-D. 12. 18; Bickerman and Sykutris, *BVSAW*, Vol. LXXX, Heft III, pp.39–41; G. L. Cawkwell, *CQ*, n.s., XIII (1963), 121–26, 131–33, 209.

On the difference between Ep. 2. 10 and D. 18. 244, see above, Chap. 8, n. 165. These differences of treatment and the differences in phraseology are sufficient to set aside the contentions of Schaefer, *NJb*, CXV, 164, and Neupert, pp.27–28, that the letter here is a slavish imitation of *De Corona*; cf. Blass, *NJb*, CXV, 543.

PARAGRAPH 10. τοὺς ἀπὸ τῶν ῾Ελλήνων . . . πρέσβεις. Elsewhere in such contexts Demosthenes uses παρά, so Schaefer, *NJb*, CXV, 164–65, sees here the hand of the forger. But ἀπό is used at Aesch. 2. 58, 61, 182. Blass, *NJb*, CXV, 543, suggests that παρά would have implied that the Greeks themselves sent the ambassadors.

PARAGRAPH 10. μόνον. Hegesippus also opposed Python, Ps.-D. 7. 18–26. Only Plut. *Dem.* 9, Philostr. *Vit. Ap.* vii. 37, and Luc. *Dem. Enc.* 32 confirm the assertion here that Demosthenes alone confuted Python; all three surely depend on Ep. 2. 10. Here again, Schaefer, *NJb*, CXV, 164–65, saw the hand of the forger. The word here, however, may be rhetorical hyperbole; if not, it means only that Demosthenes was the first to break the spell of Python's oratory, Hegesippus' proposals on the revision of the peace coming afterward (cf. Schaefer, II, 379).

PARAGRAPH 10. πρεσβείας ... καθ' ἕν. A list of Demosthenes' diplomatic missions: D. 18. 244. The writer here may be thinking beyond that list to include his mission to Olympia in 324. Since the status quo on Samos and on the exiles was being maintained, there, too, the Athenians had not lost by Demosthenes' diplomacy (but cf. Hyp. *Dem.* 18–19, Din. 1. 81–82), particularly if Demosthenes on that occasion confuted Lamachus (Plut. *Dem.* 9. 1–2; *Vit. X orat.* 845c; Schaefer, III, 318, n. 1).

PARAGRAPH 11. Cf. D. 18. 108; *Prooem.* 35. 3. *Anecdota Graeca*, ed. Bekker, I, 369, a Byzantine lexicon which drawns on early compilations (Tolkiehn, *RE*, XII, 2478), cites ἀκονῶν from "Demosthenes in a letter." Are Hyperides and Pytheas among the "toadying politicians"? See above on Ep. 3. 33–34. If Pytheas is, his imprisonment and flight occurred after the time of Ep. 2; Plut. *Dem.* 27. 1–2 implies they came well after the outbreak of the Lamian war. The rhetorical appeal to the young: Hyp. *Dem.* fr. *apud* Priscian xviii. 235 (Demosthenes using it at his trial); Hyp. *Dem.* 21–22; Aesch. 2. 180, 3. 245–46; Lyc. *Leoc.* 10; Isoc. 15. 10; etc.

In ἐφ' οἷς ... προσήκει I have taken the prepositional phrase with the main verb and regarded ἀφ' ὧν ... ἐνόμιζον as the antecedent of the relative pronoun. The antecedent could also be all the above-mentioned excellences of Demosthenes' policy. The phrase can also be taken with ἄγασθαι, "Everyone, especially the young, should feel admiration for these." Though in classic Greek this verb occurs nowhere else with such a construction (cf. Menetor Historicus *apud* Athenaeus xiii. 594c), ἐπί with the dative is frequently used in the Attic orators to express the grounds for praise or admiration (Lutz, p. 108; cf. Neupert, p. 58, Sachsenweger, p. 26).

On the construction of ἐπιτιμήσοντα, see on Ep. 3. 1, ἐπιτιμώντων.

PARAGRAPH 12. Demosthenes' liturgies: index to Schaefer, III, 465, and *Vit. X orat.* 846a, 850f–51b.

PARAGRAPH 13. παρ' ἔθος. Elsewhere in Demosthenes, the noun usually refers to the established usages of the state; e.g., D. 10. 44; 19. 2, 234; 20. 124; 22. 57; 25. 2; 54. 42. Perhaps the complaint here is that the added sentence of imprisonment was a piece of unusual severity; see above, pp. 66–67, and cf. Ep. 3. 16.

PARAGRAPH 13. κατ' ... ἁλούς. Cf. D. 24. 188.

PARAGRAPHS 14–15. Demosthenes' denial of guilt: see above on paragraph 2. 1, μηδὲν κτλ., and pp. 84–85.

PARAGRAPH 14. οὔτε ... γεγονώς. Cf. Hyp. *Dem.* 12; Dinarchus avoids the point.

PARAGRAPH 14. τῶν τε γραφέντων κτλ. On Demosthenes' measures in the Harpalus affair, see above, pp.37–43; the prosecutors' views of their effects: Din. 1. 64–71, Hyp. *Dem.* 18–19, 25, 34–36.

PARAGRAPH 14. ἀνέγκλητον. Pollux viii. 69 ascribes to Demosthenes the adjectival use of this word, found only here in the Demosthenic corpus.

PARAGRAPH 14. τῇ πρὸς ἅπαντας κτλ. The disadvantages of being the first defendant to appear in a series of trials arising from a single charge were well known. Cf. Lys. 19. 5–6. Indeed, the prosecutors try to make Demosthenes, as the first defendant, the target of the anger felt against all the defendants. To acquit him, they suggest, is to establish a precedent by which all the indictments will be discredited and all the defendants absolved (Hyp. *Dem.* 6–7; Din. 1. 105–6, 113).

PARAGRAPH 16. καλῶς ποιοῦντες. See on Ep. 3. 24.

PARAGRAPH 16. ὡς ἴστωσαν κτλ. This oath formula occurs only here in Attic prose; Plato *Phaedo* 62a and Ep. 7. 345a have it in the Boeotian dialect. However, it is common in poetry. Invocations of heroes in the Attic orators: D. 18. 208; Din. 1. 64; Lyc. *Leoc.* 1. In so elevated a passage, Demosthenes could well have used this formula (cf. Sachsenweger, pp.36–38).

PARAGRAPH 16. μαρτύρει κτλ. Cf. Hyp. *Lyc.* 14–15.

PARAGRAPH 16. ὁ ... χρόνος. Scholars have found so full an expression for "the past" intolerable and have suggested deleting either the adverb or the participle (Neupert, pp.54–55; Blass, III 1, 448, n. 5; Sachsenweger, p.27). However, "the time which has *previously* gone by" may be an expression constructed to contrast with "the unproved charge which was *recently* brought." Cf., however, D. 19. 327 and 4. 1.

PARAGRAPH 17. For the legal aspects underlying Demosthenes' imprisonment and flight, see above, pp.66–68.

Since the combination of ἑτέρωσε with οὐδαμοῖ does not recur in the Demosthenic corpus, Neupert (p.58) objected to οὐδ'

... μετέστην, and Sachsenweger (p.27) was driven to take the second adverb with the main verb, "Und nicht nach der Gegenseite schielend, ging ich irgendwohin." However, the natural meaning of Sachsenweger's construction would be an absurd denial that Demosthenes had gone anywhere. What the author intends to deny is the participle, "looking in another direction"; οὐδαμοῖ is simply the common Greek intensifying double negative (Kühner-Gerth, II, 203–206; cf. D. 18. 244, οὐκ ἄλλοθεν οὐδαμόθεν). On the connotation of ἑτέρωσε, see above, Chap. 8, rhetorical analysis of Ep. 3. 23–27.

PARAGRAPHS 18–20. See above, Chap. 6, n. 33. Some cities may have been dangerous for Demosthenes. Corinth had a Macedonian garrison, and Dinarchus, Antipater's agent (Berve, I, 242–43; II, 130), must have been powerful there in politics. The exiles in Megara (Din. 1. 58, 94) must have been enemies of Demosthenes. Boeotia, for fear of the restoration of Thebes, was strongly pro-Macedonian (Diod. xviii. 11. 3–5; Hyp. *Epit.* 11).

The hospitality of the Troezenians to the women and children evacuated from Athens before the battle of Salamis (Hdt. viii. 41. 1; Plut. *Them.* 10. 3; *Supplementum Epigraphicum Graecum*, XVIII [1962], No. 153) was an established theme in Athenian political propaganda. Anti-Macedonian propagandists may even have fabricated documents purporting to be the text of resolutions passed by the Athenians and Troezenians of yore to meet the earlier menace from the north; see Christian Habicht, "Falsche Urkunden zur Geschichte Athens im Zeitalter der Perserkriege," *Hermes*, LXXXIX (1961), 1–35. Hyperides used the theme of gratitude to the Troezenians to influence an Athenian jury (*Ath.* 32).

There were more recent instances of sympathy between Athens and Troezen. Athens, seeking allies after Chaeroneia, turned to Troezen (Lyc. *Leoc.* 42), but that city was quickly forced to yield to Philip (Aelianus *Var. hist.* vi. 1). Later, a pro-Macedonian regime there drove into exile many citizens who were hospitably received in Athens (Hyp. *Ath.* 29–35). At the time of Hyperides' speech, these exiles were still in Athens; hence Troezen probably still had a pro-Macedonian regime. Ep. 2. 18–20 suggests that the regime has been overthrown and the pro-Athenian exiles restored (as a consequence of Alexander's decree on the return of the exiles?—cf. Blass, III 2,

405–7). Troezen did join the Hellenic revolt of 323–322 (Paus. i. 25. 4; Diod. xviii. 11. 2).

Calauria became independent of Troezen in the late fourth century but the remarks here cast no light whatever on the status of the island in 323; cf. Ernst Meyer, "Troizen," *RE*, VIIA(1939), 641–43. On the alleged *vaticinium ex eventu* here, see above, pp. 68–73.

Papyri Osloenses Inv. No. 1471 preserves portions of paragraphs 18–20, [ἴδοιτ]ε ... τοσαύτην; the variants are obviously inferior to the texts of the medieval manuscripts and need not be treated here.

PARAGRAPH 19. ἐπιτιμᾶν ... ἀγνοίᾳ. The indefinite pronoun, unnecessarily deleted by Schaefer but confirmed by the papyrus, is a cognate accusative governed by the infinitive. On the double dative construction, see on Ep. 3. 1, ἐπιτιμώντων κτλ.; objections to the accusative and double dative led Sachsenweger (p.28) to render the passage, "tried to cast some reproach upon you in their ignorance of me." But the construction is unobjectionable, and Sachsenweger's interpretation forced; here, as throughout (Ep. 2. 8, 11, 26; Ep. 3. 8, 11, 13; cf. Ep. 4. 1, 7; Ep. 1. 2–3), Demosthenes uses a word connoting ignorance to describe the Athenians' treatment of him.

PARAGRAPH 20. See above, Chap. 2, n. 3. A verb of sitting is regularly used with the preposition εἰς or ἐν to express "taking asylum" as a suppliant in some holy place; cf. Th. iii. 75. 3, 5; Isaeus 5. 39; D. 18. 107; Plut. *Dem.* 29. 1. For refuge on an altar, the preposition is ἐπί with the accusative or the genitive: Lys. 2. 11; 13. 24, 52; Aesch. 1. 60; cf. *Vit. X orat.* 846e.

Although μετελθών is a verb well attested in the Attic orators, I have not been able to find a good parallel for it in fourth-century prose with the meaning it has here (either "I left" or "I resorted to"). However, that meaning fits the normal connotations of both the prefix and the root verb, and there are the earlier parallel, Hp. *Aër.* 18 (in the reading preferred by Littré), and the later, Polyb. xxvii. 16. 5. Use of the place of the shrine instead of the name of the shrine as in my alternative translation of this passage occurs in the reading of the manuscripts at D. 18. 107.

PARAGRAPHS 21–22. See above, p. 71.

PARAGRAPH 21. ὅπως. Although the use of ὅπως rather than ἵνα to introduce a pure final clause (as opposed to an object clause after a verb of striving, etc.) is comparatively rare in Plato and the Attic orators, it is not so rare as to justify any suspicion. Even in the restricted corpus of Demosthenic orations considered authentic by A. Schaefer, there are fourteen instances of ὅπως and four of ὅπως ἄν as against 253 of ἵνα; see P. Weber, *Entwickelungsgeschichte der Absichtssätze, zweite Abtheilung: die attische Prosa*, pp.15–70, and W. W. Goodwin, *Syntax of the Moods and Tenses of the Greek Verb*, p.398. Indeed, since here there are two sets of purposes expressed, it is a mark of elegance to introduce the one relating to the present situation with ὅπως, saving the other particle to introduce the one relating to the possible results of that situation in the future.

PARAGRAPH 21. ἑτέρων. See above, Chap. 8, rhetorical analysis of Ep. 3. 23–27.

PARAGRAPH 22. παρ' ὧν ... ἐμέ. The argument against Demosthenes at Hyp. *Dem.* 29–30 is similar.

PARAGRAPH 23. καλῶς ποιοῦσ'. See on Ep. 3. 24.

PARAGRAPH 23. ψηφίσασθε ... ἐμοῦ. The Oslo papyrus has τῆς πᾶσιν ὑπ[αρχούσης παρ'] ὑμῶν φιλανθρωπίας [κἀμοὶ μετά]δοτε. "Let me, too, share in the humane treatment you have accorded everyone."

PARAGRAPH 25. See above, p. 81.

PARAGRAPH 25. ⟨ὡς⟩ ἐν οὐδενὶ κτλ. The context suggests and demands Nitsche's inserted particle. Demosthenes here defends his display of emotion throughout the letter, not his career. The career no longer needs defense after paragraph 24. Haplography caused the loss of the particle.

PARAGRAPH 26. καλῶς ποιήσουσιν. See on Ep. 3. 24.

EPISTLE 4*

Concerning the Slanders of Theramenes

PARAGRAPH 1. δυστυχίαν. The word means not only inability to succeed but also being the carrier of highly contagious ill fortune. Only Demosthenes among the Attic orators uses the word in this sense (18. 270; cf. 19. 259 [the cognate adjective], 265). Theramenes, Aeschines, and Dinarchus all accuse Demosthenes of being a carrier of ill fortune. Aeschines expresses the concept by τύχη, δαίμων, and ἀλιτήριος (3. 157; see Goodwin's commentary to D. 18. 159); Dinarchus, by ἀτυχία and the cognate adjective (1. 74, 77, 91), ἀλιτήριος (1. 77), and perhaps δαίμων (1. 30). Demosthenes' own apprehensions on these lines: Plut. *Dem.* 21. 3; cf. Aesch. 3. 159.

Aeschines finds Demosthenes' contagion spreading to the entire world, but to him the disease is contracted by listening to Demosthenes' advice (Aesch. 3. 57, 114, 130–36, 157–58, 253; Demosthenes' replies: 18. 212, 252–73). To Dinarchus, mere association with Demosthenes, without listening to his advice, exposes one to infection; the safety of the city requires his complete removal (Din. 1. 30–33, 36, 64–65, 72–77, 91–93). There is no trace of the charge in Hyperides. Cf. Nicias' belief in his contagious good fortune (Th. vii. 77). See also below on paragraphs 3, 5–7, Ep. 1. 13, and above on Ep. 2. 5, τῆς δ' ἀναγκαίας.

PARAGRAPH 1. ἐργαστηρίῳ. There may be an insinuating ambiguity in this word. It often means merely "shop" or "factory," and our passage could be a close parallel to the contemptuous reference to Aeschines' servile upbringing at D. 18. 258–62. The word also means "brothel," and I have so translated it. The letter would then be

* For the historical background of Ep. 4, see above pp. 59–61.

hinting that Theramenes spent his early childhood in disgraceful surroundings, perhaps also that he was illegitimate, and certainly that he was unfit for civic life. On the other hand, Theramenes' parents in paragraph 11 are contrasted with Pausanias, the catamite. Unfortunately for the translator, no sufficiently ambiguous word exists in English. On such attacks on an opponent's fitness for civic life, see Navarre, pp. 294–96.

PARAGRAPH 2. σωθῶ. See above, Chap. 5, n. 116.

PARAGRAPH 2. περὶ ὧν ... παροινεῖ. The argument which Demosthenes used against the prominent Aeschines at 18. 270–73, that Aeschines had tacitly accepted Demosthenes' policies by not opposing them, probably had no force against the more obscure Theramenes — again the letter proves not to be a mere imitation of *De Corona*. Demosthenes used words connoting drunkenness to describe the actions of his opponents; see below on Ep. 1. 10, προποθείς.

PARAGRAPH 3. See above, pp. 59–61, 88–92, and cf. D. 18. 253.

The word "dear to the gods" does not recur in the Demosthenic corpus but is common in Isocrates, Plato, and Xenophon.

Before the battle of Chaeroneia there is no evidence of a temple and cult of Good Fortune (Ἀγαθὴ Τύχη) in Attica (the fourth-century shrine of Good Fortune in the Piraeus: *IG* II² 1035, lines 44, 48; W. Judeich, *Topographie von Athen*, p. 435; Wilamowitz, *Glaube der Hellenen*, II, 301). To get good fortune, the Athenians are told in the Delphic oracles preserved at D. 21. 51 (348 B.C.) and at D. 43. 66 (of uncertain date) to sacrifice and pray to Apollo Agyieus, Leto, and Artemis; see Parke and Wormell, II, 114–15. An inscription of 335/4, however, mentions the treasurers of Good Fortune and her *epistatai* (*IG* II² 333, fr. *c*, lines 19–20). From *IG* II² 1496, lines 76, 107, 148, we learn that sacrifices were offered to Good Fortune in 334/3, 333/2, and 331/0, the sacrifices to her coming regularly each year between the City Dionysia and the Asclepieia. The temple was also mentioned in a lost speech of Lycurgus dealing with his administration (Harpocration *s.v. agathê tychê*).

Ascribing the defeat at Chaeroneia to Fortune (D. 18. 141, 194, 207, 300, 306; 60. 21; Ep. 2. 5; Hyp. *Dem.* 30), the Athenians strove to get her on their side. Probably the oracles from Dodona and Delphi mentioned here were sought in connection with the establishment of her cult within the city and its continuing administration.

Oracles were sought in this period on the continuing administration of cults. See the mutilated *IG* II² 333, lines 19–20, 24–29, and Parke and Wormell, II, 116–17; the decree was proposed by Lycurgus. The inscription, the oration cited by Harpocration, and Lycurgus' religious interests suggest that he was responsible for bringing the cult of Good Fortune to Athens. In view of all this, "with you" is to be taken literally: Good Fortune had come to dwell in a temple in Athens after the battle of Chaeroneia with the sanction of Dodona and Delphi. Demosthenes here may also be alluding to the ordinary run of compliments accorded Athens by the Delphic oracle (Parke and Wormell, II, Nos. 16, 121, 154, 171).

The adverb ἀεί and the two present participles suggest that there has been a series of oracles since Chaeroneia. This may reflect new developments after D. 18. 253, where no such succession is suggested. Moreover, the manuscripts there do not mention the Pythian Apollo (though a marginal variant does). Demosthenes would not fail to use the testimony of a hostile witness, the "Philippizing Pythia" (Aesch. 3. 130), in his favor (cf. Neupert, p. 46). Hence, if the text of D. 18 253 is correct, here is another advance in Ep. 4 beyond *De Corona.*

There are repeated references to Zeus and Dione of Dodona in this period (Hyp. *Eux.* 24–26, and see on Ep. 1. 16). Athenians may have preferred the oracle of Dodona to the "Philippizing" Pythia; cf. Mathieu, *REA*, XXXIX, 377.

PARAGRAPH 3. προσεπισφραγιζομένους. Neupert, p. 51, objects that this word recurs in Greek literature only in Sextus Empiricus *Adv. math.* ix. 192 and Aelius Aristides *Or.* 36 (48). 106. Neupert himself, however, rendered the prefixed *pros-* by "insuper." There is no reason, then, to distinguish the word from ἐπισφραγίζομαι (Plato *Lg.* ix. 855e, xii. 957b; *Plt.* 258c). For the force of *pros-* as "in confirmation," cf. προσωμολογεῖτε in the context of D. 18. 250. According to the rules of the oracle of Apollo Koropaios, our chief source for Greek oracular procedure, the texts of the divine responses were delivered to the inquirer in writing and sealed (*IG* IX: 2 1109 of ca. 100 B.C.; M. P. Nilsson, *Geschichte der griechischen Religion*, II, 104).

PARAGRAPH 3. ὅσα . . . προλέγουσιν. The possibility that the oracles were referring to some future good fortune of Athens, one unconnected with Demosthenes' activity, must be excluded before the orator can take the oracles as judgments on his policies.

PARAGRAPH 3. προσηγορίας. The word here has its usual meaning, "name, epithet," as it does in the next paragraph. There is no reason to assume with Neupert, p. 54, that it has the otherwise unknown meaning, "sors oraculo edita."

PARAGRAPH 4. For the argument of Demosthenes' enemies, see on paragraph 1.

PARAGRAPHS 5-7. Cf. D. 18. 252-55, 270-75, 290; Aesch. 3. 132-34, and see above on paragraph 1.

In the parallels to paragraph 7 (18. 253-54, 271-72) Demosthenes does not specify who "the barbarians" are. Here he mentions first the Persians, next the two important peoples of western Asia hardest hit by the Macedonians, and finally and vaguely—because they were little known to him and his audience—the groups farther east. The Macedonian conquest of Caria was primarily an operation against Greeks and Persians; Alexander's operations against insignificant Pisidian hill tribes could pass unmentioned. On the other hand, although the submission of Cappadocia and the appointment of Sabictas as satrap (Arrian ii. 4. 2) were probably nominal, Alexander's general Antigonus prevailed over forces from Cappadocia after fighting no less than three battles (Curt. iv. 1. 34-35; W. W. Tarn, *Alexander the Great*, II, 110-11). We may assume that in these the Cappadocian losses were heavy, quite apart from those suffered by the considerable Cappadocian contingents at the Granicus (Mithrobuzanes, governor of Cappadocia, present: Arrian i. 16. 3) and Gaugamela (on the right wing, scene of heavy fighting: Arrian iii. 11. 7, 15. 1-3). Syria included the territory from the border of Cilicia to the border of Egypt (cf. Arrian ii. 25. 4); here occurred the bloody sieges of Tyre and Gaza and the punishment of Samaria; see F.M. Cross, "The Discovery of the Samaria Papyri," *Biblical Archaeologist*, XXVI (1963), 118-19.

The news of Alexander's wars in India reached Greece only shortly before the arrival of Harpalus. The author thus presents topics of interest to Athenians in 324/3.

PARAGRAPHS 8-9. Cf. D. 18. 64-65, 208, 231, 253-54, 304. The Thessalians might have been the first to block the expansion of their neighbor, Philip, who won Thessaly more by diplomacy than by force of arms (Polyaenus iv. 2. 19); see H. D. Westlake, *Thessaly in the Fourth Century B.C.*, pp. 160–216. By the time of the battle of Chaeroneia, Thessaly was under Philip's control, and Thessalian contingents seem to have fought at Chaeroneia on his side. The letter implies that the Thessalians profited from their attachment to Philip; perhaps one of their rewards was the liberal allowance of ten votes in the League of Corinth; see Westlake, pp. 207–16.

Arcadian and Argive collaboration with Philip: D. 19. 260–61; 18. 64, 304; Schaefer, II, 553–54; III, 41–47; C. Roebuck, "The Settlements of Philip II with the Greek States in 338 B.C.," *CP*, XLIII (1948), 76, 85–89; Paus. i. 25. 3; cf. Polyb. xviii. 14, and see above, p.72–73.

PARAGRAPH 10. On τοιγαροῦν, see above, p.28. For the expression, "The gods . . . are bringing the unjust slander down upon the head of the one who utters it," cf. D. 18. 290. The attack on Theramenes' character and fortune here resembles the attack on Aeschines at D. 18. 130. Now in exile, Demosthenes cannot repeat the challenge to his enemy (D. 18. 256) to compare his own fortune to that of Demosthenes.

PARAGRAPH 11. δυσχεραίνεται. The passive of this verb recurs in the Attic orators only in the Demosthenic corpus (D. 10. 44, 61. 18).

PARAGRAPH 11. ἀγάλλεται. The word does not recur in the Attic orators but is well attested in Attic prose. Construed with a dative it occurs at Th. ii. 44. 2 and Plato *Tht.* 176d.

PARAGRAPH 11. αἰσχρορρημοσύνη. Pollux ii. 129 cites this word from Demosthenes. In ancient literature it recurs only at Philodemus *Rh.*, Vol. I, p. 175 Sudhaus. Even so, the components and formation are common in fourth-century Attic, as in αἰσχροκέρδεια (D. 18. 295, 19. 28, etc.), φιλοπραγμοσύνη (D. 1. 14, 4. 42, 21. 137, 39. 1), and κακοπραγμοσύνη (D. 25. 101).

PARAGRAPH 11. ἐφ' οἷς ἀλγοῦσιν. Cf. D. 18. 128.

PARAGRAPH 11. ἀφελής. The word does not recur in the Attic orators but is used at Arist. *Rhet.* iii. 9. 5. 1409b16, Aristoph. *Eq.* 527, and Phylarchus, *F. Gr. Hist.* No. 81, F 44.

PARAGRAPH 12. Cf. D. 18. 264; 19. 309. Adjectival phrases similar to ἐν ὑμῖν: Lys. 26. 23; Isoc. 4. 65, 7. 37. ὑπόμνημα . . . κακῶν: cf. Lyc. *apud* Diod. xvi. 88. 2.

251

EPISTLE 1*

On Concord

TITLE. Aelius Aristides knew the title which Ep. 1 bears in our editions; see above, Chap. 2, n. 6. A note in the margin of **S** by a hand different from that of the scribe cites from another manuscript the title Περὶ παρασκευῆς, "On Preparation." See on Ep. 3, *Title*.

PARAGRAPH 1. τὸν ἔπειτα χρόνον. This expression for "the future" occurs in the Demosthenic corpus only here, but it occurs at Isaeus 2. 10, 9. 13; Plato *Phlb.* 39e.

PARAGRAPH 1. ἐπὶ νοῦν ἐλθεῖν. The expression recurs in the Demosthenic corpus only at *Prooem.* 25. 3. Cf. Aesch. 3. 118, ἐπῆλθε . . . ἐπὶ τὴν γνώμην (since Aeschines tolerates hiatus, there is no reason to delete the prepositional phrase with Baiter and Weidner).

PARAGRAPH 1. ἐπινοίας. This word does not recur in the Attic orators but is used by Thucydides, Xenophon, Plato, and Epicurus. Here it echoes the preceding ἐπὶ νοῦν.

PARAGRAPH 2. περὶ μὲν κτλ. See on Ep. 3. 1, περὶ μέν.

PARAGRAPH 2. ἀεὶ . . . βουλεύσασθαι. ἀεὶ is to be taken with ἔσεσθαι. Any other position for the adverb would result in hiatus.

PARAGRAPH 2. ὡς ἔχω περὶ. The same construction is found at D. 8. 73 and Aesch. 1. 8.

PARAGRAPH 3. ἔστι μέν . . . συμβουλῇ. The μέν is answered by the οὐ μὴν ἀλλά below; cf. D. 8. 38; 14. 33; 19. 201; 37. 23. Rennie construed συμβουλῇ with the infinitive preceding it and found the text "vix sanum." But the text is perfectly sound if the dative is construed with ἔργον ἐστί; the word could have no other position in the sentence

---

* For the historical background of Ep. 1, see above, pp. 61-63.

if hiatus is to be avoided. Except at 44. 29, in the rest of the Demosthenic corpus ἐμμεῖναι is used only of persons, but cf. Plato *Lg.* viii. 839c and *Phaedrus* 258b.

PARAGRAPH 3. πολλοῖς may be either masculine ("many a speaker" —resumed by λέγοντι in the next sentence) or neuter ("many a suggestion"—supplying an object for "to learn," which otherwise has none).

PARAGRAPH 3. ἐὰν ἐθελήσητ᾽ κτλ. Cf. *Prooem.* 5.

PARAGRAPH 3. ὡς σὺν (Schaefer; καὶ σὺν codd.; σὺν Wolf, Blass) κτλ. Ordinarily the "formal" infinitive is introduced by ὡς or by no particle at all (Kühner-Gerth, II, 508–9), as in the proposed emendations. If the particle in the manuscripts is to be preserved, perhaps the future perfect indicative should be read for the perfect infinitive; cf. Eur. *Medea* 625, Aristoph. *Pl.* 114. There is no parallel in the Demosthenic corpus for a perfect or passive formal infinitive, but cf. Aesch. 1. 177, Plato *Prt.* 339a, *Ion* 535a, *R.* 414a.

The use of σύν here and at paragraph 12 requires explanation in view of Tycho Mommsen's study, *Beiträge zu der Lehre von den griechischen Präpositionen*. In prose writers of the fourth century (except Xenophon), the word is almost entirely replaced by μετά except in the "inclusive" sense; the same is true of the surviving Hellenistic prose literature (not of Ptolemaic papyri: C. B. Welles, *Royal Correspondence in the Hellenistic Period*, p. lxxv). See Mommsen, pp. 1–9, 364–90, and cf. Neupert, pp. 59–60. According to Mommsen, pp. 374–75, the instance here is a stock expression retained by prose usage; cf. D. 29. 1.

PARAGRAPH 4. ἄνευ λογισμοῦ. Cf. *Prooem.* 28. 1.

PARAGRAPH 4. πέμπειν ... βελτίστων. The passage is partially preserved on *POxy.* xxxi. 2549. The variants in line 2 of the papyrus have no significance either for sense or for style.

PARAGRAPH 4. τὸ παρηκολουθηκέναι τοῖς πράγμασιν. Cf. D. 18. 172.

PARAGRAPH 4. ῥᾳδίαν κτλ. Cf. D. 1. 1.

PARAGRAPHS 5–9. See above, pp. 61–62.

PARAGRAPH 5. ὁμόνοιαν ... παρασχέσθαι. "Concord" defined: Arist. *EN* ix. 6. 1167a-b. "The city" may be dative with either the participle or the infinitive (cf. Lys. 12. 14).

PARAGRAPH 5. τὰς ἐκ τῶν κτλ. For the prepositional usage, see Lutz, p. 49; Lys. 13. 20, 50; Aesch. 2. 59, 95.

PARAGRAPH 5. ὡς τὸ μήθ᾽ κτλ. My translation follows the text of Rennie and Blass. Baiter and Sauppe's text would be rendered by "failure to act with absolute unanimity" (cf. D. 16. 24).

PARAGRAPH 6. εὐκατεργαστότερ᾽. The word is found only here in the Demosthenic corpus but occurs at Arist. *Rhet.* i. 6. 29. 1363a31; the comparative: X. *Hell.* vi. 1. 12.

PARAGRAPHS 6–7. τοῖς καθεστηκόσι. At Din. 1. 35, Demosthenes is quoted as using this expression. It appears to have been an Athenian euphemism for the Macedonian hegemony. Earlier in Demosthenes it usually means the existing order or constitution of the free Greek polis (cf. Lys. 25. 3), except perhaps at D. 6. 22. The expression probably refers to the Macedonian hegemony in the mutilated context in the speech of Leosthenes, *Hibeh Papyri*, Vol. I, No. 15, lines 57–65.

PARAGRAPH 6. πικραίνεσθαι. The word does not recur in the Attic orators. With the sense "be bitter," it occurs at Arist. *Ph.* 244b23; with the sense "feel bitterness," as here, at Plato *Lg.* v. 731d. See also on Ep. 3. 12, τῆς ἀξίας.

PARAGRAPH 7. ἀναγκαίοις τοῖς καθεστηκόσι. The context demands the sense "bound, constrained, forced." There is no other instance in the Attic orators of the word in this sense, but it is found at *Odyssey* xxiv. 210, 499. The participle has been emended by Blass; the manuscripts have συνεστηκόσι, "the conspirators, the [Macedonian] gang."

PARAGRAPH 7. ἠπιώτεροι. This word is absent from the entire corpus of the Attic orators, but it is common in Homer and the Attic dramatists. It occurs in Herodotus, and in fourth-century Attic prose the comparative itself appears at Plato *Timaeus* 85a.

PARAGRAPH 7. ἐν δυνάτῳ. For the construction, cf. ἐν ἀμφισβητησίμῳ, D. 18. 139; and ἐν κοινῷ, D. 18. 320 and 20. 24.

PARAGRAPH 7. κατὰ τῶν ἄλλων. κατά with the genitive is used in the sense of περί when a generalization is being expressed through the words πάντες or ἄλλοι (Lutz, p. 72). Cf. D. 24. 59; 37. 20; 41. 24.

PARAGRAPH 8. φημὶ δὴ χρῆναι. See Appendix VI.

PARAGRAPH 8. (μήτε πόλει) μήτε στρατηγῷ κτλ. Editors since Baiter and Sauppe have deleted the words in parentheses, and the text reads better without them. The context speaks only of the Athenians' behavior toward one another; from this, good relations with other

Greek cities are to result. The passage may have been contaminated from paragraph 6.

PARAGRAPH 8. καλῶς ποιοῦντες. See on Ep. 3. 24.

PARAGRAPH 8. ὥσπερ ἐν πλοίῳ κτλ. Cf. D. 18. 194 and the instances of the proverbial expression δεύτερος πλοῦς in the *Greek-English Lexicon s.v.* πλόος. Though κώπη is a common word, it recurs in the Attic orators only at D. 13. 14. I have been unable to find another instance in prose of κομίζεσθαι with the meaning "get through safely"; even at Ps. – D. 7. 15 the active probably means "transport" rather than "rescue." σῴζεσθαι would be an easy, though I think unnecessary, emendation.

PARAGRAPH 8. γεγενῆσθαι . . . Θεῶν. The passage has long been recognized as difficult; see Dindorf, VII, 1445. χρείαν here surely means "usefulness." I have taken the πρός phrase with the infinitive; cf. Plato *R.* 604c. One might also take it to modify the participle, translating, "its utility in the course of events has been determined by the will of the gods."

PARAGRAPH 9. τῶν ἰδίων ⟨μὴ⟩ μέμνησθε. Reiske's inserted negative is required by the context, a plea for amnesty (μὴ μνησικακεῖν—paragraph 6). "The common interest" might mean the interests of the Hellenic alliance, and "private grudges," those of the Athenians (cf. *Prooem.* 22. 1; Isoc. 5. 30). If so, a Hellenic alliance already existed at the time of the letter.

PARAGRAPH 10. The use here of ἕτερος suggests that Demosthenes is protesting again that he had been framed to please Alexander (cf. Hyp. *Dem.* 14); see above, Chap. 8, rhetorical analysis of Ep. 3. 23–27, and cf. Andoc. 2. 24, where the word refers to the public enemy Peisander. For the metaphorical use of προπίνω, cf. D. 18. 296 and 3. 22. Demosthenes was known to his contemporaries for his abstinence (D. 6. 30, 19. 46; Hyp. *Dem.* fr. *apud* Athenaeus x. 424d; Pytheas fr. *apud* Athenaeus ii. 44f). Hence, the use of the language of wine drinking to describe practices of which he disapproves is in character; cf. παροινεῖ at Ep. 4. 2. "Satisfy" ("fill up") and "mix" probably continue the drinking metaphor. Rennie, following Dobree, reads ἀποπληρῶν for the ἀναπληρῶν of the manuscripts. The manuscript reading, however, may have been just as good an Attic idiom; it need not have meant "replenish" rather than simply "fill up." Cf. D. 27. 13 and ἀναπλήρωσις at Arist. *Pol.* 1267b4 (the noun at

EN 1173*b*8 may be a Platonic technical term). μείγνυμι occurs in the Attic orators only here and at D. 60. 18 but is otherwise common.

PARAGRAPH 11. On παρασκευαί see above, p. 62–63. ἐπιστατῆσαι recurs in the Demosthenic corpus only at Ps.-D. 61. 38, but it is common in Attic (Isoc. 4. 104; 12. 154), especially in inscriptions.

PARAGRAPH 12. ὁμιλίας. See on Ep. 3. 12, τῆς ἀξίας.

PARAGRAPH 12. σὺν πολλῇ σπουδῇ καὶ πόνῳ. See on paragraph 3. The use here of σύν instead of μετά does avoid a tribrach, but elsewhere with abstract nouns Demosthenes uses μετά, never σύν. There seems to have been some tendency in Attic to use σύν where the abstract noun was modified by πολύς (very strong in Xenophon: see Mommsen, p. 363; and cf. Plato *R.* iv. 424e, vi. 492b as against Isoc. 15. 20; Arist. *Meteor.* 348*a*24 as against 367*a*4). Perhaps there was also a tendency to use σύν with σπουδή and πόνος (Plato *Lg.* vii. 818c; X. *Anab.* i. 8. 4, ii. 5. 18; *Mem.* ii. 2. 5; *Venat.* 9. 6). See Mommsen's general discussion, pp. 376–80. There are, however, examples in Demosthenes counter to both tendencies: 18. 202, 258; 21. 227; *Prooemm.* 21. 3, 53. 2.

PARAGRAPH 12. ἐφεστηκότων στρατηγῶν. Only here is this participle adjectival; Demosthenes, Aeschines, and Lysias use it to mean "those in command or authority." Hence Schaefer deleted the noun "generals" as a gloss of the less familiar word. Perhaps, however, the combination here means "the generals in charge of each department."

PARAGRAPH 12. διελυμάνθη. The word recurs at Isoc. 4. 110, but nowhere in the Demosthenic corpus.

PARAGRAPH 13. On the ascription in Athens of the Macedonian successes to *tychê*, see commentary to Ep. 2. 5. The sudden death of Alexander was taken as a sign that Fortune had finally deserted the Macedonians, and the proponents of the Hellenic revolt were quick to seize upon that notion, as in the speech of Leosthenes (*Hibeh Papyri*, Vol. I, No. 15, lines 73–78); cf. Diod. xviii. 8. 7–9. 1.

PARAGRAPH 13. καὶ γάρ ... ηὐτύχει. To Neupert, p. 28, the similarity with D. 2. 22–23 suggests the activity of a forger. But even if D. 2. 22–23 were repeated here verbatim, the description fits both Philip and Alexander so well that there is no reason to be suspicious.

PARAGRAPH 14. τούς θ' ἡγεμόνας κτλ. See above, p. 63.

PARAGRAPH 15. ὧν ἂν ἐλλίπηθ' κτλ. Cf. D. 18. 302–5.

PARAGRAPH 15. μετάγνωσις. The word occurs at Hdt. i. 87 and Philodemus *De ira*, p. 56 Wilke, but nowhere else in the Attic orators; the related verb: D. 18. 153, 21. 109.

PARAGRAPH 16. See above, p. 72.

PARAGRAPH 16. τὸν Δία κτλ. See commentary to Ep. 4. 3. The audience would surely recall the famous message of the oracle of Dodona to confirm Demosthenes' recommendations (D. 19. 298–99; Din. 1. 78, 98–99).

PARAGRAPH 16. κατὰ τῶν νικητηρίων. This construction for the object vowed, to my knowledge, is paralleled only at Plut. *Mar*. 26. 2 (cf. *Quaest. Graec.* 294b). The rarity is probably accidental; vows and oaths are closely related, and the construction is common in the Attic orators with verbs of swearing (D. 19. 292; other examples collected by Lutz, p. 72). For state vows, cf. *GHI* 144 and 146.

Appendixes

APPENDIX I

Epistles 5 and 6

E P. 5 PROBABLY WAS included, along with Epp. 1–4, in the Demosthenic corpus before the end of the third century B.C. (see above, pp. 17–18). That the letter may not be in the style of the mature Demosthenes (above, pp. 28–29) is not a conclusive proof of inauthenticity, since supposedly it was written before that style had taken form, and in any case it is a private letter, not a public speech. The ostensible purpose of Ep. 5 is an appeal to Heracleodorus, a man influential in his city, to come to the aid of Demosthenes' friend, Epitimus, who has been summarily arrested by Aratus. The supposed setting of the events is outside Athens. Demosthenes hears of the event through Menecrates and reacts by sending a letter. Menecrates is a well-attested Athenian name, whereas Aratus and Epitimus are not Athenian at all, and Heracleodorus first appears in Athenian documents in the second century B.C.; see *Pros. Att.*, *s. vv.* The Epitimus of C. Robert, "Epitimos 3," *RE*, VI (1909), 222, was probably an alien.

The events which supposedly called forth Ep. 5 are treated with bare allusions, and the ostensible purpose of the letter seems far overshadowed by the effort to display the influence of the school of Plato upon the young ambitious Demosthenes. Paragraph 3 expresses glowing admiration for the Academy, and the introductory formula εὖ πράττειν is peculiar to letters of Plato and his school and to imitations of them, being extremely rare elsewhere (earliest example in a papyrus letter: *POxy.* iv. 822, from around the beginning of the Christian era; see F. X. J. Exler, *The Form of the Ancient Greek Letter: a Study in Greek Epistolography*, pp. 23–68 and esp. p. 34). The legends associating Demosthenes with Plato lack all foundation (see above, Chap. 2, n. 1). Both the Ptolemies and the Attalids, from the third century on, offered high prices for manuscripts of choice authors. Their competitive bidding encouraged forgers to produce "collectors' items" for so lucrative a market; see

261

Galen, *Commentarius in Hippocratis De natura hominis* i. 42 (127), Vol. XV, p. 105 Kühn; ii. *prooem.* (128), Vol. XV, p. 109; *Commentarius in Hippocratis Epidemiorum* iii. 4 (239–40), Vol. XVII 1, pp. 606–7. And what could be a greater "find" than a letter in which the greatest of orators, in his youth, praises the teaching of Plato? Cf. also Lucian, *Adversus indoctum* 4.

As for Ep. 6, it, alone of all the letters, is not alluded to by any ancient source, though perhaps only because of its brevity. The setting is clearly the Lamian war of 323–322 (see Schaefer, III, 351–98, and the literature cited by Bengtson, *Griechische Geschichte*, pp. 361–62). Leosthenes has been killed and Antiphilus is in command; the member states of the Greek alliance are represented in a federal body of *synedroi* (cf. *SIG*[3] 327). On the opposite side stand Antipater and his Corinthian collaborator, Dinarchus (see Bengtson, *Die Strategie in der hellenistischen Zeit*, I, 128–32). Thus far the historical allusions of Ep. 6 are in accordance with the facts. By no means, however, are they beyond the capacities of a writer with access to the now-lost histories of the period.

Was there any time during the Lamian war when Demosthenes could have sent Ep. 6 to the Council and People of Athens? The letter purports to have been sent shortly after a battle ($\mu\acute{\alpha}\chi\eta$). The army of the Greek alliance under the command of Antiphilus fought two engagements that can be called battles. In the first, the Greek army defeated the Macedonian relief force under Leonnatus. Leonnatus himself perished, but in the process the Greeks abandoned the siege of Lamia, and Antipater succeeded in withdrawing to Macedonia where he could wait for more reinforcements from Asia. The second engagement was the battle of Crannon, 7 Metageitnion on the Athenian calendar (Aug. 6, 322, according to Meritt—see above, Chap. 5, n. 53). Though in itself Crannon was no serious defeat, after it the Greek alliance disintegrated. Little more than a month later, by 20 Boëdromion (September 18), Athens had capitulated and had been occupied by a Macedonian garrison.

After one of these battles, according to the letter, Antiphilus sent a communiqué to the *synedroi* giving grounds for hope but leaving room for vexatious propaganda by the partisans of Antipater; and Antipater himself had sent a message to Dinarchus which had been published with great effect in the cities of the Peloponnesus. Which of the two battles is meant? The letter itself suggests that the state of affairs within the Hellenic camp is a matter of concern to the Athenians. It is improbable that a communiqué sent by Antiphilus after the apparently brilliant victory over Leonnatus could have aroused such concern, though Antipater may well have sent a message then to encourage his supporters in the Peloponnesus. See Diod. xviii. 15. 3–7; Plut. *Phoc.* 25. 3; Justin xiii. 5. 14–17. On the other hand, after the battle of Crannon, there was indeed dissension in the camp of the Hellenes; a communiqué of Antiphilus, though still hopeful, could well have aroused concern in Athens and have been exploited by pro-Macedonian circles; and at this same time Antipater did use propaganda to win over the Greek cities. See Diod. xviii. 17. 6–8 and Plut. *Phoc.* 26. 1. Hence, it is far more likely that Crannon is the battle mentioned.

Furthermore, the fact that the document is a letter means that Demosthenes is outside Athens. Where could he be? The names appearing in Ep. 6 are no help; "Epinikos" is found in many parts of Greece, and "Polemaistos" is known only from here—perhaps the text is corrupt (see W. Pape, *Wörterbuch der griechischen Eigennamen, s. vv.*). If Demosthenes is writing from the Peloponnesus, surely the Athenians are better informed than he of events in the Thessalian theater of war. If he is in Thessaly, the Athenians are not only better informed than he of the state of affairs in the Peloponnesus but also receive the direct reports of Antiphilus. The letter makes it clear that Demosthenes is some distance from the site of the battle and the Greek camp; surely the Athenians had no need of eyewitnesses passed on to them by Demosthenes. If Demosthenes wrote Ep. 6 from anywhere else, he was in an even worse position to have his letter give the Athenians something which they did not already possess. Furthermore, if the battle mentioned is Crannon, it is hard to see how Demosthenes would have had time to learn of the battle, of the messages of Antiphilus and Antipater, and of the reaction in the Peloponnesus before the collapse of the Hellenic alliance made such an optimistic letter impossible. How, then, could Demosthenes have written Ep. 6?

Paul Foucart, in the only previous detailed discussion of Ep. 6 ("La sixième lettre attribuée à Démosthène," *Journal des savants*, n.s., X [1912], 49–54), suggests that Demosthenes wrote Ep. 6 from exile, after the victory over Leonnatus, and that the letter reflects the period of the orator's volunteer diplomacy in the Peloponnesus, which was to win him his restoration (Plut. *Dem.* 27. 2–4; *Vit. X orat.* 846d). He can hardly be right. When an exile or a foreigner addresses the Council and the People, he must always show that he recognizes his status and give some reason why he should receive a hearing, as in D. Epp. 1. 2–4; 2. 1–4; 3. 1; 4. 1–2; and Isoc. Ep. 8 (cf. Isoc. Epp. 1, 2. 1–2). Ep. 6 contains nothing of the kind. Furthermore, Plut. *Dem.* 27. 1–2 dates Demosthenes' diplomatic activity during the lifetime of Leosthenes (cf. Plut. *Dem. et Cic. comp.* 3. 1), and Justin xiii. 5. 9–14 seems to place it before the victory over Leonnatus. Even if this evidence is set aside, chrono-logical difficulties remain. The winter was well advanced when Leos-thenes died (Hyp. *Epit.* 23). Though Lamia had been provisioned, Antipater and his men were hard-pressed by hunger before the arrival of Leonnatus (Diod. xviii. 12. 4–13. 4). In any case the battle with Leonnatus, in which cavalry played the leading role, could hardly have taken place before the spring campaigning season. But the Peloponne-sian cities had begun to adhere to the Hellenic alliance already in December, Sicyon being the first (*SIG*³ 310; cf. Justin xiii. 5. 10). Hence, Demosthenes' diplomatic activity in exile was surely long since over by the time of the victory over Leonnatus.

Foucart saw in Ep. 6 an authentic letter of Demosthenes reworked by a rhetorical historian such as Anaximenes. This hypothesis would explain the departures from Demosthenic style. (But would an Anaxi-menes have allowed the hiatus of μοι ἃ ἔλεγεν?) The difficulties which make it improbable that Demosthenes wrote the letter also make it improbable that a historian composed it for inclusion in his narrative, for such letters can be expected to give a clear indication of their setting. In this respect, Ep. 6 compares unfavorably with the surviving examples of letters in the works of ancient historians (collected by Sykutris, "Epistolographie," *RE*, Suppl. V [1931], 208–10).

In the present state of our knowledge, Ep. 6 looks to be a fabrication. Compared to the exuberant optimism expressed by Demosthenes in Ep. 1 (see above, pp. 90–92), the cautious *dis volentibus* of Ep. 6 looks like a *vaticinium ex eventu*. (Foucart ascribes it to Anaximenes' rework-ing!) A cautiously optimistic utterance of Demosthenes after the battle of Crannon would be quite as much a collector's item as a letter in which the young orator declared his admiration for the school of Plato. How-ever, it is unlikely that Ep. 6 is a forged collector's item of the Hellenistic period. It has no stichometry, is absent from Codex Parisinus **S**, and is not attested in any ancient source; even the author of the letters of Aeschines does not allude to it (see Appendix II). All this suggests that Ep. 6 is an Atticistic rhetorical exercise of the second century A.D. or later. There are other examples of such compositions being appended to much older collections of documents; see E. Bickerman and J. Sykutris "Speusipps Brief an König Philipp," *BVSAW*, Vol. LXXX (1928), Heft III, pp. 79–80.

APPENDIX II

The Letters of Aeschines

Ps.-AESCH. EP. 11 IS written as an attack on D. Ep. 1, and such it explicitly proclaims itself to be at paragraphs 2 and 11: "ἀκούω δὲ τοὺς μὲν αὐτοῦ παρόντας, τοὺς δὲ καὶ δι᾽ ἐπιστολῶν κινεῖν τι τῶν τῆς πόλεως πραγμάτων . . . Ἄξιον δὲ καὶ ἃ λέγειν αὐτοὺς πυνθάνομαι λογίσασθαι μεθ᾽ ὑμῶν, ὡς καινὰ καὶ θαυμαστὸν ὅσον εἰς ἃ βούλονται πρᾶξαι συλλαβεῖν δυνάμενα, φάσκοντας ὑμᾶς ὁμονοεῖν δεῖν." Ps.-Aesch. Ep. 12 is an imitative counterpart of D. Ep. 2. As in D. Ep. 2 (see above pp. 56–58), the sender takes advantage of a grant of exoneration by the Athenian people to others in order to present a plea for his own family and person. The exact nature of the plea at Ps.-Aesch. Ep. 12. 15 is obscured by the corruption of the text; see *Eschine: discours*, ed. V. Martin and G. de Budé, II, 142, and *Aeschinis quae feruntur epistolae*, ed. Engelbert Drerup, pp. 47, 72. Like D. Ep. 2, Ps.-Aesch. Ep. 12 begins with a defense of the sender's career and ends with an exhortation that the influence of the writer's enemies must not prevail over the traditional virtues of the Athenians.

Ps.-Aesch. Ep. 12. 14 alludes to D. Ep. 3: "καὶ περὶ μὲν τῶν Λυκούργου παίδων Δημοσθένης ὑμῖν ἐπιστέλλει, καὶ δεῖται καλῶς ποιῶν χαρίσασθαι τὸ πατρῷον αὐτοῖς ὄφλημα." In so far as it is a plea for children, Ps.-Aesch. Ep. 12 is a counterpart also of D. Ep. 3, but the true counterpart of D. Ep. 3 is Ps.-Aesch. Ep. 3. In contrast to the bitter emotionalism of Demosthenes' pleas for vindication, Ps.-Aesch. Ep. 3 portrays the philosophic resignation of the pretended author, in language reflecting his model (compare Ps.-Aesch. Ep. 3. 1, "λοιδοροῦσι τὰς ἑαυτῶν πατρίδας, ὡς φαύλως αὐτοῖς προσφερομένας" and "ἐπείπερ ἅπαξ ἀναξίως ὧν ἐπολιτευσάμην ἠτύχησα," with D. Ep. 3. 32 and 40). Aeschines is made to refuse to indulge in such "indignant and abusive" attacks on the Council and People as are found at D. Ep. 3. 37, 42, and to console himself for

265

being in exile by considering it glorious to share the lot of Themistocles and Miltiades (in contrast to D. Ep. 3. 37–43). Ps.-Aesch. Ep. 7 is an obvious imitation of D. Ep. 4. Where Demosthenes replies to the slanders of Theramenes, Aeschines is made to reply to the slanders of Melanopus.

D. Ep. 5 probably provided the inspiration for Ps.-Aesch. Ep. 2, since the two can be shown to correspond point for point. Both begin with expressions of astonishment over news that has been brought to the writers. In the one letter Aeschines, his political career ended by exile, goes on to admonish Ctesiphon to cease hounding his aged and helpless uncle. In the other the young aspiring Demosthenes admonishes Heracleodorus to withdraw from the prosecution of his friend Epitimus, who has been summarily arrested on a grave charge. Ctesiphon's noble behaviour had inspired Aeschines to trust him; Heracleodorus' education in the noble school of Plato had inspired Demosthenes to admire him. Aeschines is made to plead with Ctesiphon not to bring disgrace and pollution upon himself by continuing his present course; Demosthenes pleads that he not be forced to change his high opinion of Heracleodorus. Aeschines admonishes Ctesiphon not to cast reproach upon him in his great misfortune ($\dot{a}\tau\nu\chi\dot{\epsilon}\sigma\tau\epsilon\rho\sigma$; compare the end of Ps.-Aesch. Ep. 2. 3 with D. Ep. 3. 43); let him be mindful that the fate (*tychê*) which befell Aeschines could fall upon him, too, as it did upon others yet more eminent. Demosthenes admonishes Heracleodorus not to despise a younger man who has not yet reached the highest ranks. Let him be mindful that he himself was such an aspiring youth before he reached his eminence; if fate (*tychê*) lends a hand, Demosthenes' talents may bring him like success.

The letters of Aeschines show no trace of D. Ep. 6. The only conceivable parallel is Ps.-Aesch. Ep. 6, which has very little if anything in common with it.

The Conditions of Ancient

Bookmaking and the Groupings of

the Demosthenic Corpus

B OOKS IN THE CLASSICAL and Hellenistic periods were written on rolls, and rolls longer than about fifty feet are extremely unwieldy. The use of the codex did not become common until much later. Hence collected editions of the works of a prolific author could not exist, except in the sense that rolls containing them could be kept in the same labeled bucket; see Frederic G. Kenyon, *Books and Readers in Ancient Greece and Rome*, pp. 17, 62, 64–65. Every extensive corpus originated as a large number of separate rolls, and rolls could easily change order and slip in and out of the buckets which contained them. The only way to fix the content and order of such a corpus was to compile a list (*pinax*) of the component works.

Sometimes the original small rolls could be conveniently grouped together into larger rolls that were still not unwieldy. There was great convenience in making some scheme of classification the basis for such a grouping. For some authors, the distribution of their works over the several papyrus rolls apparently became canonical. Such was the case with Antisthenes—see Diog. Laert. vi. 15–18; Natorp, "Antisthenes 10," *RE*, I (1894), 2541–42; Regenbogen, "Pinax," *RE*, XX² (1950), 1439.

In other cases, the original rolls might be so numerous or so large that a single bucket would not suffice, and the corpus would be sub-divided into classifications, each classified group of rolls being kept in a separate container. The classifications might then become canonical, as they did in the manuscript tradition of Demosthenes. But the order of the works within each classification was not necessarily fixed thereby. All Demosthenes' public orations (D. 18–26) are long; they could never be brought within the compass of a single roll, though under Athenian rhetorical theory they were readily recognized as a single group (see above, Chap. 7). Hence the great discrepancies in their sequence in the families of medieval manuscripts. On the other hand, the "epitropic" orations which Demosthenes used in his suits against his guardians constituted a natural classification and were brief enough to be brought within the compass of a single roll; their sequence is identical in all branches of the manuscript tradition. These facts were noted already by W. Christ, "Die Attikusausgabe des Demosthenes," *Abhandlungen der philosophisch-philologischen Classe der Königl. bayerischen Akademie der Wissenschaften*, XVI (1882), 229–33. See also E. Drerup, "Antike Demosthenesausgaben," *Philologus*, Suppl. VII (1899), 533–35, and Blass, III 1, 50–60. The same sort of group structure exists in the manuscript tradition of Isocrates; see *Isocratis opera omnia*, ed. Engelbert Drerup, I, lxxxix–xciv, and Pasquali, pp. 300–2.

The History of the Use of Greek Letter Labels

THE PROCEDURE OF dividing a work into a numbered series of "books" is well attested in Athens of the fourth century B.C.; see Wendel, *Buchbeschreibung*, pp. 54–56. But very early in the Hellenistic period the 27-letter system becomes the sole system for book ordinals; even the works of Epicurus in the Herculaneum papyri number the books by the 27-letter system. Whether the Iliad and Odyssey were divided into books in Ptolemaic Alexandria or earlier and elsewhere, the numbering of the divisions surely took place at a time when letter labels were the current form for ordinals. The vast audience which the Homeric poems commanded quickly came to recognize the letter-label designations, and these designations maintained themselves the more tenaciously because the 24 books of each poem coincided in number with the 24 letters of the alphabet. The books into which the poems of Sappho and Alcaeus were divided also probably were designated by letter labels, for there is no trace of a Book ϝ' in the fragments of either. See Edgar Lobel, Σαπ-φοῦς μέλη (Oxford: Clarendon Press, 1925), pp. xiv–xv; 'Αλκαίου μέλη (Oxford: Clarendon Press, 1927), pp. 42–46; Denys Page, *Sappho and Alcaeus* (Oxford: Clarendon Press, 1955), pp. 114–16.

The major works of Aristotle and Theophrastus were current, if at all, only within the walls of the Peripatetic school before they were published in the first century B.C. by Apellicon, Tyrannion, and Andronicus of Rhodes (Strabo xiii. 608–9; Plut. *Sull.* 26); see Paul Moraux, *Les listes anciennes des ouvrages d'Aristote*, esp. pp. 1–14, 311–21. Such an esoteric transmission explains the preservation even by late editors of the earlier method of designating the book divisions by letter labels, in contrast to the use of the 27-letter system in the works of Epicurus. It is significant, on the other hand, that the late collection of *Problemata* found in the Aristotelian corpus has its sections numbered by the 27-letter system.

Euclid used letter labels to number the propositions in his *Elements* and in so doing established the practice for mathematical works. Traces of this use of letter labels by mathematical writers can still be found in the sixth-century commentator Eutocius, but apparently in no case did the medieval scribes of our manuscript traditions understand it. They did, nevertheless, leave unmistakable traces as they tried to account for the missing stigma and the strange letters for "tenth" through "twenty-fourth" and then misread the second sequence of the alphabet ($\alpha\alpha$, $\alpha\beta$, ...) as "$\lambda\alpha'$, $\lambda\beta'$, ..." See, e.g., the apparatus to Euclid *Elementa*, ed. J. L. Heiberg (Leipzig: B. G. Teubner, 1883–85), Bks. iii, vii, x, and xi. There is no trace, however, of the use of letter labels to number the *books* of the *Elements*; to designate them Euclid seems to have used the 27-letter system.

Outside the mathematical tradition, I know of no work written after the third century B.C. which uses letter labels to designate its divisions until the rise of strong archaizing tendencies in the Roman Empire of the second and third Christian centuries, when the books of Philostratus' *Vita Apollonii* are so numbered. The tables of contents to Dio Cassius xlii–lvii and lix may or may not represent a real revival of letter labels. It is one thing to use letter labels to name separate books and another to mark each item of a list with successive letters of the alphabet.

In their official documents inscribed on stone, the Athenians refrained from using the 27-letter system for ordinals as stubbornly as for cardinals. In Hellenistic Athens itself, the practice was to write ordinals in words rather than in figures. But the temple inventories of Delos under Athenian administration in the second century B.C. (beginning in 166) number the inventoried items with letter labels and express weights and sums of money in acrophonic cardinals: see *Inscriptions de Délos*, Nos. 1400–79. This series is the last-known occurrence of letter labels in inscriptions. Letter labels were also used as mason's marks at least down to the second century B.C.; see Gardthausen, pp.358–59, and Tod, *Annual of the British School at Athens*, XLIX, 2.

Particularly instructive is the appearance of letter labels to indicate the ordinal number of the year, beginning in 271 B.C., on a series of coins minted by the first three Ptolemies. The series began at a time when the 27-letter system had not yet displaced letter labels. This one series throughout is dated by the old numeral system, but no other Greek coins are known to have been so dated. See I. N. Svoronos, *Tὰ νομίσματα τοῦ κράτους τῶν Πτολεμαίων* (Athens: P.D. Sakellariou, 1904), Vol. I, pp. 158-62,

169, 217–24, 227–28. Athenian coins from 185/4 through 88/7 use the first thirteen letters of the alphabet to indicate the month when struck, and the same system may have been used at Aradus between 138/7 and 46/5. See Margaret Thompson, *The New Style Silver Coinage of Athens* (New York: The American Numismatic Society, 1961), pp.608–13, and H. Seyrig, *Notes on Syrian Coins* ("Numismatic Notes and Monographs," No. 119; New York: The American Numismatic Society,1950), pp.23–24.

To sum up: where the numbering was for the general reader rather than for the convenience of a specialist, or where a firm tradition had not been established, the 27-letter system completely replaced both letter-labels and acrophonic numerals already in the third century B.C.

The Numerals of the Demosthenic *Prooemia*

THE MANUSCRIPTS OF the families **S** and **F** show the typical confusion around the sixth and twenty-fourth numbered pieces, as the scribes try to account for the missing digamma and misread the second sequence of letter labels as "λα´, λβ´, . . ." (see Chap. 2, n. 23). The phenomena can be seen in the apparatus of Rennie's edition and still better in the photographic edition of **S** published by Henri Omont. The numeral labels were placed in the margin alongside the first line of each prooemium, and the problem which the letter labels posed for the scribes became still more complicated when the delta of *Prooem.* 4 was mistakenly absorbed into the text and the stroke to its right misread as epsilon to yield the connective δέ. The scribe of **S** did not understand what had happened, but he accurately reproduced what lay before him, so that the delta of δέ protrudes into his left-hand margin. But with the connective, *Prooem.* 4 became fused to *Prooem.* 3. Thus, the scribe whose work is reflected by manuscripts **S**, **F**, and **Q** had to find seven *prooemia* to account for the zeta of *Prooem.* 6, which he misread as "seventh." Yet, as far as he could see, there were only five. Such scribes were not scholarly editors. They would try to solve the problem but would not trouble themselves long over it. Going back to the beginning of the *Prooemia*, the scribe looked for places where he could insert the missing figures. Evidently, he felt that μὲν οὖν was less objectionable at the head of a prooemium than δέ. Accordingly, he broke *Prooem.* 1 into two prooemia, though the second, beginning with paragraph 2, lacked the formula of address, ὦ ἄνδρες Ἀθηναῖοι. The long *Prooem.* 2 was more manageable; its paragraph 3 began with μὲν οὖν and did contain the formula of address. Applying his principle, the scribe put his digamma at ἐγὼ μὲν οὖν of *Prooem.* 4. He had now more than compensated for the missing figures, so in **S** Prooem. 5 bears no number, though the first letter protrudes as if a new piece were beginning. Interestingly, the scribe of Codex Bavaricus **B**, a thirteenth-century descendant of **F**, felt the incongruity and moved the digamma to the beginning of *Prooem.* 5. In any case, the earlier scribe had accomplished his purpose. The numeral of "*Prooem.* 7" now made sense.

The scribe had no more trouble until he reached the neighborhood of *Prooem.* 25, the letter label of which (αα) he misread as "31" (λα'). Again he manufactured new pieces, dividing the original prooemia wherever he could find μὲν οὖν. By *Prooem.* 28 he had almost caught up. The twenty-eighth letter label is αδ, and the scribe was ready to write λγ'. At this point, however, he must have realized that his "corrections" were futile. From *Prooem.* 28 on, the medieval manuscripts do not number the *Prooemia*, though the beginnings of several are signaled by a *paragraphus* or a protruding initial letter. **S** may show a trace of the original letter labels, for there seems to be a faint erased phi just before the first word of *Prooem.* 45 (the letter label of which would have been αφ), not in the margin but within the text. Curiously, in **S**, *paragraphi* appear by μὲν οὖν at *Prooemm.* 38. 2; 41. 2; and 49. 3.

The Application of B. Gaya Nuño's
Method to Epistles 1 to 6

O F THE CONSTRUCTION examined by B. Gaya Nuño (see above, p.27) Ep. 3 contains sixteen examples (paragraphs 1, 5 [two], 7, 8, 9 [two], 10, 12, 13, 18, 28, 35, 43, 45 [two]). Of these, according to Gaya's categories, eight (50%) are of type I (one of Ia, three of Ib, and four of Id); otherwise, there are one of type IIc, one of type IIIa, two of type IV (one each of IVa and IVb), one of type Va, and three of type VI (one each of VIa, VIb, and VIc). Demosthenes is remarkable for his low proportion of instances of type I, the most natural order for the construction (verb, first infinitive, second infinitive). In the orations considered by Gaya (the speeches to the Athenian Assembly and *De Corona*), type I accounts for 57.05% of the total; thus Ep. 3 is a good example of Demosthenic practice.

As for the other letters, Ep. 2 exhibits six examples of the construction (paragraphs 2, 7, 8, 15, 17, 22). Five are of type I (one of Ia, three of Ib, one of Ic) and one of type VIb. Ep. 4 exhibits one example (paragraph 6) of type Id. Ep. I exhibits nine examples (paragraphs 1 [two], 2 [two], 8 [three], 10 [two]), all of type I (one of Ia, four of Ib, two of Ic, and two of Id). The construction does not occur in Epp. 5 and 6. If Epp. 1–4 are considered as a unit, type I accounts for 71.875% of the total, a percentage higher than the average for the Demosthenic orations examined by Gaya, but lower than that for any other Attic author examined except Antiphon (66.67%). The use solely of type I in Epp. 1, 2, and 4 is not necessarily a departure from Demosthenes' usage because in such short pieces he may have felt no need for elegant variety.

Gaya also grouped the instances of the construction according to grammatical classifications. The table illustrates the comparison of the

B. GAYA NUÑO'S METHOD

	Group A	Group B	Group C	Group D	Group E	Group F
Selected orations	23.92	7.36	0.61	37.42	30.67	0.
Ep. 1	22.22	11.11	11.11	44.44	11.11	0.
Ep. 2	33.33	0.	16.67	50.00	0.	0.
Ep. 3	37.50	6.25	0.	43.75	6.25	6.25
Ep. 4	100.	0.	0.	0.	0.	0.
Epp. 1–4	34.38	6.25	6.25	43.75	6.25	3.12
Aeschines	3.48	10.34	10.34	51.72	24.12	0.
Hyperides	18.42	13.15	0.	47.36	18.42	2.63

letters with the orations examined by Gaya. The letters exhibit all the characteristics of the mature Demosthenes. Demosthenes is outstanding for the low relative frequency of group B, surpassed in the authors examined only by Andocides (7.14%) and Lycurgus (0%). Of the other writers examined by Gaya, Aeschines comes closest to Demosthenes. The one departure of the letters from the general configuration of Demosthenes lies in group E, but the high figure for that category in the orations results from the young Demosthenes' predilection for the locution "$\phi\eta\mu\grave{\iota}\ \delta\epsilon\hat{\iota}\nu$...," a predilection which fades away as the orator matures; see Gaya, pp.69–73. In *De Corona* the figure for group E is only 21.7%, and only one example of "$\phi\eta\mu\grave{\iota}\ \delta\epsilon\hat{\iota}\nu$..." in the first person occurs (paragraph 190). One may add that the peremptory locution "$\phi\eta\mu\grave{\iota}\ \delta\epsilon\hat{\iota}\nu$..." befits a confident politician advocating a policy, not a pleader in court or a fugitive writing from exile.

Gaya's researches reveal one suspicious trait, the expression "$\phi\eta\mu\grave{\iota}\ \chi\rho\hat{\eta}\nu\alpha\iota$," otherwise found only in Demosthenes' earliest orations (Gaya, p.55); but D. 18. 210 uses "$o\check{\iota}\mu\alpha\iota\ \chi\rho\hat{\eta}\nu\alpha\iota$," which otherwise is found only in the early D. 15. 8. It is surely no coincidence that the peremptory formula "$\phi\eta\mu\grave{\iota}\ \chi\rho\hat{\eta}\nu\alpha\iota$" occurs in the letters only in Ep. 1, which represents a stage at which the political situation had improved sufficiently so that Demosthenes could write with some confidence.

APPENDIX VII

Philocles

THE SOURCES which might cast light on Philocles during the years of the Harpalus affair and the Lamian war are distressingly vague. The authenticity of the most important, the speech *Against Philocles* (Din. 3), has been questioned by Chrysis Pélékidis, *Histoire de l'éphébie attique*, pp. 136–38, on the following grounds:

1. At Din. 3. 1 Philocles is declared to be *strategos* in charge of Munichia and the dockyards, whereas at Din. 3. 13 he is said to have been ready to betray Akte, which was not under his command but under the *strategos* in charge of Akte (Arist. *Ath. Pol.* 61. 1).

2. Demetrius of Magnesia (*apud* Dion. Hal. *Din.* 1, Vol. I, pp. 298–99 U.–R.) regarded Din. 1 as spurious. Hence all the orations on the Harpalus affair ascribed to Dinarchus may be spurious.

3. The speech gives no clue to the identity of the speaker.

To take (3) first, Din. 3 is the speech of a prosecutor acting on behalf of the public (see Din. 1. 1, 2. 6; *Vit. X orat.* 846c), and—in view of its structure and of Din. 3. 15—the speech of a prosecutor who spoke second or later. A public prosecutor would not necessarily identify himself in his speech. Lycurgus does not do so in *Against Leocrates*. A forgery might give more information about the speaker than do the authentic D. 23 and Lys. 31. Still less would a second or later prosecutor detain the audience with remarks identifying himself. See the authentic Lys. 27–29.

As for (2), we do not know what Demetrius thought of Din. 3, and Dionysius of Halicarnassus after quoting Demetrius' suspicion against Din. 1 shows it to be groundless.

As for (1), the expression at Din. 3. 13, "Akte and the harbors and the dockyards," is only an elaborate way of saying "the Piraeus." Munichia is missing, but it was mentioned at Din. 3. 10. Even if Akte was outside

276

Philocles' province, a speaker in 324/3 would hardly have hesitated to make the rhetorical exaggeration, "Such a man is capable of betraying the whole Piraeus." Moreover, at this time the official title of the *strategos* in charge of Munichia was "*strategos* in charge of the Piraeus," probably a survival from a few years before when there was only one *strategos* assigned to the Piraeus; see above, Chap. 5, n. 4, and Pélékidis, p. 144, n. 3. A late forger would hardly restrict Philocles' province to Munichia and the dockyards at Din. 3. 1 and then at Din. 3. 13 play upon the official title unmentioned by Aristotle at *Ath. Pol.* 61. 1. Furthermore, the language at *Ath. Pol.* 61. 1 suggests that the *strategoi* of Munichia and Akte may have been jointly responsible for the entire Piraeus. Finally, although isolated passages from Dinarchus are quoted in papyri, Din. 3 is the only one of his extant orations of which a papyrus fragment of a once-complete copy has been found (*The Antinoöpolis Papyri*, ed. C. H. Roberts, J. W. B. Burns, and H. Zilliacus [London: Egypt Exploration Society, 1950–60], II, No. 81, from the third century A.D.); see Pack, p. 37.

Thus we may accept Din. 3 as authentic and proceed to examine it for clues to the career of Philocles and the implications for the chronology of the Harpalus affair. Din. 3. 1 speaks of Philocles as *strategos* in charge of Munichia at the time of Harpalus' arrival in 325/4 (see above, p. 38). Din. 3. 15 says that after the scandal broke the People deposed Philocles from his post of "supervising the ephebes." At first sight, Dinarchus would seem to be speaking of an ephebic magistracy (see Arist. *Ath. Pol.* 42; Pélékidis, pp. 104–9, 130–31). The ephebic inscription of the tribe of Leontis from the Amphiareion might confirm this impression (published by V. Leonardos, *Arch. Ephem.*, 1918, pp. 73–100). Its left face records that the ephebes crowned the *strategos* in charge of the countryside, Leosthenes son of Leosthenes of Kephale, and the *sophronistes*, Thymochares son of Demochares of Leukonoe. The right face records that the ephebes crowned the *strategos* in charge of the Piraeus, Dikaiogenes of Kydathenaion, and the *strategos* in charge of Akte, Pherekleides son of Pherekles of Perithoidai, and the *kosmetes*, Philocles son of Phormion of Eroiadai.

No archon-date survives on the inscription. When such an array of officials appears in a document, one assumes that they are all of the same year. Since Din. 3. 1 attests that Philocles, not Dikaiogenes, was *strategos* in charge of Munichia (=*s.* in charge of the Piraeus) in 325/4, the inscription cannot refer to the officials of 325/4. Nor can it refer to the officials of 323/2 or any later year, for in 323/2 Leosthenes was killed while commanding the Athenian forces in the field at Lamia and could not have been *strategos* in charge of the countryside (see Arist. *Ath. Pol.* 61. 1). We have evidence of Dikaiogenes as *strategos* in charge of the Piraeus only for the years 324/3 and 323/2. The restored text of *IG* II² 1631, lines 214–15, shows Dikaiogenes bearing that title in 323/2. At lines 380–81, which refer to 324/3, Dikaiogenes is merely called *strategos*, but the context shows that in that year, too, his competence was over the dockyards. These facts suggest that the inscription from the Amphiareion is of 324/3, and, indeed, apart from this inscription, there is no evidence that Leosthenes was *strategos* at Athens before the outbreak of the Lamian war. This dating can be clinched provided that Din. 3. 15 is indeed speaking of an ephebic magistracy and Dinarchus' Philocles is the Philocles of the inscription, for then Philocles, with the expiration of his term as *strategos* for 325/4, would be shown to have become *kosmetes* for the ephebic year 324/3. However, Dinarchus gives neither patronymic nor demotic, and Philocles was a common name at Athens. The absence of evidence to the fact does not prove that Leosthenes and Dikaiogenes were not *strategoi* in some earlier year. The earliest possible year for the inscription would be 338, before which Thebes held the Amphiareion, and perhaps, for demographic considerations connected with the list of ephebes on the front face of the inscription, 329/8; see Pélékidis, pp. 138–39. Thus far, one may say that the identification of Philocles in the two texts and the dating of the inscription to 324/3 are possible and even probable but not proved.

If the identifications and the dating of the inscription are rejected, there is no evidence to prevent Din. 3. 15 from still referring to an ephebic magistracy. However, the scholars who reject the identification prefer to interpret Din. 3. 15 as referring to the office of *strategos* in charge of Munichia, who also could be said to "supervise the ephebes" (Pélékidis, pp. 134–35). The peculiar way of referring to the office of *strategos* may have arisen from a rhetorical parallel contrived at Din. 3. 15–16, "The People would not trust their precious sons to this man's supervision. Will you, to whom the People have entrusted our precious democratic constitution spare him?" (Cf. Pélékidis, p. 135, who suggests that the ephebes were the only troops under the command of the Piraeus generals. However, Din. 3. 10 says it was in Philocles' power to betray along with Munichia the infantry and the navy, which suggests far more than the ephebes.)

There is a lacuna at the end of Hyp. *Dem.* 18, but the beginning of the column may mean that Harpalus entered Athens late in 325/4, when Nicanor had arrived but had not formally issued his proclamations at Olympia. On any interpretation of Hyp. *Dem.* 18 it is hard to believe that Philocles could have been deposed while still *strategos* for 325/4. There would not be sufficient time left in the year for indignation to provoke Philocles' deposition before the Olympic festival to which Demosthenes himself was trusted to go as delegate (see above, Chap. 5, nn. 49, 55). It is possible, however, that Philocles was reelected *strategos* for 324/3, deposed in 324/3, and replaced by Dikaiogenes. If so, Hecatombaion 1, 324/3, is still a *terminus ante quem* for Harpalus' entry. However, Hyp. *Dem.* 18 may mean that Harpalus entered Athens early in 324/3. If so, and if Din. 3. 15 means that Philocles was *strategos* in 324/3, no such *terminus ante quem* can be derived.

Is there reason to question the identification of Dinarchus' Philocles with the one in the inscription from the Amphiareion? The principal objections to the identification are those stated by A. W. Gomme, *The Population of Athens in the Fifth and Fourth Centuries B.C.* (Oxford: Blackwell, 1933), pp. 67–69. They may be summarized as follows:

1. As propounded by Mathieu, *RPh*, 3d series, III, 162, n. 6, the identification requires that the ephebes listed on the front face of the inscription be those of two ephebic classes, the first-year ephebes who served in the Piraeus and the second-year ephebes who served in the forts of the countryside, because the two *strategoi* of the Piraeus and the *strategos* of the countryside are crowned (see Arist. *Ath. Pol.* 42. 3–4). No other ephebic inscription can be shown to bear the names of both classes of one year. Indeed, *IG* II² 1156 is a clear instance of the contrary. There is the added embarrassment that the inscription was set up at the Amphiareion, a place where the first-year ephebes had not served.

2. If the identification is correct, Philocles should not appear on the inscription as *kosmetes*. The ephebes crowned their officials at the end of the ephebic year, by which time Philocles had been deposed and, according to D. Ep. 3. 31, convicted.

Because of these difficulties, Gomme was driven to take the *kosmetes*, *sophronistes*, and Piraeus *strategoi* as those in office during the ephebes' first year of service and the *strategos* of the countryside as the one in office during their second year of service, contrary to what we assumed was natural for such an array of officials in a document. However, the presence of both the *strategos* in charge of the countryside and the *strategoi* in charge of the Piraeus does not imply that two ephebic classes are involved. The *strategos* in charge of the Piraeus and the *strategos* in charge of the countryside appear together on four other ephebic inscriptions of the period: *IG* II² 2970, as restored by F. W. Mitchel, "Derkylos of Hagnous and the Date of *I.G.*, II², 1187," *Hesperia*,

XXXIII(1964), 349–50 (of 334/3); B. D. Meritt, "Greek Inscriptions," *Hesperia*, IX(1940), 59–66, No. 8 (of 333/2); Meritt, *AJP*, LXVI(1945), 234–39 (of ca. 333/2); and J. Travlos, *Praktika*, 1954, pp. 70–71, to be published in *Arch. Ephem.* (of ca. 333/2). On the absence of the *strategos* in charge of Akte in these inscriptions, see Pélékidis, p. 144, n. 3. On all five inscriptions the *strategoi* appear in company with the ephebic magistrates (only the title of the *sophronistes* survives on *IG* II² 2970, and Travlos reports only the *sophronistes* on his inscription). Meritt, *Hesperia*, IX, 59–66, No. 8, like *IG* II² 1156, can only be a commendation of a single ephebic class and its supervisory officials on the completion of a year of service. Presumably the other four inscriptions also group the *strategoi* with the ephebic magistrates to commemorate the successful completion of a year of service. Such commendations certainly were made at the end of the ephebic year from the third century on; see Pélékidis, p. 141. However, Pélékidis there sees reason to deny that the inscription from the Amphiareion records an end-of-year commendation, for it was placed in the Amphiareion, not in the Agora or on the Acropolis. But the surviving texts of the ephebic inscriptions of the fourth century provide that the stelae be set up not in the Agora or on the Acropolis as such, and not in the places where the ephebes had served, but in shrines connected with tribal or ephebic ceremonies; cf. Pélékidis, pp. 151–52.

IG II² 1156 and Meritt, *Hesperia*, IX, 59–66, No. 8 provide that the stele be set up in the sanctuary of the eponymous tribal hero. *IG* II² 1189, a dedication of the ephebes of Hippothontis, was set up at the shrine of Eleusis in the territory of Hippothontis. Travlos' inscription, of the ephebes of Kekropis, was set up at Eleusis. The connection of the ephebes of Leontis with the Amphiareion is unknown. The Amphiareion, in the territory of Oropos, belonged to no tribe (Hyp. *Eux.* 16). Perhaps Amphiaraus was the eponym of this ephebic class; see Christian Habicht, "Neue Inschriften aus dem Kerameikos," *Mitteilungen des Deutschen archäologischen Instituts, athenische Abteilung*, LXXVI(1961), 145–46. *IG* II² 1006 (of 122/1), lines 26–28, 70–71, mentions the Amphiareion in connection with ephebic rites. The texts which Pélékidis (p. 181) uses to prove that in Hellenistic Athens the stelae were set up in the Agora are both conjectural restorations; the name of a shrine may well have originally stood in the lacunae.

In the arrays of *strategoi* and ephebic officials found in inscriptions recording end-of-year commendations one can see a sort of ephebic "board of education," of which the *strategoi* were members ex officio. The names of board members could appear whether the inscription commended first- or second-year ephebes. Cf. Pélékidis, pp. 144–45; E. Will, Review of Pélékidis, *RPh*, 3d series, XXXVIII(1964), 291. Such a board may have been a natural outgrowth of ephebic administration. Even if constituted by law, the board need not have been mentioned in Aristotle's sketchy account at *Ath. Pol.* 42; cf. Pélékidis, p. 117. Hence the fact that the inscription was set up at the Amphiareion in no way argues against the identification of Philocles and the dating in 324/3.

As for the difficulty of Philocles' deposition and condemnation, it can be shown from D. Ep. 2 that Philocles was later exonerated and perhaps reinstated; see above, pp. 48–49, 56, and Chap. 6, n. 7. Accordingly one may raise a slight objection to the supposition that Philocles was deposed as *strategos* in charge of the Piraeus for 324/3, for one might expect Philocles upon exoneration to be reinstated or reelected, yet Dikaiogenes held the post during both 324/3 and 323/2. However, Athenian voters were unpredictable.

A few other data may be used to indicate that Dinarchus' Philocles is the son of Phormion of Eroiadai. D. Ep. 3. 31 mentions Philocles among loyal and munificent patriots. Din. 3. 18 describes Philocles as rich. One would expect to find such a man, when exonerated, among the trierarchs of the Lamian war, side by side with the *strategoi* Leosthenes (*IG* II² 1631, lines 500, 601, 606, 682) and Euetion (*IG* II² 1632, lines 11–12). In fact, in the surviving lists of trierarchs appear a Philocles of Kephale (*IG* II² 1631, line 474) and a Philocles of Eroiadai (*IG* II² 1631, line 444) who paid the large total of 5300 drachmas. Of these two, Dinarchus' Philocles, who had no son (Din. 3. 18), could only be the latter (male offspring of Philocles of Kephale: *Pros. Att.*, No. 14546). Philocles son of Philotheos of Sunion, who appears as *taxiarchos* in Meritt, *Hesperia*, IX, 59–66, No. 8, does not appear in the trierarchic lists; cf. Pélékidis, pp. 135–36.

Anaximenes' Classification of Oratory

THE CLASSIFICATION OF *politikoi logoi* into genera and species seems to represent only Anaximenes' theoretical scheme. In theory, he seems to say, a speech in either of his two genera may include elements of any of his seven species (cf. Arist. *Rhet*. iii. 13. 3. 1414*b*2–4). To Anaximenes, the oratory of eulogy and disparagement came under the forensic genus if it was addressed to a court and under the deliberative if it was addressed to the Assembly or any other deliberative body of citizens. Cf. the remarks on the epideictic genus at *Rhet. ad Herenn*. iii. 8. 15: "Et si separatim haec causa minus saepe tractatur, at in judicialibus et in deliberativis causis saepe magnae partes versantur laudis aut vituperationis. Quare, in hoc quoque causae genere nonnihil industriae consumendum putemus."

In *practice*, however, Anaximenes recognized that eulogistic and depreciatory speeches, unlike those in the other species, were for the most part used for display (*epideixis*) rather than for an argument urging a practical decision in court or Assembly (*agón*; Anax. 35, p.80. 8–9 H.); cf. Arist. *Rhet*. ii. 18. 1. 1391*b*16–19, and Philodemus *Rhet*., Vol. I, pp.47–49, and Vol. II, pp.256–65 Sudh. Again, in *practice*, Anaximenes recognized that accusation or defence in a *demegoria* and eulogy or depreciation in the forensic or deliberative genera require treatment different from that which they would have received in what was their normal setting (cf. Philodemus *Rhet*., Vol. I, p.213 Sudh.). Therefore, his discussion of the persuasive and dissuasive species clearly exhausts the subject of the *demegoria*, for, in Chap. 34, he treats under those heads even the points which might be called the epideictic and forensic elements of *demegoriae*. In Chap. 35 (pp.79. 23–80. 9 H.), he explicitly indicates that the treatment of the *demegoria* is finished and that he is beginning the discussion of a distinct type. Cf. Chap. 2, p.27. 21–25 H. The end of Chap. 35 and the beginning of Chap. 36 contain a similar transition from the unnamed epideictic genus to the distinct province of forensic oratory. Thus Anaximenes' discussion of oratorical *practice* is organized as if there were three genera, despite his unwillingness to recognize epideictic speeches as *politikoi logoi*. In practice, then, even for Anaximenes, two species belong to each of the "three" genera, while his peculiar seventh species, the oratory of "exposure", can belong to any of the genera; see above, Chap. 8, rhetorical analysis of Ep. 3. 16–18. Anaximenes' peculiar exposition may be due to his failure to reconcile his resolution to restrict his discussion to *politikoi logoi* with his unwillingness to depart from school practice which taught three genera.

Aristotle, however, had different interests in writing his *Rhetoric* and introduced epideictic speeches as a third genus (see Volkmann, pp. 19–21). In the first place, unlike Anaximenes, he wished to bring all oratory, public and private, into his theoretical scheme; at *Rhet.* i. 3. 3. 1358b9–10 the deliberative genus includes both private advice and public *demegoriae*. Second, he seems to have recognized the political character of ceremonial epideictic orations like Isocrates' *Panegyricus* and the Athenian funeral orations, for several times he alludes to a public or even a political audience for epideictic speeches; see *Rhet.* i. 9. 35–36. 1367b36–1368a8; iii. 14. 2–3. 1414b29–1415a1, iii. 14. 11. 1415b30–32. But see Quint. iii. 7. 1–2.

Apologetic *Demegoriae* in Ancient
Rhetorical Exercises

ONLY THE FOLLOWING examples in Kohl's collection need be considered as possible apologetic *demegoriae*:

Number 82. Kohl finds in Sopater (Vol. IV, p.318 Walz) the theme of Pericles defending himself against the charge of having caused the Peloponnesian war. However, Sopater there is illustrating the use of argument attacking the circumstances of the accusation (*paragraphikon*); his examples are not taken from school themes but from the works of "the ancients," one being the speech of Pericles at Th. ii. 59–64. Even if, as is likely, the situation was used as a school theme, it is clearly not an imaginative invention of a rhetorician. Moreover, the speech in Thucydides is hardly an apology but a pure *demegoria*. The apologetic elements are those of the *captatio benevolentiae* required to win Pericles a hearing from a hostile audience. The main burden of the speech is to urge the Athenians to continue to adhere to his war policy. Far from denying the charges against him, he admits them, but reminds the Athenians that they had made his decisions theirs. The comment of Bruns (p.29) on this speech is instructive: "Weniger kann, wer zur Abwehr persönlicher Angriffe das Wort nimmt, nicht wohl über sich sprechen."

Number 125. Alcibiades, returned from exile and required to serve as *strategos*, demands first a chance to reply to the old charges against him (Syrianus, Vol. II, p.165 Rabe). The speaker would present no apology to the People here but would be asking for the opportunity to do so. Hence, the speech would deal purely with a matter of public policy, probably as at Th. vi. 29: "Should Alcibiades be allowed to delay the expedition and clear himself now, when public opinion is in his favor?" Thus the theme is not that of an apologetic *demegoria*.

Number 327. Kohl infers from Apsines (pp.308. 20–309. 15 H.) that D. Ep. 2 itself was used as a theme, for Apsines seems to suggest a scheme of his own for organizing the plea. The text is as follows: "... ἀπὸ τοῦ παρὰ τὴν ἀξίαν καλουμένου τὸν ἔλεον κινήσομεν. παρὰ τὴν ἀξίαν δέ ἐστι τὸ ταῦτα πάσχειν τινά, ἅπερ αὐτῷ δοκεῖ εἶναι ἧττον, οἷον τὸ πένεσθαι τοὺς ἐν πλούτῳ γεγονότας, τὸ φεύγειν δημαγωγούς, τὸ ἀτιμίᾳ περιπεπτωκέναι στρατηγούς· συνελόντι δὲ εἰπεῖν ἡ ἀπὸ τῶν βελτιόνων ἐπὶ τὰ χείρω μεταβολὴ κατὰ τὸν τόπον θεωρεῖται τὸν παρὰ τὴν ἀξίαν καλούμενον, οἷον ὁ Δημοσθένης ἐπιστέλλει πως τοῖς Ἀθηναίοις περὶ τῆς καθόδου τῆς ἑαυτοῦ· οἶμαι μὲν ὅτι καὶ αὐτὸς κινεῖ τὸν ἔλεον ἐκ τοῦ παρὰ τὴν ἀξίαν θεωρεῖσθαι· εἰ δὲ καὶ παραλέλειπται τοῦτο αὐτῷ, ὑπῆρχεν ἂν κινῆσαι τὸν ἔλεον αὐτῷ τόνδε τὸν τρόπον· 'ἀλλὰ νῦν ὁ πρότερον διοικῶν τὰ ὑμέτερα πράγματα καὶ λαμπρὸς καὶ περίβλεπτος ὢν καὶ ὑπὸ τῶν πάντων ζηλούμενος οὐ μόνον τούτων ἀφῄρημαι, ἀλλὰ καὶ τῆς πατρίδος ἐξελήλαμαι καὶ ἱκέτης ἄλλων γίνομαι ὁ τέως ἄλλους εὐεργετῶν.'"

Ep. 2 certainly was used as a theme; the author of Ps.-Aesch. Ep. 12 took it as his model. Apsines' hesitations over whether the plea *para tên axian* is to be found in Ep. 2 are strange. Hermogenes (*Id*. ii. 8, Vol. III, p.349 Walz) uses Ep. 2 as the classic example of that plea, which he treats as characteristic of the "idea" of "graveness." In any case, Ep. 2 for Apsines was a historical source, and the theme would not be imaginative fiction.

Two of Kohl's examples, Nos. 95 and 298, may be at once apologetic *demegoriae* and pure fictions.

Number 95. The Lacedaemonians demand the surrender of Pericles' person as a condition for peace; Pericles speaks in opposition (Apsines 2, p.233 H.). Thucydides mentions no such speech, although he describes an occasion on which it could have been delivered (i. 126–27). Hence the theme is in part a fiction, and the rhetorician would certainly have Pericles oppose his surrender by allusions to his glorious career. The theme, however, brings no personal accusation against Pericles and thus hardly fits the definition of apology (above, p.98).

Number 298. Philip demands the surrender of Demosthenes' person after the battle of Chaeroneia; Demosthenes speaks in opposition (Apsines 2, p.226 H.). The theme is a pure fiction, and the discredit of the failure of his policy might require a strongly apologetic speech for Demosthenes. However, two examples of the related theme, No. 299, have survived in Libanius *Decl*. 19 and 20 (Vol. VI, pp.266, 295 Foerster) According to that theme, after Chaeroneia Philip has demanded the surrender of Demosthenes' person. The People ask five days to consider.

During that time Demosthenes asks to be executed. In *Decl.* 19, Libanius portrays Demosthenes as presenting to an audience that is favorable to him (paragraph 2) the course of executing him in Athens as the best under the circumstances. Included here and there in the argument are remarks on the speaker's achievements and unsuccessful good intentions, but since no accusation is being denied and the audience is portrayed as favorable, even these remarks are not apology. In *Decl.* 20, Libanius has Demosthenes give the appearance of "due process" to his proposed execution and forestall sympathetic remonstrances by having him denounce his own career and pretend that the People are sure to vote for his surrender. This work, too, can hardly be called apologetic in nature.

Bibliography

A. EDITIONS OF THE DEMOSTHENIC CORPUS AND MANUSCRIPTS
OF DEMOSTHENES' LETTERS

Demosthenis orationes. Ed. Friedrich Blass, editio major. 3 vols. Lipsiae: B. G. Teubner, 1891–1907.

——.Ed. S. H. Butcher and W. Rennie. 3 vols. in 4. Oxonii: E typographeo Clarendoniano, 1903–1931.

Demosthenis orationum Codex Σ. published by Henri Omont. Paris: Ernest Leroux, 1892.

Ep. 1. 4. *POxy.* xxxi. 2549.

Ep. 2. 18–20, 23–25. Papyri Osloenses Inv. No. 1471, published in S. Eitrem and L. Amundsen, "Demosthenes' Epistola II," *Eranos*, LIV (1956).

Ep. 3. 1–38. No.130 of the *Catalogue of the Literary Papyri in the British Museum*, Ed. J. M. Milne (London: Published by the Trustees, 1927). Published as No. CXXXIII in F. Kenyon, *Classical Texts from Papyri in the British Museum*. Oxford: Clarendon Press, 1891.

B. TRANSLATIONS OF DEMOSTHENES' LETTERS

Auger, Athanase. Oeuvres complètes de Démosthène et d'Eschine. 6 vols. nouvelle édition. Angers: Mame, père et fils, 1804. Vol. II, pp.362–98.

DeWitt, N. W., and N. J. DeWitt, Demosthenes, VII: Funeral Speech, Erotic Essay, Exordia, and Letters. The Loeb Classical Library. Cambridge, Massachusetts: Harvard University Press; London: William Heinemann Ltd., 1949, pp.196–269.

Kennedy, Charles Rann. The Orations of Demosthenes. 5 vols. London: George Bell & Sons, 1902. Vol. V, pp.338–60.

Pabst, Heinrich August. Demosthenes Werke. 3 vols. Stuttgart: Verlag der J. B. Metzler'schen Buchhandlung, 1839–1842. Vol. III, pp. 2364–2406.

Wolf, Hieronymus. Demosthenis & Aeschinis orationes atque epistolae quae ad nostram aetatem pervenerunt omnes. 4 vols. Basileae: Per Ioannem Oporinum, 1553. Vol. I, pp.181–204. Reprinted in Dobson (see below, Section C), Vol. XVI, pp.835–51.

C. EDITIONS OF ANCIENT AND BYZANTINE TEXTS OTHER THAN DEMOSTHENES

(LCL = THE LOEB CLASSICAL LIBRARY)

Aelianus. Claudii Aeliani Varia historia. Ed. R. Hercher. Lipsiae: B. G Teubner, 1870.

Aeschines. The Speeches of Aeschines. Ed. and trans. C. D. Adams. LCL. London: William Heinemann Ltd.; New York: G. P. Putnam's Sons, 1919.

——. Aeschinis orationes. Ed. Friedrich Blass, 2d ed. rev. Lipsiae: B. G. Teubner, 1908.

——. Eschine: discours. Ed. and trans. Victor Martin and G. de Budé. 2 vols. Paris: Société d'édition "Les belles lettres," 1927–1928.

——. Aeschinis quae feruntur epistolae. Ed. E. Drerup. Lipsiae: Sumptibus Dieterichii (Theodori Weicheri), 1904.

Alcidamas. Pp.132–147 of Artium scriptores (Reste der voraristotelischen Rhetorik). Ed. L. Radermacher. ("Österreichische Akademie der Wissenschaften, philosophisch-historische Klasse: Sitzungsberichte," 227. Band, 3. Abhandlung.) Wien: Rudolf M. Rohrer, 1951.

Anaximenes. See Hammer.

Andocides. See Minor Attic Orators.

Anecdota Graeca. Ed. Immanuel Bekker. 3 vols. Berolini: Apud Nauckium, 1814–1821.

Antiphon. See Minor Attic Orators.

Aristides, Aelius. Ed. W. Dindorf. 3 vols. Lipsiae: Libraria Weidmannia, 1829.

——. Aelii Aristidis Smyrnaei quae supersunt omnia. Ed. Bruno Keil. Berolini: Apud Weidmannos, 1898.

Pseudo-Aristides. Aristidis qui feruntur libri rhetorici II. Ed. W. Schmid. Lipsiae: B. G. Teubner, 1926.
See Walz.

Aristophanes. Comoediae. Ed. F. W. Hall and W. M. Geldart. 2 vols. Oxonii: E typographeo Clarendoniano, 1902.

Aristotle. Aristoteles graece. Ed. Immanuel Bekker. 2 vols. Berolini: Apud Georgium Reimerum, 1831.

——. Aristotelis quae ferebantur librorum fragmenta. Ed. Valentinus Rose. Lipsiae: B. G. Teubner, 1886.

——. Aristote: Constitution d'Athènes. Ed. and trans. G. Mathieu and B. Haussoullier. Paris: Société d'édition "Les belles lettres," 1922.

——. The "Art" of Rhetoric. Ed. and trans. John Henry Freese. LCL. London: William Heinemann Ltd.; New York: G. P. Putnam's Sons, 1926.

Athenaeus. The Deipnosophists. Ed. and trans. C. B. Gulick. 6 vols. LCL. London: William Heinemann Ltd.; New York: G. P. Putnam's Sons, 1927–1941.

Baiter, Jo. Georg, and H. Sauppe (Eds.). Oratores Attici. 2 vols. Turici: S. Hoehr, 1845–1850.

Cicero. Brutus. Ed. and trans. G. L. Hendrickson. And Orator. Ed. and trans. H. M. Hubbell. LCL. Cambridge, Massachusetts: Harvard University Press; London: William Heinemann Ltd., 1939.

——. De inventione. Ed. and trans. H. M. Hubbell. LCL. Cambridge, Massachusetts: Harvard University Press; London: William Heinemann Ltd., 1949.

Curtius. Q. Curti Rufi Historiarum Alexandri Magni Macedonis libri qui supersunt. Ed. Edmund Hedicke, editio maior. Lipsiae: B. G. Teubner, 1908.

Demetrius. De elocutione. Ed. and trans. W. Rhys Roberts in Aristotle: The Poetics; "Longinus": On the Sublime; Demetrius: On Style. LCL. London: William Heinemann; New York: G. P. Putnam's Sons, 1927.

Didymus. Didymos' Kommentar zu Demosthenes. Ed. H. Diels and W. Schubart. ("Berliner Klassikertexte," Heft I.) Berlin: Weidmannsche Buchhandlung, 1904.

Dinarchus. Dinarchi orationes. Ed. F. Blass. 2d ed. Lipsiae: B. G. Teubner, 1888.

——. See Minor Attic Orators.

Diodorus. Diodori Bibliotheca historica. Ed. F. Vogel and C. T. Fischer. 5 vols. Lipsiae: B. G. Teubner, 1888–1906.

——. Diodorus of Sicily. Ed. and trans. C. H. Oldfather. 12 vols. LCL. Cambridge, Massachusetts: Harvard University Press; London: William Heinemann Ltd., 1933– .

Diogenes Laertius. Ed. and trans. R. D. Hicks. 2 vols. LCL. Cambridge, Massachusetts: Harvard University Press, 1958–1959.

Dionysius of Halicarnassus. Dionysii Halicarnasei opuscula. Ed. H. Usener and L. Radermacher. 2 vols. in 3. Lipsiae: B. G. Teubner, 1899–1929.

Dobson, W. S. (Ed.). Oratores Attici et quos sic vocant sophistae. 16 vols. London: J. F. Dove, 1828.

Etymologicum Gudianum. Etymologicum Graecae linguae Gudianum. Ed. F. W. Sturz. Vol. II of Etymologicon magnum. Ed. F. Sylburg. 3 vols. ed. nova correctior. Lipsiae: Weigel, 1816–1820.

Etymologicum magnum. Etymologicon magnum. Ed. Thomas Gaisford. Oxonii: E typographeo academico, 1848.

Falco, Vittorio de (Ed.). Demade oratore: testimonianze e frammenti. 2d ed. Napoli: Libreria scientifica editrice, 1954.

Fouilles de Delphes. Ed. Théophile Homolle, Tome III, deuxième fascicule: Inscriptions du trésor des Athéniens. Ed. G. Colin. Paris: Fontemoing & Cie., 1909–1913.

Galen. Claudii Galeni opera omnia. Ed. C. G. Kühn. 20 vols. Lipsiae: Libraria Car. Cnoblochii, 1821–1833.

Halm, Karl (Ed.). Rhetores Latini minores. Lipsiae: B. G. Teubner, 1863.

Hammer, C. (Ed.). Rhetores Graeci ex recognitione Leonardi Spengel, Vol. I, Pars II. Lipsiae: B. G. Teubner, 1894.

Harpocration, Valerius. Harpocrationis Lexicon in decem oratores Atticos. Ed. W. Dindorf. Oxonii: E typographeo academico, 1853.

Hermogenes. Hermogenis opera. Ed. H. Rabe. Lipsiae: B. G. Teubner, 1913.

——. See Walz.

Herodotus. Historiae. Ed. Karl Hude. 2 vols. 3d ed. Oxonii: E typographeo Clarendoniano, 1927.

Hesychius. Lexicon. Ed. Kurt Latte. Hauniae: E. Munksgaard, 1953– .

——. Hesychius Alexandrinus: Lexicon. Ed. M. Schmidt. 5 vols. in 2. Ienae: Sumptibus Friderici Maukii, 1858–1868.

Hibeh Papyri, Part I. Ed. B. P. Grenfell and A. S. Hunt. London: Egypt Exploration Fund, 1906.

Hippocrates. Oeuvres complètes d'Hippocrate. Ed. and trans. E. Littré. 10 vols. Paris: J. B. Baillière, 1839–1861.

Hyperides. Hypéride: discours. Ed. Gaston Colin. Paris: Société d'édition "Les belles lettres," 1946.

——. Hyperidis orationes sex cum ceterarum fragmentis. Ed. C. Jensen. Lipsiae: B. G. Teubner, 1917.

Inscriptiones Graecae, consilio et auctoritate Academiae Litterarum Borussicae editae. Berolini: W. de Gruyter, 1873– .

Inscriptiones Graecae, consilio et auctoritate Academiae Scientiarum Germanicae editae. Editio altera. Berolini: W. de Gruyter, 1913– .

Inscriptions de Délos, Vol. III (Nos. 1400–79). Ed. Félix Durrbach and Pierre Roussel. Paris: Librairie ancienne Honoré Champion, 1935.

Isaeus. Isée: discours. Ed. and trans. P. Roussel. Paris: Société d'édition "Les belles lettres," 1922.

Isocrates. Isocratis orationes. Ed. F. Blass. 2 vols. Lipsiae: B. G. Teubner, 1889–1895.

——. Isocratis opera omnia. Ed. E. Drerup. Lipsiae: Sumptibus Dieterichii (Theodori Weicher), 1906– .

——. Isocrate: discours. Ed. G. Mathieu and E. Brémond. 3 vols. Paris: Société d'édition "Les belles lettres," 1928–1942.

Jacoby, Felix. Die Fragmente der griechischen Historiker: 2. Teil, Zeitgeschichte. 4 vols. Berlin: Weidmannsche Buchhandlung, 1926–1930. 3. Teil, Geschichte von Staaten und Voelkern (Horographie und Ethnographie). Leiden: E. J. Brill, 1940– .

Jameson, Michael H. "A Decree of Themistocles from Troizen," *Hesperia*, XXIX (1960). Revised text: *Supplementum Epigraphicum Graecum*, XVIII (1962), No. 153.

Julius Victor. *See* Halm.

Justin. M. Iuniani Iustini Epitoma Historiarum Philippicarum Pompei Trogi. Ed. F. Ruehl. Lipsiae: B. G. Teubner, 1886.

Kock, Theodor (Ed.). Comicorum Atticorum fragmenta. 3 vols. Lipsiae: B. G. Teubner, 1880–1888.

Leonardos, Vasilios. "'Αμφιαρείου ἐπιγραφαί," *Arch. Ephem.*, 1918.

Libanius. Libanii opera. Ed. R. Foerster. 6 vols. in 7. Lipsiae: B. G. Teubner, 1903–1911.

——. Hypotheses. *In* Demosthenis orationes, ed. Butcher and Rennie (above, Section A).

Longinus. *See* Demetrius.

Lucian. Luciani Samosatensis opera. Ed. C. Jacobitz. 3 vols. Lipsiae: B. G. Teubner, 1903–1905.

Lycurgus. *See* Minor Attic Orators.

——. Lycurgue: Contre Léocrate. Ed. and trans. Félix Dürrbach. Paris: Société d'édition "Les belles lettres," 1932.

Lysias. Lysias: discours. Ed. L. Gernet and M. Bizos. 2 vols. Paris: Société d'édition "Les belles lettres," 1924–1926.

——. Ed. and trans. W. R. M. Lamb. LCL. London: William Heinemann Ltd.; New York: G. P. Putnam's Sons, 1930.

Minor Attic Orators. Vol. I: Antiphon, Andocides. Ed. and trans. K. J. Maidment. LCL. Cambridge, Massachusetts: Harvard University Press; London: William Heinemann Ltd., 1941. Vol. II: Lycurgus, Dinarchus, Demades, Hyperides. Ed. and trans. J. O.

Burtt. LCL. Cambridge, Massachusetts: Harvard University Press; London: William Heinemann Ltd., 1954.

Moeris. Moeridis Atticistae Lexicon Atticum. Ed. J. Pierson. Revised ed. Lipsiae: Sumptibus C. H. F. Hartmanni, 1831.

Müller, Carl (Ed.). Oratores Attici. 2 vols. Parisiis: Editore Ambrosio Firmin Didot, 1847–1858.

Nepos. Cornelii Nepotis Vitae. Ed. A. Fleckeisen. Lipsiae: B. G. Teubner, 1912.

Olympiodorus. Olympiodori philosophi in Platonis Gorgiam comment-aria. Ed. W. Norvin. Lipsiae: B. G. Teubner, 1936.

Oratores Attici. *See* Baiter, Dobson, and Müller.

Oxyrhynchus Papyri, The. London: Egypt Exploration Fund, 1898– .

Pausanias. Pausaniae Descriptio Graeciae. Ed. J. H. C. Schubart. 2 vols. Lipsiae: B. G. Teubner, 1891–1898.

Philodemus. Philodemi De ira liber. Ed. K. Wilke. Lipsiae: B. G. Teubner, 1914.

Philodemi. Philodemi volumina rhetorica. Ed. S. Sudhaus. 2 vols. and supplement. Lipsiae: B. G. Teubner, 1892–1896.

Philostratus, Flavius. The Life of Apollonius of Tyana, the Epistles of Apollonius and the Treatise of Eusebius. Ed. and trans. F. C. Conybeare. LCL. London: William Heinemann Ltd.; New York: The Macmillan Co., 1912.

——. Philostratus and Eunapius. The Lives of the Sophists. Ed. and trans. W. C. Wright. LCL. London: William Heinemann; New York: G. P. Putnam's Sons, 1922.

Photius. Photii opera omnia. Vols. CI–CIV of Patrologiae cursus comp-letus: series Graeca. Ed. J. P. Migne. Paris: L. Migne, 1860.

——. Photii Bibliotheca. Ed. Immanuel Bekker. Berlin: Ge. Reimer, 1824–25.

——. Photii patriarchae Lexicon. Ed. S. A. Naber. 2 vols. Leidae: E. J. Brill, 1864–1865.

Plato. Platonis opera. Ed. J. Burnet. 5 vols. Oxonii: E typographeo Clarendoniano, 1902–1906.

Plutarch. Plutarch's Lives. Ed. and trans. Bernadotte Perrin. 11 vols. LCL. London: William Heinemann Ltd.; New York: G. P. Putnam's Sons, 1914–1926.

——. Plutarchi Chaeronensis Moralia. Ed. G. N. Bernardakis. 7 vols. Lipsiae: B. G. Teubner, 1888–1896.

Pollux, Julius. Iulii Pollucis Onomasticon. Ed. W. Dindorf. Lipsiae: In libraria Kuehniana, 1824.

Polybius. The Histories. Ed. and trans. W. R. Paton. 6 vols. LCL. London: William Heinemann Ltd.; New York: G. P. Putnam's Sons, 1922–1927.

Quintilian. The Institutio oratoria of Quintilian. Ed. and trans. H. E. Butler. 4 vols. LCL. London: William Heinemann Ltd.; New York: G. P. Putnam's Sons, 1921–1922.

Radermacher, L. See Alcidamas.

Rhetores Graeci. See Hammer, Spengel, and Walz.

Rhetorica ad Herennium. [Cicero] ad C. Herennium De ratione dicendi (Rhetorica ad Herennium). Ed. and trans. Harry Caplan. LCL. Cambridge, Massachusetts: Harvard University Press; London: William Heinemann Ltd., 1954.

Rhetorische Papyri. Ed. Karl Kunst ("Berliner Klassikertexte," Heft VII.) Berlin: Weidmann'sche Buchhandlung, 1923.

Rutilius Lupus. See Halm.

Spengel, Leonhard von (Ed.). Rhetores Graeci. 3 vols. Lipsiae: B. G. Teubner, 1853–1856.

Speusippus. See Bickerman and Sykutris, below, Section F.

Stobaeus. Ioannis Stobaei Florilegium. Ed. A. Meineke. 4 vols. in 2. Lipsiae: Typis Teubneri, 1855–1857.

Strabo. The Geography of Strabo. Ed. and trans. H. L. Jones and J. R. S. Sterrett. 8 vols. LCL. London: W. Heinemann; New York: G. P. Putnam's Sons, 1917–1932.

Suda. Suidae Lexicon. Ed. Ada Adler. 5 vols. Lipsiae: B. G. Teubner, 1928–1938.

Sylloge inscriptionum graecarum, a Guilelmo Dittenbergero condita et aucta, nunc tertium edita. Ed. Friedrich Hiller von Gaertringen. 4 vols. Lipsiae: Apud S. Hirzelium, 1915–1924.

Syrianus. Syriani in Hermogenem commentaria. Ed. H. Rabe. 2 vols. Lipsiae: B. G. Teubner, 1892–1893.

Theophrastus. Characteres. Ed. H. Diels. Oxonii: E typographeo Clarendoniano, 1909.

Thucydides. Ed. and trans. C. F. Smith. 4 vols. LCL. Cambridge, Massachusetts: Harvard University Press; London: William Heinemann, 1951–1953.

Tod, M. N. (Ed.). A Selection of Greek Historical Inscriptions. 2 vols. Oxford: Clarendon Press, 1946 (Vol. I, 2d ed., 1948).

Vegetius. Flavi Vegeti Renati Epitoma rei militaris. Ed. C. Lang. 2d ed. Lipsiae: B. G. Teubner, 1885.

Walz, Christian (Ed.). Rhetores Graeci. 9 vols. Stuttgartiae: Sumptibus J. G. Cottae, 1832–1836.

Xenophon. Xenophontis opera omnia. Ed. E. C. Marchant. 5 vols. Oxonii: E typographeo Clarendoniano, 1900–1920.

D. INDICES OF CLASSICAL AUTHORS

Ast, G. A. Friedrich. Lexicon Platonicum. 3 vols. Lipsiae: In libraria Weidmanniana, 1835–1838.

Bonitz, H. Index Aristotelicus. 2d ed. Graz: Akademische Druck– u. Verlagsanstalt, 1955.

Essen, M. H. von. Index Thucydideus. Berolini: Apud Weidmannos, 1887.

Forman, L. L. Index Andocideus Lycurgeus Dinarcheus. Oxford: Clarendon Press, 1897.

Goligher, W. A., and Maguinness. Index to the Speeches of Isaeus. Cambridge: W. Heffer, 1964(?).

Holmes, David H. Index Lysiacus. Bonnae: In aedibus Friderici Coheni, 1895.

Jensen, C. See Hyperides, above, Section C.

Powell, J. Enoch. A Lexicon to Herodotus. Cambridge: At the University Press, 1938.

Preuss, Siegmund. Index Aeschineus. Lipsiae: B. G. Teubner, 1896.

——. Index Demosthenicus. Lipsiae: B. G. Teubner, 1891.

——. Index Isocrateus. ("Programm des K. hum. Gymnasiums Fürth für die Schuljahre 1903–1904 und 1904–1905.") Fürth: Buchdruckerei von L. Limpert & Sohn, 1904.

Rehdantz, C. Demosthenes' neun philippische Reden. Vol. II 2: Indices. 4th ed. rev. by F. Blass. Leipzig: B. G. Teubner, 1886.

Reiske, J. J. Indices operum Demosthenis. Ed. G. H. Schaefer. London: Black, Young, and Young, 1823.

Sturz, F. W. Lexicon Xenophonteum. 4 vols. Lipsiae: Apud Joh. Ambrosium Barth, 1801.

Van Cleef, F. L. Index Antiphonteus. ("Cornell Studies in Classical Philology," No. V.) Boston: Ginn & Company, 1895.

E. WORKS DEALING WITH THE AUTHENTICITY OF DEMOSTHENES' LETTERS

Bickerman, Elias. "Lettres de Démosthène," RPh, 3d series, XI (1937).

Blass, Friedrich. Die attische Beredsamkeit. 3 vols. 2d Ed. Leipzig: B. G. Teubner, 1887–1898.

——. "Die demosthenischen Briefe," *NJb*, CXV (1877).

——. "Ueber die Echtheit der Demosthenes' Namen tragenden Briefe," Jahresbericht über das Königliche Wilhelms–Gymnasium zu Königsberg i. Pr. Königsberg: Druck der Universitäts–Buch– und Steindruckerei von E. J. Dalkowski, 1875.

——. Blass. "Unechte Briefe," *Rh. Mus.*, L (1899).

Dindorf, W. (Ed.). Demosthenes, Vol. VII: Annotationes interpretum ad XXVII–LXI, Epist. Oxonii: E typographeo academico, 1849.

Drerup, E. Aus einer alten Advokatenrepublik: Demosthenes und seine Zeit. Paderborn: Druck und Verlag von Ferdinand Schöningh, 1916.

Foucart, C. "La VIe lettre attribuée à Démosthène," *Journal des savants*, n.s., X (1912).

Huettner, Georg. Review of Neupert, *Bursians Jahresbericht*, L (1887).

Landwehr, Hugo. Review of Neupert, *Wochenschrift für klassische Philologie*, III (1886).

Mastroianni, E. Sull' autenticità e la composizione delle epistole demosteniche 2 e 4. Santa Maria Capua Vetere: Feola, 1938.

Mathieu, G. "Notes sur Athènes à la veille de la guerre lamiaque," *RPh*, LV (1929).

——. "Quelques remarques sur Démosthène," *REA*, XXIX (1937).

Neupert, Albert. De Demosthenicarum quae feruntur epistularum fide et auctoritate. Diss. Leipzig. Lipsiae: apud Gust. Fockium, 1885.

Nitsche, Wilhelm. Demosthenes und Anaximenes. Berlin: Weidmannsche Buchhandlung, 1906. (Sonderabdruck aus der *Zeitschrift für das Gymnasialwesen*, *Jahresberichte des Philologischen Vereins* XXXII.)

——. Review of Neupert, *BPhW*, VII (1887).

Rüger, Conrad. Review of Sachsenweger, *PhW*, LVI (1936).

Sachsenweger, Horst. De Demosthenis epistulis. Diss. Leipzig. Weidae Thuringorum: Thomas et Hubert, 1935.

Schaefer, Arnold. "Sind die demosthenischen Briefe echt oder nicht?" *NJb*, CXV (1877).

Taylor, John. "Praefatio ad Aeschinis epistolas," 1759, reprinted in Dobson (see above, Section C), Vol. XII, pp. 293–96.

Treves, Piero. "Apocrifi demostenici," *Athenaeum*, n.s., XIV (1936).

——. "Epimetron arpalico-demostenico," *Athenaeum*, n.s., XIV (1936).

——. "Philokles 4," *RE*, XIX (1938).

——. Review of Sachsenweger, *Riv. fil.*, LXIV (1936).

Westermann, Anton. De epistularum scriptoribus graecis commentatio. Lipsiae: Literis Staritzii, Typogr. universit., 1851–1854.

Wilamowitz-Moellendorff, Ulrich von. "Die Amphiktionie von Kalaurea," *Nachrichten von der Königl. Gesellschaft der Wissenschaften zu Göttingen. Philologisch-historische Klasse*, 1896.

——. "Unechte Briefe," *Hermes*, XXXIII (1898).

F. OTHER WORKS

Adams, C. D. "Demosthenes' Avoidance of Breves," *CP*, XII (1917).

——. "The Harpalos Case," *TAPA*, XXXII (1901).

——. "Speeches VIII and X of the Demosthenic Corpus," *CP*, XXXIII (1938).

Aken, A. J. Die Grundzüge der Lehre von Tempus und Modus im Griechischen, historisch und vergleichend aufgestellt. Rostock: Stiller'sche Hof-Buchhandlung, 1861.

Badian, E. "Harpalus," *JHS*, LXXXI (1961).

Beloch, Karl Julius. Griechische Geschichte. 4 vols. 2d ed. Berlin and Leipzig: Walter de Gruyter & Co., 1924–1927.

Bengtson, Hermann. Griechische Geschichte. 2d ed. München: C. H. Beck, 1960.

——. Die Strategie in der hellenistischen Zeit. 3 vols. München: C. H. Beck, 1937–1952.

Bentley, Richard. A Dissertation upon the Epistles of Phalaris, Themistocles, Socrates, Euripides, &c. and Aesop's Fables. London: 1697 (Ed. Wilhelm Wagner. London: George Bell & Sons, 1883).

Berve, Helmut. Das Alexanderreich auf prosopographischer Grundlage. 2 vols. München: C. H. Beck, 1926.

Bickerman, Elias. "La Lettre d'Alexandre aux bannis grecs," *REA*, XLII (1940).

——. "Sur un passage d'Hypéride (*Epitaphios* col. VIII)," *Athenaeum*, n.s., XLI (1963).

Bickerman, Elias, and J. Sykutris. "Speusipps Brief an König Philipp," *BVSAW*, Vol. LXXX (1928), Heft III.

Blass, Friedrich (Ed.). Demosthenes: Rede vom Kranze, Part II of Demosthenes: ausgewählte Reden, Ed. C. Rehdantz and F. Blass. 2d ed. rev. by K. Fuhr. Leipzig and Berlin: B. G. Teubner, 1910.

Boëthius, Axel. Die Pythaïs: Studien zur Geschichte der Verbindungen zwischen Athen und Delphi. Uppsala: Almquist & Wiksells Boktryckeri-A.-B., 1918.

Bonner, Robert J., and Gertrude Smith. The Administration of Justice from Homer to Aristotle. 2 vols. Chicago: The University of Chicago Press, 1938.

Bourguet, E. L'administration financière du sanctuaire pythique au IVe siècle av. J.-C. Paris: A. Fontemoing, 1905.

Bruns, Ivo. Das literarische Porträt der Griechen. Berlin: Verlag von Wilhelm Hertz, 1896.

Buchner, Edmund. Der Panegyrikos des Isokrates ("Historia," Einzelschriften, Heft 2.) Wiesbaden: Franz Steiner Verlag GmbH, 1958.

Burger, Friedrich. Stichometrische Untersuchungen zu Demosthenes und Herodot: ein Beitrag zur Kenntnis des antiken Buchwesens. ("Programm des K. Luitpold Gymnasiums in München für das Studienjahr 1891/92.") München: Buchdruckerei von J. B. Lind, 1892.

Busolt, G. Griechische Staatskunde. 2 vols. (Vol. II, Ed. H. Swoboda.) München: C. H. Beck, 1920–1926.

Calhoun, G. M. Athenian Clubs in Politics and Litigation. ("Bulletin of the University of Texas," No. 262, January 8, 1913.)

Callow, Alexander B., Jr., The Tweed Ring. New York: Oxford University Press, 1966.

The Cambridge Ancient History, Vol. V: Athens, 478–401 B.C., Ed. J. B. Bury, S. A. Cook, and F. E. Adcock. Cambridge: The University Press, 1927.

Carcopino, J. L'ostracisme athénien. Paris: Librairie Félix Alcan, 1935.

Christ, W. "Die Attikusausgabe des Demosthenes," *Abhandlungen der philosophisch-philologischen Classe der Königl. bayerischen Akademie der Wissenschaften*, XVI (1882).

Colin, Gaston. "Démosthène et l'affaire d'Harpale," *REG*, XXXVIII (1925), 306–50, XXXIX (1926), 31–88.

——. Le Discours d'Hypéride contre Démosthène sur l'argent d'Harpale. ("Annales de l'Est, mémoires," No. IV.) Paris: Société d'édition "Les belles lettres," 1934.

Daitz, Stephen G. "The Relationship of the *De Chersoneso* and the *Philippica quarta* of Demosthenes," *CP*, LII (1957).

Daux, Georges. Delphes au IIe et au Ier siècle, depuis l'abaissement de l'Étolie jusqu'à la paix romaine, 191–31 av. J.-C. Paris: E. de Boccard, 1936.

Denniston, J. D. The Greek Particles. 2d ed. Oxford: Clarendon Press, 1954.

Drerup, E. "Antike Demosthenesausgaben," *Philologus*, Suppl. VII (1899).

——. Demosthenes im Urteile des Altertums. ("Studien zur Geschichte und Kultur des Altertums," Band XII, Heft 1–2.) Würzburg: C. J. Becker, Universitäts-Druckerei, 1923.

——. Review of Schwegler, *Deutsche Literaturzeitung*, XXXVI (1915).

——. "Ueber die bei den attischen Rednern eingelegten Urkunden," *NJb*, Suppl. XXIV (1898).

Dürrbach, Félix. L'orateur Lycurgue: étude historique et littéraire. Paris: E. Thorin, 1889.

Exler, F. X. J. The Form of the Ancient Greek Letter: A Study in Greek Epistolography. Diss. Catholic University of America. Washington, D. C.: 1923.

Ferguson, W. S. Hellenistic Athens. London: Macmillan, 1911.

Focke, F. "Demosthenesstudien," *Genethliakon Wilhelm Schmid*. ("Tübinger Beiträge zur Altertumswissenschaft," Vol. V.) Stuttgart: W. Kohlhammer, 1929.

Foucart, P. Etude sur Didymos. Paris: Imprimerie nationale, 1907.

Gardthausen, V. Griechische Palaeographie. 2d ed. Leipzig: Veit & Comp., 1913.

Gaya Nuño, Benito. Sobre un giro de la lengua de Demóstenes. Madrid: Instituto Antonio de Nebrija, 1954.

Glotz, G. La Solidarité de la famille dans le droit criminel en Grèce. Paris: Albert Fontemoing, 1904.

Glotz, G., P. Roussel, and R. Cohen. Alexandre et l'hellénisation du monde antique, première partie: Alexandre et le démembrement de son empire. Vol. IV of Histoire ancienne, deuxième partie: histoire grecque, Ed. G. Glotz. Paris: Les Presses universitaires de France, 1938.

Goodwin, W. W. Demosthenes on the Crown. Cambridge: At the University Press, 1901.

——. Syntax of the Moods and Tenses of the Greek Verb. 3d ed. Boston: Ginn and Company, 1890.

Habicht, Christian. "Falsche Urkunden zur Geschichte Athens im Zeitalter der Perserkriege," *Hermes*, LXXXIX (1961).

——. Gottmenschentum und griechische Städte. München: C. H. Beck, 1956.

Hemmerdinger, B. "Les Chiffres attiques du *Parisinus Gr.* 223 des Epîtres pauliniennes," *REG*, LXXVI (1963).

——. "Euthaliana," *Journal of Theological Studies*, n.s., XI (1960).

Hofrichter, Werner. Studien zur Entwickelungsgeschichte der Deklamation. Diss. Breslau, 1935.

Hudson-Williams, H. Ll. "Political Speeches in Athens," *CQ*, XLV (1951).

Jaeger, Werner. Demosthenes: the Origin and Growth of His Policy. Berkeley: University of California Press, 1938.

Judeich, W. Topographie von Athen. 2d ed. München: C. H. Beck, 1931.

Kahrstedt, Ulrich. Untersuchungen zur Magistratur in Athen. Stuttgart: W. Kohlhammer, 1936.

Kalbfleisch, K. "Plato und Demosthenes," *Rh. Mus.*, XCII (1944).

Kennedy, George. The Art of Persuasion in Greece. Princeton: Princeton University Press, 1963.

Kenyon, F. G. Books and Readers in Ancient Greece and Rome. 2d ed. Oxford: Clarendon Press, 1951.

Kirchner, J. Prosopographia Attica. 2 Vols. Berolini: Typis et impensis Georgii Reimeri, 1901–1903.

Körte, A. "Literarische Texte," *Archiv für Papyrusforschung*, VII (1924).

——. "Zu Didymos' Demosthenes-Commentar," *Rh. Mus.*, LX (1905).

Kohl, R. De scholasticarum declamationum argumentis ex historia petitis ("Rhetorische Studien," 4 Heft.) Paderbornae: Typis et sumptibus Ferdinandi Schoeningh, 1915.

Koskenniemi, H. Studien zur Idee und Phraseologie des griechischen Briefes bis 400 n. Chr. ("Annales Academiae Scientiarum Fennicae," Series B, Vol. CII, No. 2.) Helsinki: Suomalainen Tiedeakatemia, 1956.

Kramer, C. H. De priore Demosthenis adversus Aristogitonem oratione. Diss. Leipzig. Weidae Thuringorum: Thomas et Hubert, 1930.

Kroll, W. "Melete 1," *RE*, XV (1932).

——. "Rhetorik," *RE*, Suppl. VII (1940).

——. "Schiffahrt," *RE*, II^A1 (1923).

Kühner, Raphael. Ausführliche Grammatik der griechischen Sprache, zweiter Teil: Satzlehre. 2 vols. 3d ed. revised by Bernhard Gerth. Hannover and Leipzig: Hahnsche Buchhandlung, 1898–1904.

Ladek, Fr., "Über die Echtheit zweier auf Demosthenes und Demochares bezüglichen Urkunden in Pseudo-Plutarchs Βίοι τῶν δέκα ῥητόρων," *Wiener Studien*, XIII (1891).

Larfeld, Wilhelm. Griechische Epigraphik. 3d ed. München: C. H. Beck, 1914.

——. Handbuch der griechischen Epigraphik. 2 vols. Leipzig: O. R. Reisland, 1902–1907.

Lepore, E. "Leostene e le origine della guerra lamiaca," *La parola del passato*, X (1955).

Lipsius, J. H. Das attische Recht und Rechtsverfahren. 3 vols. Leipzig: O. R. Reisland, 1905–1915.

Loheit, Fritz. Untersuchungen zur antiken Selbstapologie. Diss. Rostock. Rostock: Rats- und Universitäts-Buchdruckerei Adlers Erben, GmbH, 1928.

Lutz, Leonhard. Die Präpositionen bei den attischen Rednern. ("Programm der Studienanstalt zu Neustadt a.d. H. für die Schuljahre 1886/87 und 1887/88.")

Lynch, Denis Tilden. "Boss" Tweed. New York: Blue Ribbon Books, 1927.

MacDowell, Douglas. Andokides on the Mysteries. Oxford: Clarendon Press, 1962.

Mayser, Edwin. Grammatik der griechischen Papyri aus der Ptolemäerzeit. 2 vols. in 4. Berlin.: W. de Gruyter, 1923–1934.

Meritt, B. D. The Athenian Year. Berkeley and Los Angeles: University of California Press, 1961.

——. "Athenian Calendar Problems," *TAPA*, XCV (1964).

Merkelbach, Reinhold. Die Quellen des griechischen Alexanderromans. München: C. H. Beck, 1954.

Mommsen, Tycho. Beiträge zu der Lehre von den griechischen Präpositionen. Berlin: Weidmannsche Buchhandlung, 1895.

Moraux, Paul. Les Listes anciennes des ouvrages d'Aristote. Louvain: Éditions universitaires de Louvain, 1951.

Mossé, Claude. La Fin de la démocratie athénienne. Paris: Presses universitaires de France, 1962.

Navarre, O. Essai sur la rhétorique grecque avant Aristote. Paris: Librairie Hachette, 1900.

Nilsson, M. P. Geschichte der griechischen Religion, II. 2d ed. München: C. H. Beck, 1961.

Ohly, Kurt. Stichometrische Untersuchungen. Leipzig: O. Harrasowitz, 1928.

Ostwald, Martin. "The Athenian Legislation against Tyranny and Subversion," *TAPA*, LXXXVI (1955).

Pack, Roger A. The Greek and Latin Literary Texts from Greco-Roman Egypt. 2d ed. Ann Arbor: University of Michigan Press, 1965.

Pape, W. Wörterbuch der griechischen Eigennamen. 3d ed. rev. by G. E. Benseler. Braunschweig: Friedrich Vieweg und Sohn, 1884.

Parke, H. W., and D. E. W. Wormell. The Delphic Oracle. 2 vols. Oxford: Blackwell, 1956.

Pasquali, Giorgio. Storia della tradizione e critica del testo. 2d ed. Firenze: Felice le Monnier, 1952.

Pélékidis, Chrysis. Histoire de l'éphébie attique. ("École française d'Athènes: Travaux et mémoires des anciens membres étrangers de l'École et de divers savants," Fasc. XIII.) Paris: E. de Boccard, 1962.

Pouilloux, J. "Nouveaux fragments d'un compte delphique," *BCH*, LXXV (1951).

Radermacher, L. "Der neue Äschylos," Review of Aeschyli tragoediae, edited by Ulrich von Wilamowitz-Moellendorff, *Zeitschrift für die österreichischen Gymnasien*, LXVII (1916).

Raubitschek, A. E. "The Case against Alcibiades (Andocides IV)," *TAPA*, LXXIX (1948).

Regenbogen. "Pinax," *RE*, XX² (1950).

Reincke. "Nachrichtenwesen," *RE*, XVI² (1935).

Roebuck, C. "The Settlements of Philip II with the Greek States in 338 B.C.," *CP*, XLIII (1948).

Rostovtzeff, M. The Social and Economic History of the Hellenistic World. 3 vols. Oxford: Clarendon Press, 1941.

Rupprecht, A. "Die demosthenische Prooemiensammlung," *Philologus*, LXXXII (1927).

Samuel, A. E. Ptolemaic Chronology. München: C. H. Beck, 1962.

Sauppe, H. Epistola critica ad Godofredum Hermannum, reprinted in his Ausgewaehlte Schriften. Berlin: Weidmannsche Buchhandlung, 1896.

Schaefer, Arnold. Demosthenes und seine Zeit. 3 vols. 1st ed. Leipzig: B. G. Teubner, 1856–1858. 2nd ed. Leipzig: B. G. Teubner, 1885–1887.

Schmidt, Friedrich. Die Pinakes des Kallimachos ("Klassisch-philologische Studien veröffentlicht von F. Jacoby," Heft 1.) Berlin: Verlag von Emil Ebering, 1912.

Schwahn, Walter. 'Strategos," *RE*, Suppl. VI (1935).

Schwegler, Karl. De Aeschinis quae feruntur epistolis. Diss. Giessen. Giessen: Christ und Herr, 1913.

Sealey, R. "Dionysius of Halicarnassus and Some Demosthenic Dates," *REG*, LXVIII (1955).

———. "The Olympic Festival of 324 B.C.," *CR*, LXXIV (1960).

Sijpesteijn, P. J. "Les Parchemins et les papyrus de Démosthène trouvés en Égypte," *Chronique d'Égypte*, XXXVIII (1963).

Skimina, S. État actuel des études sur le rhythme de la prose grecque: I ("Bulletin international de l'Académie polonaise des sciences et des lettres. Classe de philologie—Classe d'histoire et de philosophie," No. supplémentaire 3.) Cracovie: Imprimerie de l'université, 1937.

Snell, Bruno. Scenes from Greek Drama. Berkeley and Los Angeles: University of California Press, 1964.

Sykutris, J. "Der demosthenische Epitaphios," *Hermes*, LXIII (1928).
——. "Epistolographie," *RE*, Suppl. V (1931).
Tarn, W. W. Alexander the Great. Cambridge: at the University Press, 1948.
Tate, J. Review of DeWitt (see above, Section B), *CR*, LXV (1951).
Tod, M. N. "The Greek Numeral Notation," *Annual of the British School at Athens*, XVIII (1911–1912).
——. "Further Notes on the Greek Acrophonic Numerals," *ibid.*, XXVIII (1926–1927).
——. "The Greek Acrophonic Numerals," *ibid.*, XXXVII (1936–1937).
——. "The Alphabetical Numeral System in Attica," *ibid.*, XLV (1950).
——. "Letter Labels in Greek Inscriptions," *ibid.*, XLIX (1954).
Tolkiehn. "Lexikographie," *RE*, XII² (1925).
Treves, Piero. "Les Documents apocryphes du 'Pro Corona'," *Les Études classiques*, IX (1940).
——. "Note sur la chronologie de l'affaire d'Harpale," *REA*, XXXVI (1934).
Turner, E. G. Athenian Books in the Fifth and Fourth Centuries B.C. (Inaugural Lecture Delivered at University College, London.) London: Published for the College by H. K. Lewis & Co. Ltd., 1952.
Usteri, Paul. Ächtung und Verbannung im griechischen Recht. Diss. Zürich. Berlin: Weidmannsche Buchhandlung, 1903.
Vogel, F. "Die Kurzenmeidung in der griechischen Prosa des IV Jahrhunderts," *Hermes*, LVIII (1923).
Volkmann, R. Die Rhetorik der Griechen und Römer in systematischer Übersicht. 2d ed. Leipzig: B. G. Teubner, 1885.
Weber, P. Entwickelungsgeschichte der Absichtssätze, zweite Abtheilung: die attische Prosa. ("Beiträge zur historischen Syntax der gr. Sprache herausgegeben von M. Schanz," Band II, Heft 2.) Würzburg: A. Stuber's Verlagshandlung, 1885.
Welles, C. B. Royal Correspondence in the Hellenistic Period. New Haven: Yale University Press, 1934.
Wendel, Carl. "Das griechisch-römische Altertum," chap. ii of Handbuch der Bibliothekswissenschaft, ed. Fritz Milkau and Georg Leyh (2d ed. rev.; Wiesbaden: Otto Harrasowitz, 1955), Vol. III.
——. Die griechisch-römische Buchbeschreibung verglichen mit der des vorderen Orients. ("Hallische Monographien," No. 3.) Halle (Saale): M. Niemeyer, 1949.
Wendland, P. Anaximenes von Lampsakos. Berlin: Weidmannsche Buchhandlung, 1905.

Werner, M. R. Tammany Hall. 2d ed. Garden City, N.Y.: Garden City Publishing Company, 1928.

Westlake, H. D. Thessaly in the Fourth Century B.C. London: Methuen & Co., Ltd., 1935.

Wilamowitz-Moellendorff, Ulrich von. Der Glaube der Hellenen. 2 vols. Basel: Benno Schwabe & Co. Verlag, 1956.

Index of Greek Words Discussed

Index of References to
the Works of Demosthenes

Subject Index

For convenience in indexing, the words Demosthenes and Demosthenic have been abbreviated to D. Demosthenes' letters are cited without the designating initial.

Acrophonic numerals, 9–12, 19n, 270–71

Aeschines, as originator of rhetorical exercises on historical themes, 31; ridiculed D's "support" of Sparta, 74–75; accused D as jinx, 81, 247; in *De Corona*, 114, 127, 240, 248; use of invective, 117n; D's prosecutions of, 240–41; tolerates hiatus, 252. *See also* Aeschines, Pseudo-

Aeschines, Pseudo-, *Letters of Aeschines*, connection and comparison with D. Epp. *1–6*, 7, 49n, 78, 100, 128, 131–32, 157, 169–73, 176, 180, 265–66

Aetolians, 73, 90–91

Agen, satyric drama, 46n f.

Agis, revolt of Sparta under, 74–75; defeat in *331*, 224, 228

Alcaeus, letter labels of book divisions of, 269

Alcibiades, restoration of, 57n; Socrates' association with, 81n f.; self-defense an "apology", 101n; self-defense in year *407*, special case, 102n; sought to stand trial, 119; posthumous figure of, 120–25, 173; prosecution of son for father, 121; as a symbol, 122, esp. 122n; courts chosen for posthumous attack on, 122–23. *See also* Apology

Alexander, unexpected return from India, 37; in Carmania, 37, 46n f.; punitive action against satraps, 37, 45, 46n f.; menace to Athens, 40; death of, 44, 59, 61–62, 179, 256; decree restoring exiles, 45, 60–61, 173, 242; decree *re* island of Samos, 45n, 173, 242; deifica-

tion of, 46n, 81, 224; D "framed" to please, 57, 255; and destruction of Thebes, 74; Fortune of, 80, esp. 80n, 89, 256; D's policy toward, 80–81, 87–88; opposed twice by D, 81; D had something to fear from, 87; intercessions for men in Greek cities, 87–88, 221; no hostile mention of, in D's letters, 87–88, 147–48; demanded surrender of D in *335*, 214, 229; campaigns in India, 230; hard lot of conquered peoples, 250

Alexandria, stichometries in, 11; classification of books in corpora at, 17; Demosthenic corpus and, 17–20; Homeric poems and, 269

Amphiareion, ephebic inscription from, 38n, 65, 277–81

Amphictyony, Delphic, extradition in, 39n; ancestral sacrifices of, 50–51, 227–28; meetings of, 50–52; joined Lamian war, 72; policy of, 72nn

Anaximenes, *Philippic Histories*, 24, 33; *Technê*, 60, 100, 282–83; on *demegoriae*, 101, 106–10, 112, 117, 132, 151, 173, 282–83; genera and species of rhetoric, 101, 282–83; on apologies, 101–2; on "oratory of exposure", exposé,145; as supposed writer of Ep. *1*, 176; possibly reworked Ep. *6*, 264; classifications of oratory, 282–83

Andocides, plight and plea similar to D's, 52, 166–69; *De Mysteriis*, 113, 115; *De Reditu*, 115, 131, 152n, 166–69, 173; speech *Against Alcibiades* ascribed to 123–25.

310

Barbarians, as potential allies for Athens, 86*n* f.; victims of Alexander, 250

Bentley, Richard (*1697*), 3

Blass's law, defined, 28; in D corpus and in Epp. *1–6*, 28–29, 176–77; otherwise, in extant ancient literature, followed only by Aelius Aristides, 29, 34; D's heirs and, 34

Boeotia, in *323*, 244

Books, ancient, grouping of for publication, and classification of, 8, 17, 19, 267–68; stichometries in, 9–20

Bribe taking, *see* D, Corruption; Harpalus affair; Law; Politicians

Briefroman, 32–33

Calauria, as D's refuge in *323*, 7*n*, 68–70; D's suicide at, 64; date of independence from Troenzen, 245

Calendar, Athenian, 46*n*; and the Delphic, 51

Callimachus, and D corpus, 17–20; collection containing Epp. *1–4* antedates, 18–25

Callimedon, 230

Callisthenes, 47, 229

Cappadocians, 5*n*, 250

Captatio benevolentiae, function of prooemium, 101, 134, 284; in Epp. *1–4*, 134–139, 158, 174, 178–79; in Andoc. *2*, 167

Chaeroneia, battle of, effect on D's policy, 80–81, 88, 160–61, 216, 238; D's "cowardice" at, 81; fear of Areopagus after, 238; D and Athenians ascribe Macedonian victory to Fortune, 239; gave rise to cult of Fortune at Athens. 248–49; Thessalians at, 251

Chares, 228–30

Charidemus, fate of and authenticity of Ep. *3*, *4*, 48*n*, 228; in D. 23, 119*n*

Cicero, refers to Ep. *5*, 6; library of, 6*n*; refers to D's letters as a group, 8

Civil rights, loss of, *see Atimia*

Cleochares, on D, 83*n*, 94

Coins, numerals on ancient, 270–71

Commiseratio, in Epp. *1–4*, 150, 59, 163–66, 169

Commoratio, 142*n*, 160

Confirmatio, proof, in deliberative vs.

forensic genus, 106–9, 124, 138; in Epp. *1–4*, 140–50, 155–57, 159–65, 175; in Andoc. *2*, 168–69; in letters of Aeschines, 170–72

Corinth, in *323*, 244

Council of 500, as court, 103

Courts, Athenian, Council or Assembly as, 103, 113; public vs. private suits in, 109, 117–18, 119*n*; procedure in, 112–13; personal or political attack in, 118–19, 121–23; D's use of to advocate policies, 119*n*; arguments from probability in, 161; D avoided involvement in, 162–63, 241

Crannon, battle of and results, 89–91, 262

Deliberative oratory, *see Demegoria(e)*

Delphic oracle, follows attitude of Amphictyony, 72; condemned by D, 72, 249; on Good Fortune for Athens, 248–49

Demades, charged in Harpalus affair, 40*n* f., 42; and Antipater, 42*n* f.; and D, 42*n* f.; convicted, 44, 49*n*; possible allusion to, 44*n*, 231; confession of, 49*n* 53, 108; reputation of, 231

Demegoria(e), defined, 100–1, 103–9; parts of, *see* Anticipation, *Confirmatio*, Epilogue, Narrative, Prooemium, Proposition; apologetic, vs. forensic defense, 101–31, 155–57, 282–83; must bear on public interest, 101–2, 108, 133, 135; abuse and invective in, 102, 111, 114–16, 143; D had to use, 102, 129–30; apologetic, in rhetorical exercises, 127–28, 130, 284–86, in propaganda, 130; *See also* Apology; Forensic speech; Rhetoric

Demetrius of Phalerum, and rhetorical exercises on historical themes, 31; regime of, 72, 93; on D's character, 82

Demetrius Poliorcetes, 93

Demochares, nephew of D, possible compiler of collection containing Epp. *1–4*, 24–25; successful petition to honor D, 25, 76–77, 82–83, 87*n*, 93; death, 25; Epp. *1–4*, possibly written by or for, 33–34, 86*n*; historian, 33; motives for trying to clear D's name, 33–34, 82–83,

Panaetius, 8*n*, 81*n* f.

Particles, connective, in D's style and Epp. *1-4*, 27-28

Pélékidis, Chrysis, against authenticity of Din. *3*, 276-77; on Amphiareion inscription, 277-81

Pericles, campaign in courts against, 118-19; speech at Th. *ii. 59-64*, 173, 284; in themes for rhetorical exercises, 284-85

Peripatetic school, numerals in and transmission of works of, 12*n*, 269; on epistolography, 99, 129

Persia, Persians, D received money from, 70*n*, 74, 79, 82, 86*n*; and Ephialtes and Charidemus, 228; as victims of Alexander, 250

Personification of abstractions, 223-24

Philip, and the Greeks, 38*n*, 39, 74; right of extradition from Athens, 39, 69-70, 75; D's activity against, 74, 160, 239-42; example of in argument of Epp. *2-3*, 142, 156, 161, 215-16, 239-42; conduct after Chaeroneia, 142, 216; Python's embassy for, 240-41; and Thessaly, 250-51

Philocles, in Harpalus affair, 4, 38, 41-43, 46; *strategos* in Piraeus, 38*n*, 46, 276-81; tried before Aristogiton, 43; *kosmetes*, 46, 56, 67, 277-79; conviction and exile of, 48, 53; "abandoned" by the People, 48*n*; friends procure exoneration, 54, 56-57, 65, 93-95, 110-11, 157; identity and sources bearing on, 276-81

Philocrates, 44*n*

Philoxenus, 38

Phocion, 39, 63, 81-82, 91, 93

Piraeus, Harpalus at the, 38; Philocles *strategos* of, 38, 276-81; *strategoi* of, 38*n*, 276-81; in 3d century B.C., 93; as residence of D, 154; shrine of Good Fortune, 248; parts of, 276-77

Plato, D and, 6*n*, 261; stichometries in manuscripts of, 12*n* f.; *Apology*, 34, 71, 79*n*, 107, 113-14, 120; Ep. *7*, 126; Ep. *8*, 79*n*

Plutarch, used Ep. *2*, 6; on D's fine, 66; found Epp. *2-3* "unmanly," 94, 166; on absence of invective in *Philippics*, 114

Polemical literature, *see* Apology; Propaganda

Politicians, acceptance of gifts by, in Athens, 40-41, 84-86, 108, 137; hazards faced by, 213; D's classification of functions, 223. *See also* Assembly; Courts

Polycrates, 81*n* f., 120

Polyeuctus, 40*n* f., 42, 229

Prayers in oratory, 177-78

Prepositions in Epp. *1-4*, 27

Probability, arguments from, in Athenian courts, 161; at D's trial and in Ep. *2*, 161-62, 239

Prooemium, prooemia, collections of (not D's), 19*n*; function of in oratory, 22-23, 101*n*, 105, 145; in Andoc. *4*, 125; narrative in, 134, 136-38, 140, 167; in Epp. *1-4*, 134-40, 158-59, 174-75; 178-79; in Andoc. *2*, 167. *See also* D, WORKS, *Prooemia*

Propaganda, Philippics published as (?), 24*n*; Epp. *1-4* as posthumous, 33-34, 64-65, 70-72, 76-94, 129-31, 173; ancient, forms of, 97-132; open letters in, 97*n*, 98, 126, 150-51; for and against Socrates, 71, 79*n*, 81*n* f., 107, 114, 120, 159, 173; for and against Alcibiades, 120-25; of Isocrates, 125-26, 150-51; D speech *Apologia doron* as possible, 126. *See also* Apology

Proposition, in Epp. *1-4*, 140-42, 159, 163, 168, 175; in Andoc. *2*, 167-68

Ptolemies, as book collectors, 261-62. *See also* Egypt

Pythaïs, Athenian rite at Delphi, 50-52, 227

Pytheas, prosecutor of D, 42, 149, 226; offering sacrifices at Delphi, 50-52, 227-28; political *volte-face* of, 54, 149, 224-25, 227; imprisonment and flight to Antipater of, 56, 88*n*, 92*n*, 242; danger to Athens of, 88, 92, 230; well treated though a traitor, 147-49; bad reputation of, 149; as example (not an "attack"), 144, 149, 156, 224-28; against Alexander, 224; faced serious prosecutions, 225-26; wrote propaganda as well as speeches against D (?), 226; Treves on political status of,